Internet Email Protocols

Internet Email Protocols

A Developer's Guide

Kevin Johnson

 **ADDISON-WESLEY**

An imprint of Addison Wesley Longman, Inc.

Reading, Massachusetts · Harlow, England · Menlo Park, California
Berkeley, California · Don Mills, Ontario · Sydney
Bonn · Amsterdam · Tokyo · Mexico City

For more information, please contact:
  Corporate, Government, and Special Sales Group
  Addison Wesley Longman, Inc.
  One Jacob Way
  Reading, Massachusetts 01867

TK
5105.73
J64
2000

Library of Congress Cataloging-in-Publication Data

Johnson, Kevin.
    Internet email protocols : a developer's guide / Kevin Johnson.
       p.   cm.
    Includes bibliographical references and index.
    ISBN 0-201-43288-9 (alk. paper)
    1. Electronic mail systems.   2. Internet (Computer network)   3. Computer network
  protocols.   I. Title.

  TK5105.73.J64   1999
  004.692--dc21   99-047821

ISBN 0-201-43288-9

Text printed on recycled and acid-free paper.

1 2 3 4 5 6 7 8 9 10 – CRS – 04 03 02 01 00
First printing, October 1999

Contents

Appendices

List of Figures

List of Tables

Preface

This book is about the various protocols and standards that make up the technical side of Internet email. It describes the formatting of mail messages, including MIME—the SMTP, POP, and IMAP protocols, filtering and mailing list technologies, and security. The focus is on understanding how and why Internet email works and how it has evolved from its early forms into the "killer app" many people use on a daily basis.

Two types of applications dominate the Internet: the Web and email. Go to the computer section of any bookstore and count the number of titles devoted to the Web, including those for end-users, as well as those for developers and administrators. Now, count the titles dedicated to Internet email. You'll find the number significantly smaller, particularly for technical ones. This book attempts to remedy this, at least in some small way.

Learning how email works is not necessarily straightforward. The information is spread across a large number of documents written over a period of many years, and most of the protocols have undergone several iterations, resulting in corrections and new versions. Thus, one of the difficulties is understanding the relationship of an email document with its predecessors and successors. The information is presented here in a way that cuts across established standards by providing a current view of email technology. After reading this book, it will be much easier to put a particular RFC into perspective.

Another difficulty is that most standards aren't intended to help people learn particular protocols; they are intended to provide, at least theoretically, an exact definition of a protocol. This book presents the information in an order better suited to learning the material.

To add to these issues, there are differences and errors in the interpretation of standards and proposed standards, as well as ambiguities and errors in the documents themselves. This has resulted in various email packages implementing the standards in different ways. Key interpretations of some of the problem areas are provided as appropriate.

The bottom line is that it can be difficult to get a detailed picture of how email works. The goal here is to solve that problem.

Audience

This book is for developers, administrators, and possibly power-users, or more generally anyone with the need to understand the technical side of Internet email. Developers will find the information organized to make it easier to digest the actual standards documents. Even those developers not creating dedicated email applications should find the information useful for adding email functionality to their programs.

System administrators can use the information to help them troubleshoot and manage email systems. A system administrator's life is easier when he or she has a detailed understanding of how things are put together and how they work. Power-users can use the information to help them use email tools to the utmost. This is particularly true for the chapters that deal with mail messages, MIME, filtering, and security.

Organization

There's a natural progression to the book's structure, in which each chapter builds on information in a previous chapter or chapters. Readers new to the technical aspects of email should start at the beginning and proceed chapter by chapter. Advanced readers, of course, can read the chapters in any order.

Be aware that Chapters 2, 3, 4, and 9 contain information that is fundamental to an understanding of email. Other chapters can be safely skipped according to reader interest.

Chapter 1, Overview, provides a high-level overview and introduction to Internet email.

Chapter 2, Mail Messages, provides a detailed walk-through of the structure of email messages.

Chapter 3, Mail Transport, describes SMTP and various extensions to the protocol, and how they are used to transport email.

Chapter 4, MIME, describes MIME and how it's used to encapsulate structured or nontext data in email messages.

Chapter 5, POP, describes the POP protocol, its use, and its various extensions.

Chapter 6, IMAP, describes the IMAP protocol, its use, and several protocol extensions.

Chapter 7, Filtering, describes how email filters work, as well as various tasks that can be performed with them. The emphasis is on applying knowledge of how email works to make filtering more effective, particularly with unsolicited bulk email.

Chapter 8, Mailing List Processing, provides a detailed walk-through of mailing list processors and how email headers are manipulated to perform mailing list functions.

Chapter 9, Security, describes various aspects of email security, including authentication, digital signatures, encryption, and anonymity.

Appendix A, Example Folder Formats, describes the format of several folder formats, with an emphasis on the performance implications of their various design features.

Appendix B, UNIX Folder Locking, describes various issues related to folder locking in UNIX, which can be a particularly troublesome problem.

Appendix C, Programming Languages, surveys several common programming languages, and some of their interesting characteristics related to email.

Appendix D, IMSP, provides a brief overview of the IMSP protocol. Although it was never widely implemented and is being replaced by ACAP, its historical importance makes it worth mentioning.

Appendix E, ACAP, provides an overview of the ACAP protocol. Although not exclusively an email protocol, ACAP provides several features of interest to email developers.

Appendix F, LDAP, provides a brief overview of the LDAP protocol, which provides network-based querying and updating of directory services information.

What This Book Does Not Cover

Email is a broad topic, particularly when adjacent technologies are factored in. No book can hope to cover it all. More specifically, this book does not describe how to use, configure, or manage specific email packages. There are plenty of books out there to fulfill that need. The information here is meant to help readers learn the underlying technology implemented by email software.

Some areas of email technology are not covered—for example, the relationship between Internet email and X.400. Several advanced uses of MIME, such as transmitting voice and FAX data, are also not discussed. These areas should be easier to learn, however, with a solid understanding of the underlying technology provided here.

In addition, this book does not provide detailed information about related protocols such as TCP/IP and DNS. However, when knowledge about these protocols is important in understanding a particular topic, information is provided as necessary. Network protocols are designed in layers. Although understanding how they work is important, most Internet email can be understood without learning every other protocol in the picture.

Lastly, several algorithms related to security are not described in detail. Security is a complicated topic, requiring much more coverage than can be provided in this book.

Conventions

Examples directly related to the topic of a chapter are inset, enclosed in a box frame, and rendered with a monospace font, as shown here.

```
like this
```

If an example involves a dialog between either a client and a server or a user and a computer, the client or user inputs are set in bold. Items in a dialog that need particular attention are shown in bold italic. Summarization of information is represented in italics.

```
the client said this
the server responded with this
followed by a large amount of other information
```

Other textual examples and syntax descriptions are inset and rendered with a monospace font, with no framing box,

```
like this.
```

Most email protocols use a carriage-return (CR, US-ASCII 13, '\r') character followed by a line-feed (LF, US-ASCII 10, '\n') character to terminate lines of text. For readability, the examples in this book do not show the line terminators, except in a few instances. Each protocol has specific line termination requirements, which should be considered as implied in the examples and syntax descriptions.

While on the topic of syntax descriptions, it should be noted that some do not exactly match the ones provided in the RFCs, particularly some of the older ones, such as RFC822. In the interest of clarity, the author has chosen to provide syntax descriptions that might be easier to understand or that might resolve an ambiguity. In particular, this is the case with the use of whitespace in RFC822. The differences are generally cosmetic, but the "improved" syntax descriptions shown should be treated not as reference material but merely as an aid for learning the material.

When referenced in the body of the text, message header fields, protocol commands and parameters, and email addresses are presented in a `monospace` font.

In a few places, '␣' is used to identify a space character. It is generally limited to places where the lack of such a character would be confusing.

Many of the examples use the domain names `example.com`, `example.edu`, and `example.net`. Don't try sending email to any of these locations—it won't work. The `example` domains are set aside for use in situations in which domain names are needed but writers want to avoid the possibility of using ones that someone might use in the future.

One final note about conventions. This book uses *email* when referring to *electronic mail*. Some people might feel *e-mail* should be used instead; however, English has many word combinations that get shortened over time. Remember that *electronic mail* was initially shortened to *e-mail*. As this type of word becomes widely used, eventually the hyphen gets dropped. In fact, there are many instances where simply *mail* is used.[1] It is the author's opinion that this term is used widely enough for the hyphen to go.[2] In particular, this form has become the standard, as it were, in the email industry. Go ahead and drop it, it's just a hyphen; you won't invoke the wrath of the hyphen police.

A Few Notes about the Standards

The primary document describing the rules and guidelines for implementing Internet email protocols is the RFC, or Request for Comment. In fact, the RFC defines most fundamental protocols used on the Internet. There are thousands of RFCs available, ranging from information to required standards. Anyone who spends time with Internet protocols will eventually find their way to them because they are an important aspect of the technical underpinnings of the Internet. The creation of RFCs is described in further detail in Section 1.2.

Reference is made to a large number of RFCs, most of them directly related to Internet email, some of them are only indirectly related. This book does not replace these RFCs, it amplifies them. Although some readers might only have a passing need to understand the exact specifications of a protocol, there are bound to be situations in which referring to an RFC will resolve a question. Readers are strongly encouraged to read the RFCs and not rely solely on the information in a book.

This book includes syntax descriptions for many elements of email. In places, these descriptions deviate slightly from the exact words used in the RFC syntax specifications in the interest of clarity. The author apologizes for any inadvertent errors made in the process. On a related note, if *any* unqualified statements made in this book conflict with the standards, the standards probably win.

One last general point about the RFCs is in order. Standards and protocols evolve. As a result, updates are published as new RFCs. Readers delving into the

---

[1] Maybe by the time we're done, everyone will shorten it to just "*m*".

[2] For a second opinion, see `http://www-cs-staff.stanford.edu/~knuth/email.html`

world of Internet standards need to be aware of the historical context of a particular RFC. For example, which RFCs does it update or replace, and which RFCs update or replace the ones in question. This book references many older RFCs, particularly in the context of newer ones. There is no doubt that current RFCs will be updated by newer ones, some while this book is still new. Readers should always check to see if an RFC has been updated.

Getting the Standards

There are two primary repositories for Internet protocol specifications—one is for RFCs, the other is for Internet drafts. The RFC repository is available at

> `http://www.ietf.org/rfc.html`

This site contains an overview of the RFC repository and the standards process, answers to frequently asked questions about RFCs, and the actual repository for RFC documents.

All the RFCs referenced in this book are provided on the accompanying CD-ROM. This is intended to help people with limited bandwidth, particularly because there are so many RFCs related to Internet email.

Internet drafts (IDs) are documents intended to become RFCs eventually. They often undergo several iterations and review by many people before that happens, if indeed it ever does. The repository for Internet drafts is located at

> `http://www.ietf.org/ID.html`

Because of their dynamic nature, IDs are not provided on the CD-ROM. This should not be a problem—most readers don't need to worry about them.

This Book's CD-ROM

A CD-ROM accompanies this book. It contains all the RFCs referenced here, as well as the source code for several email packages. A thin layer of HTML is provided to aide in navigating the information. The purpose of the CD-ROM is to allow for readers to access the information without having to download it from the Internet.

Each RFC is presented in its published form, direct from the master source, with no alterations. With it is a companion HTML page, which presents some of the information contained in the master table of contents at the RFC repository. This information is available by accessing the top-level HTML pages on the CD-ROM.

The choice of software packages to include on the CD-ROM was a difficult one. Some were chosen because they are reference implementations. Some were chosen because they are classics that most people working with Internet email will deal with at one time or another. The absence of a package does not reflect the author's opinion of it. There are just too many software packages available; a line had to be drawn somewhere.

The software packages on the CD-ROM are the more recent versions available at the time of publication. Most software packages on the Internet are distributed as compressed archive files. The ones here have been uncompressed and expanded from their archive format, without modification. Note that they are provided as examples for viewing by readers. Neither the author nor the publisher provides support for them.

One final word about the CD-ROM. Over time, some of the information will become out of date. Readers are strongly encouraged to check the original sources to determine if this is the case.

Acknowledgments

Several people deserve special mention. The first ones are the many authors of email RFCs, those still with us, and those departed. This book is a tribute to their work.

The staff of Addison-Wesley is to be commended for helping in the creation of this book. Karen Gettman, the editor, not only believed the book was worth publishing, but provided insight and advice throughout the process. She also lined up some of the best reviewers I could have imagined. Mary Hart, the project editor, kept the process of routing draft submissions and reviewer comments clean and predictable. Their understanding and professionalism helped make this project manageable. Marilyn Rash, the production coordinator, kept the production phase running smoothly, even in the face of the inevitable glitches that arose. Dianne Cannon Wood, the copy editor, did an excellent job of smoothing the rough edges off the draft manuscript. In addition, the people at Interactive Composition in Portland, Oregon, are to be commended for coming through in a pinch.

I would like to thank the technical reviewers—Vic Abell, Mark Crispin of the University of Washington, Mark Ellis of Reuters, Ned Freed of Innosoft, Vic Hargrave of Endeavor Information Systems, Howard Lee Harkness, Christopher Lindsey of NCSA, Danny J. Mitzel, and Pete Wilson. Their comments and suggestions on the draft material were invaluable.

I would also like to thank several people I work with at Motorola Computer Group. Ken Ridgely, my manager, encouraged me to pursue this project and gave me flexibility with my schedule at all the right times. Being a technical manager poses special challenges; Ken is one of the best. Larry Cruz and Eric Sunderland provided feedback on early drafts of the material; their patience with these was admirable. Susan Lee Wilson provided a good sounding board for many of the problems I encountered. Her uncanny ability to ask just the right question, at just the right time, helped me solve many perplexing problems. I'd also like to thank the many people who graciously let me bend their ears about my experiences writing a book.

A few other people deserve a word of thanks. Both Randal L. Schwartz, General Manager of Stonehenge Consulting Services Inc., and Joseph Hall, author of *Effective Perl Programming,* encouraged me to believe my idea for a book wasn't farfetched and provided useful advice to a first-time author. In particular, Joseph recommended that I submit a proposal to Addison-Wesley. Without their encouragement and help, the book would never have been written. I'd also like to thank Meng Weng Wong, of `pobox.com`, for technical feedback and for chiding me on my use of my native tongue, and Sean M. Burke for opening my eyes, as it were, to the larger importance of the `Content-Language` field.

Last, but not least, I'd like to thank my wife, Kate, for understanding my desire to write this book, providing moral support during the project, and gallantly sacrificing time normally spent together. Marrying her was the best decision I've ever made.

I cannot imagine writing this book without the help of all these people. Their involvement has made this a better book.

Internet Email Protocols

Overview

Email is a set of mechanisms designed to allow computer users to send messages to one another. A user composes a piece of mail, provides one or more addresses to send it to, and then sends it. The message is delivered to its final destination, where the recipient uses a program to view it. While this process is conceptually simple, it involves a relatively sophisticated set of protocols, standards, and conventions.

Internet email is defined by a set of RFC (Request for Comment) documents, published by the IETF (Internet Engineering Task Force). It was initially designed in the early days of the Internet when most users were part of research and development efforts. As the Internet has become accessible to more and more universities, businesses, and ultimately consumers, Internet email has expanded to a point where it is one of the more common mail systems in use.

Not only was email one of the first applications widely used on the Internet, but it has shown impressive staying power. Several of the newer application protocols are gradually replacing or minimizing the use of older ones. A good example of this is the WWW (World Wide Web). The older FTP (File Transfer Protocol) is still widely used, but WWW is displacing it for many file transfers. Traditional Internet email, on the other hand, is still going strong and is showing no signs of being displaced.

Though widely used, Internet email it not the only type of email; there are several other types in use, each of which was created in different environments with different goals in mind. They won't be discussed in this book, but it's a good idea to at least know about them. Issues related to interfacing to these other types of email do come up from time to time.

Prior to a few years ago, the first exposure to email many personal computer users had was through LAN-based email packages, mainframe systems, or closed-system online services. These were often proprietary, often couldn't interoperate with other email systems, and often had limited scalability.

In an effort to create a world-wide email standard, the ISO (International Organization for Standardization) and ITU (International Telecommunications

Union) published a set of messaging standards known as X.400. Actually, this is the short name; the real name is ISO/IEC 10021, although it is rarely referred to this way. It is a very rich, powerful, and large set of standards. While there has been interest in X.400, particularly in Europe, it hasn't gained widespread acceptance across the Internet because of its size and complexity.

The explosive growth and popularity of the Internet is causing most of the other email implementations to either adapt to the Internet standards or be displaced by ones that do.

One last note. As the title suggests, this book talks about Internet email. For simplicity, however, the remainder of the book uses the words *email* or *mail* instead of *Internet email* unless a direct comparison to non-Internet email is being made.

1.1 THE VIEW FROM 10,000 FEET

So, what does email look like, and how does it operate? At the lowest levels, it can get quite complicated. At the highest level it's pretty simple, consisting of mail messages, a protocol for moving those messages from place to place, and interfaces for users to perform various related tasks.

The primary element of email is the message. Most of the protocols and specifications are centered around describing what a message can look like or how to move it from one place to another. The message is the medium, as it were.

Although email messages will be covered in detail in Chapter 2, a few basics will be covered here. A message consists of an envelope, a header, and a body. The envelope specifies the source and destination of the message. This will be covered in detail in Chapter 3. The header contains various pieces of information about the message. The body contains the information that the sender wants to communicate. Of these three components, the header and body are the only ones that most users see; the envelope is typically used only internally. The overall structure of the header and body is relatively simple, as illustrated in the following example.

```
From: bob@flugelhorn.example.com
To: joe@tuba.example.com
Subject: An ineffable email test
Date: Sat, 1 Apr 2000 12:00:00 -0700

Hey Joe,
Why do you have flour in your hair?


--
thx,
Bob
```

The header and the body are separated by a blank line. This example has four fields in the header: `To`, `From`, `Subject`, and `Date`. There are a lot of other fields that may be present in a header.

One very important aspect of email messages is the address. There are two in the previous example. Addresses are used in envelopes and headers, and relate where a message is going and where it is coming from.

While email addresses can be quite complicated, their basic structure is simple.

```
bob@flugelhorn.example.com
```

The left-hand side identifies a mailbox where the mail should be delivered, and the right-hand side identifies the machine where the mailbox resides; the '@' separates the two. Actually, this description glosses over a few details, but for now it is adequate. A more in-depth description will unfold.

A traditional message body is also very simple, consisting of a series of lines of text. While there are a few extensions defined that impose a small amount of structure on the message, it is generally free-form text data. For plain text this is more than adequate, but because email was so effective as a communication medium, people eventually wanted to send data other than plain text. Early in its history, this wasn't too much of a problem. People cobbled together several techniques that were, for the most part, workable. As time went on, however, it became obvious that something more robust was needed. As a result, MIME (Multipurpose Internet Mail Extensions) was created. These extensions define a means to encapsulate data that isn't text-oriented into email messages. They will be described in detail in Chapter 4.

An email message by itself is of limited usefulness. There needs to be a way to move it from one location to another. This work is divided into several tasks. An MTA (Mail Transport Agent) routes mail, an MDA (Mail Delivery Agent) delivers it on behalf of an MTA, and an MUA (Mail User Agent) provides an interface for the user. These tasks are typically done by different programs. While some email programs can perform more than one of these functions, it is a good idea to keep a mental distinction between them.

1.1.1 Mail Transfer Agents

An MTA receives messages from various sources. As each message is received, the MTA decides where and how the message should be routed, rewriting addresses if necessary. It then hands the message over to an MDA for delivery.

The primary mechanism for controlling the routing of Internet mail is the DNS (Domain Name Service) protocol. DNS provides a distributed database that maps domain names to several types of information, including mail-routing instructions. Most MTAs also provide their own mechanism for directly controlling routing as an adjunct to DNS routing. This is useful for local quirks or for working around temporary DNS routing problems.

In some situations it is necessary to rewrite addresses as messages are transferred from one location to the next. For example, some organizations prefer to email addresses to appear to be from one central location. Rewriting is one way this is done.

Address rewriting is also needed in some situations where email is being routed in or out of a non-Internet email system. For example, UUCP (UNIX to UNIX Copy) uses '!' as the separator for the list of machines through which a particular message needs to be routed. Since this is a different format from that of Internet email, an MTA that routes mail through these two systems needs to be able to rewrite addresses accordingly. Most, if not all, MTAs provide a way to alter the rewriting rules. Some compile the rules into the program, while others put them in runtime configuration files.

1.1.2 Mail Delivery Agents

Once an MTA has received a message, processed it, and decided where to route it, it hands it off to an MDA. The MDA is responsible for delivering a message to another location, which could be another MTA, a user's inbox, or a program that performs some special task. Based on whether the delivery attempt succeeded or generated a permanent or a temporary failure, the MTA decides whether the transaction should be considered complete, should generate an error back to the sender, or should be retried in the future.

The simplest type of MDA is the one used by some systems to deliver to a local mailbox. It simply appends the incoming message to a local user's inbox. There are, however, other things that can be done to the message at delivery time. Instead of simply appending incoming email, some MDAs provide filtering features that provide additional manipulation of incoming messages. Other MDAs can transmit the email to another machine. The possibilities are seemingly endless. One of the more common uses of MDAs, filtering, is discussed in Chapter 7.

If an MTA decides a message needs to be routed to another MTA, it hands the message over to an MDA that uses SMTP (Simple Mail Transfer Protocol), which defines a set of commands to transfer a message to a remote MTA. This MDA is often built into the MTA. SMTP and its relationship to MTAs and mail delivery are described in Chapter 3.

1.1.3 Mail User Agents

While MTAs and MDAs are responsible for routing and transporting mail messages, Mail User Agents are responsible for providing an interface for users to manage their mail. This management typically includes viewing messages, managing mail folders, and composing and sending new mail, as well as replying to messages and sending existing messages to other users. It is usually the only type of email program to which mere mortals interface directly.

In the early days of email, the MUA typically resided on the same machine where a user received his or her email. Eventually, two protocols, POP (Post Office

Protocol) and IMAP (Internet Message Access Protocol), were created to allow use of an MUA to read email that resides on remote machines.

POP provides a protocol for MUAs to download the user's inbox from a remote server. This allows the user to live on a machine that isn't always connected to the network. It is described in Chapter 5.

IMAP provides a protocol for MUAs to manipulate mail folders on a remote server. An MUA that implements the protocol can connect to a remote IMAP server and perform the various tasks that need to be done with mailboxes and messages. This allows a user's mail folders and MUA to reside on different machines. Chapter 6 describes the protocol in detail.

1.2 THE STANDARDS

As with other Internet applications and protocols, standards define how email operates. These standards are defined in a set of RFCs, which define the various protocols and formats necessary to make email work across the Internet. In order to understand how these RFCs are created and how they evolve, knowledge about the standards process is needed.

1.2.1 The Standards Process

At the top of the tree is ISOC (Internet Society). This is an international organization established to coordinate and maintain the development of the Internet. The IAB (Internet Architecture Board) is a technical advisory group chartered by ISOC to define the overall Internet architecture. Among other things, it provides oversight of the standards process and acts as the publisher of Internet RFC documents.

The IETF is the entity tasked by the IAB to design and develop the standards and protocols used on the Internet. It is divided into Areas, which are collections of Working Groups focused on a particular broad category of standards work. The current Areas are Applications, General, Internet, Operations and Management, Routing, Security, Transport, and User Services. Most of the work related to email is done in the Applications Area.

The Working Groups in an Area focus different topics of standards development. They are created and destroyed as the need for a particular topic comes and goes. Sometimes a BOF (Birds of a Feather) team is formed for a particular topic before a Working Group is created. The purpose of a BOF is to analyze a particular area of interest, determine the need for work, and possibly even create some preliminary Internet Drafts to get the ball rolling. If the topic is worthy, the BOF might evolve into a Working Group.

While a Working Group is active, it produces one or more Internet Drafts, with a final product typically being one or more RFCs. An Internet Draft of an interim document is used to communicate the work being done by the Working Group.

These drafts are reviewed by the IESG (Internet Engineering Steering Group), which decides whether or not an Internet Draft should be promoted to RFC status.

The work isn't over, however, once an RFC is created. If the specification is intended to be an Internet Standard, it then travels along a standards track where its maturity is assessed. The maturity levels are as follows.

Proposed Standard. This is the entry-level position, so to speak, for an RFC. At this point in the process, the specification is considered to be relatively stable and well understood, has been well reviewed, and is sufficiently interesting to the Internet community. The main obstacles to the next level are that the specification needs more exposure and some working implementations have to be available to confirm some of the characteristics just mentioned.

Proposed Standards should be considered stable but immature. The content of the specification might change as a result of early implementations, so caution with the use of the protocol is probably a good idea.

Draft Standard. This maturity level represents a significant status advancement for a specification. It means there is a strong belief that it is mature and usable. At this point in its life, the specification has been subjected to several implementations and scrutinized by the affected community, and any necessary adjustments have been made to it.

Implementers can normally consider a Draft Standard to be a final specification. Any further changes will probably be only to solve specific problems. It is considered reasonable to deploy an implementation of a Draft Standard in a production environment.

Internet Standard. Attaining this maturity level means the specification is seen as largely successful and that considerable experience has been obtained. A high level of technical maturity is present in the specification, and it is generally thought to be of significant benefit to the Internet.

In addition to the maturity level, each standards document is assigned a protocol status, which reflects the extent to which the protocol is required.

Required—a system must implement the protocol.

Recommended—a system should implement the protocol.

Elective—a system can decide not to implement the protocol.

Limited Use—the protocol is for use in limited circumstances, typically because it is experimental or historical.

Not Recommended—the protocol is not recommended for general use, typically because of limited functionality or because it is experimental or historical.

If an RFC is not intended to be an Internet Standard or is not yet ready for the standards track, it will be classified as one of the following types:

Experimental—typically assigned to research and development work.

Informational—typically assigned to RFCs that relate general information to the Internet community. They don't necessarily represent a consensus, nor are they intended as a recommendation.

Best Current Practice—typically assigned to RFCs that represent best current practices on the Internet. RFC1818 (Best Current Practices) describes this classification.

Historic—typically assigned to RFCs that have been superseded by newer RFCs or that, for any other reason, are considered obsolete.

Some RFCs contain requirements for unique names, numbers, and parameters. For many years, the IANA (Internet Assigned Numbers Authority), an organization funded by the U.S. government, provided coordination, allocation, and registration services for this type of information. However, since the Internet is an international entity, it was decided that an international organization should provide these services. This new organization is the nonprofit corporation ICANN (Internet Corporation for Assigned Names and Numbers).

This section has provided a very-high-level review of the standards process. Quite a few details have been glossed over. More information on the organizations that oversee the Internet can be found at their respective Web sites.

1.2.2 Augmented Backus-Naur Form

Many RFCs need to specify the syntax of information they are describing. Some early ones used BNF (Backus-Naur Form) notation for this. Eventually, a variation of BNF was devised, which allowed a more compact syntax representation. This ABNF (Augmented Backus-Naur Form) is used in a lot of email RFCs. Initially, many RFCs included a description of the ABNF syntax. To avoid duplicating the information, other RFCs often simply referenced an RFC that contained such a description.

Eventually, an RFC was created to collect the ABNF information into one central document, which all RFCs could refer to. The result was RFC2234 (Augmented BNF for Syntax Specifications).

Many, if not most, email RFCs rely heavily on ABNF. Because of this, it's important to understand what ABNF is, what is looks like, and how it works.

An ABNF syntax description is made up of a set of rules that describe the structure of a data stream. Each rule consists of a rule name, an '=' character, the specification for the rule, and a line terminator.

```
name = elements CRLF
```

A rule name consists of an initial alphabetic character, followed by any combination of alphabetic characters, numeric digits, and hyphen characters. It is case-insensitive, meaning that any combination of upper- and lower-case characters refer to the same rule.

The elements following the '=' character are a combination of other rule names, operators, individual characters, and character strings. The rule names reference other rules. The operators control how the rule names and values can be combined to form a given rule.

Individual characters are represented with a '%', a number base specifier, and a series of digits. The number base can be one of three characters, which are listed in Table 1.1. Thus, the decimal, binary, and hexadecimal representations for 42 are '%d42', '%b101010', and '%h2A', respectively.

A range of characters can be specified with a variation of this notation.

```
%d48-57
```

This example represents any character contained in the inclusive range of characters between US-ASCII '0' and '9'.

It's also possible to notate a sequence of characters. In this case, two or more characters are combined, with '.' used to separate them. The following example specifies the US-ASCII characters 'B', 'o', and 'b'.

```
%d66.111.98
```

Strings are represented as a sequence of characters inside a pair of '"' characters.

```
"Bob"
```

In ABNF, these quoted strings are case-insensitive. Thus, the string "bOB" is equivalent to the previous example. For non-case-sensitive strings, the '.' notation shown previously must be used.

TABLE 1.1 Number Base Specifiers

Character	Description
b	Binary
d	Decimal
x	Hexadecimal

At this point, it is possible to define some simple rules.

```
owner  = person
person = "bob"
```

In this example, an *owner* consists of a *person* and a *person* consists of the string "bob".

By itself, this doesn't appear to be very useful. The real power comes when the operators are added. Operators control how rule names, characters, and strings can be combined.

The concatenation operator allows a sequence of elements to be combined into an ordered list of members.

```
owner      = firstname middlename lastname
firstname  = "bob"
middlename = "gold"
lastname   = "doubloon"
```

In this example, *owner* is defined as an instance of *firstname* followed by *lastname*.

To specify alternatives, the '/' operator is used.

```
pet = dog / cat
```

This operator can also be used to combine more than two rules.

```
pet = dog / cat / iguana
```

A variation of the alternation operator can be used to add an alternative to an existing rule. In this case, '=/' is used instead of '='.

```
pet =/ rock
```

To specify repetition, the following notation is used.

```
m*m element
```

The *m* and *n* are optional decimal values, which indicate at least *m* and at most *n* occurrences of *element.*

```
1*3pet
```

This example specifies from one to three instances of *pet.*

If *m* is not specified, it defaults to 0. If *n* is not specified, it defaults to infinity. Thus, the following example specifies three or more pets.

```
3*pet
```

If *m* and *n* are the same, it means an exact value. In this case, the notation can be simplified from '*m**m' to '*n*'.

```
2pet
```

Another notation convenience is the *optional sequence*. As an alternative to using '*1' to indicate zero or one occurrence of an element, the element can be enclosed in a pair of '[ ]' characters.

```
[element]
```

A ';' character indicates comments in a syntax description. In this case, all the text on a line following the comment character is ignored up to the end of the line.

```
pets = 1*pet          ; hope you have enough iguana food
```

This allows an RFC author to embed notes about a rule in a syntax description.

Elements can also be grouped together, using parentheses, into *sequence groups,* which are treated as a single element.

```
person = firstname (middlename / initial) lastname
```

In this example, the second element can be either *middlename* or *initial.*

The following list shows the precedence of the various operators, from the highest to the lowest.

- Characters, strings, and rule names
- Comments
- Value ranges
- Repetition
- Grouping and optional sequences
- Concatenation
- Alternatives

ABNF is not complicated. It provides a standard notation to specify the grammar for various objects defined in an RFC. It plays an important role in the email RFCs, as will be seen in subsequent chapters.

1.3 A BRIEF HISTORY OF INTERNET EMAIL

Because email and its associated standards were developed over time, it is important to understand its history. Knowing the state of email at a particular point in time helps put the various standards in perspective.

The predecessor to the Internet was ARPANET. Created in 1969, it was a research and development project funded by DARPA (Defense Advanced Research Projects Agency). ARPANET laid a lot of the groundwork for the modern Internet.

In 1972, Ray Tomlinson wrote the first email program, SNDMSG, for use on ARPANET. It was very popular in the then small circle of ARPANET users. Shortly after its introduction, several other companion programs and variants cropped up. This triggered the need to develop standards to define how email would be transferred from machine to machine and to define how email messages were structured. Throughout the 70s, several documents were created to establish early standards.

The early 80s saw a certain amount of maturation in the standards. SMTP was created and is still one of the core standards for email. The email header standards also stabilized to a certain level of maturity, culminating in RFC822 (Standard for the Format of ARPA Internet Text Messages). In addition, POP was developed, which simplified the use of personal computers for handling email.

In the late 70s and early 80s, concurrent to the growth of ARPANET, several other networks sprouted up. This was partly because ARPANET was not available to all research organizations. Email played a central role in these new networks, several of which are noteworthy when talking about email.

Usenet. Based on UUCP, Usenet was initially created as a link between Duke University and the University of North Carolina. This is what most people on the Internet refer to as *news,* or *Usenet news.* It is still in wide use today on the Internet, although, for the most part, NNTP (Network News Transfer Protocol), instead of UUCP, is used as the transport mechanism. Usenet employs a message structure very similar to email.

BITNET (Because It's Time Network). BITNET was started at the City University of New York. One of its interesting features was that the only software required to participate in the network was email.

CSNET (Computer Science Network). CSNET was initially created as a link between the University of Delaware, Purdue University, the University of Wisconsin, the RAND corporation, and Bott Berenek and Newman (BBN). Its purpose was to provide network services, especially email, to university researchers who didn't have access to ARPANET.

During this time, these networks, and many others, were connected to ARPANET and to each other, forming the basis for the Internet. This period of growing inter-network connectivity culminated in 1990 when ARPANET was decommissioned. What remained was the Internet.

Another characteristic of the 80s was the development of several applications that solidified email's place on the Internet. One of them was the Sendmail MTA, one of the first MTAs to implement SMTP. Sendmail was designed to send and receive email with a variety of email communication protocols, and to this day it is the primary MTA used on the Internet. Another significant program created in the 80s was Elm. First released in 1983, this MUA was one of the first full-screen interactive email clients on the Internet. It was the choice for a lot of Internet users for quite a few years and it too, is still in use. These programs, and many others developed during this time, formed the baseline by which other email packages are judged.

An increased awareness of email security issues also developed in the late 80s. One of the most notable events occurred in 1988 when Robert Morris' *Internet Worm* wreaked havoc, crippling a large segment of the Internet by exploiting, among other things, a weakness in Sendmail. The incident was a wake-up call to the Internet community. Before, security issues had cropped up from time to time, but there was no large-scale organized response to security. The Worm was the driving force behind the creation of the CERT (Computer Emergency Response Team) organization and triggered a small renaissance in computing and networking security.

Most people on the Internet initially got connected in the 90s. The first decade saw the number of hosts grow from 4 to nearly 200; the second decade, to almost 300,000; and the third decade, to more than 19 million. The massive influx of new users has been accompanied by the continued evolution of older email programs, and a plethora of new ones.

One area that has seen particular advancement is the MUA. The wide use of personal computers triggered the creation of GUI (Graphical User Interface) interfaces for MUAs. This graphical interface, in combination with MIME, POP, and IMAP, provides a powerful communication tool for users.

The 90s has also brought about the large-scale use of unsolicited bulk email and news postings, brought to the forefront in 1994 when the law firm of Canter and Siegel posted a message to over 6,000 Usenet newsgroups advertising legal assistance for Green Card work permits in the Unites States. To the best of the author's knowledge, this was the first time the word *spamming* was used to describe large-scale unsolicited distribution of news or email. Spamming was, to put it mildly, not well received by the Usenet community—responses ranged from hate mail to death threats. The incident brought the issue of unsolicited messages to the minds of Internet users. It was also a sign of things to come—unsolicited email and news were here to stay.

So what changes are on the horizon? There are several areas of email under development. As of the writing of this book, RFC821 (Simple Mail Transfer Protocol) and RFC822 are undergoing a significant revision, intended to clarify many historical errors and ambiguities. When complete, they should help improve the quality of email software by minimizing problems related to interpretation of the older standards. Additional document types are frequently added to MIME. Progress is being made in the area of security. A new protocol, ACAP (Application Configuration Access Protocol), is being developed for accessing configuration information via the network, which will be a real boon for mobile email users. Developers are improving their understanding of what functionality is useful in MUAs. From all appearances, email will continue to evolve for some time.

1.4 SUMMARY

Email consists of four major components—mail messages, MTAs, MDAs, and MUAs. Mail messages are the paper on which messages are written. MTAs route messages, MDAs deliver them, and MUAs provide the interface for users to create and disposition them.

Internet email is defined in a set of RFCs published by the IETF. A standards process exists for the creation of new standards and the revision of old ones. This process is partially responsible for the success of Internet email.

The history of Internet email is inextricably linked to the history of the Internet. Not only was it one of the first widely used services on the Internet, and on ARPANET; it is still one of the most widely used services today.

This chapter provides a high-level view of Internet email. Subsequent chapters shift focus from the broad strokes in this chapter to the detail of specific topics.

Chapter 2

Mail Messages

The keystone of email is the mail message, around which nearly every aspect of email revolves. Understanding email requires a solid understanding of how messages are structured.

The core structure of email is defined in two primary RFCs, both of which are required reading for anyone doing anything substantial with the technical side of email.

The first one is RFC822, published in 1982. It is the current standard for Internet email messages. RFC822 defines how mail messages need to be formatted when being transmitted from host to host. Its main purpose is to provide a normalized format for mail messages so that different types of networks can transfer email from one to another. A common misconception is that it defines the format of stored email as well. This is false. While many mail packages store an Internet mail message in the same format, there's no requirement to do so.

RFC1123 (Requirements for Internet Hosts—Application and Support), published in 1989, contains important updates to many Internet standards. Section 5 of RFC1123 contains specific information about electronic mail standards.

This chapter is based primarily on the information in RFC822. In places where RFC822 is problematic, or where common usage varies, additional information is provided as needed.

2.1 THE MESSAGE

At the highest level, a mail message is very simple. It consists of a series of text lines, each of which is terminated with a CR (carriage-return) character followed by an LF (line-feed) character. When CR and LF are combined in this way, they form CRLF (carriage-return–line-feed). The contents of each line consists of US-ASCII characters. US-ASCII is a 7-bit variant of the ASCII (American Standard

Code for Information Interchange) character set. MIME adds the ability to specify alternatives, but all the examples in this chapter use US-ASCII.

Unfortunately, the RFC822 definition of a line raises some issues. Namely, RFC822 allows message lines to contain US-ASCII 0, CR, and LF characters. US-ASCII 0 presents a problem for many programming libraries, since it is commonly used internally to represent the end of a line. CR and LF characters are problematic as well, since in various combinations they are used for line termination on various operating systems. Developers are strongly encouraged to disallow US-ASCII 0 in email messages. This goes for single CR or LF characters as well; they should be used only in CRLF line terminators.

RFC822 doesn't specify any limits on line length or message length. Most of the length limitations related to email messages are specified in the RFCs for SMTP. In line with the Robustness Principle,[1] the limits are stated as maximum lengths an email program is allowed to generate. Email software should not, within reason, impose any limitations on the sizes it can accept.

The SMTP standard imposes a limit of 1,000 characters per line, including the line termination characters. For readability, lines should be shorter than 80 characters, including the CRLF.

There is no specified limit to the number of lines in a mail message, but some software packages and some transport mechanisms, such as SMTP, impose limits of their own. These and related limits on mail messages are described in Chapter 3.

The overall format of the lines of text in a mail message is reminiscent of a standard office memorandum. At the beginning of the message is a collection of lines called the *header*. It contains information such as who sent a message, who it is being sent to, when it was sent, and the subject. The header has a defined format designed to allow programmatic parsing of the header data. This enables MTAs, MDAs, and MUAs to analyze and act on information in a mail message.

Following the header is a blank line, used to separate the header from the remainder of the message. Following the blank line is a set of lines called the *body*. The body is the payload—the actual information to be related to recipients of the message. Figure 2.1 shows a simple email message with each of the top-level elements identified. While the header is required, the body is optional. Also, the blank line is optional if the body isn't present.

Messages were designed to be easy to parse at a high level, without the need to know too much of the underlying structure. RFC822 even provides a grammar definition for developers who need to perform a high-level parse of messages.

---

[1] "Be liberal in what you accept, and conservative in what you send." Although its exact origins are unknown, the Robustness Principle was deemed important enough to be mentioned in Section 1.2.2 of RFC1122 (Requirements for Internet Hosts—Communication Layers).

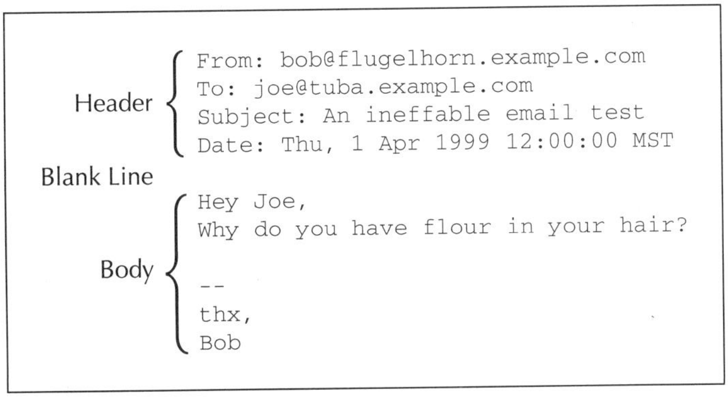

```
          ⎧ From: bob@flugelhorn.example.com
          ⎪ To: joe@tuba.example.com
  Header ⎨ Subject: An ineffable email test
          ⎩ Date: Thu, 1 Apr 1999 12:00:00 MST

Blank Line

          ⎧ Hey Joe,
          ⎪ Why do you have flour in your hair?
          ⎪
    Body ⎨ --
          ⎪ thx,
          ⎩ Bob
```

FIGURE 2.1 A Simple Email Message

2.1.1 The Body

The body will be described first, since it is simpler than the header. The body conveys the actual message sent to a recipient. Pure RFC822 message bodies are merely a series of text lines, which have no additional structure or meaning imposed on them.

Because additional structure is sometimes desirable, several ad-hoc conventions have evolved over the years, outside the scope of the message format standard. One of the most commonly encountered body structures is the email signature, a series of lines, typically three to five, at the end of the message body that convey information about the sender.

There is no standard for how email signatures are structured or what they contain. Typically they contain information such as the person's preferred name, job title, and business affiliation and often personal commentary and humor.

For more information about signatures, one needs to look at the documents that define the format of Usenet News messages. One document, referred to as "son-of-RFC1036,"[2] contains a definition for a signature separator for news articles that many email users have adopted. Here, the signature is preceded by a delimiter line consisting of the string '--␣'. Having a well-defined delimiter line allows MUAs to provide additional visual cues to the user about the message being presented, such as displaying the signature in a different color. This signature separator is by no means ubiquitous, so there is no way for MUAs to reliably detect ad-hoc email signatures.

Another ad-hoc convention that gained wide use early in the history of Internet email was the use of encoding programs to convert binary data into a format safe

---

[2] This document was written by Henry Spencer, as an update to RFC1036 (Standard for Interchange of USENET Messages). The update was never published as an RFC, but is considered one of the primary documents defining Usenet news. It is available at `ftp://zoo.toronto.edu/pub/news.txt.Z`.

for email transport. A common technique was to use a program such as uuencode to encode the binary data into printable US-ASCII characters.

Another useful capability was identified earlier in the history of email—encapsulating several email messages into one aggregate message, called a *digest*. A digest is often used on high-volume mailing lists to reduce the quantity of mail messages being delivered to inboxes.

Each of these conventions suffers from one common problem—they were never adopted as standards and are not defined in RFC822. General solutions to these problems had to wait for the creation of MIME, which is discussed in detail in Chapter 4.

2.1.2 The Header

The lines of a header are grouped into fields, which provide information about the piece of mail that is intended for both users and programs.

Each field is made up of one or more lines of text. For fields spanning more than one line, the additional lines start with whitespace and are called *continuation lines*. Section 2.2.5 describes continuation lines in greater detail.

Fields

Each header field is made up of a field name, optional whitespace, a colon, optional commented folding whitespace, and an optional field body. The field body can also contain leading whitespace.

```
field = field-name *WSP ":" [[CFWS] field-body] CRLF
```

Whitespace will be described in more detail in Section 2.2.1.

To simplify syntax descriptions, future examples will dispense with the trailing CRLF, except where it is fundamental to an understanding of a particular item.

The following example shows a typical field.

```
Subject: a question about the fuel injectors
```

There is usually no whitespace between the field name and the colon.

The *field-name* consists of a sequence of any printable US-ASCII characters, except the space character or ':'. Most field names consist of a series alphanumeric characters, often interspersed with dash characters.

```
From:
Status:
Subject:
X-Mailer:
```

TABLE 2.1 Standard Header Fields

Field Name	Description
From	The creator of the message
Sender	The sender of the message
Reply-To	The address to send replies to
To	Primary recipients of the message
Cc	Secondary recipients of the message
Bcc	Blind Carbon Copy recipients of the message
Message-ID	The message's unique identifier
In-Reply-To	The message being replied to
References	All messages ancestors
Date	The date the message was created
Received	MTA footprint
Return-Path	The address of the originator
Subject	The subject of the message
Comments	Miscellaneous comments regarding the message
Keywords	Topical keywords related to the message
Encrypted	Encryption information (obsolete)
Resent-*	Fields created when redistributing
X-*	Extension Fields

Since the set of allowable characters is broader than what is shown in the previous examples, here are some valid field names using other characters.

```
X-(foo):
X-"Quotification":
X-#(@#*&@#$!:
X-$obj->$key:
```

RFC822 defines a standard set of fields for mail messages. Table 2.1 lists those fields, which will be described in detail in Section 2.3. In truth, there are many other fields, but these form the foundation for basic email.

While field names are relatively straightforward, field bodies are another story. At the highest level, field bodies consist of a sequence of US-ASCII characters. There are, however, several aspects to them not covered by this description, including the use of whitespace, parenthetical comments, quoting, and field folding. These details are described in Section 2.2. In addition, the contents of a field body depend on the field name, with each type of field having a specific format. The format of the standard fields is described in greater detail in Section 2.3.

Required Fields

In the two dozen fields defined in RFC822, very few header fields are actually required. The message must specify the date it was created on, using a `Date` or

Resent-Date field. It must also specify a mailbox for the person or program creating the message, using the From field.

RFC822 requires a recipient field. This can be a To, Cc, or Bcc field, or its Resent-* equivalent.

In addition to the header required in sent messages, all MTAs that process a message must add a Received line at the beginning of each header. This adds information describing the path a message took to reach a recipient.

Recommended Order of Fields

With only a few exceptions, the fields in a header aren't required to be in any particular order. The exceptions are the Received, Return-Path, and Resent-* fields. As a message passes through a series of MTAs, each MTA prepends a Received field to the message. The Return-Path is prepended by the final MTA prior to final delivery. Because these fields provide tracing information for diagnosing problems, their placement must not be altered. Any Resent-* fields added to a message should also be prepended.

RFC822 recommends the following order.

```
Date
From
Subject
Sender
To
Cc
...
```

In practice, there is no compelling need or requirement to follow this order. In fact, browsing through an arbitrary collection of mail messages reveals that the order varies widely. While the fields inserted by MTAs, mailing list processors, and MDAs are typically prepended and appended, the order of the rest of the fields typically isn't fixed.

Multiple Occurrences of Fields

RFC822 allows for multiple occurrences of any of the fields. With the exception of the Received and Resent-* fields, however, multiple occurrences are discouraged. With some fields, the meaning of multiple occurrences is intuitively obvious. For example, multiple To fields obviously means the same as when all the members of those fields are contained in one field. Multiple occurrences present difficulties with many other fields, however. For example, how should multiple Date fields be handled?

In general, there are two common ways for an MUA to handle errant multiple instances of fields. It can use the first one encountered or the last one encountered.

It's not uncommon to find MUAs that use a mix of these two methods, depending on the field in question.

Some readers might be wondering whether errant messages should just be rejected. This is generally a bad idea because it violates the Robustness Principle, which suggests that it's better for email software to deal with the problem gracefully instead of throwing the message away or bouncing it back to the sender.

Structured and Unstructured Fields

So far in this chapter, very little has been said about the content of a field. This is about to be rectified by a detailed look at each of the standard fields. Before the detail, however, one last concept needs to be mentioned—structured and unstructured fields.

Structured fields have a specific format parsers might need to detect. The `Sender` field is a good example of this; here the content of the field is a mailbox, which has a discrete structure.

An unstructured field contains arbitrary data with no defined format. For example, a `Subject` field contains arbitrary text, which has no inherent structure. The only fields that are unstructured are `Subject`, `Comments`, extension fields, nonstandard fields, and certain instances of `In-Reply-To` and `References`. All other fields are structured.

2.2 INSIDE FIELDS

While the higher-level structure of messages is relatively simple, the structure of some fields can be complicated. Before delving into the details of each standard field, several elements common to most fields need to be understood.

2.2.1 Whitespace

There are several places in fields where whitespace, which plays an important role in the formatting of fields, can be used. The rules in RFC822 for the placement of whitespace are difficult to digest. In an attempt to simplify the syntax notation, RFC822 left the notation for whitespace out of the main syntax descriptions for fields. Readers have to interpolate the rules from the main text of the standard into the syntax descriptions. Even with years of experience, it's often necessary to review the standard for clarification of some of the finer points. Because of the difficulty of whitespace handling in RFC822, there have been many mistakes made by developers over the years.

One of the ways to avoid difficulties with whitespace is to be conservative in its use. Rather than try to stretch the intent of RFC822, it is often better to use whitespace only as needed. A review of existing email implementations shows that most developers follow this strategy.

There are generally three types of whitespace, each with specific uses and places where they are allowed.

Simple Whitespace

The simplest form consists of a single space (US-ASCII 32) or tab (US-ASCII 9) character. These form the basis of the other forms of whitespace.

```
WSP  = SP / HTAB
SP   = %x20
HTAB = %x09
```

RFC822 calls this an *LWSP-char*.

Folding Whitespace

This form combines simple whitespace and CR and LF characters. RFC822 refers to it as *linear-white-space*. Folding whitespace is semantically equivalent to simple whitespace. It is used to implement field folding, which is discussed in Section 2.2.5.

The syntax allows the occurrence of lines made up entirely of white space characters. This should be considered an anomoly in the syntax, and should be avoided.

The definition for folding whitespace is as follows:

```
FWS = 1(*[CRLF] WSP)
```

This amounts to various combinations of CRLF and WSP characters.

Commented Folding Whitespace

This form integrates comments into folding whitespace. Comments are described in Section 2.2.3. Like folding whitespace, commented folded whitespace is semantically equivalent to simple whitespace.

RFC822 doesn't explicitly include a syntax for commented folding whitespace. The following syntax, however, describes the various possible combinations of folding whitespace and comments.

```
CFWS = *([FWS] comment) (([FWS] comment) / FWS)
```

2.2.2 Atoms

Several places in structured fields use sequences of certain basic characters. These sequences are called *atoms*. The syntax for atoms is as follows.

```
atom     = 1*<any CHAR except specials, SP, or CTL>
specials = "(" / ")" / "<" / ">" / "@" / "," / ";" /
           ":" / "\" / <"> / "." / "[" / "]"
CTL      = %d0-31 / %d127
```

This doesn't tell the entire story, however. Because whitespace can occur on either side of an atom, the following syntax is more accurate.

```
atom = [CFWS] 1*<any CHAR except specials, SP, or CTL> [CFWS]
```

There are some places where a '.' character is used in concert with atoms. To simplify the syntax descriptions, a *dot-atom* token is useful.

```
dot-atom      = [CFWS] dot-atom-text [CFWS]
dot-atom-text = 1*atext *("." 1*atext)
```

This is used in several places in this chapter.

2.2.3 Comments

A *comment* is a sequence of characters surrounded by parentheses.

```
(this is a comment)
```

In the places where comments are interpreted, they can be replaced with a single space character and nothing is supposed to break. This is not to say comments don't contain information useful to a human reader, but as far as the semantic meaning of a field is concerned, the comment doesn't exist and isn't supposed to be acted upon. Thus, it is typically used to add additional information not part of the formal definition of a field.[3]

The syntax for comments is as follows.

```
comment  = "(" *([FWS] ccontent) [FWS] ")"
ccontent = ctext / quoted-pair / comment /
           linear-white-space
ctext    = <any CHAR except "(", ")", "\", and CR>
```

Comments are interpreted only in structured fields. They can be present in other places but aren't interpreted as comments.

RFC822 is rather liberal about where comments can occur. Inside structured fields they can occur between tokens or wherever *linear-white-space* is allowed.

---

[3] These comments are not related to the Comments field described in Section 2.3.6.

In addition to not being interpreted in unstructured fields, comments are also not interpreted in quoted strings, which are described in Section 2.2.4. If present, they are considered part of the text of the quoted string.

```
"The (comment) is part of the string"
```

Comments cannot be used inside atoms. Placing a comment inside an atom would split the atom, so to speak.

```
not(reallyth)at(h)om(es)ic(k)
```

Because each comment is equivalent to a space character, the result is as follows.

```
not at om ic
```

Comments can also nest, which means that they can contain other comments.

```
(These (comments) nest inside ((other) comments))
```

Nested comments are the primary hangup for people trying to write email parsers based on regular expressions. Simply put, there is no regular expression capable of matching nested parenthetical clauses of arbitrary depth.

2.2.4 Quoting

Because some characters have special meaning in certain places, two quoting mechanisms are provided for escaping the special meanings. There are two types of quoting: single-character and quoted strings.

A single-character quote is where a character is preceded with '\'. This is similar to the character escaping found in many programming languages. It is only allowed in quoted strings, domain literals, comments, and *msg-id* tokens.

```
"Thus \" the raven"

(this is a comment with a \( character in it)
```

A quoted string is used to quote items in other constructs—that is, the string is wrapped with '"' characters. It should also be used if a sequence of adjacent characters needs to be quoted.

As with single-character quoting, there are limits to where quoted strings may be used, but they are much less severe. Quoted strings cannot be used in domain names, portions of `Received` fields, and *date-time* tokens.

Just as there are places where comments aren't interpreted, there are places where quoted strings aren't interpreted: unstructured fields, field names, comments, and message bodies.

```
Comments: "this time for sure"

X-"yowza": pretty weird, huh?

From: joe@tuba.example.com (the one that "works")
```

Each of the preceding examples shows valid use of quotes, but since the quotes are not used in places where they are interpreted, they don't perform the quoting one would normally expect. To further illustrate the point, let's look at two examples. The first one shows that quoting doesn't escape anything in a field name.

```
X-"yow:za": too weird
```

This is a valid field, but the interpretation is probably not what was intended. The first ':' character, not the second one, is considered to be the separator between the field name and field body.

```
X-"yow: za": too weird
```

Because the quotes aren't interpreted, the ':' isn't escaped.

As another example, here is a quoted string in a comment.

```
From: joe@tuba.example.com
       (the one after the one that works ":-)")
```

Again, because a quoted string isn't interpreted inside a comment, the ')' isn't escaped. As a result, the first ')' is actually considered to be the match for the preceding '(', while the remaining '")' is considered to be outside the comment.

```
From: joe@tuba.example.com ")
```

This probably wasn't the intention. The point to remember is that there are places where quoting works and places where it doesn't, so be careful.

2.2.5 Field Folding

Because lines in a mail message are not allowed to be longer than 1,000 characters, and because long lines can be difficult for humans to read, it is possible to split a field into multiple lines for readability. This is called *folding*. It is allowed in both structured and unstructured fields.

Folding is a good example of the importance of human readability to the creators of the mail message standards. It was built into the standard so that the length of lines could be kept in the range of 72 to 76 characters. Doing this helps make email messages easier to read.

Folding consists of inserting a CRLF and one or more whitespace characters at strategic points in a field. The lines following the first line are called continuation lines.

As an example, the following field is not folded.

```
To: joe@tuba.example.com, mary@glockenspiel.example.com
```

Here is an example of the field with folding.

```
To: joe@tuba.example.com,
    mary@glockenspiel.example.com
```

Strictly speaking this example doesn't need to be folded because the length is small enough to fit on one line. In this case, however, folding helps make the list of recipients a little more readable.[4]

While RFC822 is liberal about where folding can occur, it does recommend folding at higher syntactic points rather than at arbitrary points. For example, in the previous illustration the folding occurred after the comma. It's also possible to fold after a '@' character.

```
To: joe@tuba.example.com, mary@
    glockenspiel.example.com
```

---

[4] Note that while individual lines have limits imposed when being passed through SMTP servers, there is no limit on the length of folded header fields. Developers need to make sure their software can handle this situation.

While this is syntactically correct, it's harder to read than the previous example. It's also prone to misunderstanding by users not paying attention. It should be avoided when possible.

An interesting anomaly can occur with the definition of folding whitespace in RFC822—it's possible to have continuation lines in a field that are empty except for whitespace characters.

```
To:

␣
␣
␣␣mary@glockenspiel.example.com
```

This is valid as long as an apparently blank line actually has whitespace at the start of the line. Even so, despite the fact that it's legal in RFC822, it should be avoided. It's not unusual to find email programs, particularly smaller utility scripts, that don't process it correctly.

Taking a folded field and collapsing it into one line is called *unfolding*. This can be done by converting the folding whitespace characters to space characters.

2.2.6 Case Sensitivity

Field names are case-insensitive, which means that it is equally valid to write `Subject` as `SUBJECT`, `subject`, or even `sUbJeCt`.

The title-cased form—`Subject`—is generally considered canonical and should be used when creating messages. This is not a requirement, just a good idea. The most common exception to this canonicalization is with fields containing abbreviations or acronyms. For example, the field `Message-Id` is often normalized as `Message-ID`, and the field `Mime-Version` is often normalized as `MIME-Version`. Because case doesn't matter in field names, neither form is wrong.

Most users prefer a consistent format for field names. A message header with incongruent capitalization looks cluttered and is harder to read. Because of this, MUAs often canonicalize field names when presenting them to the user.

Compared to field names, case dependence for field bodies is slightly more complicated. In general, the case of words in field bodies is immaterial; however, there are places where it does matter and must be preserved.

- `Subject` field bodies
- `Comments` field bodies
- Quoted strings
- Domain literals

- Comments
- The *local-part* part of addresses (except `postmaster`, which is case-insensitive)

2.2.7 Backspaces

Backspace characters (US-ASCII 8) are allowed in several places in headers, but are rarely used today. There is one issue to be aware of—backspace characters are not allowed to "back up" beyond the boundary of the entity they are being used in.

There are several places where this applies. Inside parenthetical comments, backspaces are not allowed to cross the comment's left boundary. The same holds true for domain literals and quoted strings. In addition, backspaces are not allowed to back up past the colon in a field or cross the blank line header separator in a message body.

2.3 STANDARD FIELDS

There are a lot of fields. Thus, it is not unusual to find hundreds of different field names in a large collection of mail folders, although most of them can be ignored most of the time. The set of fields defined in the email standards are the ones to focus on; they provide the core set needed for basic email services. Thankfully, the number of standard fields is relatively small.

RFC2076 (Common Internet Message Headers) is a good document to review. It contains information on fields frequently appearing in email headers. It also includes reference information regarding where the fields are defined and discusses their current status.

This section describes the fields defined in RFC822, as well as a few other frequently encountered fields. Fields defined in other standards, such as MIME, will be discussed in later chapters.

A syntax description is included with each field. In order to simplify the notation, whitespace is not shown between the field name and the colon.

```
"field-name:"
```

As described earlier in this chapter, the actual syntax is

```
field-name *WSP ":" [CFWS]
```

2.3.1 Originator Fields

The fields used to specify who or what sent a message are called *originator fields*. There are several of them, each with a slightly different purpose.

From

```
"From:" mailbox-list
```

Normally, the `From` field contains a single mailbox identifying the person or process that generated a message.

```
From: larry@ictus.example.com
```

While rarely encountered, the syntax permits a comma list of mailboxes to be included in the field. This indicates that a message is from multiple people. The definition of *mailbox-list* is as follows.

```
mailbox-list = mailbox [CFWS] *("," [CFWS] [mailbox])
```

This amounts to a comma list of mailboxes, with accommodations made for commented folding whitespace and multiple consecutive commas. RFC822 uses a slightly different notation for indicating a comma list of mailboxes.

```
1#mailbox
```

While this is more compact, it's not included in RFC2234. This book uses RFC2234's more verbose notation.

The topic of mailbox names, and addresses in general, is rather involved. Because of this, it is covered in detail in Section 2.5.

If multiple mailboxes are provided in the field, the message must also contain a `Sender` field.

Sender

```
"Sender:" mailbox
```

The `Sender` field is used to note that the sender of a message is different from the creator of the message.

```
From: system-scanner@ictus.example.com
Sender: root@ictus.example.com
```

At first glance, the field might seem redundant, but it isn't. It can be used, for example, when a message is being sent by a person other than the original creator of the message, such as when a secretary sends a message on behalf of a manager.

RFC822 stipulates that the field must be used if multiple addresses are present in the `From` field, to help identify the originator of the message.

There is one very important point to make about this field. It was intended to be added at the point of origination, not to be used by subsequent receivers of a message. Some mailing list processors use this field to indicate that a message has been reflected through a mailing list. Technically speaking, this is an incorrect use, since it prevents using the field for its original purpose at the point of origination. This topic is covered in greater detail in Chapter 8.

Reply-To

```
"Reply-To:" mailbox-list
```

The `Reply-To` field is used to control where replies to a message should be sent.

```
From: larry@larryhome.example.com
Reply-To: larry@ictus.example.com
```

This field has a problematic past. RFC822 doesn't specify its use very rigorously. The result has been a variety of uses.

The `Reply-To` field can override the `From` field. It is often used by users with more than one computer who want replies to all messages to go to one computer.

Some mailing lists use this field to divert replies to the list. Because `Reply-To` usually overrides the reply behavior of MUAs, generally all replies go back to the list instead of back to the author of the message. Issues with this technique are discussed in Section 8.2.1.

This field is also occasionally used to specify the exact list of recipients for a reply, regardless of the `To` and `Cc` fields. This is similar to the first use mentioned above, but with multiple recipients in the `Reply-To` field.

```
To: joe@tuba.example.com, larry@ictus.example.com
Cc: bob@flugelhorn.example.com
Reply-To: joe@tuba.example.com, larry@ictus.example.com
```

In this example, the `Reply-To` field indicates that `bob@flugelhorn.example.com` should not be included as a recipient if a reply is generated. This could be used, for example, in situations where a person receives a courtesy copy of a specific message but should not be included in a subsequent conversation thread.

2.3.2 Receiver Fields

The fields used to specify the recipients of a mail message are called *receiver fields*. Like originator fields, there are several different fields, because there can be several types of recipients.

To

```
"To:" address-list
```

The To field indicates the primary recipients of a message.

```
To: mary@glockenspiel.example.com, harry@gong.example.com
```

The syntax for *address-list* is similar to that of *mailbox-list*.

```
address-list = address [CFWS] *("," [CFWS] [address])
```

The details of the syntax are described in Section 2.5.

Cc

```
"Cc:" address-list
```

The Cc field is used to specify secondary recipients of a message. In line with its original memorandum analogy, Cc is an abbreviation for *carbon copy*.

```
Cc: slim@bassoon.example.com, harry@gong.example.com
```

Bcc

```
"Bcc:" (address-list / [CFWS])
```

Bcc is an abbreviation for *blind carbon copy*. It is similar to Cc, except that the recipients listed in the To and Cc fields are not shown the recipients listed in the Bcc field.

```
Bcc: ludwig@althorn.example.com
```

There are three ways Bcc fields are handled. In the first way the originating MUA reviews the field contents, strips the contents or deletes the field, and then uses the information to generate separate dialogs to the MTA for the destinations listed in the original field.

The second way of handling the field is for the originating MUA or MTA to delete or strip the field for the recipients listed in any To and Cc fields. The recipients listed in Bcc get a copy of the message with the original Bcc field intact. This technique suffers from the problem that the originator might not want the recipients listed in the Bcc field to know what other Bcc recipients the message was sent to.

The third way is a combination of the first and second. The originating MUA or MTA strips or deletes the field for the copies being sent to the To and Cc recipients. It sends a separate message to each Bcc recipient showing only that particular recipient in the Bcc field.

2.3.3 Reference Fields

Some fields provide information that uniquely identifies a message and associates a reply with its parent message.

Message-ID

```
"Message-ID:" msg-id
```

The Message-ID field uniquely identifies a piece of mail. The field is generated either by the MUA or by the first MTA the message passes through.

```
Message-ID: <19990401114213.48293.1@gong.example.com>
```

Because the field uniquely identifies each piece of email, it needs to be unique across both space and time—in other words, across the entire Internet and across the entire history of the Internet. To accomplish this, the field value is fashioned after an email address, with a '@' dividing the value into two parts.

```
msg-id = [CFWS] "<" local-part "@" domain ">" [CFWS]
```

Even though *local-part* and *domain* allow the use of commented folding white-space, it should not be used, particularly since it's not necessary.

The left-hand side, *local-part,* contains a string of characters to uniquely identify the message on the machine where it was created. The right-hand side specifies that machine.

In the example given at the beginning of this section, the right-hand side consists of the following string.

```
gong.example.com
```

The left-hand side varies considerably, depending on the software generating the data. It's usually based on the date and time. On machines where multiple processes can be running simultaneously, a process identifier is often added. To handle the possibility of multiple messages being created within one time unit on the machine, a sequence number is often used. This number is incremented for each message in a session to prevent duplicate message identifiers from being generated within a particular process. The combination of these three mechanisms generally prevents duplicate message identifiers from being generated on a particular machine.

In the example given at the beginning of this section, the left-hand side of the unique identifier consists of the following string.

```
19990401114213.48293.1
```

The *date-time* portion of the string is '19990401114213'. In this case, the string consists of four digits for the year and two digits each for the month, day of the month, hour, minutes, and seconds. The process identifier information is '48293', and the sequence number is '1'.

There is no requirement to use the technique described here. The key requirement is that the value must be unique. Any technique capable of generating unique values for a particular machine can be used.

The Message-ID field has several uses. For one, MUAs that create indexes of folder contents can use it to track messages in a folder. It is also used when creating a threaded view of a folder. In addition to being able to sort on simple criteria like date-sent, subject, or originator, it can be used with the In-Reply-To and References fields to create the tree-like folder summary often seen in newer MUAs and news readers.

As a side note to developers, there is no guarantee that the field value will be unique. Care is needed when using it to manage folder indexes and message threads. Developers must make sure their software can cope with situations where the field is missing or contains a duplicate value.

In-Reply-To

```
"In-Reply-To:" *(phrase / msg-id)
```

The `In-Reply-To` field contains information used to identify what message or messages the current message is a reply to. It is used in combination with the `References` field to allow MUAs to present tree-like displays of conversation threads.

```
In-Reply-To: <19990401114213.48293.1@gong.example.com>

In-Reply-To: Your message of "Sun, 07 Mar 1999 10:23:23 -0700."
             <19990401114213.48293.1@gong.example.com>

In-Reply-To: Harry's message of Sun, 07 Mar 1999 10:23:23 -0700
```

Something to note about this field is that the definition for it in RFC822 doesn't quite match its usage. The syntax for the field allows multiple identifiers or phrases, which means the message is in reply to multiple messages. In practice, this field seldom contains more than one message identifier.

Three formats are used for the field. If a message identifier is present by itself, it identifies the message that this message is a direct reply to.

```
In-Reply-To: <19990401114213.48293.1@gong.example.com>
```

There can also be a sequence of words either before or after the message identifier. In this case, the sequence is typically used to provide some additional information associating the message with its predecessor. This additional text frequently contains the date and time of the original message, but this is by no means required.

```
In-Reply-To: Your message of "Sun, 07 Mar 1999 10:23:23 -0700."
             <19990401114213.48293.1@gong.example.com>
```

The third format for the `In-Reply-To` field consists of text with no message identifier. It cannot be used to allow the MUA to associate the reply with the original message, but is intended to be a helpful piece of information for users.

```
In-Reply-To: Harry's message of Sun, 07 Mar 1999 10:23:23 -0700
```

In general, the *msg-id* format for this field is recommended, since it allows email programs to programmatically link related messages together.

References

```
"References:" *(phrase / msg-id)
```

The `References` field lists the ancestors of a message. It's used as an adjunct to the `In-Reply-To` field.

```
In-Reply-To: <19990402091245.1928.1@triangle.example.com>
References: <19990401114213.48293.1@gong.example.com>
            <19990402143437.18392.1@triangle.example.com>
            <19990402091245.1928.1@triangle.example.com>
```

When a message is a reply to a reply, the previous `In-Reply-To` field is appended to the existing contents of the `References` field. The `References` field is created if it doesn't already exist.

An example might be helpful. Say a message gets sent with the following message identifier.

```
Message-ID: <19990401114213.48293.1@gong.example.com>
```

A reply to that message generates a new message identifier and uses the previous identifier to seed the contents of the `In-Reply-To` and `References` fields.

```
Message-ID: <19990402091245.1928.1@triangle.example.com>
In-Reply-To: <19990401114213.48293.1@gong.example.com>
References: <19990401114213.48293.1@gong.example.com>
```

This is illustrated in Figure 2.2.

At this point, the `In-Reply-To` and `References` fields are redundant, but both should be used because of how the fields are used with multiple layers of replies.

FIGURE 2.2 References in an Initial Reply

A reply to this second message would, again, cause a new message identifier to be generated and the previous identifier would be used to populate the In-Reply-To field. The previous identifier would be appended to the contents of the References field.

```
Message-ID: <19990403101116.983.2@gong.example.com>
In-Reply-To: <19990402091245.1928.1@triangle.example.com>
References: <19990401114213.48293.1@gong.example.com>
           <19990402091245.1928.1@triangle.example.com>
```

Figure 2.3 shows the linkage between the three messages.

Why is this field even needed? After all, the other messages in a thread reference their parent message, so why have a seemingly redundant field? Consider situations where the immediate parent of a reply hasn't yet been received or perhaps has been deleted from the mailbox. Having the References field allows an MUA to build message threads even if not all the intermediate replies are present, as is illustrated in Figure 2.4. As with the In-Reply-To field, use of the *msg-id* form is recommended.

2.3.4 Trace Fields

Trace fields create an audit trail for a message. They relate information about when a message was sent, what path it took, and the return path back to the originator.

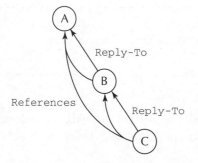

FIGURE 2.3 Multiple References

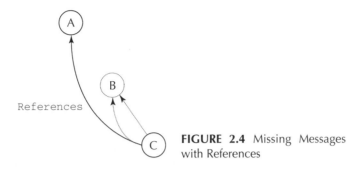

FIGURE 2.4 Missing Messages with References

Date

```
"Date:" date-time
```

The `Date` field contains the date and time an email was created.

```
Date: Sat, 2 Oct 1999 08:35:07 -0700
```

There have been instances where the `Date` field has been used to note what time a message was transported, but this is an incorrect interpretation of its purpose. It is intended to indicate what time a message was put into a form ready for transport. As an example, with MUAs that allow email to be composed while the machine is not connected to a network, there can be a noticeable amount of time between when a message was created and when it is submitted to an MTA for delivery. The creation date is definitely called for in this situation. The date and time a message was given to an MTA will be noted in a `Received` field.

A more detailed description of the format of *date-time* is provided in Section 2.7.

Received

```
"Received:" ["from" CFWS domain CFWS]
            ["by" CFWS domain CFWS]
            ["via" CFWS link CFWS]
            *("with CFWS protocol CFWS)
            ["id" CFWS (string / msg-id) CFWS]
            ["for" 1*(CFWS mailbox) CFWS]
            ";" CFWS date-time
```

The `Received` field contains a record of a particular MTAs handling of a mail message.

```
Received: from flugelhorn.example.com by tuba.example.com
         with SMTP id HAA19482
         for <joe@tuba.example.com>; Mon, 4 Oct 1999 08:33:48 -0700
Received: by flugelhorn.example.com (8.8.7/8.8.7) with smtp
         id CAA17583; Mon, 4 Oct 1999 08:33:47 -0700
```

Each MTA that handles a message must prepend a `Received` field to each header it processes. The result is a list of fields describing the path the message took to get to its final destination. This can be especially useful when tracking down a variety of email problems. Because this field can be so important, Section 2.6 is devoted to it.

Return-Path

```
"Return-Path:" ("<>" / route-addr)
```

The `Return-Path` field indicates the path back to the originator of the message. It is populated with the data provided in the SMTP `mail` command, which is discussed in Section 3.2.

```
Return-Path: <>

Return-Path: <joe@tuba.example.com>

Return-Path:
   <@c.example.com,@b.example.com,@a.example.com:guido@a.example.com>
```

`Return-Path` is added by an MTA when a message leaves the world of SMTP or when final delivery is made.

The syntax for *route-addr* is described in Section 2.5.

RFC822 doesn't provide the ability to use '<>' for a value in a `Return-Path` field. RFC1123 updated the syntax by adding '<>' and stating that notification of delivery failures is not allowed when the field is set to the null path. This prevents loops when a piece of email is generated by an MTA to report a problem.

2.3.5 Resent Fields

One of the techniques for resending a received message to another set of recipients is *redistribution*. This technique keeps the entire original message intact and simply generates new versions of the fields necessary to resend it. The fields added to the redistributed message all start with the string `Resent-`, which avoids collisions with the previous fields. Any fields without a `Resent-*` equivalent can't be added in the redistributed message.

The following is a list of all the valid `Resent-*` fields.

- `Resent-From`
- `Resent-Sender`
- `Resent-To`
- `Resent-Cc`
- `Resent-Bcc`
- `Resent-Date`
- `Resent-Message-ID`
- `Resent-Reply-To`

Technically speaking, the `Resent-Reply-To` is redundant. The `Resent-From` field should be used instead.

If a resent message needs to be resent again, the fields are simply prepended to the message. There is no conflict with multiple occurrences of these fields.

One thing to note is that there are no `Resent-*` equivalents for extension fields (`X-`). Thus, there is no way to override extension fields when redistributing.

A more detailed description of the use of these fields is provided in Section 2.4.2.

2.3.6 Other Fields

There are several fields that don't fit into a specific category but are important nonetheless.

Subject

```
"Subject:" *([FWS] text)
```

The `Subject` field is straightforward. It describes what the message is about.

```
Subject: Object definitions
```

The definition of *text* is as follows:

```
text = <any CHAR, including bare CR and bare LF, but not including CRLF>
```

When replying to a message, MUAs often prefix 'Re:␣' to the beginning of the subject text to mark the message as a reply. This is purely for the convenience of the user.

```
Subject: Re: Object definitions
```

MUAs also frequently alter the subject text when a message is being forwarded. There is more variety here than with replying. The most common method is to insert something like 'Fw:␣', 'Fwd:␣', or '[fwd]␣' at the beginning of the subject text.

```
Subject: Fw: Object definitions
```

Some MUAs add more detail, such as the sender of the forwarded message.

```
Subject: [joe@tuba.example.com: Object definitions]
```

Comments

```
"Comments:" *([FWS] text)
```

The Comments field allows a comment to be added to a message. It isn't used as much as some of the other standard fields.[5]

```
Comments: use this document as a starting point
```

One of its more common uses is to add some sort of comical remark or warning.

```
Comments: insert pithy comment here
```

Another use is to add information about where readers can get a copy of the sender's public encryption key.

```
Comments: Public Key at http://example.com/~bob/public-key.pgp

Comments: finger bob@tuba.example.com for public key
```

---

[5] One thing to be aware of is that Comment is sometimes used instead of Comments.

Some add-on packages use the `Comments` field to include information about the package. Emacs' Hyperbole, for example, inserts the following string to indicate that the user's email processing has extra features that it can handle.

```
Comments: Hyperbole mail buttons accepted, v04.023.
```

Keywords

```
"Keywords:" phrase *([CFWS] "," [CFWS] phrase)
```

The `Keywords` field allows a set of keywords to be added to the message for use with topical search engines.

```
Keywords: printers, drivers, linux
```

Since few MUAs implement topical indexes, this field is rarely used.

Encrypted

```
"Encrypted:" word *FWS ["," *FWS word]
```

The `Encrypted` field never quite caught on, and it is rarely, if ever, seen in modern Internet email. There are better defined ways to send encrypted email, described in Chapter 9.

2.3.7 Extension Fields

Email is a moving target. Because of this, developers sometimes need to create new nonstandard fields. There is a risk that a nonstandard field could conflict with a new standard field at some point in the future. Extension fields minimize this problem. RFC822 mentions the use of `X-` at the beginning of field names to indicate that a field is an extension.

In theory, extension fields allow people to create new fields without the risk of the field name being used in a subsequent message standard. In practice, many have become de-facto standards, complicating the original definition of this field type. Also, many extension fields are widely used, but have no standard definition. This creates ambiguities in processing them. One of the long-term trends in Internet email standards is to reduce the use of extension fields. In many cases, they present more problems than solutions.

There are several relatively common extension fields worth mentioning.

X-Loop

```
X-Loop: product-announcements@example.com
```

The X-Loop field is frequently used by filters and mailing list processors to prevent mailing loops. A filter or mailing list processor can add an X-Loop field to each message it handles. If it encounters a message containing its particular value in the field, it assumes a loop is in process and so processes the message differently.

X-Mailer

```
X-Mailer: CroMagnonMail v14.3
```

The X-Mailer field indicates what MUA was used to generate the message. It is probably the most widely used extension field.

Though not required in any of the standards, MUA developers should have their software add an appropriate X-Mailer field to all out-bound messages. The field should contain not only the name of the package but also the version number. If the package runs on multiple platforms, noting the platform on which the MUA is running can be helpful as well.

X-MIME-Autoconverted

```
X-MIME-Autoconverted: from quoted-printable to 8bit
                      by example.com id BAA02049
```

Newer versions of Sendmail can be configured to perform 8-bit to 7-bit and 7-bit to 8-bit conversions on MIME messages. If this feature is enabled, it will automatically perform these conversions and add an X-MIME-AutoConverted field to note the fact.

X-UIDL

```
X-UIDL: 12db69e63ad9ba04f7513b0fffa73d63
```

The `X-UIDL` field is used by some POP daemons to store the unique identifier for a message. The daemons insert it into messages in a user's inbox. It should never be included in a message being transmitted.

The use of unique identifiers in POP will be discussed in Chapter 5.

2.3.8 Nonstandard Fields

There are several fields frequently encountered that are not part of standard email, many of which are worth looking at.

Status

```
Status: O
```

The `Status` field isn't part of the standards. Some MUAs insert it into messages in mail folders to store information such as whether a message has been read, is new, or has been replied to, but it should never be included in a message being transmitted.

A `Status` field consists of one or more status characters, each of which indicates a specific piece of status information. Table 2.2 summarizes the more common status characters encountered. Not all MUAs support all the fields, and some MUAs use other characters.

TABLE 2.2 Characters in Status Fields

Character	Description
D	marked for Deletion
N	New
O	Old
R	Read or downloaded
U	Unread or not downloaded

A message can be considered *New* if no Status field is present in the message. The 'O' character requires a little explanation. When an MUA that uses the Status field opens a folder, it reviews the contents of the field. For a particular message, if the field is not present or if it is present and contains an 'N', the message is considered *New*. When the MUA closes the folder, it sets 'O' flag in the field if the message was not processed. Thus, 'O' flag can be interpreted as 'untouched and not new'.

As mentioned earlier, not all MUAs using this field implement all the flags. The most common ones are 'O' and 'R'.

The meaning of the various combinations of status characters is straightforward. For example, 'ND' means the message hasn't been read and is also marked for deletion. As another example, 'RD' means the message has been read, or downloaded, and is marked for deletion.

A few combinations are contradictory and shouldn't occur. *New* and *Old* are obviously contradictory when combined, as are *Read* and *Unread*.

Because the field is intended only for use within mail folders, it should never be transmitted in a mail message. Therefore, it is perfectly reasonable for an MDA to delete Status fields when processing incoming messages.

Content-Length

```
Content-Length: 2112
```

A few MUAs use a Content-Length field to note how large a message is. The SVR4 flavor of UNIX also uses it by default. This allows the MUAs to store the messages in a format that is a variant of the standard mbox format, except that lines in message bodies starting with 'From␣' don't need to be escaped.

This is another field that isn't part of the standards. It is only used in mail folders, and thus, like the Status field, should never be transmitted in a mail message.

2.4 SOME EXAMPLES

Email messages, particular headers, can be fairly complex. It's easier to pick apart even the most complicated headers if the processes a message goes through are understood. To illustrate this, this section walks through a few examples.

2.4.1 A Simple Message

Here is a simple mail message that will be passed from its originator to its recipient.

```
To: joe@tuba.example.com
Subject: another question

Why is the frobnazoid gefargled again?

--
thx,
bob
```

There is a header, a blank line, and a message body. In the header there is a `To` field and a `Subject` field. Following the header is the blank line used to separate the header from the body. The remainder of the message is the body.

This constitutes a complete message as created by a user. Before it can be sent off, however, it needs a few more things. It doesn't yet have all the required fields.

To prepare the message for sending, the MUA adds a few fields, including the remainder of the required fields and a few nonrequired ones.

A `Date` field is added to specify when the message was sent. The MUA usually inserts this field automatically. A `From` field is added to specify who sent the message. Again, MUAs typically insert this field automatically, but many provide the ability to customize the field contents. A `Message-ID` field is added to specify a unique identifier for the message. If the MUA doesn't generate this field, the first MTA to process the message will probably generate one automatically. An `X-Mailer` field is added to specify what program was used to generate the piece of mail. This field isn't part of the standards, but almost all MUAs add it.

```
Date: Mon, 4 Oct 1999 08:33:45 -0700
From: bob@flugelhorn.example.com
To: joe@tuba.example.com
Subject: another question
Message-ID: <19991004083345.18492.1@flugelhorn.example.com>
X-Mailer: MondoMail v42.86
```

At this point, the mail message has all the requirements of valid email. It is ready to be given to an MTA for transport.

Each MTA that processes the message prepends a `Received` field to it. This provides trace information for anyone troubleshooting problems. In addition to the `Received` fields, the final MTA prepends a `Return-Path` field to the message.

The message now appears as it would at its final destination.

```
Return-Path: <bob@flugelhorn.example.com>
Received: from flugelhorn.example.com by tuba.example.com
        with SMTP id HAA19482
        for <joe@tuba.example.com>; Mon, 4 Oct 1999 08:33:48 -0700
Received: by flugelhorn.example.com (8.8.8/8.8.8) with smtp
        id CAA17583; Mon, 4 Oct 1999 08:33:47 -0700
Date: Mon,  4 Oct 1999 08:33:45 -0700
Message-ID: <19991004083345.18492.1@flugelhorn.example.com>
From: bob@flugelhorn.example.com
To: joe@tuba.example.com
Subject: another question
X-Mailer: MondoMail v42.86
```

2.4.2 Redistributing

Once a user has received a message he or she might want to send it to another
recipient or set of recipients. The simplest technique for doing this is redistributing.[6]
In this case, the entire original message is resent to another set of recipients. New
versions of the To, Cc, Bcc, Sender, Reply-To, Date, and Message-ID fields
are added to the message with Resent- inserted at the beginning of each of those
fields to allow the entire original message to be sent without alteration.

```
Resent-Date: Tue, 5 Oct 1999 13:02:17 -0700
Resent-From: joe@tuba.example.com
Resent-To: sally@oboe.example.com
Resent-Message-ID: <19991005130217.962.2@tuba.example.com>
Received: from flugelhorn.example.com by tuba.example.com
        with SMTP id HAA19482
        for <joe@tuba.example.com>; Mon, 4 Oct 1999 08:33:48 -0700
Received: by flugelhorn.example.com (8.8.8/8.8.8) with smtp
        id CAA17583; Mon, 4 Oct 1999 08:33:47 -0700
Date: Mon,  4 Oct 1999 08:33:45 -0700
From: bob@flugelhorn.example.com
To: joe@tuba.example.com
Subject: another question
Message-ID: <19991004083345.18492.1@flugelhorn.example.com>
X-Mailer: MondoMail v42.86
```

---

[6] This goes by different names in various MUAs. The most common are *bounce, resend,* and *distribute.*
Each of these terms has problems in general usage. *Bounce* is commonly used to note email that can't get to
its final destination and subsequently *bounces* back to the sender. *Resend* seems to imply the original sender
resending a piece of email. *Distribute* is also used to describe distributing a piece to a list of users, such as
is done by a mailing list processor. Many end-users find all these terms confusing. The problem is further
aggravated by the fact that not all MUAs provide a function to perform this task.

Unfortunately, RFC822 is vague about how `Resent-*` fields should be added to a message. For example, no information is provided about where in the header they should be inserted. To further aggravate the problem, RFC822 states that the behavior of multiple instances of `Resent-*` fields is undefined. Because of these shortcomings, in general case it's not possible to programmatically analyze `Resent-*` fields.

2.4.3 Forwarding

The primary limitation of redistributing a message is that there is no way to add additional material to the message. *Forwarding* is an alternative that solves this problem.

There is nothing particularly noteworth about the header of a forwarded message. No special processing is necessary to construct forwarded headers, although an MUA might slightly alter the subject to indicate to the new recipient or recipients that it's a forward.

```
Fw: Where are my shoes?

Fwd: Where are my shoes?

[fwd] Where are my shoes?

Where are my shoes? (fwd)

[bob@flugelhorn.example.com: Where are my shoes?]
```

Why so many variations? Well, the standards don't specify any requirements for the `subject` field when replying or forwarding. However, over the years users have found it useful to know when a message is either of those two types, so various techniques have been created.

One thing worth mentioning at this point is that it is not possible to programmatically detect all forwards.

While the header for a forwarded message is straightforward, the body is another story. There are several ways a forwarded message can be incorporated into the new message because RFC822 doesn't specify forwarding behavior. Actually, it does talk about forwarding, but it incorrectly uses the word *forwarding* when it should use the word *redistributing*.

One of the options to be dealt with a forwarded message is the decision of which header fields to include in it. Sometimes the entire set of headers is desired, sometimes only a partial set.

Simple Message Encapsulation

A common technique for incorporating the original message is to wrap it in a pair of strings, called an encapsulation boundary. This is an example.

```
------- Start of forwarded message -------
I'll be out of town next week.
Make sure the next meeting goes on without me.
------- End of forwarded message -------
```

Here's a variation on the same theme that references the originator of the forwarded message in the first string.

```
----- Forwarded message from original-from -----
I'll be out of town next week.
Make sure the next meeting goes on without me.
----- End of forwarded message -----
```

Another variation is to preface the message with something like 'Forwarded message:' and then insert the original message with '>␣' at the start of every line.

```
Forwarded Message:
> I'll be out of town next week.
> Make sure the next meeting goes on without me.

George,

Looks like you're going to need to be ready to present next week
after all...
```

With the simple encapsulation techniques just described it's impossible to extract a forwarded message 100% of the time. A wide variety of start and finish strings are used to mark the boundaries of the original message—in particular, differing numbers of dashes, differing amounts of whitespace separating the dashes and the text, different capitalization, and even different wording. To further aggravate the problem, it's possible for the encapsulated message to contain text that would confuse an extraction program.

To reliably extract a message from a forward, a more predictable encapsulation technique is required.

RFC934

RFC934 (Proposed Standard for Message Encapsulation) defines an extension very similar to the first technique described above, except that additional steps are taken to prevent the text of the message from interfering with the identification of the boundary strings. While this extension isn't widely used, it's a good example of providing a simple encapsulation layer on top of the core message format.

In RFC934 an encapsulation boundary is defined as any line beginning with a dash character, with no limit on its length or on what characters follow the dash. To handle messages containing lines already starting with a dash, RFC934 defines a technique called *character-stuffing*. Each line in the message starting with a dash is prepended with a dash and a space character ('-␣'). A program needing to extract a message identifies lines starting with these characters as part of the original message and clips off the extra characters. The following example contains an RFC934 encapsulated message.

```
To: mary@glockenspiel.example.com
From: joe@tuba.example.com
Subject: bob's message to me

I think his eyes were bigger than his stomach.

- -------------------------
To: joe@tuba.example.com
From: bob@flugelhorn.example.com
Subject: I'm stuffed

I think I ate too much.

- --
thx,
bob
- -------------------------

--
thx,
joe
```

Extraction yields Bob's original message.

```
To: joe@tuba.example.com
From: bob@flugelhorn.example.com
Subject: I'm stuffed

I think I ate too much.

--
thx,
bob
```

MIME

The most resilient technique is MIME. It provides a media type particularly suited to this task—`message/rfc822` entities—which allow any MIME-compliant MUA to extract the encapsulated message without ambiguity. MIME will be described in detail in Chapter 4.

2.4.4 Replying

In addition to redistributing or forwarding, users can also reply to a message. This is similar to forwarding, but the headers are handled differently.

The header of a reply looks very much like the header of the original message. There are new `Date`, `Message-ID`, and `X-Mailer` fields. Since it's a reply, the contents of its `From` and `To` fields are reversed. An `In-Reply-To` field is added, as is a `References` field. Finally, the `Subject` field is the same except for a 'Re:␣' preceding the original subject.

```
Date: Wed, 6 Oct 1999 14:22:36 -0700
Message-ID: <19991006142237.9823.1@tuba.example.com>
From: joe@tuba.example.com
To: bob@flugelhorn.example.com
Subject: Re: another question
In-Reply-To: <19991004083345.18492.1@flugelhorn.example.com>
References: <19991004083345.18492.1@flugelhorn.example.com>
X-Mailer: WaWaPeddleMail v1.0.1.0
```

Unlike the original message, where portions of the header were provided by the user, almost the entire header of a reply is generated by the MUA. One possible exception to this is where the user might want to edit the recipients fields to alter who is included in the reply.

There is only one recipient in the original message in this simple example. If there is more than one, the user might want to adjust the recipient list for his or her reply. Some MUAs assist by providing *Reply* as well as a *Reply All* function.

There is quite a bit of divergence here in MUAs, primarily because there are many different scenarios for replies and differing opinions of what users want to do when replying.

The next issue to deal with is the inclusion of the original message. Two styles of inclusion are generally used. The first one, described in son-of-RFC1036, is to prefix each line of the original text with a string of characters to visually identify it as included. This allows the replier to interject statements between the lines of the original message. With the original text prefixed, the replier's statements are easy to spot. The second style includes the body of the original message between a pair of surrounding lines similarly to what is often done when forwarding messages.

For the prefix style, the most common prefix string is '>␣'. To illustrate, here is a message body to use as a starting point.

```
Meet me for lunch tomorrow.
We need to discuss the strategy you defined.
```

The respondent could reply as follows.

```
> Meet me for lunch tomorrow.
> We need to discuss the strategy you defined.
I can't. I'm in meetings all day tomorrow.
Let's shoot for Wednesday.
```

The text of the original message is clearly visible, as is the response.

The prefix-string technique can be used multiple times to accommodate responding to a reply.

```
> > Meet me for lunch tomorrow.
> > We need to discuss the strategy you defined.
>
> I can't. I'm in meetings all day tomorrow.
> Let's shoot for Wednesday.

ok
```

It's not uncommon to see prefixes other than '>', such as ':', '|', or '|'.

An interesting variation on the prefix-string technique is to include a string in the prefix to identify the sender of the original text.

```
mary> Meet me for lunch tomorrow.
mary> We need to discuss the strategy you defined.

bob> I can't. I'm in meetings all day tomorrow.
bob> Let's shoot for Wednesday.
```

Actually, there are two variants of the prefix-string style. One, the example shown above, has flattened nested reply text. The other is closer to the original style, but has a tendency to use a lot of real estate for heavily nested conversation threads.

```
bob>mary> Meet me for lunch tomorrow.
bob>mary> We need to discuss the strategy you defined.

bob> I can't. I'm in meetings all day tomorrow.
bob> Let's shoot for Wednesday.
```

As presented so far, the included message text doesn't indicate who sent the message being replied to. This is particularly important in conversation threads carried out between more than two people. While a pointer to the information is in the In-Reply-To and References header fields, having to navigate the headers to get this information can be burdensome. It might not even be possible if part of the conversation thread isn't available to the user.

To solve this problem, it's not uncommon to prefix the included message with an *attribution* string to note who sent the original message. The attribution usually includes the name or email address of the person the message is a reply to and often the date and time of the original message. It might also add a little levity to a conversation. By the way, there's no defined standard for this string, so trying to parse it for meaning is probably pointless.

```
Bob Flower <bob@flugelhorn.example.com> wrote:
> The meeting this week has been moved to Wednesday.

On 4/3/1999 at 7:31 AM -0700, Bob Flower wrote:
> The meeting this week has been moved to Wednesday.

Earlier this morning, Bob barked:
> The meeting this week has been moved to Wednesday.
```

Attributions can also be used in nested replies.

```
On 4/4/1999 at 9:42 AM -0700, Joe wrote:
> Mary Quintessence wrote:
>> On 4/3/1999 at 7:31 AM -0700, Bob Flower wrote:
>>> The meeting this week has been moved to Wednesday.

>> Can we just postpone it until next week?

> I vote yes...
```

They can be a little cumbersome to sift through, but are helpful when trying to dissect an involved conversation in a mail message.

One final thing to mention about this style of message inclusion is the problem of paragraph filling and automatic word wrapping. Currently there is no standard for what prefix character is used with inclusions, so there is no foolproof way of properly wrapping long lines or filling paragraphs for included text.[7] This problem is particularly troublesome with MUAs that insist on performing these actions automatically. What results is filled paragraphs with inclusion strings sprinkled throughout or dangling words with the wrong prefix string.

Here is an example of how incorrect paragraph filling can look.

```
> How did the meeting go? I couldn't attend because of a
scheduling > conflict.
```

Here's one with overly simplistic paragraph filling or word wrapping.

```
> How did the meeting go? I couldn't attend because of a
scheduling
> conflict.
```

These are definitely not the desired results given the original text.

```
> How did the meeting go? I couldn't attend because of a scheduling
> conflict.
```

As mentioned earlier, the second style for message encapsulation in replies includes the original text in a fashion similar to that used when including forwarded

---

[7] As this book was being written, an Internet draft was being developed to address this problem.

text in a message. The text is inserted as is, and leader and trailer strings are added to act as boundaries for it.

```
----- Original Message from original-from -----
original message text
----- End of Original Message -----
```

This style has several issues, the most pronounced being the cumbersome nature of responding to specific items in the included text. If responses are included inline with the included text, it is difficult to differentiate new text from old. The only practical alternative is to leave the inserted text intact and add remarks before or after it.

Another issue is that users often leave the entire piece of included text intact without pruning any unnecessary text. This leads to bloated messages, particularly with extended conversation threads.

On the plus side, automatic paragraph filling tends to be less of a problem with this style of message inclusion. This is because the line lengths aren't increased as a conversation thread develops and because no prefix characters are being used to confuse a paragraph fill function.

The preference for style of message inclusion in replies varies from person to person. It's been the author's experience that new users prefer the forwarding style while users experienced in carrying on extended conversations via email prefer the prefix style. In either case, the preferences tend to be strong.

With the text of the original message appropriately incorporated into the reply, and the header properly constructed, the message is ready to be transmitted. There are no surprises here. As the messages pass through MTAs, each MTA prepends a `Received` line to the header, with the final MTA also prepending a `Return-Path` field.

```
Return-Path: <joe@tuba.example.com>
Received: from tuba.example.com by flugelhorn.example.com
         with smtp id CAB23718
         for <bob@flugelhorn.example.com>
         ; Wed, 6 Oct 1999 14:22:40 -0700
Received: by tuba.example.com (8.8.8/8.8.8) with smtp
         id HAA19984; Wed, 6 Oct 1999 14:22:39 -0700
Date: Wed, 6 Oct 1999 14:22:36 -0700
Message-ID: <19991006142237.9823.1@tuba.example.com>
From: joe@tuba.example.com
To: bob@flugelhorn.example.com
Subject: Re: another question
In-Reply-To: <19991004083345.18492.1@flugelhorn.example.com>
References: <19991004083345.18492.1@flugelhorn.example.com>
X-Mailer: WaWaPeddleMail v1.0.1.0
```

There's an important subtlety regarding replies to resent messages. If a message contains `Resent-*` fields, the reply should be based not on them but on the original fields. RFC822 doesn't restrict the use of the `Resent-*` fields in this way, but they are used in a variety of ways. There's no general way to determine how the `Resent-*` fields are used, so it's difficult to provide a general reply function based on them.

2.5 EMAIL ADDRESSES

Email addresses have been used several times in this chapter, but not much explanation has been provided about what they are and how they are made up. This section explores them in greater detail.

There are two primary types of address to understand in email—mailboxes and group lists. All the syntax elements related to addresses in headers are based on these two constructs.

2.5.1 Mailboxes

A mailbox is the form of email address most users are familiar with. There are two variations: simple and route. RFC822 uses *addr-spec* to identify simple addresses and *route-addr* to identify route addresses.

```
mailbox = addr-spec /
          [phrase] route-addr
```

Simple Addresses

A simple address is the prototypical email address, and all the other forms are variations of it. It consists of a mailbox name, an '@', and an FQDN (Full Qualified Domain Name). The simple mailbox, or *addr-spec*, is at the core of all email addresses.

```
addr-spec = local-part "@" domain
```

The *local-part* specifies the mailbox on a destination machine, while the *domain* specifies the destination machine name. The syntax for *local-part* is deceptively simple.

```
local-part = word *("." word)
word       = atom / quoted-string
```

The vast majority of email addresses consist of a series of dot-separated atoms.

```
bob@flugelhorn.example.com
bob.flower@flugelhorn.example.com
```

CFWS can occur on either side of an atom, so it's possible for it to occur in *syntref*. As a general rule, however, this should be avoided. As will be seen later in this section, there is a better way to provide additional information in an address.

```
joe.(gold)doubloon@tuba.example.com
```

Quoted strings can also be used for *local-part* in situations where one or more characters present in the name of the mailbox are not valid in the other two forms of *local-part*.

```
"Joe G. Doubloon"@tuba.example.com
```

The syntax for *local-part* also allows various combinations of dot-separated atoms and quoted strings. The previous example could be specified as follows.

```
"Joe G"." Doubloon"@tuba.example.com
```

This form is seldom used, and should be avoided. If *local-part* needs quoting, it's best to enclose it in one set of quotes.

None of the email standards impose any semantics on *local-part*, which means its interpretation is up to the machine where the mailbox resides.

This lack of imposed semantics allows something very interesting to be implemented—*subaddresses*. These are a way of partitioning *local-part* using specific characters. The two most common separator characters are '-' and '+'. This allows users to categorize incoming email. The first segment identifies the base address for a mailbox; the subsequent segments identify subaddresses for that mailbox.

```
joe-hotcars
joe-doglovers
```

For example, a software vendor has created a single mailbox for a product, with subaddresses for specific topics related to it.

```
mondomail-announcements
mondomail-betatesters
mondomail-bugs
mondomail-help
mondomail-sales
```

One last item to mention regarding *local-part* is case sensitivity. By the letter of the law, the information in *local-part* is case-sensitive. Thus, Joe is a different mailbox than joe. There is one exception this: postmaster is a special mailbox defined in the email standards to which error messages related to email can be sent. `Postmaster` is case-insensitive, meaning `pOStMAstEr` is equivalent to `postmaster`.

While *local-part* is case-sensitive in the standard, most MTAs implement it to be case-insensitive. This is for good reason. Users would find it frustrating to receive errors for an email address that simply used a different case.

The *domain* portion of *addr-spec* indicates where email for a specific mailbox can be sent to facilitate delivery. RFC822 defines *domain* as follows.

```
domain     = sub-domain *("." sub-domain)
sub-domain = domain-ref / domain-literal
domain-ref = atom
```

This isn't quite right, however. The *sub-domain* and *domain-literal* elements aren't mixed together in a domain name. A more accurate syntax is as follows.

```
domain = dot-atom / domain-literal
```

The most common form used is *dot-atom,* which is based on the notation used by the DNS protocol. DNS and its relationship to email are explained in Chapter 3, but domains need to be discussed here.

The *dot-atom* specifies a path down a tree of hierarchical domains, such as the one shown in Figure 2.5. Each dot acts as a separator, similar to those found in a directory tree in a filesystem, except that the segments are in reverse order compared to a filesystem directory name.

An FQDN is written by traversing down the tree, using a dot to separate the elements of the name.

```
tuba.example.com
```

The next form of *domain* to look at is *domain-literal,* which is used to specify a literal address of the machine in question. Specifying the destination machine as a literal bypasses DNS, normally used to translate a domain name into an IP (Internet Protocol) address. The most common use of this form is where either the

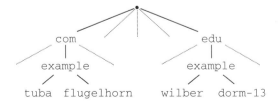

FIGURE 2.5 Example Domain Hierarchy

hostname is unavailable or unknown or the normal email routing mechanism is broken. In general, *domain-literals* should be used only for debugging problems and temporarily working around problems with name resolution.

The syntax for domain literals is very liberal.

```
domain-literal = [CFWS] "[" *([FWS] dcontent) [FWS] "]" [CFWS]
dcontent       = dtext / quoted-pair
dtext          = <any CHAR except "[", "]", "\", and bare CR>
```

The contents inside the enclosing '[ ]' characters is rather liberals, too. This was intentional. Remembering that mail messages are a format for transporting mail, there's nothing in the standard that stipulates the transport method. While SMTP is the most common, there's no reason that another transport can't be used. The *domain-literal* syntax is liberal so that it can accommodate any transport.

For many years, the only domain-literal most people encountered was the familiar dotted-quad version of an IP address.

```
joe@[10.1.1.1]
```

A new version of IP, IPv6 (Internet Protocol—Version 6), is being developed for use on the Internet. Instead of a 32-bit value, it uses a 128-bit value. In addition, the text representation of the 128-bit address is different. If the traditional dotted-quad notation were used, an IPv6 address would contain 16 segments.

```
254.220.186.152.118.84.50.16.254.220.186.152.118.84.50.16
```

This would be cumbersome, to say the least. To shorten the address and speed up parsing the information, the decision was made to use a different notation for text representation, which is described in RFC1884 (IP Version 6 Addressing Architecture). The previous example is represented as follows.

```
FEDC:BA98:7654:3210:FEDC:BA98:7654:3210
```

RFC1884 improves upon this by allowing consecutive sequences of zero bits to be compressed in the address string. As an example, the following address contains a significant number of zero bits.

```
1080:0:0:0:8:800:200C:417A
```

This can be compressed as follows.

```
1080::8:800:200C:417A
```

The IPv6 version of a loopback address can be compressed even more.

```
::1
```

This new format requires a different notation for domain literals in email addresses. Unfortunately, the liberal syntax in RFC822 doesn't provide any guidance for specifying them in IPv6. Without an explicit tag identifying the type of address contained in the domain literal, the only way to detect the difference between an IPv4 and IPv6 address is to check for '.' or ':' characters. This doesn't solve the general problem. A future update to RFC822 will probably provide a tag for identifying the address type.

Route Addresses

The second form of a *mailbox* is a route address, which allows the sender to specify a series of machines to use for the route a message will take to a destination.

```
route-addr  = [CFWS] "<" [route] addr-spec ">" [CFWS]
route       = [CFWS] domain-list ":" [CFWS]
domain-list = "@" domain *(*(CFWS / ",") [CFWS] "@" domain)
```

The following is an example of a route address.

```
<@c.example.com,@b.example.com,@a.example.com:guido@a.example.com>
```

Specifying the route in the address is called *source routing*, since the source of the message specifies the route the message will take. This form of address is rarely seen and should not be used. Many email implementations ignore the source route information completely.

Route addresses with no source routing information are commonly found on the Internet.

```
<guido@a.example.com>
```

The syntax for a *mailbox* allows a *phrase* to be used in front of a route address. RFC822 doesn't indicate that *phrase* is optional, but RFC1123 corrects this.

```
[phrase] route-addr
```

The *phrase* allows additional information to be included with the address, most commonly a human-readable name.

```
Joe Doubloon <joe@tuba.example.com>
```

2.5.2 Group Lists

The mailbox notation described in the previous section specifies a single destination. Group lists provide a way to notate a set of destinations treated as a single unit.

```
group         = display-name ":" [mailbox-list / CFWS] ";" [CFWS]
display-name = phrase
```

The *display-name* portion holds the name of the list. A list of mailboxes is placed between the ':' and ';' characters.

```
To: Tiger Team: joe@tuba.example.com,
                mary@glockenspiel.example.com;
```

Group lists do not nest. Thus, the following example is invalid.

```
To: Tiger Team: joe@tuba.example.com,
                mary@glockenspiel.example.com,
                Previous Tiger Team: bob@flugelhorn.example.com,
                                     larry@ictus.example.com;
```

Group lists are used not so much for their original purpose but commonly as a way to specify an address without disclosing the recipients. This is possible because the portion between the ':' and ';' characters is optional. The following example is a valid group list.

```
To: Undisclosed-Recipients:;
```

It is often used for such things as product announcements to avoid having the actual recipients visible in the outgoing message.

```
To: Acme New Product Announcement:;
```

2.6 RECEIVED FIELDS

The `Received` field deserves special attention. Not only is it one of the most complex fields, it is also one of the most important to understand for diagnosing email problems.

In its full glory, `Received` can get quite complicated. Starting at the top and working down will help sift through the complexity. By the end of this section, the reader will have a good understanding of how the field is structured and how it can be used to diagnose various email problems.

2.6.1 Field Elements

The top-level syntax for the field is as follows.

```
"Received:" ["from" CFWS domain CFWS]
            ["by" CFWS domain CFWS]
            ["via" CFWS atom CFWS]
            *("with CFWS atom CFWS)
            ["id" CFWS (string / msg-id) CFWS]
            ["for" 1*(CFWS mailbox) CFWS]
            ";" CFWS date-time
```

All the subfields except *date-time* are optional. In general, the set of subfields depends on the MTA that prepends the `Received` field.

While the overall structure is fairly simple, each of the subfields has a few twists.

From

This subfield specifies the name of the sending machine. RFC822 used a simple *domain* element for it.

```
from tuba.example.com
```

Most MTAs add a parenthetical comment after *domain* to provide additional information. If present, the comment typically contains a domain literal of the IP address of the peer on the TCP (Transmission Control Protocol) connection, and the domain name resulting from a DNS lookup of the address is frequently included.

```
from tuba.example.com (tuba.example.com [10.1.1.1])
```

This additional information is useful for troubleshooting various email problems.

By

This subfield specifies the name of the receiving machine.

```
by flugelhorn.example.com
```

Via

This subfield was originally supposed to note the physical mechanism over which the message was sent. RFC822 lists ARPANET and Phonenet[8] as example values. RFC1700 (Assigned Numbers) lists UUCP as the only valid value. A review of existing practice shows via more commonly used to note what program was used to transmit the message or what gateway software it was transmitted through.

```
via rsmtp
via smap (3.2)
via sendmail
```

With

This subfield was originally intended to note the mail or connection protocol used to transfer the message between two MTAs. Unlike other subfields in Received, this one may be used multiple times to note a set of protocols used, although it seldom is.

RFC822 lists SMTP and X.25[9] as example values, while RFC1700 lists only SMTP and ESMTP as valid. Again, a review of existing practice shows that the use of with is generally in line with the intent of the standard; however, the list of protocols is larger than that in RFC822 and RFC1700. The following examples are typical of what is seen in this subfield:

```
with smtp
with esmtp
with P:bsmtp/R:internet/T:mxsmtp
with uucp
```

Id

This subfield is used to note the unique identifier the MTA used for the message when processing it. It can be quite handy, since most MTAs keep a log of the messages handled, and it allows the message to be linked with MTA log entries.

Section 5.2.8 of RFC1123 updates the format of this subfield, stating that it is not required to contain a '@'. Since the definition of *msg-id* is '*<addr-spec>*',

---

[8] Phonenet was the dial-up portion of CSNET.

[9] X.25 is a communications protocol developed by CCITT (Consultative Committee for International Telephone and Telegraph). It is common in Europe, but is gradually being displaced by other protocols.

one would tend to think this means that '*<local-part>*' is the alternative format described in RFC1123. In practice, however, the surrounding angle brackets are often not included, resulting simply in *local-part*.

```
id HAA19482
```

For

This subfield is used to record the recipient address given in the `rcpt` command in the SMTP dialog. RFC1123 updates `for` to allow a list of entries if multiple `rcpt` commands are given. Details on the `rcpt` command are presented in Chapter 3.

```
for <joe@tuba.example.com>
;
```

This subfield specifies the date and time the `Received` line was inserted into the header. The format of *date-time* is described in Section 2.7.

```
; Tue, 28 Sep 1999 12:23:46 -0300
```

The following example shows a `Received` field with all of its subfields.

```
Received: from tuba.example.com
          by lab-rat.example.com
          via smap
          with esmtp
          id HAA19482
          for <wilber@lab.example.com>
          ; Tue, 28 Sep 1999 12:23:46 -0300
```

2.6.2 Comments

In real email messages many of the `Received` fields contain comments. These are used to relate extra information not included in the base definition for the field.

While comments are, strictly speaking, transparent to the structure of fields, it is very common for them to convey crucial information for diagnosing problems. An important point to remember is that `Received` fields are intended to be read by humans. Because of this, MUA developers have been liberal in using comments to add useful information not covered by the standard.

```
Received: from ictus.example.com ([10.2.3.1]) by tuba.example.com
          (Mail-Monster MTA v1.2.3 license (AA38921-1/234/9Z)
          8/14ZA7I1W9) with SMTP id BAA12938;
          Tue, 28 Sep 1999 12:23:46 -0300

Received: from oboe.example.com (sally@oboe.example.com
          [10.1.3.2]) by example.com (8.8.8/8.8.7) with ESMTP
          id CAA19283; Wed, 3 Feb 1999 17:56:25 -0500 (EST)

Received: from tuba.example.com (tuba.example.com [10.1.1.1])
          by example.com (8.8.8/8.8.5) with ESMTP id LAA32871
          for <bob@tuba.example.com>
          ; Sat, 3 Jan 1998 16:03:04 -0800 (PST)
```

2.6.3 Machine Parsing

Because there is a lot of potentially useful information in a series of `Received` lines, the urge can be strong to programmatically parse the information to help diagnose problems. On the surface, this seems like a workable idea—machine-parse the field and analyze the information using various heuristic rules. Unfortunately, it's a little more complicated. As mentioned earlier, there is a lot of variety in `Received` fields. In addition, very little of the data in comments is controlled by any standards.

Another problem is the inconsistent contents in some of the subfields. The `via` and `with` subfields illustrate this vividly.

Despite the problems just mentioned, it is technically possible to programmatically parse `Received` fields to a limited degree. What isn't possible is to parse them in a way that allows all the information to be used consistently by a program. The closest one can get is to include more and more logic related to exceptions.

2.6.4 Diagnosing Problems

`Received` fields are a fertile source of troubleshooting information. To reinforce the reader's understanding of them, this section walks through some ways to use them to diagnose simple email problems.

Delivery Delays
Email can traverse multiple machines in order to get from an origin to a destination, so it's possible for it to be delayed as it moves from machine to machine. The `Received` field provides a very simple way to determine the amount of time between hops.

As an example, say email from some remote locations seems to take an inordinately long time to arrive. Because `Received` fields include date-stamps for each

TABLE 2.3 Date and Time Information

Machine	Date and Time
oboe.example.com	Wed, 29 Sep 1999 12:56:24 -0700
tuba.example.com	Wed, 29 Sep 1999 12:51:02 -0700
exthub.example.com	Tue, 28 Sep 1999 06:26:41 -0700
wilber.example.edu	Tue, 28 Sep 1999 06:25:10 -0700

of the machines a message passes through, they are a likely place to find some answers.

A review of the header of the most recent message sent reveals the following `Received` lines.

```
Received: from tuba.example.com (tuba.example.com [10.1.1.1])
          by oboe.example.com (8.8.8/8.8.8) with ESMTP id BAA05527
          for <sally@oboe.example.com;
          Wed, 29 Sep 1999 12:56:24 -0700 (MST)
Received: from exthub.example.com (exthub.example.com [10.1.2.3])
          by tuba.example.com (8.8.8/8.8.8) with ESMTP id HAA26572
          ; Wed, 29 Sep 1999 12:51:02 -0700
Received: from wilber.example.edu (wilber.example.edu [10.10.3.1])
          by exthub.example.com (8.8.8/8.8.8) with ESMTP
          id IAA25252; Tue, 28 Sep 1999 06:26:41 -0700
Received: (from anne@slip-152.east.example.edu)
          by wilber.example.edu (8.8.8/8.8.8) id QAA01421;
          Tue, 28 Sep 1999 06:25:10 -0700
```

Table 2.3 condenses these fields down to the relevant date and time information.

The time between when `exthub` received the message and when `tuba` received the message accounts for the majority of the total elapsed time. This means `exthub` and `tuba` are the two machines worth investigating. The message could have been delayed by problems on `exthub` or because `tuba` was asking `exthub` to defer it.

Something to be aware of when doing this type of analysis is that there's no guarantee that the date-stamps on each of the machines will be accurate. A convenient solution to this problem is the *daytime* TCP service. If the machine in question has this service enabled, it's possible to connect to port 13 on the remote machine to see what it thinks the current time is.[10]

---

[10] Because the output from the daytime port is the local time at the server, it's necessary to compensate for the time-zone when comparing it to the time on a local machine. The time-zone offset in daytime, however, will usually match the offset in the `Received` field.

```
$ telnet tuba.example.com daytime
Trying 10.1.1.1...
Connected to tuba.example.com.
Escape character is '^]'.
Sun Feb 15 13:48:31 1998
Connection closed by foreign host.
$
```

This information can be used by email administrators to identify differences in system time for the machines listed in `Received` fields. For the information shown in Table 2.3, it might be a good idea to check the daytime service on `exthub`. If the system clock is seriously wrong, the information in the `Received` field will be misleading, resulting in troubleshooting efforts being aimed at the wrong machine. If, for example, the clock on `exthub` was behind by approximately six hours, the problem could actually be on `wilber`.

Spoofed Email

Internet email provides no built-in means for authentication. Thus, it is possible to create a piece of email that appears to be from a different person. This is referred to as *spoofing*. There are mechanisms that solve this problem, but it is important that administrators be able to detect spoofing when analyzing messages.

The `Received` fields in a message can sometimes be used to detect trivial spoofing techniques. For example, an atypical piece of email may appear to have come from a certain person. If there is a possibility of spoofing, the extra information gleaned from the SMTP connection often contained in `Received` fields may provide some clues.

A review of the header for the piece of email in question reveals the following `Received` lines.

```
Received: from ictus.example.com (ictus.example.com [10.2.3.1])
        by tuba.example.com (8.8.8/8.8.8) with ESMTP
        id BAA62840 for <bob@tuba.example.com>;
        Wed, 29 Sep 1999 12:13:14 -0700
Received: from bells.example.com (bubezleeb@dorm-13.example.edu)
        by ictus.example.com (8.8.8/8.8.8)
        id DAA01465; Wed, 29 Sep 1999 12:12:50 -0700
```

The items of interest are the comments following the `from` subfields. The MTA has inserted additional information based on the SMTP connection. In the first `Received` line, the information in the first set of comments specifies the machine name and the IP address on the other side of the SMTP connection. This was done by getting the IP addresses of the remote side of the TCP connection and then using DNS to convert the IP address into a domain name.

The first `Received` field appears to be in order; the information matches. The second `Received` field is another story. The contents of the `from` subfield don't match the contents of the adjacent comment, which means that the MTA on `ictus.example.com` had a different view of the machine connected to it than was presented in the dialog from the SMTP `helo` command.

Another thing to note about the comment string in the second `Received` field is that the hostname looks more like an email address. This is a tell-tale sign of the use of the *ident* protocol, defined in RFC1413 (Identification Protocol),[11] which is used to detect the username on the other side of a connection. While it isn't always implemented, in this case it is. The additional information confirms the likelihood that the email was spoofed.

The techniques described here cannot catch all instances of spoofed email, but they can catch a significant percentage. Completely detecting and preventing spoofed email is much more involved. Chapters 3 and 9 include information on more sophisticated techniques.

2.7 DATE-TIME FIELDS

Several of the structured fields contain *date-time* elements in their definition, which while not overly complicated, are worth walking through. Since they are programmatically analyzed, it is important that they be correct.

The *date-time* element is a good example of the importance of the human readability of headers. Using a pure integer would have been more bullet-proof and easier to implement, but it would have been a lot less readable by humans.

The top-level definition of a *date-time* field is as follows.

```
date-time = [day-of-week "," ] date time
```

The syntax for *day-of-week* is

```
day-of-week = [CFWS] day-name [CFWS]
day-name = "Mon" / "Tue" / "Wed" / "Thu" / "Fri" / "Sat" / "Sun"
```

The syntax for *date* is

```
date       = day month year
day        = [CFWS] 1*2DIGIT [CFWS]
month      = CFWS month-name CFWS
month-name = "Jan" / "Feb" / "Mar" / "Apr" / "May" / "Jun" /
             "Jul" / "Aug" / "Sep" / "Oct" / "Nov" / "Dec"
year       = [CFWS] 2*4DIGIT [CFWS]
```

---

[11] The ident protocol, while useful, shouldn't be relied on in all cases. The quality of the data is subject to the trustworthiness of the machine on the other side of the network connection.

The syntax for *date-time* allows a copious amount of commented folding whitespace. It is strongly recommended that this extra whitespace be avoided, as it's not typically needed.

The *year* value deserves special attention. RFC822 defines it with a two-digit year.

```
1*2DIGIT month 2DIGIT
```

The format was updated in RFC1123 to cope with the Y2K (Year-2000) problem.[12] Email programs are still required to handle two-digit years, but it is recommended that they only transmit or generate four-digit years.

After the *date* portion comes *time,* defined as follows.

```
time = time-of-day zone
```

The *time-of-day* token is defined as

```
time-of-day = hour ":" minute [":" second]
hour        = [CFWS] 2DIGIT [CFWS]
minute      = [CFWS] 2DIGIT [CFWS]
second      = [CFWS] 2DIGIT [CFWS]
```

The three segments of *time-of-day* must be 2-digit values. In addition, the total value must be semantically valid. For example, 99:99:99 is not valid.

The final item to deal with in *date-time* is the *zone* element. The syntax is as follows.

```
zone = [CFWS] ((("+" / "-") 4DIGIT) /
              "UT" / "GMT" /
              "EST" / "EDT" / "CST" / "CDT" /
              "MST" / "MDT" / "PST" / "PDT" /
              1ALPHA)
```

RFC822 defines three formats for *zone* values: numerals, time-zone acronyms, and 1-letter military designators.

A numeric time-zone is a positive or negative number noting the time-zone offset from UT (Universal Time).[13] For example, Phoenix, Arizona, is at an offset of -0700 from UT. The numeric representation for UT is +0000.

The value -0000 is used to indicate some operational difficulty with the time-zone on the local machine, such as an unknown or invalid one.

---

[12] This was an insightful change considering that RFC1123 was published in 1989, well ahead of many Y2K efforts.

[13] Universal Time (UT) and Greenwich Mean Time (GMT) are one and the same. GMT is simply the old designation for UT.

TABLE 2.4 Time-Zone Acronyms

Time-zone	Full Name	Offset
UT	Universal Time	+0000
GMT	Greenwich Mean Time	+0000
EDT	Eastern Daylight Savings Time	-0400
EST	Eastern Standard Time	-0500
CDT	Central Daylight Savings Time	-0500
CST	Central Standard Time	-0600
MDT	Mountain Daylight Savings Time	-0600
MST	Mountain Standard Time	-0700
PDT	Pacific Daylight Savings Time	-0700
PST	Pacific Standard Time	-0800

The acronym for time-zones consists of alphabetic tags that stand for specific offsets. This is the form people in North America are familiar with. Table 2.4 lists the acronyms valid in *date-time* values.

The military version uses a single character to note the offset from UT. Unfortunately, there was an error in the specification of this in RFC822. As pointed out in section 5.2 of RFC1123, RFC822 reversed the east/west directions when describing military time-zones. Because of this error, RFC1123 states that all military time-zone codes should be considered equal to the numeric offset `-0000`.

RFC1123 expands on the time-zone issue by recommending that the numeric time-zones be used. The main benefit to the numeric form is that international users don't have to remember time-zones they aren't familiar with.

2.8 SUMMARY

Email messages are the cornerstone of Internet Email. They provide the *lingua franca* for messages exchanged between users. RFC822 and portions of RFC1123 define the format messages must have when being transmitted from one location to another. Without a common format, it would be nearly impossible for email to work on the Internet.

An email message is a text-oriented piece of data consisting of a header and a body. The header provides a machine-parsable, yet human-readable, data structure for relating a considerable amount of information about a message. The body contains the actual data being sent.

Each header contains a set of fields. These fields provide the essential information needed to process a message. While the number of fields is relatively small, the structure of some of the fields is relatively complicated. This complexity accounts for most of the difficulty encountered when learning how mail messages are structured.

There are four fundamental types of message. New messages are created from scratch; redistributed messages are built by adding `Resent-*` fields to an existing message; forwarded messages are created by encapsulating an existing message inside the body of a new message; and reply messages are created by incorporating some, or all, of the text of a previous message into a new message and referencing the `Message-ID` of the previous message in the `In-Reply-To` and `References` fields of the new message.

With an understanding of email messages, the reader is ready for the next step—understanding how messages are transferred from one location to another.

Chapter 3

Mail Transport

An email message in isolation is of limited use. To harness the real power of email, users need to be able to send a message somewhere. This leads to the second primary aspect of email—transport, specifically, the SMTP protocol. This chapter provides a description of how the protocol works, the commands it provides, the basic mail transactions possible, and the SMTP extension mechanism.

Many people do not realize that the earliest protocol used for transporting Internet email was FTP. Shortly after the first email software was created, commands were added to FTP to improve its use in transporting email, and it was used through the remainder of the 70s.

The first RFC to implement a protocol dedicated to transferring mail was RFC772 (Mail Transfer Protocol), published in 1980. The components related to mail transfer were moved out of FTP as part of the protocol cleanup done during the migration from ARPANET to the Internet. This RFC was updated in 1981 with RFC780 (Mail Transfer Protocol).

Shortly after RFC772 was published, some nonessential elements were removed from the protocol based on input from the Internet community at the time. The result was RFC788 (Simply Mail Transfer Protocol), published in 1981, which defined SMTP.

In 1982, RFC821 was published, replacing RFC788 as the specification for SMTP. It has served as the core definition for several years. In 1989, RFC1123 was published to clarify and improve several protocols, including SMTP.

After years of use, it became evident that several features would be useful to add to SMTP. Rather than creating a new version of the protocol, an extension mechanism was created. In 1993, RFC1425 (SMTP Service Extensions) was published. This provided a framework for adding new extensions to the protocol without breaking existing implementations. RFC1425 was updated in 1994 by RFC1651 (SMTP Service Extensions) and again in 1995 by RFC1869 (SMTP Service Extensions). The extension mechanism has proven to be very effective in adding new functionality to SMTP without affecting the core protocol. Section 3.5 describes several of the more common extensions in use.

Together, RFC821, RFC1123, and the service extensions have been the basic specification for SMTP for many years. In fact, the SMTP extension mechanism has become important enough that this chapter describes parts of that mechanism while describing the core SMTP protocol.

3.1 INTERFACE MODEL

At the highest level, SMTP is implemented as a communication protocol between two machines—a client and a server. In its simplest form, a message is sent from a user on one machine to a mailbox on another machine, as illustrated in Figure 3.1. SMTP is used by the two servers to transfer the message.

This description doesn't tell the entire story, however. The various actions performed when transferring a message are handled by different agents. These agents are shown in Figure 3.2.

In practice, most MTAs are designed with SMTP delivery built in. As a result, Figure 3.2 can be simplified as shown in Figure 3.3. This is the style used in later diagrams in this book.

SMTP is a *store-and-forward* protocol, meaning that it permits a message to be sent through a series of servers in order to be delivered to an end destination. Servers store incoming messages in a queue to await attempts to transmit them to the next destination. The next destination could be a local user or another mail server, as shown in Figure 3.4.

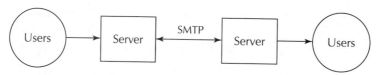

FIGURE 3.1 High-Level SMTP Interface Model

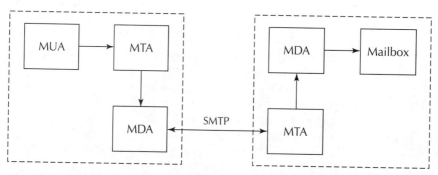

FIGURE 3.2 Agents Involved in Mail Transfer

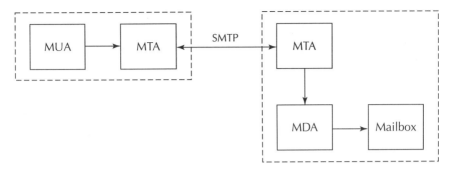

FIGURE 3.3 Simplified Diagram of Mail Agents

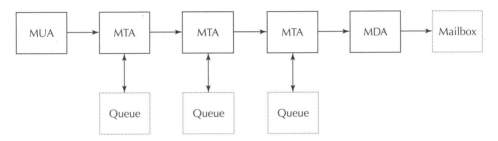

FIGURE 3.4 Store and Forward

If the downstream MTA is temporarily unavailable, the MTA simply keeps the message in the queue and tries to deliver it later.

To transfer a message, a server encapsulates it in a data object consisting of the message and an envelope. This is similar to a regular postal letter, which is enclosed in an envelope; the post office uses the information written on the envelope to route the message rather than look at the message itself. Like its namesake, the email envelope specifies source and destination information necessary for delivering a message. At first glance, it would seem that the envelope is redundant; after all, the message header contains this same information. However, using a separate envelope allows the message to be treated as an opaque object, eliminating the need for the MTA to analyze its contents. It also allows the source and destination to be different from what is contained in the message.

To process the envelope and message, servers maintain three buffers. The *reverse-path* buffer holds the source address for a mail message, which is where email messages detailing delivery problems are sent. The *forward-path* buffer holds the list of recipients a message is being delivered to. The *mail-data* buffer holds the message being transmitted.

Understanding these three buffers, and the relationship between the envelope and the message, is very important for understanding how mail transactions work. Various commands affect the buffers. These effects are described in Section 3.2.

In addition to the source and destination information, it's possible for SMTP extensions to add pieces of information to the envelope. The most important set of additions is described in Section 3.5.6.

3.1.1 Commands and Replies

SMTP is a text-oriented, command-based protocol. The client issues a command; the server processes it and sends a reply back to the client, as shown in Figure 3.5. This dialog continues until the session is terminated.

By default, the command sequence is synchronous, meaning that a response for the previous command must be received before the next command can be issued. Section 3.5.2 describes a protocol extension, pipelining, which loosens this "lock-step" requirement.

Each line transmitted, in either direction, is terminated with a CR character followed by a LF character. Command lines and each line of a reply can be no more than 512 characters long, including the CRLF.

There are 14 commands in the core protocol. Of these, 8 are required, which are listed in Table 3.1. Each command line sent from a client consists of a 4-character command followed by an optional set of arguments. One additional command will be described with the core SMTP commands—ehlo, a variant of `helo` used with the SMTP service extensions.

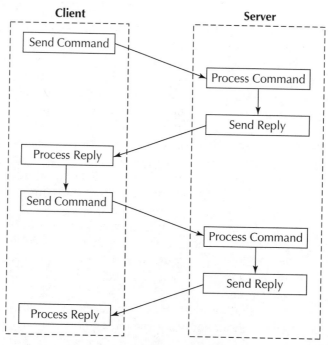

FIGURE 3.5 Synchronous Dialoging in SMTP

TABLE 3.1 Core SMTP Commands

Command	Required?	Description
quit	Yes	Terminate the session
help		Request help with SMTP commands
noop	Yes	No-Operation
vrfy	(Yes)	Verify an address (not required to be enabled)
expn		Expand an alias
helo	Yes	Client greeting to server
mail	Yes	Specify sender of a mail message
rcpt	Yes	Specify recipients of a mail message
data	Yes	Send message data
rset	Yes	Reset the session state
send		Specify sender of a message to be sent to user terminal
soml		Send or Mail
saml		Send and Mail
turn		Swap client/server roles

All the commands are case-insensitive. A few have additional arguments that do not represent variable data; these, too, are case-insensitive. For example, see the `mail` and `rcpt` commands in Section 3.2.

After processing a command, the server sends a reply back to the client. The primary purpose of a reply is to relate success or failure status information. It is a structured piece of data designed to be both machine-parsable and human-readable. Replies come in two forms—single-line and multiline. The format for a single-line reply is as follows.

```
reply = reply-code SP human-readable-text
```

The first portion is a 3-digit numerical reply code. A single space character follows it, and the remainder of the line is the human-readable portion. Some commands, like `vrfy`, impose constraints on the text format, but it is always intended to be readable by humans.

This reply format is a remnant of the protocol's roots in FTP, which uses a similar one. Interested readers might want to compare the reply mechanisms in RFC821 and RFC959 (File Transfer Protocol).

Here is an example SMTP reply.

```
250 Requested mail action okay, completed
```

The human-readable portion typically contains descriptive text associated with the reply number. The purpose of the text is to provide users with a readable description of problems encountered. In general, it is not designed to be machine-parsed.

RFC821 provides standard text strings to go with each of the reply codes. In general, the standard text is used, but variations are not uncommon. The standard text for the 250 reply code is a good example. The text portion of this reply is often reduced to a simple acknowledgment of success.

```
250 ok
```

This is a perfectly acceptable deviation from the standard text. Developers need to be careful, however, about being too liberal in diverging from the text specified in RFC821. There are instances where it makes sense to diverge, but the defined text should be used where possible.

Clients should be prepared to handle reply lines that don't provide the human-readable text or even the space character after the reply code. Despite the fact that the space character and human-readable text are required, some servers have been known not to issue them.

Replies can also span multiple lines. The format is very similar to that of a single-line reply, except that the space character is replaced with a '-' on all but the last line. The '-' serves as an indicator to the client that there are more reply lines coming. The following example shows a client sending an ehlo command and the server sending a multiline response.

```
ehlo tuba.example.com
250-flugelhorn.example.com
250-size 10485760
250 8bitmime
```

Reply Code Digits

The three digits of a reply code each convey different levels of information. The first digit is the most significant, conveying the overall success or failure of the command. The defined values for the first digit are shown in Table 3.2.

With a positive preliminary reply, the command succeeded but the server is expecting additional confirmation from the client. No SMTP commands use this reply category. A positive completion status means the command succeeded and the server doesn't require any additional confirmation for it. The 250, shown earlier, is an example of this reply type. A positive intermediate reply indicates the command succeeded and the server is prompting for additional data. Currently, data is the only command that uses this type. After the client issues the data command, the server issues a 354 reply, which is a prompt for the message

TABLE 3.2 First Digit of Reply Code

First Digit	Description
1	Positive preliminary reply
2	Positive completion status
3	Positive intermediate reply
4	Transient negative reply
5	Permanent failure

payload. See the description of the `data` command in Section 3.2 for an example of this reply.

A transient negative reply indicates a temporary failure. The command has failed, but attempting it at a later time might succeed. Lack of disk space is typically a temporary problem. Since the problem will probably be rectified, the server can issue a `452` reply, which tells the client to try again later. A permanent failure means a command failed and retrying isn't expected to work. Examples include syntax errors and unknown users.

The second digit specifies a category for the reply. Only four values are used, shown in Table 3.3. The value `0` relates to the syntax of a command. Permanent failures are the only replies that use it; requests for additional information use the value `1`, which is only used by replies to `help` commands. Replies related to the communication channel include the connection greeting, the `quit` command, and notification that the server is shutting down the connection. The final category for the second digit is the mail system. This one has the most variety. The other value for the second digit occurs only with 3 to 5 commands; this value occurs with 12.

While the first and second digit have specific meanings associated with the values, the third digit is a little different. It provides a finer level of granularity for various combinations of the first two digits. There is no specific meaning for a particular value of the third digit. It serves only to differentiate a specific

TABLE 3.3 Second Digit of Reply Code

Second Digit	Description
0	Syntax
1	Responses to requests for additional information
2	Communications Channel
5	Mail system

combination of the first two. As an example, the following list shows a variety of transient negative replies related to the mail system.

```
450 Requested mail action not taken: mailbox unavailable
451 Requested action aborted: local error in processing
452 Requested action not taken: insufficient system storage
```

Compare this to a list of replies using the same value for the third digit.

```
220 domain Service ready
250 Request mail action ready, completed
450 Mailbox busy
500 Syntax error, command unrecognized
550 Mailbox not found
```

Even though all these replies use 0 as the third digit, they have nothing in common. To emphasize the point, the first digit is the only one that should be used to detect the success or failure of an SMTP command. The second and third digits can be used to fine-tune the processing of the reply code, but shouldn't be used to detect success or failure.

Generic Reply Codes

A subset of the reply codes is applicable to nearly all the commands. The most common one is 250, which indicates a positive completion status.

```
250 ok
```

At the opposite end of the spectrum are reply codes that note failure of one form or another. The 421 reply code indicates a transient error with the SMTP service, typically that the service is going offline temporarily.

```
421 domain Service not available, closing transmission channel
```

Reply codes related to syntax errors are also common to most commands. They are generally permanent errors.

```
500 Syntax error, command unrecognized
501 Syntax error in parameters or arguments
502 Command not implemented
504 Command parameter not implemented
```

RFC821 allowed servers to return 500 for all the commands, even required ones. Server implementations should use 502 for required commands that are disabled, but client implementations can still expect 500 from older servers.

Issues with Reply Codes

There are a few issues regarding reply codes to be aware of. Some of them might not be obvious to the casual observer.

Certain reply codes can convey different error conditions when used in different contexts. For example, 553 has two distinct meanings depending on the command being replied to.

```
vrfy john
553 User ambiguous
```

```
rcpt to:<roland@fido.lab.example.com>
553 sorry, that domain isn't in my list of allowed recipient hosts
```

While this isn't a problem, software that parses reply codes shouldn't read too much into them. There's really only one dependable rule about reply codes—the first digit is used to indicate the success, transient failure, or permanent failure of a command. Software should use this digit only to determine the status of a command.

In addition to overloaded reply codes, nonstandard reply codes have been introduced from time to time. Developers should create new reply codes only through the standards process. Failure to do so can cause problems with implementations that interpret the reply at a greater level of detail than is called for in the standard.

Another issue is the lack of sufficient reply codes for reporting delivery problems. The majority of the codes were designed for protocol interactions and mail system problems. Over the years, this has proven to be a problem, since there are many types of delivery problems.

To avoid overloading the reply codes any further, particularly for delivery problems, an enhanced mechanism was devised. In 1996, RFC1893 (Enhanced Mail System Status Codes) was published. It was designed to be used with RFC1894 (An Extensible Message Format for Delivery Status Notifications) and with the SMTP extension defined in RFC2034 (SMTP Service Extension for Returning Enhanced Error Codes), which are both described in Section 3.5.

3.1.2 SMTP Sessions

An SMTP session can be divided into several phases—determining which machine to connect to, establishing a connection, initializing the session, performing various transaction dialogs, and session shutdown.

Determining the Destination

Once an MTA decides a message is ready to be delivered, it must determine where to deliver it. At first glance, this might seem trivial; after all, the right-hand side of an email contains an FQDN. As it turns out, this process is more complicated than simply connecting to the machine referenced in the email address.

As mentioned earlier, SMTP was designed as a store-and-forward protocol. This includes the ability for machines to act as gateways or relays for other machines—a consequence of the early history of email, when other email-based networks, such as CSNET, were connected to ARPANET. To accomplish this connectivity, gateway machines were created to translate between the different types of email networks. To get email servers to route email for an external network through the gateways, the query process for SMTP was made slightly different from regular DNS lookups.

RFC973 (Domain System Changes and Observations) defines the changes made to DNS to handle the current technique for routing email. RFC974 (Mail Routing and the Domain System) defines how MTAs should use those changes. Updates to the DNS protocol, RFC1034 (Domain Names—Concepts and Facilities) and RFC1035 (Domain Names—Implementation and Specification) integrated the changes to the protocol described in RFC973. Since the process defined in RFC974 was acceptable, it wasn't updated at that time.

There are two ways to determine which remote host should be contacted for an SMTP dialog. The first is only used by MUAs when submitting a message to any other MUA. The second is used by MTAs when connecting to any other MTA.

With the first technique, a client performs a DNS query, requesting an A (Address) record for its SMTP relay. If the response provides multiple A records, the client should attempt to identify the address that is closest to it, particularly if one of the addresses is on the same physical network as the client.

With the second technique, the first step is to perform a DNS query, requesting MX (Mail Exchanger) information for the FQDN in the right-hand portion of the email address.

At the highest level, there are three possible outcomes of the DNS query. The MTA might not get an answer from the DNS server, in which case the server should either try another DNS server or defer the delivery of the message. If the DNS server does respond, the answer could be "no such domain." In this case, the message is undeliverable, so the sending MTA should bounce the message back to the sender with a 550 permanent failure.

The third possibility is that the DNS server responds with DNS information about the FQDN in the request. The server can send back a CNAME (Canonical Name) record or zero or more MX records. CNAME records identify machine aliases. The value of a CNAME record points to the real name of a FQDN. In this case, the MTA needs to requery DNS for information about the canonical name of the machine. This process continues until the server identifies an FQDN that doesn't have a CNAME record associated with it.

There's a complication with processing CNAME records. Special care needs to be taken to avoid long sequences of nested CNAME lookups, particularly if a loop in the CNAME records is present. Implementations typically limit the number of CNAME indirections to around 10. If this limit is exceeded, the server treats it as a DNS failure.

At this point, the MTA has a list of zero or more MX records, which contain several pieces of information. Two fields are of particular interest: mail exchanger and preference. The mail exchanger field contains the fully qualified name of a host capable of serving as a mail exchanger for the given FQDN. The preferences field indicates how preferable that host is compared to other possible mail exchangers.

```
$ nslookup -q=mx www.example.com
Server: localhost
Address: 127.0.0.1

Authoritative Answer:
example.com    preference = 10, mail exchanger = smtp1.example.com
example.com    preference = 30, mail exchanger = smtp3.example.com
example.com    preference = 20, mail exchanger = smtp2.example.com
$
```

DNS provides the ability to set default MX information for an entire domain with the use of *wildcard MX* records. If this type of record is present in the DNS server's database, and the query matches the wildcard, the server will synthesize an MX record based on the DNS query. For example, if a wildcard MX record exists for `*.example.com`, and a client requests information for `tuba.example.com`, the server will reply with MX information for `tuba` with information based on the wildcard record. This is transparent to the SMTP client, since the DNS server provides an answer based on the SMTP client's question.

RFC974 also describes the use of WKS (Well Known Service) records when determining where to route a message. RFC1123 deprecated these, so they should no longer be used.

If the query doesn't contain a CNAME record or any MX records, the MTA considers the FQDN to be the best place to deliver the message. In this case, it performs an address lookup to determine the IP address of the machine. With that in hand, it connects to the remote server on TCP port 25 and carries on whatever SMTP dialog is necessary to transfer the message.

If the DNS query returns at least one MX record, the next step is to prune the list to remove undesirable entries. If the sending MTA finds itself in the list of MX records, it removes itself from the list. It also removes any records with a higher preference value than any occurrences of itself. In the previous example, if `smtp2` were performing the query, it would remove itself and `smtp3`.

If, after removing the undesirable MX records, the remaining list is empty, an error has occurred. An empty list implies that there are no acceptable hosts to act as a mail exchanger. Generally, the correct action is to generate a bounce message back to the sender with a description of the problem. This behavior is different from the one described in RFC974, which left the decision of how to handle the exception to developers.

If the list of MX records is not empty, the MTA sorts it by preference value. It now has a list of machines willing to accept email for the target destination sorted by preference. The next step is to iterate through the sorted list, progressing from the lowest to the highest preference, looking for a machine willing to accept a connection.

If a set of records has the same preference value, the MTA picks one record at random, unless there's a compelling reason to select a specific one, such as network proximity.

In order to connect to a machine, the client must determine the machine's IP address. At this point, the client has an FQDN for a mail exchanger. It then queries the DNS server, asking for address information about that mail exchanger.

If the mail exchanger has multiple network interfaces, it's possible that the DNS query will return multiple A records. In this case, the client can attempt to connect to each of the addresses, looking for one that works. The DNS server is supposed to order this list by decreasing preference, so the client must try the records in the order presented. If a DNS server cannot determine the preferred order, it is supposed to randomize the list. The client is still required to try the records in the order presented.

It's possible, as has been seen, for an FQDN entry to contain several types of records. At this point, the client is interested only in A records for the mail exchanger. Some administrators have been tempted to point MX records at CNAME records in an attempt to simplify the administration of DNS. This is the wrong thing to do. All mail exchanger records should point to hosts with A records.

It's a good idea for all hosts to have an MX record, even if that record simply points back to the host. DNS is a distributed network database. In general, clients query local DNS servers, which then query remote servers. To improve performance, the local server caches answers from remote servers. If a host doesn't have any MX information, every connection attempt can result in one or more resolver queries, looking for MX information. Adding the extra MX information can reduce DNS traffic and improve performance for an MTA.

Establishing a Connection

Compared to the steps involved in determining what host to connect to, establishing an SMTP connection is very simple. The client creates a TCP connection to the server on port 25, the standard SMTP port.

The session startup consists of a sequence of steps that establish a connection between the client and server and the initial dialog the machines have. This will be described in detail in Section 3.3. Once the session is established the client might decide to perform an authentication process. RFC821 doesn't provide any authentication, but extensions have been developed to do so. These are described in Chapter 9.

Upon getting the connection request, the server machine starts SMTP to process the connection. At this point, the TCP connection is established.

Session Initialization

After initializing itself, the server process outputs a connection greeting to the client. This is normally a 220 reply formatted as follows:

```
greeting = "220" SP domain [SP text]
```

The client should wait until the connection greeting is seen before sending any commands to the server.

```
220 tuba.example.com Service ready
```

The greeting frequently includes a field indicating which flavor of SMTP the server supports.

```
220 tuba.example.com SMTP Service ready
```

```
220 tuba.example.com ESMTP Service ready
```

Some SMTP clients use this information to determine whether the server supports the SMTP service extensions, although this technique is technically incorrect. The client should instead use a fall-back technique, where it issues a `ehlo` command, then issues a `helo` command if the `ehlo` command fails. Some older SMTP servers disconnect if the `ehlo` command fails. To make sure the fall-back technique is resilient, SMTP clients should be prepared to reestablish the connection and issue a `helo` command if this occurs.

The greeting can also include information about the name and version number of the server software. There are two schools of thought on the choice of which one to use. One school thinks providing the information is helpful when debugging problems.

```
220 flugelhorn.example.com MondoMail v4.2
```

The other school thinks providing the information allows intruders to deduce what attacks might be more successful. Which is right typically depends on the environment. The previous example provides the name of the software package as well as the version. The following example gives minimal information for would-be attackers.

```
220 bassoon.example.com ESMTP
```

The 220 reply code isn't the only type of greeting a server can provide. A couple of other reply codes are available for indicating problems with the session.

To note a temporary problem, the server can respond with a 421 reply code. After issuing this reply, the server closes the connection.

```
421 tuba.example.com Service not available
```

Some MTAs use this reply code when there are too many concurrent SMTP connections in use. Since this is a temporary condition, the server issues this response to get the client to defer the message.

A subtle point is worth mentioning about this temporary reply. An SMTP client is supposed to iterate through its list of target machines until a delivery attempt succeeds. There are differing opinions about whether connecting to a server issuing a temporary failure in its connection greeting qualifies as a successful delivery attempt. The heart of the problem is the definition of "successful." One school of thought is that the next address should be attempted, since the server issuing the temporary failure is speaking only for itself, not the other possible mail exchangers. The other school of thought is that attempting to connect to the other target machines consumes excess resources, so a temporary failure in the connection greeting should result in a deferral.

This issue applies to machines with multiple addresses as well. If a machine has a large number of interfaces and is down, attempting to connect to each of its interfaces is a futile exercise. To address this problem, some MTAs can short-circuit the list of IP addresses to reduce the time spent attempting to connect to machines that are unavailable.

For a permanent problem, the server can respond with a 554 reply, which notes, in the case of a connection greeting, that no SMTP service is available on this machine.

```
554 No SMTP service available
```

In this case, the server doesn't drop the connection. Instead, it keeps it open until a `quit` command is issued. Any commands issued prior to the `quit` command are met with a `503` error.

If the server responds with a `220` reply for the initial greeting, the client sends a `helo` or `ehlo` command to identify itself. To complete the connection establishment dialog, the server replies to the `helo` or `ehlo` command with a status code.

```
220 flugelhorn.example.com ESMTP
ehlo tuba.example.com
250-flugelhorn.example.com
250-vrfy
250 help
```

In this case, the `ehlo` command was used. This caused the server to respond with a multiline `250` reply code listing the service extensions supported. At this point, the session is in what is referred to in RFC821 as the *Initial State*.

If a client uses `ehlo` and the server supports an authentication extension, the client may wish to authenticate to the server. This is describe in further detail in Chapter 9.

Transaction Dialogs

Once the session is established and any optional authentication has been performed, the two machines are ready to move mail from the client to the server with sequences of commands grouped together to perform mail transactions. In addition, several commands perform miscellaneous tasks not directly related to completing a mail transaction.

Session Shutdown

When the client is ready to terminate the conversion, it issues a `quit` command. The server responds with a success reply code, and the two disconnect.

3.1.3 Protocol States

A mail transaction consists of a specific set of commands executed in a specific order. To ensure that this order is maintained, the current state of the session is tracked by both the client and the server. The state diagram for these transactions is illustrated in Figure 3.6.

The client drives the session by issuing commands; the session changes state if the associated command succeeds; otherwise, it stays the same. The server responds

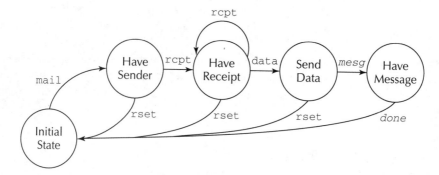

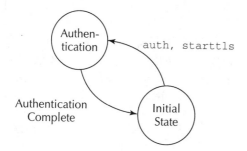

FIGURE 3.6 Top-Level State Diagram

FIGURE 3.7 Adding Authentication
to the State Diagram

with a 503 reply code if a command is sent that is inappropriate for the current
state.

```
503 bad sequence of commands
```

The client can exit the session at any time by issuing a quit command.

If an authentication mechanism is used, the changes to the state diagram focus
on the initial state. Figure 3.7 illustrates the addition. The actions performed while
authenticating are specific to a particular authentication extension.

3.2 STANDARD COMMANDS

This section describes the standard commands provided by RFC821. The general
commands are presented first, followed by the mail transaction commands. Lastly,
several commands not widely used in modern email implementations are described.

Readers can reinforce their understanding of the SMTP commands by interacting
with a local SMTP server. This can be done via the **telnet** command to connect
directly to the SMTP port on a machine.

```
$ telnet localhost 25
Trying 127.0.0.1
Connected to tuba.example.com.
Escape character is '^]'.
220 tuba.example.com ready.
SMTP dialog
quit
221 Closing connection
Connection closed by foreign host.
$
```

3.2.1 Quit

```
"quit"
```

The quit command terminates the session.

```
quit
221 tuba.example.com Service closing transmission channel
```

The server should respond with a 221 reply code to acknowledge the termination, then close the connection.

3.2.2 Help

```
"help" [SP string]
```

The optional help command is used to ask the server to send back various types of helpful information.

```
help
214-GreebleMail version 3.2.1
214-Commands:
214- DATA EHLO EXPN HELO HELP MAIL
214- NOOP QUIT RCPT RSET VERB VRFY
214-For more help, try "HELP <command>".
214-To report implementation bugs send email to:
214 greeble-bugs@example.com
```

In this example, the server responded with a summary of available commands as well as other general information about the software.

The command can also take an optional argument, which can be either an *atom* or a quoted string. It is typically used to request help on a particular SMTP command.

```
help rcpt
214-RCPT TO: <recipient>
214-Specifies the recipient for the next message.
214 Can be used any number of times.
```

In this example, with the request to provide additional information on `rcpt`, the server responded with a summary of the command usage as well as a brief description of the command.

One last thing worth mentioning about `help` is that it was designed to be read by humans rather than parsed by machines. As a result, there is no defined format for `help` output, except that the lines must adhere to the format defined for multiline replies.

3.2.3 Noop

```
"noop"
```

This command does nothing. More specifically, it has no effect on the session state or transaction buffers. The server normally responds with a `250` reply code to acknowledge its success in doing nothing.

```
noop
250 ok
```

While RFC821 doesn't specify any arguments for the `noop` command, it's probably a good idea for servers to accept, and ignore, them.

```
noop arf
250 ok
```

The utility of the `noop` command might not be intuitively obvious at first glance; after all, it doesn't do anything. It does, however, have a use—because the command doesn't alter the state of the session, the client can use it to test the connectivity to the server. Thus, SMTP servers that maintain persistent connections to other servers can verify that a connection is still intact.

3.2.4 Verify

```
"vrfy" SP string
```

The `vrfy` command is used to confirm if the given argument identifies a valid user or mailbox. It can also be used, in some implementations, to identify a list of possible matches if the given string is ambiguous.

There are two general styles of the argument. The most common is a simple mailbox name.

```
vrfy joe
250 Joe Doubloon <joe@tuba.example.com>
```

Notice that the reply includes an email address inside a pair of '<>' characters. This is intended to allow programs to parse the reply and extract the value.

On some implementations, the argument to `vrfy` can contain a domain name. This format can be useful for SMTP servers willing to relay email for other machines or domains.

```
vrfy joe@tuba.example.com
250 <joe@tuba.example.com>
```

RFC821 doesn't mandate this behavior. In fact, the syntax specified in RFC821 doesn't allow the '@' to be used, but MTA developers discovered that allowing it was useful in situations where a server was handling mail for more than one domain. Without the '@' confirming addresses for those other domains was impossible. It's not uncommon to find MTAs that implement this feature.

There are a variety of replies to this command. To convey success, several of the `25x` series of replies are possible. The primary reply is `250`, as shown near the beginning of this section.

One success reply code not seen very often is `251`. This is used when a server wants to state that the specified mailbox has moved to another location but mail to it will be forwarded.

```
251 User not local; will forward to forward-path
```

This reply is associated with an equivalent reply for the `rcpt` command. Even though it provides a convenient way for indicating that a recipient has moved to a different location, it isn't used very much because very few email packages programmatically use output from the `vrfy` command. The command is typically used only by humans.

The primary failure reply for the `vrfy` command is `550`.

```
550 Mailbox not found
```

Another failure reply is `551`, which, like `251`, is used when a mailbox has moved to another machine. The primary difference here is that the server uses a failure reply to indicate its unwillingness to forward messages for that recipient.

Since RFC821 doesn't allow the '@' character, some MTAs will not process it. In the following example, the MTA implements the letter of the RFC821 law, viewing '@' as an invalid character.

```
501 Syntax error in parameters or arguments
```

In the example below, the MTA does not check addresses containing '@', but has checked the address specified in the `vrfy` command and is willing to attempt delivery to it.

```
252 Possible remote address not checked
```

Some administrators prefer that the `vrfy` command disclose less information. Many MTAs accommodate this by providing the ability to configure the output of the command—a permanent failure, for example.

```
502 VRFY locally disabled
```

Another possibility is to have the MTA issue a success reply but to disclose no information. As with the previous example use of `252`, the MTA performs some validity checking on the address to determine whether it is structurally valid. The success reply means that the address is valid and the MTA will accept it. Whether the message will be delivered is another story.

```
252 Cannot VRFY user, but will accept message and attempt delivery
```

The use of the generalized *string* for the argument is intentional. This allows MTA developers to implement more sophisticated uses for the command.

The simplest response to `vrfy` could be a single-line reply stating that the request is ambiguous.

```
vrfy joe
553 User ambiguous
```

It could also respond with a list of possible values.

```
vrfy jo
553-Ambiguous; Possibilities are
553-Joe Doubloon <joe@tuba.example.com>
553 Josephine Snide <jsnide@tuba.example.com>
```

If MTAs implement this feature in the `vrfy` command, RFC821 requires the string "User ambiguous" in the first line of the reply. This allows clients to detect the ambiguity and provide a more detailed description of the error to a user. In particular, it allows the client to translate the error message into another language or to provide the list of alternative addresses for further processing. Despite the fact that the first digit of a reply code is the only value that should be used to indicate success or failure, it's possible for MUAs to use the entire reply to tune their interactions with users. This is an acceptable use of the second and third reply code digits. As a side note, clients should probably just scan for "ambiguous" in the first line. This will increase the likelihood of detecting the feature if the wording is slightly different.

There is one additional thing worth mentioning about the 553 reply code. The standard definition for 553 is as follows.

```
553 Requested action not taken: mailbox name not allowed
```

While this is rarely encountered in server implementations, it serves as a good example of sanctioned use of alternate reply code text.

3.2.5 Expand

```
"expn" SP string
```

MTAs typically provide a mechanism to associate an email address with a list of members. This type of mailing list is described in Chapter 8. The `expn` command expands the given argument as a mailing list pointing to a list of constituent members.

As an example, say an MTA server has a mailing list containing three members.

```
golf-club: joe@tuba.example.com,
           bob@flugelhorn.example.com,
           larry@ictus.example.com
```

The expn command can be used to expand the list to show its members.

```
expn golf-club
250-<joe@tuba.example.com>
250-<bob@flugelhorn.example.com>
250 <larry@ictus.example.com>
```

The reply may also contain the full names of the users in the list.

```
expn golf-club
250-Joe Doubloon <joe@flugelhorn.example.com>
250-Bob Flower <bob@tuba.example.com>
250 Larry Point <larry@ictus.example.com>
```

The expn command is often disabled on SMTP servers, particularly those directly accessible from the Internet, because most administrators feel it discloses too much information. There are several reply codes possible when expn is disabled. The choice depends on the implementation.

```
252 Cannot EXPN mailbox, but will accept address
```

The response in this example is similar to the equivalent one shown for the vrfy command. The MTA has performed checks on the argument and determined that the argument appears structurally valid; however, it will not expand the list.

In the following examples, the MTA has responded with a permanent error stating that the command is either not recognized or not implemented. This is legal because the command is optional.

```
500 Syntax error, command unrecognized
```

```
502 Command not implemented
```

Since expn can be a useful diagnostic tool, some MTAs allow it be to be enabled if the request is coming from particular machines and disabled if it is coming from other machines. In this case, the server can respond with a 550 reply if the client is denied access.

```
550 Access denied
```

The `vrfy` and `expn` commands can be very useful diagnostic tools. Unfortunately, abuses of these commands have resulted in many, if not most, sites disabling them, particularly on machines directly accessible to the Internet.

One final note about `expn` is that not all mailing lists are expandable with it. If a mailing list is implemented outside an MTA, the MTA will probably not have access to the data to perform the expansion.

3.2.6 Hello

```
"helo" SP domain

"ehlo" SP domain
```

The `helo` command is used by the client to identify itself to the server. The second form of the command, `ehlo`, serves the same basic function but indicates to the server that the client might want to use the SMTP service extension mechanism as defined in RFC1869. While `ehlo` is not part of the core SMTP protocol defined in RFC821, it's common enough to warrant discussion with the `helo` command.

The *domain* argument in either of the two commands is used by the server to populate the `from` subfield in a `Received` field, as described in Section 2.6. Many servers double-check this information by doing DNS queries to translate the given domain name to an IP address and translating that IP address back to a domain name. If any anomalies are found during that process, the server can indicate them in parenthetical comments in the `Received` field.

```
Received: from flugelhorn.example.com ([10.1.1.2]) by tuba.example.com
          with SMTP id HAA19482
          for <joe@tuba.example.com>; Mon, 4 Oct 1999 08:33:48 -0700
```

One of the side effects of `helo` and `ehlo` is that the transaction buffers and session state are reset, as with the `rset` command. Clients are allowed to issue these commands at any point in a session, but since some servers don't allow this, it probably should be avoided.

The following example illustrates the simplest form of the `helo` command. The client issues a `helo` using its FQDN for the *domain* argument. The server responds with a `250` reply containing its domain name. Once the `helo` command is complete, both the client and server are ready to proceed with the rest of the SMTP dialog.

```
helo tuba.example.com
250 flugelhorn.example.com
```

The 250 response from the server can contain more than just the server's FQDN. The following example shows a response that includes the results of an Ident query against the client, as well as the IP address the server detected for the client.

```
250 ictus.example.com Hello joe@tuba.example.com [10.1.1.1]
```

The second form of the command, ehlo, was originally introduced in RFC1425 as an alternative to helo. A client can issue this command to see if the server supports the SMTP service extensions. If so, the server responds with a multiline reply containing the list of extensions supported. The service extensions are described in detail in Section 3.5.

```
ehlo tuba.primenet.com
250-flugelhorn.example.com
250-8bitmime
250-size
250-dsn
250-onex
250-etrn
250-xusr
250 help
```

In this case, the server responds with a series of 250 lines, using a dash on all but the last line to indicate that multiple lines are being output. The first line contains the FQDN of the server, as with the helo form of the reply. The rest contain the keywords for the extensions the server supports.

MTA developers are strongly encouraged to implement the ehlo and associated SMTP service extensions. If a server responds to a ehlo command with a permanent failure code, the client should then send a helo command. Some SMTP clients use string 'ESMTP' in the 220 connection greeting to determine whether ESMTP is supported. Technically, this is incorrect; the client should use the fall-back technique just described.

There are several possible failure replies for these commands. As with all commands, a 421 can be issued if the server is going down and needs to abruptly terminate the session.

If the domain name given as the argument to the command is too long, a 501 can be issued.

```
501 Path too long.
```

A `550` error can be issued if the server wants to reject the incoming machine for security reasons.

```
550 Access Denied.
```

RFC821 requires that `helo` be issued before any mail transactions are performed. Obviously, the use of SMTP service extensions expands this to include the use of `ehlo`. It's not unusual to find servers that don't require the `helo` command. It should, however, be issued to avoid interoperability problems. If a server does require it, something similar to the following reply might be seen.

```
503 Polite people say HELO first.
```

3.2.7 Mail From

```
"mail" SP "from:" reverse-path [SP mail-parameters]
```

```
"mail" SP "from:<>"
```

The `mail` command specifies the sender portion of the envelope. It is also the first command in a mail transaction. It resets any state tables and data buffers so that a new transaction can be started.

```
mail from:<joe@tuba.example.com>
```

The *reverse-path* argument must be a valid mailbox name with the following syntax.

```
reverse-path   = path
path           = "<" [at-domain-list ":"] mailbox ">"
at-domain-list = at-domain *("," at-domain)
at-domain      = "@" domain
```

The argument usually consists of a simple *mailbox* enclosed in '<>' characters. It must be no longer than 256 characters.

The *reverse-path* argument is used to populate the reverse-path buffer for the mail transaction. In the event of a delivery failure, this address will be used as the recipient for a delivery failure notification. When '<>' is used instead of *reverse-path,* the transaction is a bounce message. This is discussed in Section 3.4.7.

The *at-domain-list* portion of the syntax is for source routes, which have been deprecated. MTAs are allowed to ignore source route information when processing *path* parameters. As an example, the following address illustrates a source route.

```
<@c.example.com,@b.example.com,@a.example.com:guido@a.example.com>
```

The source route information can be removed, resulting in the following:

```
<guido@a.example.com>
```

The optional *mail-parameters* argument is used with SMTP extensions. RFC821 doesn't include this feature. It was added as part of the SMTP service extension mechanism and is described in Section 3.5.

The *mail-parameters* argument is used only when the `ehlo` command initiates the session, not `helo`. The syntax is as follows.

```
mail-parameters = *(SP keyword "=" value)
keyword         = (ALPHA / DIGIT) *(ALPHA / DIGIT / "-")
value           = 1*<any CHAR except "=", SP, and %d0-31>
```

The contents of *keyword* and *value* depend on the extensions being used. These are discussed in Section 3.5.

If the `mail` command succeeded, the server issues a 250 reply. This indicates that the session is ready to proceed to the next state.

```
mail from:<joe@tuba.example.com>
250 ok
```

There are several possible failures for the command. The 451 reply code is used when a general internal error has occurred in the server. The 452 reply code indicates a failure due to a lack of disk space. Since these are 4xy series reply codes, the error is transient; the client should keep the message queued and defer delivery.

Permanent failures also come in several forms. If the server doesn't want to grant access, it can issue a 550 error.

```
mail from:<wilber@dorm.example.edu>
550 access denied
```

For syntax errors, the server can respond with a 553 error.

```
mail from:<joe@tuba.example.com>
553 mailbox syntax incorrect
```

For a variation of the previous error, the server can respond with a 552 error if the length of the envelope sender is too long.

```
552 exceeded storage allocation
```

3.2.8 Recipient

```
"rcpt" SP "to:" forward-path [SP rcpt-parameters]
```

This command specifies a recipient for the mail message. The server appends the contents of the *forward-path* argument to the forward-path buffer.

```
rcpt to:<joe@tuba.example.com>
250 ok
```

The syntax for the *forward-path* and *rcpt-parameters* arguments is the same as that of the *reverse-path* and *mail-parameters* arguments in the mail command. The length limitations are also the same.

The rcpt command can be called multiple times for a given transaction. A server is required to support at least 100 recipients in the forward-path buffer.

The *forward-path* can be used to populate the for subfield in the Received line, if the mail transaction is a final delivery into a mailbox. This is described in Section 2.6.

```
Received: from flugelhorn.example.com by tuba.example.com
          with SMTP id HAA19482
          for <joe@tuba.example.com>; Mon, 4 Oct 1999 08:33:48 -0700
```

The mail command must be issued and a successful reply must be received before the rcpt command can be successfully invoked. If this is not the case, the server must respond with a 503 reply to indicate that the command is out of sequence.

Like the *mail-parameters* argument for the `mail` command, the optional *rcpt-parameters* argument is used with SMTP extensions, but only when `ehlo` initiates the session.

The `rcpt` command has the largest sets of reply codes. This is because of the large number of errors related to recipient addresses that can occur.

As with the `vrfy` command, the definition of the `mail` command in RFC821 allows the 251 reply to be used when the recipient's email is automatically forwarded to another destination. Also as with the `vrfy` command, this use isn't encountered very often. As a consequence, the most common reply code used with this command is 250.

The usual permanent failure reply is 550, which is used when the client is attempting to send to a nonexistent mailbox.

```
550 No such user.
```

There is one address that must never generate this reply—`postmaster`. All SMTP servers are required to provide a mailbox with this name. The purpose is to provide a destination to which problems can be reported. Unlike other mailbox names, which can be case-sensitive, this mailbox name is case-insensitive.

Another permanent failure is the 551 reply, which can be used when a recipient has moved to another location and the server wants to provide the new location to the sender.

```
551 User not local; try <clyde@northforty.example.com>
```

If the data being sent exceeds available storage, the server can reply with a 552 reply.

```
552 Message is too large
```

Problems with the recipient address can be indicated with a 553 reply.

```
553 Address too long
```

There are also several possible transient failures. If, for whatever reason, a recipient's mailbox is temporarily unavailable, the server can respond with a 450 reply.

```
450 Mailbox locked - try later.
```

The server can also use 451 or 452 to indicate errors in processing the request, as with the `mail` command. It can also reject the command with a 550, just as with the `mail` command. In addition, the server can respond with one of the standard permanent failure replies, `421`, `500`, or `501`.

3.2.9 Data

```
"data"
```

This command is used by the client to provide the RFC822 mail message for a mail transaction. The server populates the mail-data buffer with the data submitted with the command.

The reverse-path and forward-path buffers on the server side must be populated before `data` can be processed. This means a `mail` command and at least one `rcpt` command must be issued first. If not, the server must respond with a `503` reply to indicate that the command is out of sequence.

This command works a little differently from the other SMTP commands. After it is issued, the server normally responds with a `354` reply code. This indicates that the server is ready for the client to send the data. In addition to the common failure replies, the server can also respond with `451` or `554`, depending on whether the failure is considered transient or permanent, to indicate some internal problem.

```
451 Requested action aborted: local error in processing

554 aliasing/forwarding loop broken
```

If the server replies with a `354` reply code, the client sends the data, which is an RFC822 message. When done, the client indicates that the transmission is complete by sending a single period on a line by itself. At this point, the server responds with a reply code to indicate the success or failure of the message transmission.

```
data
354 Start mail input; end with <CRLF>.<CRLF>
To: larry@ictus.example.com
From: joe@tuba.example.com
Date: Fri, 15 Dec 2000 14:20:02 -0700
Message-ID: <20001215142002.2432.2@tuba.example.com>

Where are the blank transparencies?
.
250 ok
```

Because a period is used to terminate the message, steps must be taken to prevent a similar line in the data from prematurely terminating the transmission.

When sending the data to the server, the client checks each line of the message. If a line starts with a period, another period is added to the beginning of that line. Referred to as *dot-stuffing,* this eliminates the possibility of a line being sent that consists of a single period. When processing the lines from a `data` command, the server checks each one. If a line starts with a period, one period is deleted from the beginning of the line. This converts the data to its original form.

To illustrate this, the following message body contains several types of lines with dot characters.

```
This line won't be dot-stuffed.
... but this one will.
```

Dot-stuffing this text results in the following.

```
This line won't be dot-stuffed.
.... but this one will.
```

When the server receives this data, it strips off the first character in the lines if that character is a period. The result is a duplicate of the original data.

There are two major constraints on the data sent to a server. The first is that, by default, it must be 7-bit US-ASCII, although, if both the server and the client support the 8bit-MIMEtransport SMTP extension, described in Section 3.5.3, 8-bit data can be sent. The other limitation is that lines can be no more than 998 characters in length, not including the trailing CRLF. While servers should be able to accept longer lines, clients should not expect it. The MIME extensions, described in Chapter 4, can be used to cope with these limitations.

Servers must be able to process messages at least 64K octets in length. However, it is recommended that they be able to handle messages of arbitrary length, although practical matters such as disk consumption must be taken into account. An extension is available that allows a server to advertise what size messages it is willing to accept. It is described in Section 3.5.1.

As a general rule, MTAs should not analyze the contents of a message provided with the `data` command. In particular, they should not reject a message because of apparent errors in the header. One exception to this recommendation is when a message is being submitted by an MUA. MTAs are allowed to analyze the header in order to correct fields or to determine whether the message should be rejected. This is discussed in further detail in Sections 3.4.10 and 3.5.8.

When the server is done receiving the message, it sends a status reply to the client. If the command succeeded, the server responds with a `250` reply and clears the transactions buffers. It then submits the transaction to a delivery queue for further processing, which is described in Section 3.3.

There are several reasons the `data` command can fail. The following list illustrates some of the more common ones.

```
552 Requested mail action aborted: exceeded storage allocation
554 Local configuration error
451 Requested action aborted: local error in processing
452 Requested action not taken: insufficient system storage
```

The text in `data` failure replies can vary widely for a variety of reasons.

3.2.10 Reset

```
"rset"
```

This command resets the state of the connection.

```
rset
250 ok
```

On receiving it, the server clears its reverse-path, forward-path, and mail-data buffers, and also resets the session state to be equivalent to when the `helo` command was issued. This essentially aborts any current transaction.

3.2.11 Send

```
"send" SP "from:" reverse-path
```

This command is similar to the `mail` command, except that it sends a message to a user's terminal, if it is active, instead of delivering it to the user's mailbox.

```
send from:<joe@tuba.example.com>
250 ok
```

Rarely seen in modern SMTP implementations, this command is a vestige of early email on ARPANET. Clients should avoid using it. Servers may implement it, but they should do so it as described in RFC821. If the SMTP service extensions are implemented, the server should also advertise the command in its response to an `ehlo` command.

3.2.12 Send or Mail

```
"soml" SP "from:" reverse-path
```

This command will output the message to a recipient's terminal if the user is active; otherwise, it will deliver it to the recipient's mailbox. Like the `send` command, this one should be avoided.

```
soml from:<joe@tuba.example.com>
250 ok
```

3.2.13 Send and Mail

```
"saml" SP "from:" reverse-path
```

This command is similar to the `send` and `soml` commands. It will output the message to a recipient's terminal if the user is active and deliver it to his or her mailbox. Like the other two commands, it should be avoided.

```
saml from:<joe@tuba.example.com>
250 ok
```

3.2.14 Turnaround

```
"turn"
```

The `turn` command allows the roles of client and server to be reversed. After its successful completion, the server issues SMTP commands and the client processes them.

This command was not originally intended to be used with TCP because there is no authentication mechanism built into TCP or SMTP. Since most SMTP services run on TCP, the command has some severe security problems in most environments. Many MTAs do not even implement it.

To address `turn`'s shortcomings, an SMTP extension, `etrn`, was defined to provide the general equivalent of the `turn` command without the security problems. It is discussed in greater detail in Section 3.5.4.

3.2.15 Local Extension Commands

In addition to the standard commands, RFC821 also provides a way to add local extension commands. Any commands starting with 'x' are considered local extensions. There will never be a standard SMTP command that starts with 'x'.

Here is an example of a mythical local extension command.

```
xstatus
250-queue empty
250
```

3.3 MAIL TRANSACTIONS

There are basically three mail transactions performed with SMTP—mailing, relaying, and forwarding. They provide the building blocks for all Internet email message transmissions.

3.3.1 Mailing

The fundamental mail transaction performed with SMTP is sending a message from a source machine directly to a destination. All the other transactions are variations on this theme. As a result, this section contains the most detail; following sections describe the variations.

To describe this primary transaction, the mailing of the message in Section 2.4.1 will be walked through. The user Joe wants to send the message to Bob. The first step is to identify which host should be contacted for the transfer. Once this is done, the client connects to that host on TCP port 25.

On accepting the client connection, the server sends a connection greeting.

```
220 flugelhorn.example.com Service ready
```

The client parses the greeting and is ready to proceed with the mail transaction since the greeting reply code indicated success. The first command to issue is `mail`.

```
mail from:<joe@tuba.example.com>
250 ok
```

This causes the server to reset the reverse-path, forward-path, and mail-data buffers. The server then sets the reverse-path buffer to the value specified by the `mail` command and responds to the client with an appropriate reply code.

At this point, the sender has been identified and the server is ready to accept a list of recipients.

```
rcpt to:<bob@flugelhorn.example.com>
250 ok
```

The server appends the value specified in the `rcpt` command to the forward-path buffer. It then responds to the client with a reply code.

In this example, there is only one recipient on the server. If there were more than one recipient, the `rcpt` command would be issued for each of them, with the specified values appended to the forward-path buffer.

With the sender and recipients specified, the next step is to transmit the message data. This is done using the `data` command.

```
data
354 Start mail input; end with <CRLF>.<CRLF>
Date: 4 Oct 1999 08:33:45 -0700
From: bob@flugelhorn.example.com
To: joe@tuba.example.com
Subject: another question
Message-ID: <19991004083345.18492.1@flugelhorn.example.com>
X-Mailer: MondoMail v42.86

Why is the frobnazoid gefargled again?

--
thx,
bob
.
250 ok
```

In this example, the client sent a `data` command, which the server responded to with a `354` reply, indicating it was ready to receive the message. The client then sent the message, ending the transmission with a period. The server used the information to populate its mail-data buffer, then sent a reply code to the client. No dot-stuffing was required because no line in the mail message started with a period.

Once the data has been transmitted to the server, and the server has acknowledged the transfer with a successful completion status, the client can safely delete its copy of the message from its send queue. The server has accepted responsibility for the message.

The server now has three choices for processing the message. It can relay it to another MTA, forward it to another MTA, or deliver it to a local mailbox. The first and second choice are described in Sections 3.3.2 and 3.3.3. In any case, the MTA prepends a `Received` field to the header. A `Return-Path` field is also prepended when delivery is to a local mailbox.

To deliver the message to a local mailbox, the MTA first determines which mailbox should receive the message. There are several techniques to do this. Most MTAs provide the ability to map virtual mailboxes to real mailboxes. For example, the virtual mailbox 'bob.flower' might be mapped to 'bob'. Some MTAs also provide subaddresses, as described in Section 2.5.1. In either case, the specified mailbox is mapped into the actual mailbox, then handed over to an MDA for local delivery.

The simpler MDAs just append the message to a recipient's inbox. Some of the more sophisticated ones provide filtering as part of local delivery, described in Chapter 7. Some implementations use LMTP (Local Mail Transfer Protocol), which is described in Section 3.5.7.

On UNIX, the inbox is usually located in a central spool directory containing inboxes for all users on the machine. The directory location varies between UNIX implementations, but common ones include /usr/spool/mail, /var/spool/mail, and /usr/mail. Each inbox is named the same as the corresponding user account. In the case of our user Bob, this would be something like /usr/spool/mail/bob. The mailbox is usually in the mbox format, described in Appendix A.

The spool directory technique for user inboxes suffers from two problems. The first is that with a large number of users on the machine, the directory can contain many files. This can significantly affect performance because of the way UNIX stores file information in directories. For that reason, many large sites use a *hash spool* to subdivide the inboxes into multiple subdirectories. The most common way of doing this is to create a series of subdirectories using the first letter of the user account names, then a series of subdirectories underneath those using the first two letters of the names. The inboxes are then placed in these subdirectories accordingly. For example, the inbox bob is placed in /usr/spool/mail/b/bo/bob. This reduces the number of files in specific directories.

There are several potential security problems with inbox spool directories. These problems are described in Section 9.1.4. One common solution is to deliver mail not to an inbox spool directory but to a user's home directory.

If other messages destined for the current server are queued up on the client, additional mail transactions can be performed to empty the queue. In this example, there is no other work to be done, so the client tells the server to close the session.

```
quit
221 flugelhorn.example.com Service closing transmission channel
```

After issuing the reply code to the quit command, the server issues a 221 reply and closes the connection, thus ending the conversation.

3.3.2 Relaying

Instead of performing a local delivery, it's possible for an MTA to relay the message to another machine, if it's configured to allow this. Relaying is merely a variation of the process for sending a single message described in the previous section. In this case, the relay machine acts as the server to accept the message. Then it acts as a client and transmits the message to another destination machine. The message is deposited in a send queue between the two steps to make the process more reliable. Without queuing, a system failure could cause the mail to get lost.

Two primary places where relay machines are typically used are security firewalls and relay servers for MUAs. With firewalls, a relay can be used as an intermediate point for incoming email. This provides an opportunity to scrutinize and log the mail for security purposes and to impose centralized security policies on it.

The other common use of relaying is found with relay servers for MUAs. Most personal computers do not have a resident full-featured MTA. This requires their MUAs to hand the message off to a machine that does. While it's possible for an MUA to implement the entire set of features mentioned in the previous section, most simply include enough code to hand a message off to a relay server.

Other than for the two uses just mentioned, relaying is usually undesirable. To minimize unsolicited bulk email, some administrators configure their MTAs to block incoming email from certain sites by not allowing certain IP addresses or domain names to connect to mail servers. However, relaying can circumvent this blocking by having the email pass through an intermediate site. Since the intermediate site is the one connecting to the local machine, the blocking mechanism will not catch the problem.

For this reason, most MTAs allow administrators to control the circumstances under which relaying is permitted. There are two aspects to control—the incoming hosts that can relay and the destinations to be relayed to. A local MTA serving a collection of end-users is configured to allow relaying for hosts on the local network. This allows the end-user MUAs to use the local mail server as an out-bound mail spool. In the case of an Internet firewall mail server, the MTA is configured to allow relaying only into the local network and not to other sites on the Internet. When a message has been rejected for this type of policy reason, the server can issue a permanent failure reply to the client.

```
rcpt to:<wanda@example.net>
550 Access denied. Relaying not permitted.
```

In recent years, it has become standard policy to implement these limitations on relaying. Chapter 7, Section 7.4.1, discusses the topic in more detail.

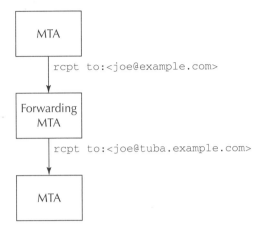

FIGURE 3.8 Forwarding a Message

3.3.3 Forwarding

Forwarding is similar to relaying.[1] An intermediate server receives a mail message and retransmits it to another destination. The difference is that instead of passing the message through with the same recipient in the envelope, the MTA changes envelope recipients to other values before passing a message to the next MTA, as illustrated in Figure 3.8. Some MTAs also provide the ability to alter addresses contained in the message header.

The previous figure illustrates translating one single address to another single address. The address translation can also result in an incoming envelope recipient being expanded into a list of out-bound envelope recipients. If the envelope sender is changed to the owner of the list, the result is a *mailing list,* which is described in Chapter 8.

3.4 OPERATIONAL CONSIDERATIONS

While SMTP is relatively simple, developing a robust SMTP implementation is complicated. This section describes several aspects of SMTP that deserve particular attention.

3.4.1 Protocol Nonconformance

As with most protocols, some implementations have interoperability problems. Since SMTP is a communications protocol, designed to freely transfer messages from place to place, implementations should strive to increase interoperability.

---

[1] This is not the same forwarding described in Chapter 2.

As an example, some SMTP servers only accept upper-case commands. Since SMTP verbs are supposed to be case-insensitive, this is a violation of the protocol specification, and SMTP clients that normally transmit commands in lower-case will not be able to carry on a successful conversation with such nonconformant servers.

The Robustness Principle tells us that the client should attempt to deal with this problem gracefully, rather than failing outright. In this example, there is no requirement for servers to adapt but it might be a good idea. There are two things the client can do. First, it can always send commands in upper-case. However, while this solves the immediate problem, it doesn't handle the possibility that there are servers that only accept lower-case commands—no known servers exhibit this behavior, but it's possible. The second solution is for the client to notice that otherwise normal commands are generating errors and change case when talking to the server.

```
220 bork.example.com
helo tuba.example.com
500 Command unrecognized
HELO tuba.example.com
250 bork.example.com
```

In general, SMTP clients and servers should be tolerant of nonconformance and attempt to work around it. There are times, however, when it is acceptable to reject such behavior. For example, if a client sends 8-bit data without negotiating an 8-bit communication channel using the `8bitmime` extension, described in Section 3.5.3, the server can decide to either strip the eighth bit or reject the message.

The decision to accept or reject nonconformant behavior is not always clear-cut. The final judgment should be based on experience and a clear understanding of the consequences.

3.4.2 Reliability and Responsibility

One overriding design and development goal should exist for any email software—reliability. Email has become an integral part of the modern computing environment, and a lot of people rely heavily on it. Lost email can cause severe frustration for users and administrators. As with the telephone, users have come to expect reliable delivery. This level of expectation leads to the cardinal rule of email software development.

Don't Lose the Mail!

If a server responds to a `data` command with a `250` reply code, it is saying, in effect, that it is accepting responsibility for the message and will either send it to the next destination or generate a bounce message detailing a failure in its attempt to do so. This responsibility should not be taken lightly. All reasonable attempts should be made by email software to correctly and safely process mail.

3.4.3 Queuing

Since SMTP is a store-and-forward protocol, a message might need to be passed through several machines in order to reach its final destination. Because any machine can be temporarily unavailable, each client needs to maintain a queue for out-bound messages. If a server is temporarily unavailable or if it reports a transient error, the client keeps the message in its queue for later processing. A message is not removed from the queue until it is successfully transmitted to the server, a permanent error is detected, or the message has been in the queue for an excessive amount of time. As mail is received, it is stored for safekeeping, then relayed or forwarded to the next destination.

Good queuing is critical to an MTA. The primary requirement is that it be reliable. Any queue code must be very careful about handling the queue and must check the return status of any system calls used to implement it. In addition, most MTAs use synchronized writes, or a similar mechanism, to ensure that data is actually written to disk instead of having it linger in disk buffers in memory. This minimizes the chance of losing data from a catastrophic system failure once a message has been received from a machine upstream.

3.4.4 Sending

As described earlier in this chapter, the mechanics of a mail transaction are relatively straightforward. However, a few additional issues related to sending mail are worth mentioning.

The client should coalesce recipients when sending them the same message. If a specific message is being sent to three recipients on the same machine, there should be one transaction with three `rcpt` commands, not three separate transactions. This is particularly important because some modern MTAs are capable of storing the message once with pointers into the individual recipient mailboxes to minimize storage requirements.

Another optimization involves the client's out-bound message queue. To reduce the overhead associated with establishing a connection, the client should try to send all messages in the queue destined for the current server. This reduces the number of times a client needs to connect to a given server.

When processing a new out-bound message, a useful performance optimization is to check the status of the most recent conversation to the destination machine. If, for example, a previous email to a particular machine got deferred for connectivity reasons, the client might want merely to add the new message to the out-bound queue. The idea is that if it failed only a few minutes ago, it will probably fail again until some more time has elapsed.

Any deferred messages in the queue will eventually need to be retried. Most MTAs use a progressive retry time on deferred messages, meaning that every time a particular message gets deferred, its retry time increases. This provides a compromise between trying to get a message to its destination as soon as possible and frequently retrying to connect to a host that is down for an extended period. The idea is that most host outages are relatively short. In the case of a short outage, an initial short retry increases the likelihood that the message will get dequeued quickly. In the case of a longer outage, eventually the MTA will slow down its attempts to resend the message, reducing the overhead associated with the connection attempt. RFC1123 recommends an initial retry duration of 30 minutes.

As a general rule, messages that stay in the queue at least 4 to 5 days are considered undeliverable. At this point, a bounce message is generated to the sender about the delivery problem. Bounce messages are discussed in Section 3.4.7. Some MTAs even send a warning message to the sender if a message has been in the queue for several hours. This notification provides the sender the opportunity to investigate the problem, if so inclined.

Many MTAs have the ability to send multiple messages simultaneously to a remote machine by establishing multiple connections to it. Since modern machines have quite a bit of capacity, this is good way to dequeue a large set of messages for a particular destination. However, it bears mentioning that not all machines are capable of handling this type of aggressive behavior. The more sophisticated dequeuing techniques include the ability to ramp up the number of simultaneous connections from an initial one to the maximum configured number. This prevents the sending machine from overwhelming remote machines if a large number of messages are queued up for the remote machine.

3.4.5 Receiving

Most MTAs handle incoming and outgoing email with separate processes, which seems reasonable considering the differences in the two tasks. If not done correctly, however, this can result in an MTA not capable of taking care of a very useful performance optimization. If an MTA has deferred mail queued for a particular destination, and that destination sends a piece of mail, the MTA can assume that that destination has become available. This means the queued mail can now be delivered.

In situations where the mail has been queued long enough to result in an elevated retry time, the next normal retry time could be several minutes or more. If the sending side of the MTA can be notified that the remote machine is now up, it can expedite the delivery of the queued mail, reducing the amount of time the deferred mail is queued.

TABLE 3.4 SMTP Timeouts

Event	Timeout (minutes)
initial 220 greeting	5
mail command	5
rcpt command	5
data initiation	2
TCP block	3
data termination	10

3.4.6 Timeouts

RFC821 doesn't specify any timeouts for various operations in SMTP. RFC1123 adds information on this issue. All SMTP programs should implement a timeout mechanism to prevent an SMTP session from hanging indefinitely. On the server side, the only protocol requirement is a timeout of at least five minutes for waiting for commands from the client.

On the client side, there are more timeouts to deal with. The minimum values specified in RFC1123 range from two to ten minutes, depending on the items being discussed. Table 3.4 summarizes these values.

In addition to protocol timeouts, two timeouts related to queue management are worth mentioning. One is when any message stuck in an out-bound queue for an extended period needs a delivery failure notification sent back to the sender. This period may be at least 4 to 5 days. Another one some MTAs implement is a warning to senders that a particular message has been in an out-bound queue for an excessive amount of time. Rather than a notification of delivery failure, this is a warning message, apprising the sender of the situation.

3.4.7 Bounces

Because SMTP is a store-and-forward mechanism and messages can travel through multiple MTAs, there needs to be a way to notify a sender of a delivery failure after an MUA has submitted a message for delivery. In typical email fashion, this is done with email messages. If, for whatever reason, a message can't be delivered and the failure is considered permanent, a message detailing the problem is generated and sent to the sender.

To create a bounce message, the server generates a new message using the envelope sender of the failed delivery as the recipient. It also sets the sender of the bounce message to '<>' to indicate that the message is a bounce.

```
mail from:<>
250 ok
rcpt to:<original-sender>
250 ok
```

Setting the sender in the `mail` command to '`<>`' effectively sets the sending address to nowhere. This can prevent delivery problems while trying to deliver a bounce message. If a problem is encountered, the result is another bounce, referred to as a double bounce. In that event, the bounce message is sent to `postmaster`.

The next step is to generate a mail message describing the delivery error. This is a regular mail message, with a few specific items related to the bounce. The `To` field is set to the sender of the original message. The `From` field is set to a destination associated with bounces, with the *local-part* portion frequently set to `MAILER-DAEMON`. The `From` field is populated in this way in case the recipient of the bounce message tries to reply to it. Since the real sender in the envelope is set to '`<>`', this provides a real destination to reply to, just in case. In addition to these fields, the `Subject` line is populated with an explanatory note.

```
From: Mail Delivery Subsystem <MAILER-DAEMON@tuba.example.com>
To: larry@ictus.example.com
Subject: Warning: could not send message for past 4 hours
```

Bounce message text can come in many forms. Each MTA package has its formatting, but typically the text provides a human-readable description of the problem, a transcript of the SMTP dialog, and often a copy of the original message.

The following example is from Sendmail and shows a failure trying to deliver to an unknown user. It contains a note of when it received the original message, a specific error message, a transcript of the SMTP session, and a copy of the original message.

```
The original message was received at Sat, 13 Mar 1999 18:38:49 -0700
from daemon@tuba.example.com

    ----- The following addresses had permanent fatal errors -----
<notauser@ictus.example.com>
    (expanded from: <notauser@ictus.example.com>)

    ----- Transcript of session follows -----
... while talking to ictus.example.com.:
>>> RCPT To:<notauser@ictus.example.com>
<<< 550 <notauser@ictus.example.com>... User unknown
550 <notauser@ictus.example.com>... User unknown

    ----- Original message follows -----
```

The example below is from the Postfix MTA. Like the example for Sendmail, it shows a bounce message for attempting to deliver to an unknown user, with an introductory explanation of the bounce mail, the specific error condition, and the original message.

```
This is the Postfix program at host lab.example.com.

I'm sorry to have to inform you that the message returned
below could not be delivered to one or more destinations.

For further assistance, please contact <postmaster@lab.example.com>

If you do so, please include this problem report. You can
delete your own text from the message returned below.

                    The Postfix program

        --- Delivery error report follows ---

<notauser@lab.example.com>: unknown user: "notauser"

        --- Undelivered message follows ---
```

An important thing to notice about the previous examples is the variety of the output from different MTAs. This variety presents a problem—it's just not possible to programmatically parse all bounce messages reliably. RFC1891 (SMTP Service Extension for Delivery Status Notifications) and RFC1894 solve this problem with an extension for generating machine-parsable delivery notification messages. It is described in further detail in Section 3.5.6.

3.4.8 Loop Detection

If two machines each think email for a particular user needs to be forwarded to the other machine, the result is a mail loop. The email will be sent back and forth because each machine thinks the mail belongs on the other machine. Mail loops need to be detected and broken.

Several things can cause a mail loop. The two MTAs could be configured to forward the email to each other. Improperly configured Sendmail .forward files, for example, can cause this problem quite easily. Certain types of DNS updates also can cause this because of the caching nature of DNS. A naive email robot can as well cause it.[2]

Bounce loops are a particularly frustrating type of loop, created when a bounce generates a bounce, which then causes another bounce. When a bounce message

---

[2] Email robots are discussed in Chapter 7.

is generated, the return path in the envelope is supposed to be set to '<>'. Bounce messages are not supposed to be generated for bounces. Properly written software will detect a double bounce and notify a postmaster. If the software doesn't do this, a loop is created.

Left unchecked, a mail loop can cause a piece of mail to ricochet between a set of machines indefinitely. There are several ways to prevent this from happening.

The simplest way to detect loops, used by many MTAs, is to count the number of Received fields. The number that will trigger a mail loop varies between MTA implementations, and many, if not most, MTAs provide configurable parameters to control this feature. Determining a good value can be difficult. Setting it too high can result in valuable resources being consumed; setting it too low can cause legitimate email to be bounced. In the general case, it's probably not a good idea to set it any lower than 25. In many environments setting it upwards of 100 might be prudent.

```
Received:  from tuba.example.com by ictus.example.com
           ; Mon, 4 Jan 1999 12:15:09 -0700 (MST)
Received:  from ictus.example.com by tuba.example.com
           ; Mon, 4 Jan 1999 12:15:07 -0700 (MST)
Received:  from tuba.example.com by ictus.example.com
           ; Mon, 4 Jan 1999 12:15:05 -0700 (MST)
Received:  from ictus.example.com by tuba.example.com
           ; Mon, 4 Jan 1999 12:15:03 -0700 (MST)
```

This technique, while easy to implement, suffers from a few problems. The first one is that email will still loop until the hop count is reached. A loop occurring on a high-volume email server can be very disruptive. The second problem is with picking an acceptable hop count. Setting the number too low will result in valid email not getting delivered; setting it too high will increase the amount of time before the loop is broken.

Ideally, a loop should be detected and broken immediately. Some email packages add an additional field to a message header. If they see a message with the field already there, they assume a loop has occurred and take appropriate action. This technique is commonly found in mailing lists and auto-responding programs like vacation scripts and mail robots.

```
X-Loop: product-announcements@example.com
```

There are variations on this theme. Some MTAs, for example, prepend a Delivered-To field whenever a message is delivered to a mailbox, including aliases that are expanded into other mailboxes. Like X-Loop, this marks the message as being delivered to a particular mailbox. If the package that added the field receives the message again, it will detect the mail loop and generate an error message.

3.4.9 Security

The topic of security is covered in Chapter 9, but there are some points worth mentioning while talking about SMTP. For several reasons email has a history of security problems. The primary reason is that email is a ubiquitous service—even the most conservative firewalls allow it to traverse their boundaries. This ubiquity makes email a tempting target for some attackers. The problem is worsened by the fact that email is complicated; writing a strong email package is not a trivial task, and exploitation of certain types of weaknesses, such as stack overflows, can be devastating.

Another problem to cope with is information disclosure. The vrfy and expn commands can provide information many administrators do not want revealed. Also, to aid in troubleshooting, some MTAs include product name and version information in connection greetings. If a weakness is found in a particular product, it is often easy to find servers running that software. To address this concern, most MTAs provide configuration options to control the amount of information a product discloses.

There is one place where information disclosure is difficult to solve—Received fields. Some stricter security environments prefer to make no information available about the internal architecture of a network, including the names of machines users live on as well as the route a message takes leaving a network. Thus they route all out-bound email through a gateway that strips the Received headers from messages. This solves the information disclosure problem, but creates another one. Since the Received fields from internal machines are now gone, it can be difficult to troubleshoot certain problems. One solution is to have the gateway maintain logs of all the messages it processes and all the Received fields it deletes from headers. Unfortunately, at a high-volume site, this can consume significant disk space.

Another security problem with email is lack of authentication in the core protocol. This means that spoofing is relatively easy. While email experts can detect most spoofing attempts, most end-users can not.

Message integrity also is a problem. Email has no built-in methods for ensuring that a message is not altered before it reaches its final destination. This makes it impractical to use email in its raw form for legally binding transactions.

All is not lost, however. There are extensions available that can significantly reduce the authentication and integrity problems just mentioned. Chapter 9 describes these extensions, as well as other security extensions for other parts of email.

3.4.10 Message Submission

SMTP was designed as a transfer protocol. The standard included specific prohibitions against MTAs altering the contents of a message except to prepend fields such as `Received` and `Return-Path`.

In addition to being used to transfer a message from one MTA to another, SMTP is also used by MUAs to submit a message for transmission. Unfortunately, MUAs are prone to configuration errors, which can result in invalid messages. To compensate, most MTAs perform some modest hygiene on submitted messages, including inserting missing fields, canonicalizing addresses in originator and recipient fields, and rewriting addresses so email appears to be from a central server. While not technically conformant, these actions are accepted as necessary to ensure the proper operation of email services.

Some MTAs can be invoked from a command line. One common option is to have the MTA deduce the envelope information from the message header. This is convenient for the MUA, but it is prone to errors if the MTA doesn't process the header correctly. It is much better if the MUA can provide the exact envelope contents to the MTA.

In general, the envelope sender should be derived from the identity of the user operating the MUA. The `From` field should be used if this is not possible. If the identity of the user can be determined, it should be used to populate the `Sender` field if it differs from the `From` field, removing any existing `Sender` field.

`Bcc` fields deserve special care, since they provide the ability to carbon-copy a set of recipients without the knowledge of the other recipients.

`Bcc` fields have a problematic history. Now they are normally handled by the MUA. In the early days, however, this wasn't always true, so many, if not most, MTAs have the ability to process them.

Handling `Bcc` fields is fairly simple. Prior to submitting the message for transport, the MUA scans the header, looking for them. If any are found, it removes them and then continues normal processing of the message.

There is a special case to be aware of. If there are no other recipient fields, deleting `Bcc` fields results in an invalid message, since the message now has no recipient fields. In this case, the MUA should add a `To` field with an empty group list.

```
To: Undisclosed-Recipients:;
```

Some MUAs do not do this, and MTAs try to compensate for this incorrect behavior by adding a recipient field. Unfortunately, some MTAs add an `Apparently-To` field instead of a To field. This is incorrect, since Apparently-To is a nonstandard field.

There is another problem to be aware of. Some implementations split the recipients into two sets when processing the Bcc field. One set contains all the recipients not being blind-carbon-copied; the other set contains all the blind-carbon-copy recipients. The first set receives a copy of the message with the Bcc field deleted; the second set receives a copy with the field intact. The problem is that all the recipients in the second set see the list of members in the second set. Some people are not bothered by this but others think it discloses too much information to the Bcc recipients.

RFC2476 (Message Submission) provides a solution for many of the problems with using SMTP to submit messages. It is described in Section 3.5.8.

3.5 SMTP EXTENSIONS

Over the years, several potential improvements to SMTP were identified. However, one of the primary difficulties with enhancing SMTP is doing it in such a way that older implementations will not break. To address this problem, a mechanism was devised that provides the ability to add new extensions, without compromising backward compatibility. This section describes that mechanism, as well as the most common extensions.

RFC1425, published in 1993, provided the ability to add new features to SMTP. It was updated in 1994 by RFC1651 and in 1995 by RFC1869.

The extension mechanism had to address several issues in order to avoid breaking older implementations. There had to be a safe way for implementations to signal support for SMTP extensions. There also had to be a way to add new extensions, since future additions would be inevitable.

The first issue was resolved by introducing a new command, ehlo, which, as described in Section 3.2, is a variation of the helo command. A client can issue ehlo instead of helo to signal its support for the extensions. If the server does not support them, it responds with a syntax error reply code. The client can then revert to the older helo command and resume the dialog.

The second issue, extensibility, was resolved by adding the ability to identify which extensions were supported. If the server responds positively to the ehlo command, it will provide a list of supported extensions in the reply. As new extensions are added, clients can identify server support for them by analyzing the server reply.

The extensions define a core set of keywords that can be used in an ehlo response. These represent optional commands in SMTP. Providing them in the response to an ehlo command allows a client to detect whether they are available without needing to execute them.

```
250-send
250-soml
250-saml
250-expn
250-help
250 turn
```

As with most aspects of the email standards, in addition to the standard extensions nonstandard extensions can be created by prefixing them with 'x'. Two examples of this are the `xone` and `xusr` commands implemented in Sendmail.

Some of the extensions add parameters to the `mail` and `rcpt` commands that specify options to the commands. Generally these parameters are case-insensitive. To accommodate additional parameters, the extensions also increase the command length limitations where appropriate. If a syntax error is found in a parameter, a server should respond with a `501` error.

There are a variety of extensions available. The remainder of this section describes some of the more common ones in use.

3.5.1 Message Size Declaration

This extension, defined in RFC1870 (SMTP Service Extension for Message Size Declaration), allows a server to decline a message based on site-wide policies, sender-based policies, and per-recipient policies.

With the availability of MIME and the ease with which it allows large amounts of data to be sent via email, it is not unusual to see mail message sizes in megabytes. Given this, it is easy for servers to run into space problems. This extension was created to handle larger messages.

A server announces its support for the extension by adding the `size` keyword to its response to an `ehlo` command. This sets a maximum message size the server will accept. Without this extension, the client will not know if a message transmission failed for lack of space until the entire message has been transmitted.

```
ehlo tuba.example.com
250-flugelhorn.example.com
250 size 1048576
```

In this example, the server is announcing its willingness to handle messages up to 1 megabyte in size.

The numeric argument to the `size` keyword is optional. If no argument is specified, the server is indicating that it supports the extension but it's not advertising a limit.

To use the extension, the client can add an additional parameter to `mail` commands to specify the estimated size of the message to be transmitted.

```
mail from:<joe@tuba.example.com> size=241293
250 ok
```

If the message is larger than the maximum size the server allows, the server can respond with a permanent failure reply code.

```
mail from:<joe@tuba.example.com> size=17283982
552 Requested mail action aborted: exceeded storage allocation
```

Since this is a permanent failure, the client should generate an appropriate failure notification.

The server can also use the information provided in the `mail` command to impose size constraints per recipient. To do this, the server makes note of the value in the `size` parameter. When a `rcpt` command is issued, the server checks the value provided with the `mail` command against the recipient. If the declared size is larger than allowed, the `rcpt` command is rejected.

```
mail from:<joe@tuba.example.com> size=241293
250 ok
rcpt to:<sally-beeper@oboe.example.com>
552 Requested mail action aborted: Exceeded storage allocation
```

If the client sends a message larger than the advertised limit, the server can reject the message. In this case the server should continue to accept the entire message and respond with a failure when the client is done sending.

If the server temporarily lacks the storage space to accept the message, but ordinarily would be willing to accept it, it can respond with a temporary failure reply code.

```
mail from:<bob@tuba.example.com> size=241293
452 Requested action not taken: insufficient system storage
```

In this case, the client should defer the message and try later.

3.5.2 Command Pipelining

This extension, defined in RFC2197 (SMTP Service Extension for Command Pipelining), allows the client to issue a series of SMTP commands without waiting for replies from the server. This reduces some of the latency involved in the lock-step dialogs normally used in SMTP.

A server announces its support for the extension by adding the `pipelining` keyword to its response to an `ehlo` command.

```
ehlo tuba.example.com
250-flugelhorn.example.com
250 pipelining
```

The client can now send multiple commands in one TCP send operation before waiting for the reply codes for each of the commands.

To illustrate the differences between a traditional SMTP dialog and a pipelined one, the following dialog uses the traditional lock-step style.

```
mail from:<joe@tuba.example.com>
250 ok
rcpt to:<bob@flugelhorn.example.com>
250 ok
rcpt to:<vera@flugelhorn.example.com>
250 ok
data
354 Start mail input; end with <CRLF>.<CRLF>
the message
.
250 ok
quit
221 flugelhorn.example.com Service closing transmission channel
```

This dialog requires the client to wait six times for responses from the server. With pipelining, the dialog could be as follows.

```
mail from:<joe@tuba.example.com>
rcpt to:<bob@flugelhorn.example.com>
rcpt to:<vera@flugelhorn.example.com>
data
250 ok
250 ok
250 ok
```

```
354 Start mail input; end with <CRLF>.<CRLF>
the message
.
quit
250 ok
221 flugelhorn.example.com Service closing transmission channel
```

Here, the client needs to wait only twice for responses from the server. On high-latency links, this extension can provide a significant performance increase.

The client cannot merely send the entire set of commands for an SMTP dialog. Certain commands require it to wait for a response from the server—in particular, ehlo, data, vrfy, expn, turn, quit, and noop. These commands involve a possible change of transaction state based on their success or failure. Any extension command not covered by the RFC is assumed to require a response from the server, unless its RFC explicitly specifies pipelining.

3.5.3 8-bit MIME Transport

Defined in RFC1652 (SMTP Service Extension for 8bit-MIMEtransport), this extension provides a way for 8-bit data to be transmitted in message bodies.

A server announces its support for the extension by adding the 8bitmime keyword to its response to an ehlo command.

```
ehlo tuba.example.com
250-flugelhorn.example.com
250 8bitmime
```

The extension provides an additional parameter, body, to the mail command, the value for which can be 7bit or 8bitmime.

```
mail from:<joe@tuba.example.com> body=8bitmime
250 ok
rcpt to:<bob@flugelhorn.example.com>
250 ok
data
354 send 8bitmime message, ending in <CRLF>.<CRLF>
the message
.
250 ok
```

It is sometimes used in conjunction with 8-bit content transfer encoding, described in Section 4.3.3.

3.5.4 Remote Message Queue Starting

This extension, defined in RFC1985 (SMTP Service Extension for Remote Message Queue Starting), allows a client to request that the server start processing any queue entries destined for the client. This provides an alternative to the `turn` command described in Section 3.2.

A server announces its support for the extension by adding the `etrn` keyword to its response to an `ehlo` command.

```
ehlo tuba.example.com
250-flugelhorn.example.com
250 etrn
```

The extension adds an additional command, `etrn`, the syntax for which is as follows.

```
"etrn" [option-char]node-name
```

The *node-name* argument specifies the name of the machine on which to start queue processing.

```
etrn tuba.example.com
250 ok
```

If the server accepts the command, it will trigger a queue run for any messages spooled for the given machine. Because a queue run can take quite a while to finish, the server immediately sends the reply code, before processing the queue. It then triggers a separate process to perform the queue run.

SMTP servers that can't trigger the queue processing for a particular destination or domain are allowed to simply trigger the entire queue, but the optimal method is to start queue processing for a specific destination.

There are several reply codes a server can use to note successful execution of the command. The basic reply is a regular `250` error formatted as follows.

```
250 ok, queuing for node node-name started
```

This code works if the server can't calculate the number of messages queued for the destination. With knowledge of the queue size, the server can respond with more informative reply codes.

```
251 ok, no messages waiting for node node-name

252 ok pending messages for node node-name started

253 ok n pending messages for node node-name started
```

As with other SMTP commands, there are possible failure replies. If, for whatever reason, a failure occurs in an attempt to initiate a queue run, a `458` reply can be given.

```
458 Unable to queue messages for node node-name
```

If the server has security policies that prevent an `etrn` request from being honored, it can respond with a `459` reply.

```
459 Node node-name not allowed: reason
```

Since both of these replies are transient errors, the client can try later, as appropriate.

The optional *option-char* argument provides two additional operating modes for the command. The syntax is as follows.

```
option-char = "@" / "#"
```

The '@' option character allows the client to trigger a queue run for an entire domain.

```
etrn @example.com
250 ok
```

This will result in queued messages for `example.com` and any machines in that domain, such as `tuba.example.com` and `flugelhorn.example.com` being processed.

Another option character that isn't used very much, '#', provides the ability for non-Internet-based mail queues to be processed. RFC1985 uses the example of a UUCP queue. Other types of queues are theoretically possible but not common.

3.5.5 Enhanced Status Codes

This extension, defined in RFC2034, establishes a set of enhanced reply codes to provide more informative descriptions of errors. RFC2034 doesn't define these codes, only the extension mechanism for using them in SMTP. The codes are defined in RFC1893 and were originally designed for use in delivery status notifications, described in Section 3.5.6.

While SMTP reply codes are workable for reporting problems with the mail transport system, the added demands of reporting delivery status information present a dilemma for email protocol designers and software developers. There are just too many reasons a delivery can fail. There are only about a dozen useful reply codes, and an uncontrolled use of reply codes in implementations presents a significant problem to correct.

RFC1893 provides a solution for expanding the scope of reply codes without breaking existing implementations. Originally designed for the DSN (Delivery Status Notification) extension, RFC2034 allows MTAs to use the codes in normal operations. This section describes the enhanced status codes and their use with the enhanced status codes extension.

Enhanced status codes use the familiar 3-segment design of traditional SMTP reply codes, but are extended for more capacity. Instead of a 3-digit integer, an enhanced status code consists of 3 integers separated by the '.' character.

```
2.1.5
```

The formal syntax for the codes is as follows.

```
status-code = class "." subject "." detail
class       = "2" / "4" / "5"
subject     = 1*3DIGIT
detail      = 1*3DIGIT
```

The first segment can be '2', '4' or '5'. These digits have the same interpretation as the first digit of a traditional SMTP reply code—namely, success, transient failure, and permanent failure.

The second digit consists of one to three digits and it indicates the component, or subsystem, being referenced in the status code. Table 3.5 summarizes the defined values for this digit.

TABLE 3.5 Second Digit of Enhanced Status Codes

Value	Description
0	Other or Undefined
1	Addressing
2	Mailbox
3	Mail System
4	Network and Routing
5	Mail Delivery Protocol
6	Message Content or Media
7	Security or Policy

TABLE 3.6 Network and Routing Enhanced Status Codes

Value	Description
X.4.0	Other or undefined network or routing status
X.4.1	No answer from host
X.4.2	Bad connection
X.4.3	Directory server failure
X.4.4	Unable to route
X.4.5	Mail system congestion
X.4.6	Routing loop detected
X.4.7	Delivery time expired

The third digit, the *detail,* is combined with the second digit to provide a specific error message. RFC1893 defines 49 combinations of the first and second digit and provides descriptions of each. Rather than enumerate all of them, a typical set, the network and routing codes, is shown in Table 3.6. The other categories are similar. When a particular two-digit combination is combined with the first digit, the result is a complete enhanced status code.

To announce its support for the extensions, a server adds `enhancedstatus-codes` to its response to a `ehlo` command.

```
ehlo tuba.example.com
250-flugelhorn.example.com
250 enhancedstatuscodes
```

This extension redefines a portion of the syntax for SMTP response lines. All 2xx, 4xx, and 5xx SMTP responses except the initial greeting and responses to `helo` and `ehlo` are prefixed with an enhanced status code followed by one or more spaces.

```
220 flugelhorn.example.com ready.
ehlo tuba.example.com
250-flugelhorn.example.com
250 enhancedstatuscodes
mail from:<joe@tuba.example.com>
250 2.1.0 originator ok
rcpt to:<bob@flugelhorn.example.com>
250 2.1.5 recipient ok
rcpt to:<vera@flugelhorn.example.com>
550 5.1.1 mailbox "vera" does not exist
data
```

```
354 Start mail input; end with <CRLF>.<CRLF>
the message
.
250 2.6.0 message accepted
quit
221 2.0.0 flugelhorn.example.com closing transmission channel
```

Notice that the enhanced status codes were not issued with the connection greeting, the response to `ehlo`, or the `data` command.

Clients don't need to do anything to enable this feature. Servers supporting the extension simply provide the information. If the server announces it in support response to an `ehlo` command, the client can expect to find the enhanced codes in the reply text.

An enhanced code in a reply must generally agree with the SMTP reply code. For example, a 2.x.y enhanced status code can be used only with a 2xy SMTP reply code.

3.5.6 Delivery Status Notifications

This extension, defined in RFC1891, controls notification of delivery status information.

Neither the core mail message format nor SMTP provide much detail to guide implementers regarding delivery status information. Delivery failures generate bounce messages, but minimal requirements are placed on the contents of the messages. As a result, the format of bounce messages varies wildly across software packages. In addition, no guidelines are provided for implementing such things as delay warning messages and success notifications.

For that reason, it is nearly impossible to implement programmatic handling of delivery status information based solely on the core standards. To address this problem, a suite of RFCs was written to define DSN services. These services consist of an SMTP extension, enhanced status codes, and associated MIME media types. The enhanced status codes, defined in RFC1893, were described in Section 3.5.5. The MIME portions, defined in RFC1892 (The Multipart/Report Content Type for the Reporting of Mail System Administrative Messages) and RFC1894, are described in Chapter 4, since knowledge of MIME is necessary to understand them. This section describes the overall design of the mechanism, as well as the SMTP extension that controls its use. These portions are defined primarily in RFC1891.

There are five notifications defined for DSN: failure, delay, success, relay, and expansion.

A failure is defined as an inability to deliver a message to a recipient. The reporting MTA has encountered a permanent failure attempting to deliver a message or has given up attempting to deliver it.

A delay means that the reporting MTA has been unable to deliver a message but will continue to try. This could be the result of a temporary error reply in an SMTP transaction or a temporary failure to connect to a remote MTA.

A success means that the message has been either delivered to the final recipient or, in the case of a mailing list, delivered to the mailing list processor.

A notification of relay can be generated if a message has been relayed or gatewayed into an environment that doesn't support DSN services.

An expansion notification indicates that a message has been successfully delivered to a recipient address and forwarded by the reporting MTA beyond the destination specified in the envelope. It can be used when a message is expanded to multiple recipients by an MTA alias. This does not include being expanded by a mailing list processor, which is covered by a success notification.

A server announces its support for the extension by adding a `dsn` keyword to `ehlo` responses.

```
ehlo tuba.example.com
250-flugelhorn.example.com
250 dsn
```

When a message is submitted to an initial MTA supporting the extension, the client selects the desired DSN options. These options determine what type of DSN actions are performed, including notification of delivery failure, a delay in delivery, and successful delivery.

The DSN options are controlled by specifying optional parameters to the `mail` and `rcpt` commands. As the message is transferred through a series of MTAs, an attempt is made to propagate the parameters. When a delivery is made, the options are used to determine the type of delivery notification. Under certain circumstances delivery notification can be generated from an intermediate MTA.

To prevent DSN loops, the envelope sender in a DSN must be set to '<>'. Just as regular bounces should not be generated for transactions where the envelope sender is '<>', those types of transactions should also not result in a DSN, and the postmaster for the reporting machine should be notified in a way that will avoid this.

Four parameters are provided with the DSN extension and summarized in Table 3.7. They should be viewed as extending the SMTP envelope, since they are propagated like the regular envelope information described in Section 3.1.

Notify

The first parameter of interest is `notify`. It can be provided with a `rcpt` command to control which type of events should trigger a DSN. Three types of notifications can be triggered: success, failure, or delay. The other two types, relay and expansion, cannot be specifically requested by an MUA.

TABLE 3.7   DSN Parameters

Parameter	Command	Description
notify	rcpt	Select which results trigger a DSN
orcpt	rcpt	Original Recipient
ret	mail	Select whether full message or headers are returned
envid	mail	Envelope identifier

There are several types of delivery this extension is interested in. A local delivery means that the message has been placed in a recipient's mailbox. If IMAP or POP is used, delivery occurs when the message is available to the IMAP or POP server, not when the message is retrieved by the user. For messages submitted to mailing lists, delivery occurs when the message is available to the list exploder.

The syntax for the parameter is as follows.

```
notify-esmtp-value  = "never" / 1#notify-list-element
notify-list-element = "success" / "failure" / "delay"
```

Each of the values is case-insensitive, and duplicates are not allowed. Also, the comma list of *notify-list-element* tokens is slightly different from other comma lists in mail messages. In this application, no whitespace is allowed between the values.

```
rcpt to:<joe@tuba.example.com> notify=success,failure,delay
250 ok
```

The value 'never' indicates that a DSN should not be returned to the sender regardless of the delivery status.

```
rcpt to:<joe@tuba.example.com> notify=never
250 ok
```

This is particularly useful for bulk mail or vacation auto-responders, where the delivery status of a message isn't important.

If the notify parameter contains 'failure', a DSN should be generated if delivery fails for whatever reason. This is the default if the notify parameter isn't used.

```
rcpt to:<joe@tuba.example.com> notify=failure
250 ok
```

The MTA must not generate a DSN to the sender if 'failure' is present. It may, however, send a failure notification to postmaster as long as that notification doesn't result in a DSN. In this situation, the notify parameter should be set to 'never'.

If the notify parameter contains 'delay', a DSN should be generated if delivery is delayed. The amount of time that constitutes a delay is server-dependent.

```
rcpt to:<joe@tuba.example.com> notify=delay
250 ok
```

If 'delay' is not present, but the parameter is, an MTA must not generate a delay DSN. If the parameter isn't provided, the server is free to choose whether a delay DSN is issued.

If the notify parameter contains 'success', a DSN should be generated if the message is successfully delivered.

```
rcpt to:<joe@tuba.example.com> notify=success
250 ok
```

If the parameter is present in an incoming message, an MTA must propagate it to downstream MTAs. If the parameter wasn't supplied, it must not be added if the message is sent to another MTA.

So far, the discussion has assumed that all downstream MTAs support DSN. What if a message is sent to an MTA that doesn't support it?

If the notify parameter contains 'success' and the transaction succeeds for a particular recipient, the client must issue a relayed DSN. This informs the sender that the message is being relayed to a non-DSN host, so further DSN information will not be available.

If a transaction fails when submitting a message to a non-DSN MTA and the notify parameter contains 'failure', the client must send a failed DSN to the sender. If that transaction has 'never' in the parameter, no DSN should be generated in any case.

Orcpt

It's possible for a recipient address to change as a message is forwarded though an MTA. Since the original recipient value can be important information when diagnosing an email problem, the orcpt parameter is provided to the rcpt command to allow the original recipient information to be propagated.

```
rcpt to:<joe@tuba.example.com> orcpt=rfc822;joe@example.com
250 ok
```

The syntax for `orcpt` is as follows.

```
orcpt-parameter            = "orcpt=" original-recipient-address
original-recipient-address = addr-type ";" xtext
addr-type                  = atom
```

The *addr-type* token consists of an address type registered with the IANA. RFC1894 defines the value 'rfc822' for this parameter.

The *xtext* token contains the encoded value for the original recipient address. Since it's possible for a message to originate from a non-SMTP environment that allows nonprintable characters in an address, an encoding scheme is provided for the parameter value.

Octets less than US-ASCII 33 and greater than US-ASCII 126 must be encoded, as do any '=' characters. An octet can be encoded by converting it to a '+' character followed by the character's upper-case hexadecimal equivalent. Because the '+' character is special, it must be escaped as '+2B'. There is no prohibition on what characters can be encoded, so implementations can encode other characters as well.

The address `larry+golf@ictus.example.com` could be encoded as follows.

```
orcpt=rfc822;larry+2Bgolf@ictus.example.com
```

If an `orcpt` parameter was present when a message was received, an `orcpt` parameter must be generated and populated with the received 'orcpt' value, if the message is sent to another destination. If the parameter wasn't present when the message was received, it may be added. In this case, it is populated with the value of the `rcpt` command from the incoming message.

Ret

Traditional bounce messages often include a copy of the original message being processed when the problem occurred. To reduce network traffic, some traditional bounces contain the header instead of the entire message. This is often an acceptable alternative, since the header generally has the most important information for diagnosing problems. The key point is that the choice isn't up to the client; it's up to the server.

The DSN extension provides a `ret:` parameter to allow the client to select how much of the original message will be included in a DSN. The parameter can be supplied to the `mail` command. There are two options for `ret`: the entire message or just the header. To have a server return the entire message, the parameter is set to 'full'. ·

```
mail from:<bob@flugelhorn.example.com> ret=full
250 ok
```

A value of 'hdrs' has a server return just the message header.

```
mail from:<joe@tuba.example.com> ret=hdrs
250 ok
```

If the parameter is not specified by the client, the server may choose either option.

An MTA must propagate the parameter value when transferring a message to another MTA. If no 'ret' was present when a message was received, the MTA is not allowed to add one when sending the message.

Envid

Since the entire point of a DSN message is to provide machine-parsable delivery status notification, MUAs might want to associate a DSN with the initial SMTP transaction that sent the message. This can be done by providing an *envelope identifier* parameter, `envid`, to a `mail` command. The syntax is as follows.

```
envid-parameter = "envid=" xtext
```

The *xtext* token can up be up to 100 characters in length. It provides an identifier for MUAs to recognize a DSN for a particular message.

```
mail from:<joe@tuba.example.com> envid=612E01AC4
250 ok
```

This parameter is propagated in the envelope as a message and is transferred to its final destination. If a DSN is generated, the value is included in the DSN message returned to the sender.

The DSN extension provides a useful way to generate machine-parsable delivery status notifications. Clients can use the information to associate a particular message with an error message. In addition, the detail available in a DSN can make it easier for email administrators to diagnose problems. As will be seen in

Chapters 7 and 8, it can also be useful for programs that have to programmatically process bounce messages.

3.5.7 LMTP

Most MTAs initiate local delivery by invoking an MDA program, passing the message to the program, and monitoring the exit status of the program to determine whether the delivery was a success, temporary failure, or permanent failure. This method has two significant problems. First, the exit status provides only a single value, which usually means the MDA can be used to deliver email only to one recipient. Second, it is difficult to support the DSN extensions. This is particularly frustrating with MDAs that perform filtering, since they do not have access to additional DSN information in an envelope.

LMTP, a protocol described in RFC2033 (Local Mail Transfer Protocol), was published in 1996. It is an informational protocol, which developers are under no obligation to implement; however, it does provide an interesting solution to the problems just mentioned.

LMTP is a derivative of the SMTP protocol, with support for the SMTP extension mechanism. It acts in much the same way, using `mail`, `rcpt`, and `data` commands to transfer a message, but there are a few noticeable differences. For instance, instead of `helo` and `ehlo`, it uses a `lhlo` command, to which the server responds with the same type of multiline response seen with a SMTP `ehlo` command.

```
220 tuba.example.com LMTP server ready
lhlo tuba.example.com
250-pipelining
250 size
```

LMTP servers must support the pipelining and enhanced status codes extensions. They should also support the 8-bit MIME extension.

Another difference between SMTP and LMTP is in the `data` command. SMTP `data` returns only one reply; LMTP `data` returns a reply for each of the `rcpt` commands that were successful. The replies are sent in the order the `rcpt` commands were issued. The following example illustrates this.

```
mail from:<larry@ictus.example.com>
250 ok
rcpt to:<joe@tuba.example.com>
250 ok
rcpt to:<snord@tuba.example.com>
550 No such user
```

```
rcpt to:<root@tuba.example.com>
250 ok
data
354 Start mail input; end with <CRLF>.<CRLF>
the message
.
450 Mailbox locked - try later.
250 ok
```

Notice the two 250 responses after the message is sent to the LMTP server. There were three rcpt commands issued, but one of them failed. The first recipient, Joe, had a lock problem, so the server responded with a temporary failure. The second recipient succeeded, resulting in a 250 reply.

Another significant difference between SMTP and LMTP is that the latter is expressly forbidden to use port 25. An LMTP server is typically invoked as a normal MDA, as described in the start of this section. Rather than simply passing the message to the MDA command, the MTA interacts with it using the LMTP protocol, propagating DSN information if appropriate. Instead of the exit status of the MDA, the MTA uses the LMTP reply codes to determine the status of the delivery attempt. Since the MTA receives individual status replies for multiple recipients, it can use one LMTP transaction to deliver a message to multiple recipients, reducing the number of commands it must invoke to perform local delivery.

3.5.8 Submit

As mentioned in Section 3.4.10, SMTP has several constraints that present difficulties when MUAs use it for initial message submission. RFC2476 provides a solution to many of these constraints by defining an MSA (Mail Submission Agent) service. This is an adjunct to existing MTAs. The idea is to separate the tasks of initial message submission and message transfer to allow submitted messages to be scrutinized in sufficient detail without adding the functionality to dedicated MTAs.

The RFC allows MUAs to use TCP port 587 to communicate with an MSA. SMTP is used with the addition of the service extension mechanism defined in RFC1869. The RFC also allows port 25 to be used if the machine providing that service isn't being used for transfer services, or if a way to keep the two services separate is used. This differentiation of services makes it easier to provide MSA services without affecting transfer services.

An MSA is allowed to reject a message for a variety of reasons, including structure defects, insufficient authentication, or site policy. A 554 response code with an enhanced status code of 5.6.0, should be used for rejections unless a more specific response is possible.

An MSA is also allowed to enforce who is, or is not, allowed to submit messages. This includes access based on network address, domain, or authentication ·

information. It should use a 550 reply code with a 5.7.1 enhanced status code if it rejects a submission for this reason. In addition, a publicly accessible MTA is not allowed to require authentication, but an MSA is. If an MSA is configured to impose policy based on the recipient, it can issue a 550 reply code with a 5.7.1 enhanced status code when rejecting such messages. The ability to require authentication can be extremely useful, as will be seen shortly.

Besides enforcing security policies, one of the most important things an MSA can do is enforce the structural integrity of messages and ensure that certain information is present. For example, it's not unusual for MUAs to submit messages with addresses that aren't fully qualified. An MSA must ensure that all domain names in the envelope are fully qualified. In addition, it is allowed to coerce addresses in the header into fully qualified values.

The MSA also is permitted to check and enforce the syntax of addresses. Indeed, it should reject any message with an illegal address syntax in the envelope. If the MSA detects a problem with the mail and rcpt addresses, it should reject the message with a 501 reply code. If it detects an address problem in the message header, it should use a 554 reply code with a 5.6.2 enhanced status code.

In fact, an MSA can check for general structural defects in a submitted message. If the payload provided with a data command has syntactic errors or violates site policy, it can be rejected with a 554 reply code. If it violates site policy, a 5.7.0 enhanced status code is used. If it contains syntax errors, a 5.7.1 code is used.

The MSA is allowed wide latitude in making other alternations. Based on the history of MTAs in the role of MSA, several additions have been found useful.

If the identity of the sender is known and is not given in the From field, the MSA can add a Sender field with the correct information. It is also allowed to replace the contents of an existing Sender field. Thus, if an MSA requires authentication, all outgoing messages can contain definitive information about who sent them. This can significantly reduce spoofing.

If the Date field is missing or incorrect, the MSA can add or replace the information. This can be useful, for example, with mobile users, where the time-zone is often incorrect. It's also useful in ensuring that the Date field is structurally valid.

Since Message-ID is very good at tracking down problems and providing accurate message threading in MUAs, the MSA can rectify any problems with this field.

MSAs can provide more sophisticated manipulation of messages. They can coerce transfer encodings in MIME entities, if necessary. They can also digitally sign messages to verify their authenticity and encrypt them to ensure privacy.

These examples illustrate some of the possibilities of MSAs. However, because of the many things an MSA can do, logging is important. If the MSA encounters a configuration error, a malicious user, or some systemic problem with email services, appropriate logging will help identify the cause.

3.6 SUMMARY

SMTP is the primary means of transmitting messages on the Internet. Using a store-and-forward architecture, it provides email connectivity for millions of users.

SMTP is a command-oriented protocol with a relatively small number of core commands. The commands are combined to form the three basic types of transactions: mailing, relaying, and forwarding. These transactions, when combined with the store-and-forward nature of SMTP, provide the fundamental service.

In order to extend the capabilities of the protocol without breaking existing implementations, an extension mechanism was devised that allows cooperating SMTP processes to use the features available in the various extensions. This mechanism has proven to be a very successful enhancement to SMTP, and as a result many extensions are available and most of them are used on a regular basis.

On the surface, the protocol appears simple. After all, there are a small number of commands whose syntax is relatively easy to learn. Under the surface, however, the requirements placed on SMTP services are rather stringent because email has to be reliable.

With an understanding of how email is transferred across the Internet, it's time to shift focus back to the email message, with MIME. The limitations placed on email messages are in no small part due to the limitations of SMTP. One of the keys to the next chapter is remembering that SMTP is used to transmit messages.

Chapter 4

MIME

As email became a viable medium for transmitting messages, users naturally wanted to expand its capabilities to transmit more than just simple text. It would be useful, for example, for email to transmit such things as arbitrary binary data, references to non-email resources, and collections of data.

RFC822 messages in their basic form cannot handle these additional capabilities. Overcoming this limitation required recognizing the shortcomings of RFC822 and creating extensions to cope with them.

The characters available for RFC822 messages are limited to US-ASCII, which does not support all of the characters used in many non-English languages. While this was tolerable in the early days, it became an issue as more international users joined the Internet. Someone named André might find it annoying that he must spell his name Andre in email messages.

In addition to being limited to US-ASCII, RFC822 has no way to identify the structure of the data in the message body. If a sender sends a message containing, for example, an HTML (Hypertext Markup Language) file, it is up to the recipient to notice that the data can be viewed by an HTML browser. If the format of the data is identified in the message, the MUA can take whatever steps necessary to present the data in that way.

Users occasionally want to send multiple pieces of data in one email message, but a plain RFC822 message body is a single, uninterpreted, data chunk. While it is possible to manually insert separator strings between the different pieces, a standard way to programmatically, and reliably, separate them would be useful.

Finally, message bodies are limited to relatively short lines of 7-bit data. There are SMTP extensions that allow the transmission of binary data, but some non-Internet gateways cannot handle it. In addition, because RFC822 messages are text-based, MUAs need a way to identify binary data in order to handle it properly. Safe transmission of nontext email messages requires extra steps, regardless of the mail environments they are traversing.

MIME provides a way to deal each of these limitations. Some might argue that the MIME extensions are one of the primary reasons that email is as popular as it is.

4.1 PREDECESSORS TO MIME

MIME is not the first technique created to deal with some of the shortcomings of flat text-based messages. In fact, it has several predecessors.

In 1980, RFC767 (Structured Format for Transmission of Multi-Media Documents) was published as an experimental method for handling multimedia messages. This RFC, as well as the meeting minutes in RFC807 (Multimedia Mail Meeting Notes) and RFC910 (Multimedia Mail Meeting Notes), makes compelling reading for those readers interested in the issues early researchers sought to address.

The final multimedia solution took a longer path. Instead of the fairly complete solution to multimedia email in RFC767, most early techniques were ad hoc. Over time, they were replaced with MIME.

A good example of those ad-hoc techniques is the early use of the uuencode and uudecode programs, which are part of the UUCP package. They provided the ability for a sender to encode binary data into a text format generally suitable for email transport and for the receiver to decode it into its original binary form. Prior to MIME, this scheme was the most common way of distributing binary data via email.

Uuencoding is fairly simple. The encoding scheme consists of mapping groups of three bytes into groups of four printable US-ASCII characters. An encoded file consists of an header line, the encoded data, and a trailer line.

```
begin 644 bullet.png
MB5!.1PT*&@H''''-24A$4@@''''X'''."','''HEMWC'''';U!,5$7$Q,3K
MF++WK@:::;K-3_K-4'K+5/K'D'K#S/K'RGK'"?IAE7hau?>?53>>4W='"':0439
M5$k40D#0'B3-1#_!''!W'6D.Z0SBW6D*Q'!Z<'!>4/#"$-RE[''!)=)1Y8''|\\
M''HO''@D''48''48''0''''=T)AJ'''''7123E,'0.;89@'''!MT15AT4V]F
M='=<F4'9VEF,G!N9R'P+C8@*&)E=&$$IJMUID@'''&=)1$%4>)R%SDD.@"'4
M'U"<OZ"(BH|'R.''_,VH$W=K=2Y.F"'/V&$,,,88>84[@)KV.'8]5'50+F*?0YI4
M@S+3(Y9!4=YR.K"'Y^-VP/1J-2MP|LP)8QQZ^YM$Z>7[?3>Mm']-j;5L_N]>
46('&;';J>;('''''245.1*Y"8(*M
'
end
```

The header line consists of three space-delimited words: the string 'begin', the UNIX permission value, and the filename. The permission value indicates what permissions the decoded file should have. The filename indicates the decoded file's preferred name. The trailer line contains the single word 'end'.

The uudecode method suffers from a serious drawback—the filename is the only information provided to indicate what type of data is contained in the encoded chunk. Many data types have associated filename extensions—for example, a file named `canyon.jpg` is probably a JPEG file—but some data types do not have them. To aggravate the problem, some filename extensions are used by multiple data types; for example, `file.doc` can be from a couple of word processors.

Interoperability is another problem with some implementations of uudecode. Since no standard exists for the uuencode format, there have been several broken implementations, which is particularly astounding considering the fact that uuencode was widely used prior to the broad availability of MIME. The filename problem, in combination with the lack of a standard format, virtually eliminates uuencode as a primary way to encapsulate data in email messages.

In 1988, RFC1049 (A Content-Type Header Field for Internet Messages) was published to solve these problems. It uses a `Content-Type` header field to provide several pieces of information for determining the type of data contained in the message body. Readers already familiar with MIME might recognize this as a MIME field. In fact, the MIME field by the same name is a variant of `Content-Type`. MIME has displaced RFC1049 to the point where the older form is rarely seen. The syntax for the RFC1049 form of the field is as follows.

```
"Content-Type:" type [";" ver-num [";" 1#resource-ref]] [comment]
```

The *type* subfield identifies what type of data is contained in the message. The initial RFC allowed `postscript`, `scribe`, `sgml`, `tex`, `troff`, `dvi`, and 'x-' extensions.

The *ver-num* subfield contains version information to assist in the selection of the proper processing software, if it's an issue.

The *resource-ref* subfield indicates the names of any macro packages used in the preparation of the document. For example, a Troff document might need to be handled by the Eqn package to process equations embedded in it.

Finally, the *comments* subfield provides the opportunity to include additional commentary. It is enclosed in parentheses as an RFC822 comment.

```
Content-Type: troff; null; eqn (RF analysis)
```

RFC1049, while addressing part of the problem, left several issues unresolved, most notably, the lack of support for multipart attachments or non-US-ASCII data. Another significant shortcoming was the lack of extensibility. The initial list of documents formats could be expanded, but it wasn't designed for scalability.

More work was needed to provide a robust and scalable architecture. The result of that additional work is the modern MIME extensions.

4.2 OVERVIEW OF MIME

MIME is a relatively new addition to the world of Internet email. In 1992, a series of RFCs was published to provide its first definition.

- RFC1341 (MIME: Mechanisms for Specifying and Describing the Format of Internet Message Bodies)
- RFC1342 (Representation of Non-ASCII Text in Internet Message Headers)
- RFC1343 (A User Agent Configuration Mechanism for Multimedia Mail Format Information)
- RFC1344 (Implications of MIME for Internet Mail Gateways)

In 1993, RFC1521 (MIME Part One: Mechanisms for Specifying and Describing the Format of Internet Message Bodies) and RFC1522 (MIME Part Two: Message Header Extensions for Non-ASCII Text) were published as updates to the previous RFCs. They provided minor clarifications and corrections. Finally, in 1996, a series of RFCs was published as another round of clarifications and corrections.

- RFC2045 (MIME Part One: Format of Internet Message Bodies)
- RFC2046 (MIME Part Two: Media Types)
- RFC2047 (MIME Part Three: Message Header Extensions for Non-ASCII Text)
- RFC2048 (MIME Part Four: Registration Procedures)
- RFC2049 (MIME Part Five: Conformance Criteria and Examples)

This chapter concentrates on this most recent set of MIME RFCs.

Additional documents provide enhancements to the core MIME specification. Several of the enhancements are described in this chapter, which also indicates where further information can be obtained. Before a detailed description can be provided, a few terms must be introduced that are central to an explanation and understanding of MIME.

RFC2130 (The Report of the IAB Character Set Workshop Held 29 February–1 March) provides, among other things, a set of recommendations to the IAB, IANA, and the IESG related to character sets in Internet protocols. One of the items included in the report is an architectural model of the components required to specify the transmission of text-based information. This model is also helpful for understanding how MIME works because it defines the various components and describes their relationship to each other.

TABLE 4.1 Architectural Model for Text Transmission

Seven Layers
Layout
Culture
Locale
Language
Transfer syntax
Character encoding scheme
Coded character set

The model consists of seven layers, listed in Table 4.1, from the highest to the lowest. The layers are separated into two major categories. The top four layers address user interface issues. The layout layer relates to the display of information to a user, such as fonts and paragraph line wrapping. The culture layer concerns cultural preferences, such as spelling and word choice. The locale layer addresses choices related to location-specific display of data, such as date, time, and monetary formats. The final upper layer indicates the language used in transmitted text.

The bottom three layers relate to accurately transmitting character set data in a transmission protocol. These are MIME's primary focus. In order to understand them, it is probably best to start from the bottom up.

The coded character set layer provides a mapping from a set of abstract characters to a set of integers. For example, the letter 'A' is assigned to the integer 65 in US-ASCII.

US-ASCII is the most common coded character set. Others include the ISO-8859 (Information Processing—8-bit Single-Byte Coded Graphic Character Sets) series, which provide mappings for European countries, and ISO-10646 (Information Technology—Universal Multiple-Octet Coded Character Set (UCS)—Part 1: Architecture and Basic Multilingual Plan), which defines a mapping for characters from most of the world's languages.

The next layer identifies the character encoding scheme, which provides a mapping between a coded character set, or several of them, and a set of 8-bit octets. Some readers might be wondering how this differs from the coded character set layer. As it turns out, this layer serves a very useful purpose. US-ASCII is a 7-bit coded character set; the ISO-8859 family are 8-bit sets. These map into octets in a one-to-one manner. Coded characters sets such as ISO-10646, however, are larger than 8 bits. Since the atomic unit in modern networking protocols is 8 bits, a process to map other data unit sizes into 8 bits is needed. Examples include ISO-2022 (Information Technology—Character Code Structure and Extension Techniques) and UTF-8 (UCS Transformation Format 8).

Finally, there is the transfer encoding syntax layer. This provides a mapping from a coded character set, and possibly a character encoding scheme, to a format suitable for a specific protocol. RFC821, for example, requires data to be in a 7-bit format. Any data not in that format must be encoded to order to be usable with SMTP.

These layers are used in concert to provide a particular transformation. As an example, a particular document might contain ISO-10646 data. If it is to be transmitted via SMTP, it first needs to be converted to UTF-8, which maps it to an 8-bit format. If the resulting data contains any characters outside of the 7-bit range required by SMTP, it needs to be encoded down to 7-bit data.

The core MIME extension provides a framework for labeling the various transformations in the bottom three layers of the architectural model. Other extensions to MIME are starting to address some of the upper layers as well. Keeping the architectural model in mind will help when learning MIME.

The primary object dealt with in MIME is the *entity,* which consists of the body of a message and the MIME-specific fields in the message header. By definition, an RFC822 message is a MIME entity if it contains certain MIME-specific header fields.

```
To: joe@tuba.example.com
From: larry@ictus.example.com
MIME-Version: 1.0
Content-Type: text/plain

Joe,
This is an example MIME entity.
```

The header of an entity contains fields used to describe the contents of the body. This includes, among other things, information describing the type of data included in the body, the coded character set used in the original data, and the encoding technique used to coerce the data into a format acceptable for RFC822 messages.

```
Content-Type: text/plain; charset=iso-8859-1
Content-Transfer-Encoding: quoted-printable
```

Like RFC822 message bodies, an entity body carries the data payload. It is essentially a regular RFC822 body with the added complication that the data might be encoded.

Conceptually, the encoding process is fairly simple. It consists of the following steps.

1. *Identify the format of the data.* In order to determine what transformations to apply to the data, the data type needs to be established, such as a JPEG graphics image, a word-processor file, or a plain text file. The coded character set used in the data also needs to be identified, since it might need to be coerced into 7-bit format.

2. *Convert local form to canonical form.* The canonical form for lines of text in RFC822 ends with CRLF. Some operating systems use a different convention. For example, UNIX uses LF and Mac-OS uses CR. When encoding the text data into MIME, lines must be converted to the canonical form defined by RFC822.

3. *Apply transfer encoding.* The data might be in a format unsuitable for RFC822 text bodies. If so, it might need to be encoded.

4. *Insert encoded data into the entity.* Once the data has been prepared, it is ready to be inserted into a MIME entity. The fields mentioned below are populated, and the encoded data is inserted into the entity body. The final result is a valid MIME entity, ready for use in RFC822 messages.

To reverse the process, the encoded data is extracted from the entity, decoded, and then converted to the canonical form for the operating system to which it is being written.

Some MIME entities contain multiple parts, called *body parts,* which are also entities. Figure 4.1 illustrates this visually.

Because each entity contains a header and body, the diagram in Figure 4.1 can be expanded to illustrate the relationship between entities, headers, and bodies as shown in Figure 4.2. With these terms defined, it is possible to begin exploring the various elements of MIME messages in detail.

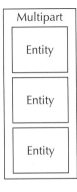

FIGURE 4.1 Multipart Entities

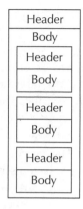

FIGURE 4.2 Multipart Headers and Bodies

4.3 MIME HEADERS

The MIME extension is controlled through a set of MIME-specific header fields, which are additions to those provided in RFC822. They are generated by a sending MUA when a message is composed. A receiving MUA uses them to decide how to extract any entities contained in the message.

4.3.1 MIME-Version

The `MIME-Version` field is used to identify which version of MIME was used when the encapsulation was performed. The creators of MIME foresaw the possibility that the extensions might need to be altered in the future. Dramatic changes could prove to be very difficult, and adding the version number allowed such changes to be added without the problem of backward compatibility.

This is the only field required to be present for a message to be considered a MIME message. In addition, all MIME-conformant MUAs must insert this field in all messages they generate.

The field is defined as follows.

```
"MIME-Version:" 1*DIGIT "." 1*DIGIT
```

The first segment of the number indicates the major version number; the second segment indicates the minor release level. Only one version number is currently defined—1.0.

```
MIME-Version: 1.0
```

Because there is only one version number in use, there is no standard method of handling future versions.

4.3.2 Content-Type

The `Content-Type` field, the workhorse in MIME, describes the data contained in a particular MIME entity. It is a generalized version of the `Content-Type` field mentioned in Section 4.1.

The field value consists of three segments: a media type, in two segments, and an optional semicolon-separated list of parameters.

```
"Content-Type:" type "/" subtype *(";" parameter)
```

Media Types

The media type indicates the specific data format contained in the entity. The *type* parameter indicates the major classification for the media type. The *subtype* provides an additional level of classification. Both of these elements are case-insensitive.

An example is in order. One of the major classifications is `text`, but because there are various types of text data, a subtype is needed to be more specific. The most common subtype used with `text` is `plain`, resulting in `text/plain`.

```
Content-Type: text/plain
```

One small complication worth mentioning is that the media type is occasionally specified incorrectly.

```
Content-Type: text
```

Sometimes this form of the field is provided with no `MIME-Version` field. In this case, it should be interpreted as an RFC1049 form. Unfortunately, it is sometimes seen with an accompanying `MIME-Version` field. Technically speaking, the field is incorrectly formatted, but, erring on the side of forgiveness, the field should be considered to have an implicit value of `text/plain`.

Many of the common media types encountered in this field are described in Section 4.4.

Parameters

Most of the media types have associated parameters that control their interpretation. Each parameter consists of an attribute name and value, separated by a '=' character.

```
parameter = attribute "=" value
```

An *attribute* name consists of what RFC2045 describes as a *token*. This can contain any US-ASCII character except SPACE, control characters, or any of the following characters:

```
()<>@,;:\"/[]?=
```

If any of these characters are present in *value*, it must be quoted as a *quoted-string*.

A parameter value can consist of a *token* or a *quoted-string*. The *quoted-string* is used in situations where a value needs to contain characters not allowed in a *token*.

```
Content-Type: message/external-body;
              access-type=mail-server;
              server="lists@example.com"
```

This example shows a `Content-Type` field with two parameters. The value for the `server` parameter is quoted because it contains an '@' character, which is not allowed in the unquoted form.

It is not uncommon to see quoted values where they are not necessary. Strictly speaking, the quoting isn't necessary in this instance, since none of the characters in the value are disallowed in the unquoted form. Even so, while not necessary, it isn't wrong.

```
Content-Type: text/plain; charset="us-ascii"
```

Parameter names are case-insensitive. Case sensitivity of parameter values depends on the parameter name. In addition, it doesn't matter in what order parameters are listed.

As another example of the Robustness Principle, any unrecognized parameters should be ignored. This makes MIME software more resilient to change and to errors in other software.

4.3.3 Content-Transfer-Encoding

Many data formats can contain byte values outside the range of characters allowed in a mail message. Many can also contain lines of data longer than what is allowed. Some data formats don't even have the concept of a line in their definition. The `Content-Transfer-Encoding` field addresses these issues.

MIME defines five values for this field: `7bit`, `8bit`, `binary`, `base64`, and `quoted-printable`. Each is case-insensitive. All MIME-conformant MUAs must be able to process every one of these encodings.

Of the five values, the first three are referred to as identity encodings. This means that no encoding of the data has been performed—they only indicate whether the entity contains 7-bit, 8-bit, or binary data has been established. The other two encodings, `base64` and `quoted-printable`, indicate that the data has been transformed into a format suitable for transport across a communication channel that restricts the values allowed in the data. The primary example of this is SMTP, which normally restricts data to 7-bit values.

7bit

```
Content-Transfer-Encoding: 7bit
```

The `7bit` encoding scheme is used for data consisting of lines no longer than 998 octets of 7-bit data, terminated by CRLF. This is generally equivalent to standard RFC822 lines of text. The octets in a line can be any value less than ASCII 128, not including US-ASCII 0, CR, or LF characters. This is the default encoding. If no `Content-Transfer-Encoding` field is provided, `7bit` is assumed.

8bit

```
Content-Transfer-Encoding: 8bit
```

Like `7bit`, `8bit` can be used to encode data consisting of lines no longer than 998 octets of data, terminated by CRLF, but unlike `7bit`, octets higher than US-ASCII 127 are allowed. In addition, while CR and LF are not allowed, just as with `7bit`, US-ASCII 0 is allowed. The `8bitmime` SMTP extension, described in Section 3.5.3, can be used to transport messages that use this encoding scheme.

Binary

```
Content-Transfer-Encoding: binary
```

The `binary` encoding scheme is used for arbitrary 8-bit data, with no restrictions on line length or on allowed characters. There are currently no places where `binary` encoding is valid in a top-level MIME entity. Where it becomes useful is in the `message/external-body` media type, which is described in Section 4.4.4.

Base64

```
Content-Transfer-Encoding: base64
```

The `base64` encoding scheme is used to encode binary data into a format suitable for transport via Internet email. Like the uuencode technique mentioned in Section 4.1, it does this by converting groups of three 8-bit bytes into groups of four printable characters.

The first step is to take a group of three 8-bit bytes and convert them into four 6-bit numbers, as illustrated in Figure 4.3. Say the three bytes values are 183, 40, and 244. Applying the conversion shown in Figure 4.3 results in the 6-bit numbers 45, 50, 35, and 52, as illustrated in Figure 4.4.

These numbers are then converted to US-ASCII using the characters in Table 4.2. These were chosen because they are immune to corruption when going through external email gateways. In the current example, mapping the 6-bit numbers into `base64` results in the printable characters 't', 'y', 'j', and '0'. Thus, encoding the 3-byte sequence 183, 40, and 244 in `base64` results in the 4-character printable US-ASCII sequence 'tyj0'.

This process is repeated for the entire sequence of bytes being encoded. As the encoded data is generated, CRLF characters are inserted into the output stream to keep line lengths under 76 characters, which is necessary because binary data typically isn't line-oriented; CR and LF characters are encoded the same way other characters are encoded. In decoding, the CRLF characters are removed, so the result is an exact duplicate of the original data.

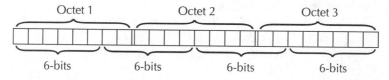

FIGURE 4.3 8-Bit to 6-Bit Conversion

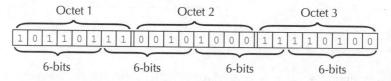

FIGURE 4.4 Converting 3 Octets

TABLE 4.2 6-Bit `base64` Encoding

6-bit value	Char	6-bit value	Char	6-bit value	Char	6-bit value	Char
0	A	16	Q	32	g	48	w
1	B	17	R	33	h	49	x
2	C	18	S	34	i	50	y
3	D	19	T	35	j	51	z
4	E	20	U	36	k	52	0
5	F	21	V	37	l	53	1
6	G	22	W	38	m	54	2
7	H	23	X	39	n	55	3
8	I	24	Y	40	o	56	4
9	J	25	Z	41	p	57	5
10	K	26	a	42	q	58	6
11	L	27	b	43	r	59	7
12	M	28	c	44	s	60	8
13	N	29	d	45	t	61	9
14	O	30	e	46	u	62	+
15	P	31	f	47	v	63	/
						pad	=

One final detail in `base64` encoding remains—padding. Since the encoding scheme uses groups of three 8-bit bytes as input, special steps need to be taken if the length of the data being encoded is not a multiple of three. The last iteration of the encoding process might not have a complete group of three bytes, in which case either one or two bytes will be left over.

When there is one extra byte, the 3-byte group is created by appending two more 0-value bytes; two encoded characters are generated, and two '=' characters are appended.

In the case of two extra bytes, one extra 0-value byte is appended, three encoded characters are generated, and one '=' character is appended.

Quoted-Printable

```
Content-Transfer-Encoding: quoted-printable
```

The `quoted-printable` encoding scheme is designed to encode data consisting primarily of text. It is particularly useful in situations where line lengths exceed 80 characters. Despite the fact that RFC821 allows lines up to 1,000 characters in length, not all non-Internet email programs handle them correctly. Another problem frequently encountered on non-Internet email packages is the addition or removal of trailing whitespace. With standard flat RFC822 text bodies, these problems can often be overlooked; human readers simply adapt to the changes in format. With structured data, however, this is unacceptable. Software that needs to interpret the data might misinterpret spurious trailing whitespace. The `quoted-printable` encoding scheme provides a resilient way to encode an entity in a way that is immune to these problems.

In `quoted-printable` encoding, individual characters are encoded instead of groups, as in `base64` encoding. Any individual character can be replaced with its two-digit hexadecimal equivalent by prefixing it with a '=' character. As an example, the hexadecimal value of the ESCAPE character is '1B'. Prefixing it with '=' results in '=1B', which is ESCAPE's `quoted-printable` encoding.

One interesting use of character encoding is the escaping of lines starting with 'From␣'. This string is used as a message separator in the standard UNIX mail folder format. Escaping strings such as this reduces the chance of the message being broken by simple-minded message software.

```
=46rom now one, let's use a different trucking company.
```

Any 8-bit character can be encoded using this scheme, with one exception— CRLF used as a line break in the original data format must be represented as a CRLF in the `quoted-printable` encoding.

To reduce the chance of gateways breaking messages, the encoding scheme does not allow lines to be longer than 76 characters, not including the trailing CRLF. Because of this, *soft line breaks* are provided, which disappear when the line is decoded. A soft line break is encoded as an '=' at the end of a line.

```
There is only one =
line in the original text.
```

This example will be decoded as follows.

```
There is only one line in the original text.
```

Since most US-ASCII characters don't normally need to be encoded, `quoted-printable` encoding allows them remain unencoded. Thus, US-ASCII characters 33 through 60 and 62 through 126 can be used directly. This amounts to the entire set of printable US-ASCII characters except SPACE (US-ASCII 32) and '=' (US-ASCII 61).

The SPACE and TAB characters can be used in their unencoded form except as the last character in an encoded line. Any trailing whitespace in the original data must be encoded in the final result. This stipulation deals with the fact that some email gateways are known to strip whitespace from the end of lines, while some others are known to add it.

```
This line has whitespace at the end.=20=20=20
```

Since `quoted-printable` encoding does not allow whitespace at the end of a line, any trailing whitespace present must be removed when decoding the data, under the assumption that a gateway added it.

This small set of simple encoding rules can be combined in various ways as necessary. To illustrate this, the following example uses a little of everything.

```
To illustrate the =
various rules for encoding,
=20the=20following=20=
example uses a little of=0D=0Aeverything
```

The result after decoding is as follows.

```
To illustrate the various rules for encoding,
the following example uses a little of
everything.
```

MIME `quoted-printable` encoding is relatively immune to damage from external email gateways; however, this immunity can be improved slightly. Some gateways are run on operating systems not based on US-ASCII or a variation of it. For example, there are still mainframes around that use EBCDIC (Extended Binary Coded Decimal Interchange Code), a charset from IBM. The problem with gatewaying between US-ASCII and EBCDIC is that several characters in US-ASCII are not contained in common variants of EBCDIC. Encoding the following list of characters will reduce the possibility of an EBCDIC-based gateway losing information:

```
!"#$@[]\^'{|}~
```

X-Uuencode

```
Content-Transfer-Encoding: x-uuencode
```

Despite the fact that MIME has virtually eliminated the need for uuencoding data, uuencoding is still encountered. The nonstandard `x-uuencode` content transfer encoding tag is often used to identify it in MIME entities.

The body of an entity tagged with `x-uuencode` contains traditional uuencoded data. It also commonly includes a `name` parameter in the `Content-Type` field that corresponds with the filename identified in the uuencoded data.

```
Content-Type: image/png;
              name="bullet.png"
Content-Transfer-Encoding: x-uuencode

begin 644 bullet.png
MB5!.1PT*&@H'''''-24A$4@''''X''''."','''HEMWC''''';U!,5$7$Q,3K
MF++WK@::;;;K K-3_K K-4'K+5/K'D'K#K#S/K'RGK'"?IAE7HAU?>?53>>4W='"':0439
M5$$K40D#0'B3-1#_!''!W'6D.Z0SBW6D*Q'!Z<'!>4/#"$-RE[('!!')=)1Y8''|\\
M''HO''@D''48''48''0''''=T)AJ'''''7123E,'0.;89@'''!MT15AT4V]F
M='=<F4'9VEF,G!N9R'P+C8@*&)E=&$$$$IJMUID@'''&=)1$%4>)R%SDD.Q@"'4
M'U"<0Z"'"(BH|'R.''_,VH$$SW=K(=2Y.F"/&/V&$$$,188$>84[@)KKKV.'8]5'50+F*?0YI4
M@S+3(Y9!4=YR=R.K"K"C.C'Y^-VP/1.J-2MP\LP,J)]8QZQQZQ"CYM$$$Z>7[?3>MM'-J;5L_N]_
46('&;';J>;('''''245.1*Y"8(*M
'
end
```

4.3.4 Content-ID

The `Content-ID` field provides a way to uniquely identify a MIME entity, similarly to how `Message-ID` uniquely identifies a mail message. It provides a way for media types to reference other MIME entities and is optional for all media types except `message/external-body`.

```
"Content-ID:" msg-id
```

The *msg-id* has the same syntax as the `Message-ID` field. Like `Message-ID`, it must be unique across space and time. The description of the `message/external-body` media type in Section 4.4.4 contains an example of this field.

4.3.5 Content-Description

The `Content-Description` field allows a text description to be associated with a MIME entity.

```
"Content-Description:" *text
```

This can be useful when the contents of the entity might not be immediately obvious to a recipient.

```
Content-Description: View-cells from last meeting
```

4.3.6 Content-Disposition

Early MIME implementation in MUAs often took a very simple approach to presenting an interface for attachments to users. Single entities were often displayed inline if they were text. Entities such as graphics were often presented as an icon or menu selection that the user could activate to launch an external viewer. Multipart entities were often presented as a list of icons or menu items that the user could select manually.

As MIME implementations matured, one of the interface improvements introduced was the display of attachments inline. As it turns out, however, broadly deciding to display certain media types inline raises some issues. In the case of graphic images, inline display is very convenient if the image is a reasonable size. With large images, it can be cumbersome; programs specializing in the media type in question are often more appropriate in these instances. Also, not all attachments are intended to be viewed inline; sometimes the sender intended them as peripheral data.

RFC2183 (Communication Presentation Information in Internet Messages: The Content-Disposition Header Field) provides a way to deal with these issues. It defines the `Content-Disposition` field, which can be used to control whether an entity should be treated as inline data or as a peripheral attachment.

The `inline` disposition type indicates the preference for the entity to be displayed inline in the message body. Possible examples include small graphic images and HTML material.

The `attachment` disposition type indicates the preference for display outside of the normal message body. A common example is large graphic images whose size is not suited to the display capabilities of a normal MUA.

There are several parameters available with this field. The most common one is `filename`, which provides a way to suggest a filename for the entity.

```
Content-Disposition: attachment; filename=render99071601.jpg
```

There is no requirement to use the filename supplied; it is merely a convenience for the user.

Any directory component in the parameter should be ignored. Thus, on a UNIX machine, if the parameter is set to '`/tmp/render99071601.jpg`', the '`/tmp/`' portion should be disregarded. This is true on any operating system, whatever the directory notation.

TABLE 4.3 Disposition Parameters Related to Dates

Parameter	Description
creation-date	The date the file was created
modification-date	The date the file was last modified
read-date	The date the file was last read

For security reasons, the filename should be treated with care. If it is not handled properly, it is possible to overwrite existing files, which could result in a security breach. There are several techniques to minimize the problem. If all extracted attachments are placed in a separate subdirectory, the chances of overwriting a file are eliminated.[1] In the case of UNIX operating systems, refusing to honor filenames starting with the '.' character prevents the possibility of creating files such as '.exrc'. Another useful technique is to refuse to honor filenames containing nonprintable or other problematic characters.

A size parameter is available to indicate the size of the entity. It is a convenient way to determine whether sufficient space exists to process the entity without scanning through the entire entity to calculate its size.

```
size=189283
```

Three other parameters provide information regarding various date characteristics of the attachment. They are listed in Table 4.3.

4.3.7 Content-MD5

```
"Content-MD5:" md5-digest
```

RFC1864 (The Content-MD5 Header Field) defines the Content-MD5 field, which can be used to add an MD5 (Message Digest Algorithm 5) integrity check to messages. This check verifies that a received message has not been inadvertently altered during transmission to its destination.

RFC1321 (The MD5 Message-Digest Algorithm) describes the algorithm used to generate an *md5-digest*. The algorithm generates a 128-bit message digest, or fingerprint, of the message. It is designed such that it is computationally unlikely for two messages to have the same digest value. RFC1864 describes how to encode an MD5 digest in a Content-MD5 field.

---

[1] With the exception of overwriting other extracted attachments.

To generate the digest, the message is first padded at the end so that its length is 64 bits short of being a multiple of 512 bits. This padding consists of a single '1' bit, followed by a series of '0' bits. It is always added, even if the length is already 64 bits short of being a multiple of 512 bits.

As an example, if a message is 21,414 bytes, the padded message will be 21,440 bytes since 21,440 equals $(512 \times 12) - 64$.

A 64-bit version of the message length (before padding) is then appended. The bits are appended as two 32-bit integers and low-order first.

Since the padding in the previous step created a message that was 64 bytes short of a multiple of 512, and this step adds 64 bits, the resulting message is an exact multiple of 512.

The algorithm uses four 32-bit integer buffers to calculate the message digest. The buffers are initialized with a specific value, then the message is taken through an algorithm, described in RFC1321, which condenses it into the four buffers.

The final output of the message digest algorithm is a 128-bit digest value, created by combining the four 32-bit buffers. Each of these buffers is output as a series of 8-bit values, with the least significant byte going first and the most significant byte going last.

Once the 128-bit digest is generated, it needs to be converted into a printable US-ASCII string, safe for email transport. The digest is converted to US-ASCII using `base64` encoding.

```
Content-MD5: cBcSKQBRbjNBaCyiRDkZzg==
```

As mentioned earlier, messages can sometimes be altered when passing through various email gateways. Any and all damage will result in a mismatch between the message and the digest value. Entities with the `Content-MD5` should use `quoted-printable` or `base64` encoding to reduce the risk of accidental damage from gateways.

The `Content-MD5` field doesn't guarantee that the digest for a message has not been altered; it merely indicates whether a message has been accidently altered. Thus, it is unsuitable as proof that the message is in its original form. More resilient mechanisms, which provide stronger assurances, are described in Chapter 9.

4.3.8 Content-Language

The `Content-Language` field is defined in RFC1766 (Tags for the Indentification of Languages). It provides the ability to indicate the language used in an entity.

On the surface, indicating the language might seem like a mere convenience to users. After all, many languages are relatively easy to identify visually. In practice, however, programmatically identifying a language can be difficult. This is particularly important for speech synthesis and braille translation, where identification of the language can improve the conversion process.

The field value consists of a command list of language tags.

```
"Content-Language:" language-tag [CFWS] *("," [CFWS] language-tag)
```

Each *language-tag* identifies a particular written or spoken language only—computer languages are explicitly excluded from use.

```
Content-Language: en-US
```

This identifies the entity as containing information in the U.S. variant of English.

```
language-tag = primary-tag *("-" subtag)
primary-tag  = 1*8ALPHA
subtag       = 1*8ALPHA
```

Whitespace is not allowed inside *language-tag*.

Applications should always treat language tags as a single token. Unlike media types or directory paths, the tag segments do not necessarily represent a particular path down a language tree. The notation is simply an administrative convenience.

The *primary-tag* token typically indicates the high-level name of the language. RFC1766 predefines several sets of *primary-tag* values. Two-letter codes are considered values from ISO-639 (Code for the Representation of Names of Languages). Examples include 'en' for English, 'fr' for French, and 'de' for German.

The primary tag 'i' is reserved for IANA-defined registrations, which can handle languages not handled by ISO-639. There are only three registered tags of this type: 'i-navaho', 'i-mingo', and 'i-default'. The first two identify Native American languages; the third was defined in RFC2277 (IETF Policy on Character Sets and Languages) for situations where the language, or language preferences of the user, cannot be identified.

The primary tag 'x' is reserved for private use. It provides a way for developers, for instance, to use a temporary language until a tag can be registered. Using any other values for a primary tag requires an update to RFC1766.

The subtags following the primary tag typically convey such things as country and dialect. Except when used with 'x' primary tags, they must be registered values. With only one exception, any subtag code can be registered with the IANA. In the first subtag, all two-letter tags are interpreted as ISO-3166 (Codes for the Representation of Names of Countries) codes.

Like many pieces of information in mail messages, a tag is case-insensitive. However, two case conventions are worth mentioning. In ISO-639 and ISO-3166 language names are lower-case, while country codes are upper-case.

The interpretation of the list of language tags in a Content-Language field depends on the information being tagged. For a single-part entity, such as a plain-text message, it indicates the set of languages needed for a complete understanding of the entity.

```
Content-Type: text/plain
Content-Language: en
```

Multiple tags can be used for multiple languages in a particular entity.

```
Content-Type: application/pdf
Content-Language: en, fr
```

In this example, the data is an Adobe PDF (Portable Data Format) file containing English and French information.

A tag can also be used with media types not based on written text. For example, with movie data it can indicate that the dialog is in the specified language.

```
Content-Type: video/mpeg
Content-Language: fr
```

With multipart entities, there are two places the tag can be used: in the top-level header and in each body part. In the top-level, it indicates the set of languages used in all the body parts; in a body part, it indicates the set of languages used in that particular part. This is illustrated in Section 4.4.5.

4.3.9 MIME Extension Fields

'Content-' is reserved as the prefix for future MIME fields. This allows email software to identify new fields without needing to understand them.

4.4 MIME MEDIA TYPES

As mentioned in Section 4.3.2, a media type is divided into two segments—a type and a subtype. RFC2045 defines eight top-level media types: text, image, audio, video, application, message, and multipart. An additional type, model, was added by RFC2077 (The Model Primary Content Type for Multipurpose Internet Mail Extensions). Each of these major types provides a structure for their respective data. MIME media types have proven effective enough that other technologies, such as the World Wide Web, have adopted them for specifying data types.

4.4.1 Text

The text type is used for text-based content. Any of the subtypes in this category theoretically can be read without requiring an application to format the data.

TABLE 4.4 ISO-8859 Charsets

Charset	Description
ISO-8859-1	Latin alphabet No. 1
ISO-8859-2	Latin alphabet No. 2
ISO-8859-3	Latin alphabet No. 3
ISO-8859-4	Latin alphabet No. 4
ISO-8859-5	Latin/Cyrillic alphabet
ISO-8859-6	Latin/Arabic alphabet
ISO-8859-7	Latin/Greek alphabet
ISO-8859-8	Latin/Hebrew alphabet
ISO-8859-9	Latin alphabet No. 5
ISO-8859-10	Latin alphabet No. 6
ISO-8859-13	Latin alphabet No. 7
ISO-8859-14	Latin alphabet No. 8 (Celtic)
ISO-8859-15	Latin alphabet No. 9

A `charset` parameter is available to all the subtypes in this media type category to indicate the charset of the original data.

```
Content-Type: text/plain; charset=us-ascii
```

This example indicates that the original data was US-ASCII prior to be encapsulated into the MIME entity.

If the parameter is not specified, the default value is US-ASCII. This is by far the most used, but there are many others available. The IANA provides a repository of the allowable charsets.[2]

The most common alternatives to US-ASCII are the ISO-8859 set of charsets, which are listed in Table 4.4. All of them are supersets of US-ASCII. The additional characters are in the range between US-ASCII 128 and US-ASCII 255.

Of these charsets, ISO-8859-1, Western European, is the most common. Table 4.5 shows the additional characters it makes available.

There's no doubt that the Internet is going international. RFC2130 recommends that all new protocols, and new versions of older protocols, use ISO-10646 as the default charset. As mentioned earlier in this chapter, ISO-10646 defines a

---

[2] http://www.isi.edu/in-notes/iana/assignments/character-sets.

TABLE 4.5 ISO-8859-1 additions to US-ASCII

	0	1	2	3	4	5	6	7	8	9	10	11	12	13	14	15
128																
144																
160		¡	¢	£	¤	¥	¦	§	¨	©	ª	«	¬	—	®	¯
176	°	±	²	³	´	µ	¶	·	¸	¹	º	»	¼	½	¾	¿
192	À	Á	Â	Ã	Ä	Å	Æ	Ç	È	É	Ê	Ë	Ì	Í	Î	Ï
208	Ð	Ñ	Ò	Ó	Ô	Õ	Ö	×	Ø	Ù	Ú	Û	Ü	Ý	Þ	ß
224	à	á	â	ã	ä	å	æ	ç	è	é	ê	ë	ì	í	î	ï
240	ð	ñ	ò	ó	ô	õ	ö	÷	ø	ù	ú	û	ü	ý	þ	ÿ

multi-octet coded character set, UCS (Universal Character Set), which encompasses the characters in most of the world's writing systems. Two encodings are defined: UCS-4 is 4-octet, and UCS-2 is 2-octet.

Another standard worth mentioning is Unicode, created by the Unicode Consortium.[3] This standard is compatible with ISO-10646. The primary difference is that it defines character properties and includes helpful information for developers. Also, it does not use the UCS-4 encoding, although it defines the same set of characters defined in ISO-10646.

Because many communication mediums handle only 7- and 8-bit characters, three UTF (UCS Transformation Format) standards are provided. UTF-7 (UCS Transformation Format 7) maps UCS-2 data to a 7-bit format; UTF-8 maps UCS-2 or UCS-4 data to an 8-bit format; and UTF-16 maps UCS-4 data into UCS-2.

UTF-8 is documented in RFC2044 (UTF-8, a Transformation Format of Unicode and ISO 10646). UCS characters are encoded into sequences of one to six octets, based on what range a specified UCS character is in. The mapping between UCS-4 and UTF-8 is shown in Table 4.6.

An important characteristic of UCS and UTF-8 is that the lower 127 characters of UCS match the characters in 7-bit US-ASCII, as do their UTF-8 equivalents. This was intentional. If all the characters in a message are in this range, no transfer encoding is needed.

Looking at Table 4.6, it is interesting to note that the other UCS characters all map to UTF-8 characters with the eighth bit set. These characters require some type of encoding. If the majority of characters are in the range of US-ASCII characters, then `quoted-printable` encoding is sufficient. If the majority is outside that range, `base64` is called for.

---

[3] http://www.unicode.org/.

TABLE 4.6   UTF-8 Encoding

UCS-4 range (hex)	UTF-8 Octet Sequence (binary)
00000000–0000007F	0xxxxxxx
00000080–000007FF	110xxxxx 10xxxxxx
00000800–0000FFFF	1110xxxx 10xxxxxx 10xxxxxx
00010000–001FFFFF	11110xxx 10xxxxxx 10xxxxxx 10xxxxxx
00200000–03FFFFFF	111110xx 10xxxxxx 10xxxxxx 10xxxxxx 10xxxxxx
04000000–7FFFFFFF	1111110x 10xxxxxx . . . 10xxxxxx

In addition to UTF-8, another transformation format is available for UCS—UTF-7, which is defined by RFC2152 (UTF-7 A Mail-Safe Transformation Format of Unicode). As mentioned earlier, UTF-7 results in 7-bit US-ASCII data.

One set of characters can always be mapped into their equivalent US-ASCII values. These include the letters 'a' through 'z' and 'A' through 'Z', the 10 digits '0' through '9', and the following characters.

```
'(),-./:?
```

Another set of characters can optionally be mapped directly into their US-ASCII equivalents.

```
!"#$%&*;<=>@[]^_;{|}
```

The choice as to whether they should be depends on the situation.

Any sequence of characters can be encoded using a modified encoding. A '+' character is used to signal the start of an encoded sequence. Subsequent characters are considered encoded until the first character outside the set of modified base64 characters is encountered. The modified base64 characters include all the characters in regular base64 except '='.

To encode the data, the base64 algorithm is used except for the '=' character. Instead of '=', zero bits are appended to the data to pad it to a base64 character boundary. When decoding, any bits left over when building the 16-bit characters are discarded.

There are several special cases to take into account. If an encoded sequence ends with a '–' character, the '–' is discarded. If the first character after an encoded sequence is a '–', it is preceded by another '–' so that the actual '–' is not discarded. Thus, the '–' character is used as a terminator for encoded sequences. This is necessary when the character following the encoded sequence would otherwise be considered part of it.

Another special case is '+–'. This can be used to encode the '+' character.

The space, tag, CR, and LF characters can be directly mapped to US-ASCII, but special care is needed. If a particular content transfer encoding is used, the characters must be handled according to its rules.

When generating the `charset` parameter, message composition software should set its value to the lowest value that specifies a correct charset. For example, if a message composed in German contains none of the additional characters in ISO-8859-1 and can be completely represented using US-ASCII characters, the `charset` parameter should not be set to `iso-8859-1`. Not all MUAs can natively handle all charsets and they often resort to external programs to present the message to a user. Thus, the user could be presented with a needless invocation of an external program if the charset is overspecified.

Plain

```
Content-Type: text/plain
```

The `text/plain` media type identifies an entity consisting of regular printable US-ASCII data with no structured content. With a `Content-Transfer-Encoding` field set to `7bit` and with the default `charset`, this field is analogous to the message body defined in RFC822.

Enriched

```
Content-Type: text/enriched
```

The `text/enriched` media type, defined in RFC1896 (The Text/Enriched MIME Content-Type), provides a simple markup language for creating text that has justification, color, and font changes. It was originally designed as an interim solution until a more robust alternative, like HTML or XML (Extensible Markup Language), became widely deployed.

Enriched text should look familiar to readers familiar with HTML, SGML (Standard Generalized Markup Language), or XML. Its markup tags provide a set of commands to control the appearance of text, as in the following example.

```
A Really <bold><bigger><bigger>Big</bigger></bigger></bold> Announcement!
```

This could be rendered as follows.

A Really **Big** Announcement!

TABLE 4.7   Summary of `text/enriched` Commands

Command	Description
param	Provide parameters to commands
bold	Embolden text
italic	Italicize text
underline	Underline text
smaller	Reduce size of text
bigger	Increase size of text
fixed	Use fixed-width text
fontfamily	Use specified font
color	Use specified color
center	Center text
flushleft	Left-justify text with a ragged right margin
flushright	Right-justify text with a ragged left margin
flushboth	Fully-justify text
nofill	Display text with no paragraph filling
paraindent	Control margin positions
excerpt	Display text as excerpted material
lang	Set language to one listed in RFC1766

Table 4.7 provides a summary of the markup tags available in `text/enriched` entities.

HTML

Another common media type is `text/html`. As one would expect, it is used to identify entities containing HTML data.

```
Content-Type: text/html

<html>
  <head>
    <title>A Web Page</title>
  </head>
  <body>
    <h1>The Obligatory Web Page<h1>
  </body>
</html>
```

RFC822-Headers

RFC1892 defines the `text/rfc822-headers` media type. It was originally created for use with DSN messages. The body of the entity is a message header. No parameters are defined for this media type.

```
Content-Type: text/rfc822-headers

Return-Path: <bob@flugelhorn.example.com>
Received: from flugelhorn.example.com by tuba.example.com
         with SMTP id HAA19482
         for <joe@tuba.example.com>; Mon, 4 Oct 1999 08:33:48 -0700
Received: by flugelhorn.example.com (8.8.8/8.8.8) with smtp
         id CAA17583; Mon, 4 Oct 1999 08:33:47 -0700
Date: Mon, 4 Oct 1999 08:33:45 -0700
Message-ID: <19991004083345.18492.1@flugelhorn.example.com>
From: bob@flugelhorn.example.com
To: joe@tuba.example.com
Subject: another question
X-Mailer: MondoMail v42.86
```

There is a media type defined for messages, `message/rfc822`, but it should not be used if the data is just a message header with no body.

4.4.2 Image, Audio, and Video

These three major media types handle graphic, audio, and movie data, and are relatively straightforward. Since the data is usually binary, the encoding is usually `base64`.

```
Content-Type: image/jpeg
Content-Transfer-Encoding: base64

base64-encoded jpeg data
```

RFC2046 defines a core set of media types for these categories. This set, shown in Table 4.8, is by no means exhaustive but merely an initial list.

Any unrecognized media types in these categories should be treated as `application/octet-stream`, described in Section 4.4.3. This will at least allow a user to save the data to a file.

4.4.3 Application

This major media type contains any media types related to specific application file formats. It has the largest number of subtypes of any of the major types.

TABLE 4.8   Initial Image, Audio, and Video Media Types

Media Type	Description
image/jpeg	JPEG Graphics File
image/tiff	TIFF Graphics File
audio/basic	8-bit ISDN mu-law Audio File
video/mpeg	MPEG Movie File

Octet-Stream

```
Content-Type: application/octet-stream
```

The `application/octet-stream` media type is used to indicate that an entity contains arbitrary data—a raw stream of octets. It is useful when the content type is unknown or when there is no defined media type for the data. Essentially it is a last resort for describing an entity.

Any unrecognized media type should also be treated as an `application/octet-stream` entity. All MUAs are required to understand this field. This allows any MIME type to be handled, albeit in a potentially degraded mode, regardless of whether the MUA supports a particular media type.

A few optional parameters are available for providing more detail about the entity. The `type` parameter allows information to be included about the data type in the entity. It is designed for humans rather than for machine parsing.

```
type="new 8-dimensional NP solver"
```

For data not aligned on 8-bit boundaries, a `padding` parameter is available. This can be used to specify the number of bits appended to the data to align it to an 8-bit boundary when encapsulating it into the entity.

```
padding=3
```

Two other parameters are seen occasionally in older MIME messages. The `conversions` parameter, defined in RFC1341, provides a way to specify a set of conversions applied to the data in the process of encapsulating it into an entity. It has been deprecated and should rarely be seen.

RFC1341 also defined a `name` parameter to suggest a filename for the entity. This parameter has been deprecated in favor of the `Content-Disposition` field described in Section 4.3.6.

PostScript

```
Content-Type: application/postscript
```

The `application/postscript` media type identifies the contents of an entity as PostScript code.

Because an `application/postscript` entity contains executable code, it is imperative that its contents arrive at the destination without being damaged. For this reason, it is frequently encoded with `quoted-printable` to insulate it from damage due to line length limitations and characters known to incur damage crossing external gateways.

Sometimes, it is necessary to encode the data in `base64` because of the ability of PostScript code to contain raw binary data. If the percentage of nonprintable characters is excessive, resorting to `base64` will result in a smaller encoded entity.

This media type raises a few security issues resulting from the power of PostScript. For one, the language has file operators intended to be used by printers to manage their disks, but they are often available on graphical PostScript previewers. Some of these operators, such as 'deletefile', 'renamefile', 'filenameforall', and 'file' can be used maliciously.

Secondly, the language allows changes to be made to the global environment in the printer. This allows malicious programs to interfere with printer operation.

Finally, it is possible for PostScript programs to consume large amounts of system resources, such as memory and CPU cycles. It's also possible to write PostScript code that loops indefinitely. Any of these can cause performance problems and denial-of-service attacks.

RFC2046 includes more detail on these security problems. Luckily, most PostScript previewer implementations have options to disable operations considered unsafe. Administrators should scrutinize PostScript viewers to determine whether they are being invoked in a way that will minimize these security problems.

Applefile

```
Content-Type: application/applefile
```

Files on the Mac-OS operating system are a little different than those on other operating systems, and so special media types have been defined for handling them.

A Mac-OS file consists of two parts, called forks. The data fork contains the actual data and generally corresponds to a file on other operating systems. The resource fork contains a collection of attribute/value pairs that include pieces of code, icon images, and other attributes related to the file.

Because other operating systems and networking protocols don't have multisegmented files, MAC data is usually encoded when transferred across the network. Three formats are commonly used: AppleSingle, AppleDouble, and BinHex. AppleSingle is an Apple Computers format that represents Mac-OS files as one stream of bytes. AppleDouble is a derivative of AppleSingle that separates the resource fork from the data fork. BinHex provides 7-bit encoding for Mac-OS files.

RFC1740 (MIME Encapsulation of Macintosh Files—MacMIME) defines the MIME media types `application/applefile` and `multipart/appledouble`. The former is used to encapsulate AppleSingle data; the latter, to encapsulate AppleDouble data.

This section describes how AppleSingle data is encapsulated in a MIME entity. Encapsulating AppleDouble requires the use of a multipart entity, so it is described in Section 4.4.5. BinHex is described in the section following this one.

An AppleSingle file contains the filename and file type embedded in the data. However, a `name` parameter is provided for the `Content-Type` field so a hint can be provided to the user on the receiving end. This is particularly useful if the receiving MUA doesn't natively support Apple files. Also, an AppleSingle file contains binary data, so `base64` encoding might need to be used.

```
Content-Type: application/applefile;
            name="My Trans-Am"
Content-Transfer-Encoding: base64

AppleSingle file data
```

For interested developers, Appendix A of RFC1740 contains a description of the AppleSingle format.

Despite the fact that this media type allows native Apple files to be safely transmitted in email messages, the normal media types should be used whenever possible. For example, if the data is a JPEG file, it should be sent as an `image/jpeg` entity.

Mac-binhex40

BinHex 4.0 has been a popular method for encoding native Mac-OS files for transport. RFC1741 (MIME Content Type for BinHex Encoded Files) defines an `application/mac-binhex40` media type for encapsulating this data format in a MIME entity.

This media type is a variation of `application/applefile`, except that no encoding is necessary since the data is already safe for transport.

```
Content-Type: application/mac-binhex40;
              name="ta.hqx"

BinHex 4.0 data
```

For interested developers, Appendix A of RFC1741 includes a description of BinHex encoding. As with the `application/applefile` media type, traditional MIME media types should be used if at all possible.

4.4.4 Message

This major type provides a category for entities consisting of email messages.

RFC822

```
Content-Type: message/rfc822
```

The `message/rfc822` content type provides a convenient way to encapsulate a mail message inside another mail message. All MIME-conformant MUAs must support it.

As an example of this encapsulation, take the following message.

```
From: larry@ictus.example.com
To: bob@flugelhorn.example.com
Date: Sun, 3 Oct 1999 14:45:51 -0700

We have a problem!
The freight-forwarder lost the truck.
```

Instead of using one of the encapsulation techniques described in Section 2.4.3, it's possible to encapsulate the message inside another message.

```
From: bob@flugelhorn.example.com
To: joe@tuba.example.com
Date: Sat, 3 Oct 1998 15:36:26 -0700
Subject: larry found a problem
MIME-Version: 1.0
Content-Type: message/rfc822

From: larry@ictus.example.com
To: bob@flugelhorn.example.com
Date: Sun, 3 Oct 1999 14:45:51 -0700

We have a problem!
The freight-forwarder lost the truck.
```

This media type provides a convenient way to encapsulate messages when forwarding them to other recipients. As described in Section 2.4.3, encapsulating forwarded messages can be problematic. Using this media type allows encapsulated messages to be programmatically extracted in a consistent manner, without the complications mentioned for the other techniques. If additional commentary needs to be added, it's possible to bundle both the forwarded message and the commentary in a `multipart/mixed` entity. Section 4.4.5 describes this in detail.

Only a subset of the `Content-Transfer-Encoding` values can be used with this media type: `7bit`, `8bit`, and `binary`. At first glance, this might seem a bit odd. Why limit the encoding allowed? The thing to remember here is that the payload is an RFC822 message. Since, by definition, that data will already be in a format acceptable for email transport, possibly with its body encoded in `quoted-printable` or `base64`, there is no need to add another layer of encoding.

Partial

The `message/partial` media type provides a way to split a large entity into multiple pieces. Each part can be transmitted separately and reassembled on the receiving end, providing a way to send large chunks of data in situations where intermediate systems have limitations on message size.

Like `message/rfc822` media types, this type limits the allowable values for the `Content-Transfer-Encoding` field. In this case, the field value can only be `7bit`.

Another limitation is that fragments must be split on line boundaries. This makes sense considering that a boundary string must start at the beginning of a line. The mechanics necessary to allow splitting in the middle of a line would present an unnecessary complication.

Three parameters are used with this media type. An `id` parameter identifies the members of a set of `message/partial` entities. Each member has the parameter set to the same value, the syntax for which is identical to the one for a `Message-ID`.

This unique identifier allows MUA software to identify each fragment in a set of partials.

```
id="29128jas28@tuba.example.com"
```

A `total` parameter provides an integer to indicate how many `message/partial` entities to expect. This parameter must be present in the final entity. It is optional in the other entities, but it's not a bad idea to include it.

```
total=3
```

A `number` parameter provides an integer to indicate which position a fragment occupies in a sequence of entities. The numbering starts with 1.

```
number=2
```

These three parameters are designed so that it is possible for an MUA to reassemble the message regardless of the order in which the fragments are received.

As an example, the following two messages contain the pieces of a 2-part `message/partial` message.

```
From: joe@tuba.example.com
To: bob@flugelhorn.example.com
Date: Mon, 15 Mar 1999 16:03:14 -0700
Message-ID: <1998072314021511.1@tuba.example.com>
Subject: video of meeting (multiple parts)
MIME-Version: 1.0
Content-Type: message/partial; id="28a3ja198a@tuba.example.com";
              number=1; total=2

Message-ID: <1998072314022512.1@tuba.example.com>
Subject: video of meeting
MIME-Version: 1.0
Content-type: video/mpeg
Content-Transfer-Encoding: base64

first half of base64-encoded mpeg data
```

A few things are worth pointing out about this example. Notice the lack of content transfer encoding in the top header. It isn't necessary because the underlying message has already been encoded in a format suitable for transport. Also notice that both the outer and inner message headers have different `Message-ID` fields. This is because they are distinct messages.

Compared to the first fragment, subsequent fragments are fairly simple. The second half of the data would look something like the following. It simply consists of a regular message header and a body that contains the second data fragment.

```
From: joe@tuba.example.com
To: bob@flugelhorn.example.com
Date: Mon, 15 Mar 1999 16:03:14 -0700
Message-ID: <1998072314021511.2@tuba.example.com>
Subject: video of meeting
MIME-Version: 1.0
Content-Type: message/partial; id="28a3ja198a@tuba.example.com";
              number=2; total=2

second half of base64-encoded mpeg data
```

The final message is assembled by combining information for each of the fragments. The data from the two fragments is extracted and combined into a new message.

To assemble the header, all the fields from the first partial, except the `Subject`, `Message-ID`, `Encrypted`,[4] `MIME-Version`, and `Content-` fields, are combined with the corresponding fields in the first fragment entity to create the header of the final message. The fields of interest from the header of the first `message/partial` consist of the following.

```
From: joe@tuba.example.com
To: bob@flugelhorn.example.com
Date: Mon, 15 Mar 1999 16:03:14 -0700
```

Notice how none of the MIME headers are carried forward. The same is true for the `Subject` and `Message-ID`. These fields will be provided by the header in the entity of the first fragment.

```
Message-ID: <1998072314022512.1@tuba.example.com>
Subject: video of meeting
MIME-Version: 1.0
Content-type: video/mpeg
Content-Transfer-Encoding: base64
```

The body of the new message is a concatenation of the bodies from the complete set of message fragments. Combining the body parts and merging the two sets of headers result in the following message.

---

[4] Even though the `Encrypted` field has been deprecated, it's mentioned in RFC2046 for thoroughness.

```
From: joe@tuba.example.com
To: bob@flugelhorn.example.com
Date: Mon, 15 Mar 1999 16:03:14 -0700
Message-ID: <1998072314022512.1@tuba.example.com>
Subject: video of meeting
MIME-Version: 1.0
Content-type: video/mpeg
Content-Transfer-Encoding: base64

first half of base64-encoded mpeg data
second half of base64-encoded mpeg data
```

What is extracted can be any valid MIME-enabled RFC822 message.

External-Body

```
Content-Type: message/external-body
```

The `message/external-body` media type provides a way to access information outside of the message. In this case, instead of the actual data, the entity contains information that describes how to retrieve the data. This media type is a particularly useful alternative to `message/partial` if the information can be made available using one of the mechanisms supported by the `message/external-body` media type.

The body for this media type is slightly different from that for the other media categories. In this case, it contains another header that contains MIME fields related to the data being referred to. Following the extra header is a blank line and a body, just like a normal message. Here the body isn't real; it's a *phantom body,* which only one of the access-types, `mail-server`, uses.

```
Content-Type: message/external-body;
              access-type=local-file;
              name="/home/joe/sounds/snurf.au"

Content-Type: audio/basic
Content-Transfer-Encoding: binary
Content-ID: <19990302143214.3@tuba.example.com>

Phantom Body
```

The `Content-Type`, `Content-Transfer-Encoding`, and `Content-ID` fields are the most common fields used in this subheader. The `Content-Type` field is optional if the media type is plain text and the charset is US-ASCII. Content transfer encoding is also optional if the encoding is 7-bit.

The `Content-ID` field is required in all cases. It is useful for MUAs that cache information from messages, where the field value is used as a key into the cache. Keeping a cache allows the MUA to minimize the retrieval of data already retrieved.

Several parameters are used with this media type. The most fundamental is `access-type`, which indicates what method should be used to access the external data.

```
access-type=ftp
```

An optional `expiration` parameter is available to specify when the external data is expected to expire. The syntax for the value is the same as the *date-time* construct in RFC822.

```
expiration="Tue, 4 May 1999 13:23:41 -0700"
```

Since the expiration date is generated on the sending machine, the information is based on the date on that machine. MUAs and users should be aware of this when dealing with the information.

One final note about this parameter—its absence doesn't mean the data will never expire; it just means no parameter was specified.

Another parameter, `size`, is available as an option. It provides a way to indicate the size of the data. The size is measured in octets and is calculated before any content encoding is performed. The purpose of this parameter is to provide information to recipients to help assess the impact of retrieving the data.

One more optional parameter is available, `permission`, which indicates whether the recipient can expect to be able to update the data. The value can be 'read' or 'read-write', and the default permission is 'read'. As with many other parameters, the value is case-insensitive.

In addition to informing a user whether the data is writable, this parameter can also impact caching in MUAs. If the data is read-only, the caching algorithms can assume that it isn't likely to change. If a user retrieves the information via the MUA, a cache might be implemented to store the information in case the user wants to retrieve it at a later date. Normally, the data's expiration date would be the primary factor in deciding when to flush it from the cache. On the other hand, if the data is marked writable, an MUA can decide to ignore a locally cached copy of it, because it is unknown whether the user has updated it.

Access-Type=FTP

The FTP access-type is used to specify a file that is accessible via FTP. It requires two parameters: `site` specifies the site where the data is located, and `name` specifies the name of the file to retrieve.

```
Content-Type: message/external-body;
              access-type=ftp;
              site=ftp.example.com;
              name=README
```

A file is often located in a subdirectory. Because of the different notations used for directories on different operating systems, the directory is specified as part of the filename. The `directory` parameter provides this information, simplifying the processing of the filename and directory information.

```
directory="/pub/packages"
```

FTP also has commands to change the mode used to transfer the information. These modes are 'ascii', 'ebcdic', 'image', and 'local$n$'. A `mode` parameter is provided to specify the mode of transfer. Its value is the same as those specified in FTP.

To illustrate the use of parameters, here is an example that uses most of them.

```
Content-Type: message/external-body;
              access-type=ftp;
              site=ftp.example.com;
              name=mondomail.tgz;
              directory="/pub/packages";
              mode=image;
              size=3829381
```

This field could be translated into the following FTP dialog.

```
$ ftp ftp.example.com
Connected to ftp.example.com.
220 ftp.example.com FTP server ready
Name: joe
331 Password required for joe.
Password: xxxxxxxx
230 User joe logged in.
ftp> cd /pub/packages
250 CWD command successful.
ftp> image
220 Type set to I.
ftp> get mondomail.tgz
200 PORT command successful.
250 Opening BINARY mode data connection for mondomail.tgz.
226 Transfer complete.
3829381 bytes received in 5.04 secs
ftp> quit
221 Goodbye.
$
```

With the exception of the login and password data, the entire dialog is controlled by the parameters specified in the `Content-Type` field. For security reasons, there are no parameters for including the login and password input. An MUA implementing this feature must prompt the user for the information.

Access-Type=ANON-FTP

This access-type is exactly like the `ftp` access-type, except that the FTP dialog will be carried out as an anonymous FTP session.

Using the previous example, if the `access-type` is set to `anon-ftp`, the login and password information can be replaced with the following.

```
Name: anonymous
Password: joe@tuba.example.com
```

Access-Type=TFTP

This access-type references data available via TFTP (Trivial File Transfer Protocol), defined in RFC783 (TFTP Protocol (revision 2)). It isn't used very much. Other than the protocol, the only differences between this access-type and the `FTP` access-type are the login sequence and the values of the `mode` parameter. The valid `mode` values are 'netascii', 'octet', and 'mail', with the default being `netascii`.

Access-Type=Local-File

This access-type is used to reference a file on the local machine. It provides two additional parameters: `name`, which specifies the name of the file to retrieve, and `site`, which specifies a mask to indicate where the local file access is valid. The value of the `site` parameter can be either an FQDN or a wildcard domain name. If the client machine name matches that value, the local file access is valid. Wildcards allow the '*' character to be used in a domain name to indicate a match on *anything;* thus, '*.example.com' matches anything inside the `example.com` domain. Theoretically, a single '*' character may be used to match all machines everywhere, but it's unlikely to be valid outside a specific site.

```
Content-Type: message/external-body;
              access-type=local-file;
              name="/net/home/bob/status/current.txt";
              site="*.example.com";
              expiration="Tue, 11 May 1999 23:59:59 -0700"
```

In this example, the entity is intended only for machines located inside the `example.com` domain. Also, it is due to expire on May 11, 1999, right before midnight, Mountain Standard Time.

Access-Type=Mail-Server

This access-type is used to reference data available from a mail server, typically a mailing list processor or an email-based data archive. It allows a piece of email to be used as instructions for retrieving a piece of information from the server or performing a transaction on the server.

A `server` parameter is required to specify the email address to send the mail server request to. Its value needs to be a valid RFC822 *addr-spec*.

```
server="lists@example.com"
```

Since an unquoted '@' is not allowed in a parameter value, a standard Internet email address needs to be quoted.

An optional `subject` parameter is provided to set the value of the `Subject` field sent to the mail server.

```
subject="send index"
```

In this case, since a SPACE character is present in the value, it needs to be quoted.

There is no standard for interacting with mail servers, so this media type doesn't provide a set of parameters to configure the dialog. Instead, it uses the phantom body to hold mail server command text.

```
Content-Type: message/external-body;
              access-type=mail-server;
              server="lists@example.com"

Content-Type: text/plain
Content-ID: <1998041562071534.2@example.com>

get list-of-lists
```

To initiate a data retrieval, the MUA generates a new piece of mail using the information from the message. The `server` parameter is used to populate the `To` field; if a `subject` parameter is present, it is used to populate a `Subject` field. If the phantom body isn't empty, it is used to populate the body of the new message. The `Content-ID` field is typically used to keep a record of outstanding retrieval requests. When a response from a mail server is received, the MUA can refer to a list of outstanding retrieval requests and check off the appropriate entry.

In the previous example, the following partial message would result.

```
To: lists@example.com

get list-of-lists
```

Additional fields, such as `From`, `Date`, and `Message-ID` are also inserted to make a complete message. At this point, the message is ready to be sent to the mail server.

Access-Type=URL

Newcomers to email might wonder why there are so many access-types provided, when most could be replaced with a reference to a URL (Uniform Resource Locator). When MIME was first created, in 1992, the World Wide Web was not as widely deployed as it is now. In 1996, RFC2017 (Definition of the URL MIME External-Body Access-Type) was created to rectify the problem of not having a URL access-type for `message/external-body` entities.

This access-type requires a `url` parameter to specify how the data can be retrieved. The normal syntax for a URL is defined in RFC1738 (Uniform Resource Locators). There is a slight complication with standard URLs when used in MIME parameters—they can be an arbitrary length and contain arbitrary characters. Because MIME parameters are subject to length and charset limitations, a URL is altered to fit into a form acceptable for email.

- All occurrences of nonprintable characters, SPACE characters, '"', '\', and 8-bit characters are checked to make sure they are encoded.
- The resulting URL is broken into substrings of 40 or fewer characters.
- The list of substrings is inserted into the `url` parameter, with each substring separated by RFC822 linear whitespace.
- The parameter value is then quoted because it contains whitespace and the *tspecial* characters ':', and '/'.

After this transformation, the URL is in a format suitable for folding.

```
Content-Type: message/external-body;
              access-type=url;
              url="http://www.example.com/support/docs
                  /MondoMail/index.html"

Content-Type: text/html

Phantom Body
```

To extract a URL, the process is essentially reversed, except that the final URL does not need to have any unsafe characters decoded.

```
http://www.example.com/support/docs/MondoMail/index.html
```

Access-Type=x-*

In addition to the defined access-types, MIME also provides a way to add experimental extensions. As with many elements in MIME, any access-type prefixed with 'x-' is considered experimental. This prefix will never be used in a standard access-type.

Delivery-Status

```
Content-Type: message/delivery-status
```

Section 3.5.6 described an SMTP extension for providing DSN reports. Part of the extension defines a `message/delivery-status` media type, which is defined in RFC1894. This media type is used in a `multipart/report` entity, described in Section 4.4.5, to provide a machine-readable delivery report.

To explain this media type, a few terms must be introduced. The MTA to which an MUA submits a message is called the *original MTA*. An MTA that generates a DSN is called the *reporting MTA*. And the MTA that gave the message to the reporting MTA is called the *received-from MTA*. If a message cannot be transferred to a particular MTA, that MTA is called the *remote MTA*. Figure 4.5 illustrates the relationship between these machines.

The `Content-Type` field for a delivery report uses no parameters. In addition, 7-bit data is usually contained in the entity, so content transfer encoding is normally not needed.

The delivery report information is contained in a set of headers in the entity body. The formatting rules for these fields are the same as for normal RFC822 header fields, including folding and parenthetical comments. In addition, most of the values in the fields are case-insensitive.

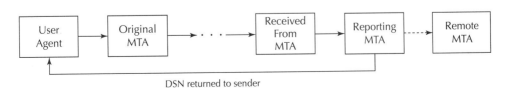

FIGURE 4.5 Delivery Report Machines

Since the fields must be in 7-bit US-ASCII, it is sometimes necessary to encode data in them. Some require *xtext* encoding, which is described in Section 3.5.6.

The fields are separated into two categories: those associated with the message and those associated with specific recipients.

```
Content-Type: message/delivery-status

per-message fields

per-recipient fields

...
```

The fields in the *per-message* section provide a context for the DSN message, which includes an indication of the original envelope identifier, a date field, and a field identifying the various MTAs related to the delivery report. The syntax for this section is as follows.

```
per-message-fields = [original-envelope-id-field CRLF]
                     reporting-mta-field CRLF
                     [dsn-gateway-field CRLF]
                     [received-from-mta-field CRLF]
                     [arrival-date-field CRLF]
                     *(extension-field CRLF)
```

The only required field is `Reporting-MTA`, which indicates the MTA that attempted to perform the operation described in the DSN.

```
reporting-mta-field = "Reporting-MTA:" mta-name-type ";" mta-name
mta-name-type       = atom
mta-name            = *text
```

The *mta-name-type* indicates the type of name being listed in the field. The *mta-name* subfield contains the name of the MTA and is formatted according to the value contained in *mta-name-type*. If the reporting MTA can determine its FQDN via DNS, the *mta-name-type* subfield must contain dns. In this case, the *mta-name* subfield will contain the FQDN of the reporting MTA.

```
Reporting-MTA: dns; tuba.example.com
```

If the reporting MTA cannot determine its Internet name via DNS, *mta-name* can contain a string identifying the MTA, but *mta-name-type* must *not* contain dns.

In this case, RFC1891 recommends populating *mta-name-type* with `x-local-hostname`.

If an SMTP transaction included an `envid` parameter supplied with the `mail` command, the delivery report must include an `Original-Envelope-ID` field.

```
original-envelope-id-field = "Original-Envelope-ID:" envelope-id
envelope-id                = *text
```

If the transaction didn't include an `envid` parameter, this field is not included in the report.

```
Original-Envelope-ID: 612E01AC4
```

While most of the fields are case-insensitive, this one is not. The case of the envelope identifier in the *envid* parameter must be preserved. Additionally, an `envid` parameter can be encoded as *xtext*. This field is not encoded, so an MTA needs to decode any *xtext* encoding when transferring the information to the report field.

If the DSN report is a translation of a status notification from a foreign email system, a `DSN-Gateway` field must be provided. This indicates the name of the machine that performed the transaction from the foreign status notification format into the Internet DSN format.

```
dsn-gateway-field = "DSN-Gateway:" mta-name-type ";" mta-name
```

The format of the *mta-name-type* and *mta-name* subfields is similar to that for the `Reporting-MTA` field, except that *mta-name-type* is typically `smtp`.

The `Received-From-MTA` field indicates which MTA gave the report MTA the message.

```
received-from-mta-field =
        "Received-From-MTA:" mta-name-type ";" mta-name
```

The format of the subfields is the same as that of the `DSN-Gateway` field, including the use of `smtp` in the *mta-name-type* subfield.

The *mta-name* should be populated with the domain name provided with the `helo` or `ehlo` command. The exact value should be used, which includes preserving the case of the value, since case is significant in some mail systems. In addition, RFC1894 recommends including the address of the machine in a parenthetical comment with the *mta-name*.

```
Received-From-MTA: smtp; flugelhorn.example.com ([10.1.1.2])
```

This field is roughly equivalent to a `from` subfield of a regular `Received` field, except that it's designed to be compatible with the DSN extension.

An optional `Arrival-Date` field can be used in the per-message set of fields to indicate the date and time the reporting MTA received the message.

```
arrival-date-field = "Arrival-Date:" date-time
```

The format of *date-time* is the same as that of the *date-time* described in Section 2.7, with one exception—the time-zone must be numeric.

```
Arrival-Date: Mon, 4 Oct 1999 08:33:45 -0700
```

After the defined per-message fields, MTAs can add extension fields. These follow the same format as that of the `X-` extension fields for mail messages, described in Section 2.3.7.

To show how these per-message fields can be combined, the following example presents a typical set.

```
Original-Envelope-ID: 481F92ER0
Reporting-MTA: dns; ictus.example.com
Received-From-MTA: smtp; flugelhorn.example.com
Arrival-Date: Sun, 3 Oct 1999 14:45:51 -0700
```

A DSN contains information about delivery attempts for one or more recipients. Each recipient is represented in a set of `per-recipient fields`.

```
per-recipient-fields = [original-recipient-field CRLF]
                       final-recipient-field CRLF
                       action-field CRLF
                       status-field CRLF
                       [remote-mta-field CRLF]
                       [diagnostic-code-field CRLF]
                       [last-attempt-date-field CRLF]
                       [final-log-id-field CRLF]
                       [will-retry-until-field CRLF]
                       *(extension-field CRLF)
```

If an `orcpt` parameter was provided with the `rcpt` command, an `Original-Recipient-Field` must be present.

```
original-recipient-field =
        "Original-Recipient:" addr-type ";" generic-address
```

The *addr-type* subfield indicates the type of address contained in *generic-address*. Both subfields are normally populated with the values contained in the `orcpt` parameter from the SMTP `rcpt` command.

```
Original-Recipient: rfc822; joe@example.com
```

The above example is the result of creating an `Original-Recipient` field from the following `rcpt` command.

```
rcpt to:<joe@tuba.example.com> orcpt=rfc822;joe@example.com
```

A value of `unknown` should be used if the *addr-type* cannot be determined. If an `orcpt` parameter was not provided in the SMTP transaction, the field should not be present in the DSN report.

A `Final-Recipient` field is used to identify a recipient for a particular set of `per-recipient` fields. This field is required.

```
final-recipient-field = "Final-Recipient:" addr-type ";" generic-address
```

The *addr-type* subfield indicates what type of address is contained in the field. In the case of Internet email, this should be `rfc822`. The *generic-address* subfield contains the mailbox address of the recipient provided in the `rcpt` command when the delivery was attempted. It must appear exactly as presented there. For example, the previous `rcpt` example would result in the following `Final-Recipient` field.

```
Final-Recipient: rfc822; joe@tuba.example.com
```

An `Action` field indicates the type of action the DSN is reporting for the recipient listed in the `Final-Recipient` field. This field is also required.

```
action-field = "Action:" action-value
action-value = "failed" / "delayed" / "delivered" /
               "relayed" / "expanded"
```

These actions correspond to the five notification types mentioned in Section 3.5.6.

```
Action: failed
```

The third required field is `Status`, which indicates the delivery status of a message for a recipient.

```
status-field = "Status:" status-code
status-code = DIGIT "." 1*3DIGIT "." 1*3DIGIT
```

The *status-code* value is populated with an RFC2034 enhanced status code. Whitespace and comments are not allowed within it, but a comment is often used after it to convey the text portion of the status response.

```
Status: 5.1.1 (bad destination mailbox address)
```

A `Remote-MTA` field can be included to indicate the name of the remote MTA from which the reporting machine received a delivery status.

```
remote-mta-field = "Remote-MTA:" mta-name-type ";" mta-name
```

The field contents are similar to the contents of a `Reporting-MTA` field. This field is used only if the reporting MTA received status from a remote machine.

```
Remote-MTA: flugelhorn.example.com
```

For failed or delayed transactions, a `Diagnostic-Code` field is provided to indicate the exact status message issued by the MTA.

```
diagnostic-code-field = "Diagnostic-Code:" diagnostic-type ";" *text
```

While the `Status` field contains a machine-readable enhanced status code, the *text* in it conveys the actual text emitted by an MTA for a delay or failure. This additional information may be helpful for email administrators when diagnosing problems. The *diagnostic-type* subfield indicates what type of MTA provided the information. It is usually `smtp`.

```
Diagnostic-Code: smtp; 550 mailbox "moab" does not exist
```

The `Last-Attempt-Date` can be used to indicate the date and time of the most recent attempt to deliver, relay, or gateway a message.

```
last-attempt-date-field = "Last-Attempt-Date:" date-time
```

As with `Arrival-Date`, the format of *date-time* is the same as for a message `Date` field.

```
Last-Attempt-Date: Sun, 3 Oct 1999 18:45:58 -0700
```

As an extra piece of information for email administrators, a `Final-Log-ID` field can be added to the recipient.

```
final-log-id-field = "Final-Log-ID:" *text
```

RFC1894 contains a couple of small errors regarding `Final-Log-ID`. The syntax for a per-recipient field in Section 2.3 of that document doesn't list it, and a formatting error between Sections 2.3.7 and 2.3.8 makes its description hard to find.

```
Final-Log-ID: 4C3D03157
```

If a message is delayed, a `Will-Retry-Until` field can be added to indicate when the MTA will give up attempting to deliver it.

```
will-retry-until-field = "Will-Retry-Until:" date-time
```

To illustrate how these fields are combined, the following example shows a complete delivery status entity.

```
Content-Type: message/delivery-status

Original-Envelope-ID: 481F92ER0
Reporting-MTA: dns; ictus.example.com
Received-From-MTA: smtp; dorm.example.edu
Arrival-Date: Sun, 3 Oct 1999 14:45:51 -0700

Original-Recipient: rfc822; joe@example.com
Final-Recipient: rfc822; joe@tuba.example.com
Action: delayed
Status: 4.3.1
Diagnostic-Code: 450 Mailbox full
Last-Attempt-Date: Sun, 3 Oct 1999 18:45:58 -0700
Will-Retry-Until: Fri, 8 Oct 1999 14:45:51 -0700

Final-Recipient: rfc822; moab@tuba.example.com
Action: failed
Status: 5.1.1
Diagnostic-Code: 550 mailbox "moab" does not exist
```

This media type provides a machine-readable format that allows MUAs, and other programs with a need to parse the information, to unambiguously extract delivery status information sent from an MTA.

4.4.5 Multipart

The `multipart` major type provides a way to encapsulate multiple entities in a single entity. Figure 4.1 illustrated this graphically.

The body of a multipart entity consists of an optional preamble, one or more body parts—each preceded by a boundary line—and an optional epilogue.

A boundary line consists of two dashes followed by a unique string and optional whitespace. The unique string is specified with a boundary parameter in the `Content-Type` field. It should be set to a value that, when combined with the dashes, will not occur in the body part.

```
Content-Type: multipart/mixed; boundary=zxf918
```

The syntax of the boundary parameter is designed to be relatively immune to issues with external email gateways.

```
boundary       = 0*69bchars bcharnospace
bchars         = bcharnospace / " "
bcharnospace   = DIGIT / ALPHA / "'" / "(" / ")" / "+" / "-" / "," /
                 "-" / "." / "/" / ":" / "=" / "?"
```

To understand the definition, imagine that the definition for boundary were as follows.

```
boundary = 0*70bcharnospace
```

This is like the real definition, except that instead of 69 *bchars* and one *bcharnospace,* it consists of 70 *bcharnospace* characters. The definition of *bcharnospace* is simple enough—it is a list of allowable characters. Because trailing whitespace is sometimes added by external email gateways, the boundary string needs to be defined in such a way that trailing whitespace added by gateways can be identified and ignored. To accomplish this, the first 69 characters are allowed to be either *bcharnospace* or spaces. The final character must be a *bcharnospace,* which does not contain a space. This might seem overly complex, but it is essential to providing a boundary string that is relatively immune to damage while being sent through external gateways.

While whitespace is allowed in boundary strings, experience has shown it to be problematic. It is prone to parsing errors in email software and should be avoided, since it is easy to generate boundary strings without it.

With the boundary value defined, a boundary line can be created by combining the boundary parameter with two leading dashes.

```
--zxf918
```

The boundary line preceding each part separates each part from the previous one.

```
--zxf918
body part 1
--zxf918
body part 2
```

To signal the end of a collection of body parts, a closing boundary line follows the final one. It consists of a regular boundary string followed by two dashes.

```
--zxf918
body part 1
--zxf918
body part 2
--zxf918--
```

The body parts contain a looser form of RFC822 messages; they don't necessarily require RFC822 fields. One interesting characteristic of this looser form is that header portions can be blank if no entity fields need to be provided. A blank line must still be present so that the MUA can tell that there is no header.

```
--zxf918
```

headerless body part 1
```
--zxf918
```

headerless body part 2
--zxf918--

The preamble and epilogue are dead space on either side of the body parts. The epilogue is typically left empty, while the preamble is often used to convey information to non-MIME users, most commonly that the email message is formatted using MIME.

```
Content-Type: multipart/mixed; boundary=zxf918

This is a MIME-encapsulated message.

--zxf918
body part 1
--zxf918
body part 2
--zxf918--
```

Because a body part is an RFC822 message, multipart entities can also nest. The following example illustrates one `multipart/mixed` entity embedded inside another one.

```
Content-Type: multipart/mixed; boundary=zxf918

--zxf918
outer body part 1
--zxf918
Content-Type: multipart/mixed; boundary=qvz412

--qvz412
inner body part 1
--qvz412
inner body part 2
--qvz412--
--zxf918
outer body part 2
--zxf918--
```

If a `Content-Disposition` field is used with multipart entities, the field applies to the entire set of parts.

As with the `message/rfc822` media type, `7bit`, `8bit`, and `binary` are the only content transfer encoding values that are allowed in the upper level of a multipart entity.

Mixed

The `multipart/mixed` entity is, by far, the most common multipart entity encountered. For interpreting it, an MUA considers each of its body parts discrete, with no specific relationship to the others, even though there might actually be relationships between them.

Multipart subtypes not supported by an MUA should be treated as a `multipart/mixed` entity. This allows the MUA to present the data to the user, albeit in a degraded mode, rather than failing to work. All MUAs must support the `multipart/mixed` media type, which ensures that all multipart entities can at least be presented to the user.

Alternative

The `multipart/alternative` media type is used for a collection of parts that are alternative formats for the same piece of original data. In general, the parts are listed in increasing order of preference; in other words, the most preferable is last. The MUA is allowed to pick the best choice for the particular environment or user preference.

```
To: joe@tuba.example.com
From: larry@ictus.example.com
Subject: System Status
MIME-Version: 1.0
Content-Type: multipart/alternative; boundary=ahD03

--ahD03
Content-Type: text/plain; charset=us-ascii

                        Everything is broke.

--ahD03
Content-Type: text/enriched

<center><color><param>red</param>Everything is broke.</color>
</center>

--ahD03--
```

In this example, the `multipart/alternative` entity contains a plain-text and an enriched-text entity. The latter will be presented to the user if the MUA supports it; otherwise, the MUA will present the `text/plain` entity as a fall-back.

In addition to the `boundary` parameter defined in RFC2046, RFC1766 added another parameter to a multipart alternative entity, `differences`, which assists MUAs in differentiating alternative entities when the `Content-Language` field is used.

This parameter can contain one of two values, `Content-Type` and `Content-Language`, which control the technique an MUA should use when determining which subpart of a multipart alternative entity to display. If no `differences` parameter is present, the default is `Content-Type`.

```
Content-Type: multipart/alternative;
              boundary=qpa94hj1as290uf;
              differences=Content-Language;
Content-Language: en, de, fr

--qpa94hj1as290uf
Content-Language: en

English text
--qpa94hj1as290uf
Content-Language: fr

French text
--qpa94hj1as290uf
Content-Language: de

German text
--qpa94hj1as290uf--
```

In this example, three alternative entities are provided, with `Content-Language` being used to control which one is displayed to the user.

As with the `multipart/mixed` media type, MUAs are required to support `multipart/alternative`. They are also required to avoid presenting the redundant body parts. Unfortunately, it's not uncommon to find simpler MIME implementations that do not support it.

Digest

The `multipart/digest` media type is used to encapsulate a set of `message/rfc822` entities in one mail message. MIME-conformant MUAs are required to implement it. It provides a reliable mechanism for encapsulating digests of email messages, which were mentioned in Section 2.1.1.

```
From: joe@tuba.example.com
To: bob@flugelhorn.example.com
Date: Tue, 16 Jun 1998 15:32:15 -0700
Subject: digest of my conversation with larry
MIME-Version: 1.0
Content-Type: multipart/digest;
              boundary="sjf9381"

--sjf9381

From: larry@ictus.example.com
To: joe@tuba.example.com
Date: Mon, 15 Jun 1998 07:02:23 -0700
Subject: problem with server

data

--sjf9381

From: joe@tuba.example.com
To: larry@ictus.example.com
Date: Mon, 15 Jun 1998 07:19:56 -0700
Subject: Re: problem with server

data

--sjf9381--
```

This example shows a `multipart/digest` entity containing two `message/rfc822` entities. The most important thing to notice is the presence of a blank line following each boundary line. Remembering that a body part contains a looser form of RFC822 messages, note that the digest body part in this example is actually a headerless message. The blank line is the separator between a blank header and the entity body. Compare this to the contents of a `message/external-body` entity, particularly one with a mail-server access-type.

The default value for the `Content-Type` field in a multipart digest is `message/rfc822` rather than `text/plain`. This means there is no need to include anything in the header; therefore, the header can be empty. It must, however, still exist.

Although the default media type for a digest body entity part is `message/rfc822`, it's possible for the media type to be set to something else.

```
--sjf9381
Content-Type: text/plain

data

--sjf9381--
```

Nevertheless, this shouldn't be necessary because there are other media types more suitable to this type of structure.

Parallel

```
Content-Type: multipart/parallel
```

The `multipart/parallel` media type is structured the same as `multipart/mixed` except that its parts are intended to be processed in parallel. This media type is rarely used, and many MUAs do not support it.

Report

The SMTP DSN extension, described in Section 3.5.6, uses MIME to format messages when generating delivery notifications. The top-level entity for these messages is a `multipart/report`, which is defined in RFC1892.

The syntax for the media type is similar to that for the `multipart/mixed`. Two parameters are required, `boundary` and `report-type`. There are no optional parameters.

The `boundary` parameter is the same as the one used for a `multipart/mixed` entity. The `report-type` describes what type of delivery report is contained in the entity.

This entity has two or three subparts. The first contains a textual description of the delivery report and is intended for human consumption. Thus, the information should be easy for users to understand. Intended for users with MUAs that don't support the `multipart/report` media type, this subpart can, in general, have any MIME content type, charset, or language settings. In fact, in international environments it's even possible for it to be a `multipart/alternative`, with the error message in multiple languages.

The second subpart also contains a report, but is machine-parsable for automated processing. The third subpart, which is optional, can contain either a copy of the message or a copy of its headers. The `report-type` parameter in the top-level `Content-Type` field specifies what type of entity is present in the subpart. The most common type of report is a `message/delivery-status`. In this case, the `report-type` parameter is set to `delivery-status`.

```
Content-Type: multipart/report;
              boundary=ha0qweh123;
              report-type=delivery-status
```

Other report types can be defined through the IETF standards process. For example, RFC2298 (An Extensible Message Format for Message Disposition Notifications) defines a media type for providing message receipt notifications.

The optional third subpart can contain either a `message/rfc822` or a `text/rfc822-headers` entity. It's technically possible for the original message to be identified through the `Original-Recipient` and `Original-Envelope-ID` fields in the second subpart. This third subpart was provided for when the sender doesn't provide an envelope identifier.

The following example shows the overall structure as it appears in a message.

```
Content-Type: multipart/report;
              boundary=ha0qweh123;
              report-type=delivery-status

--ha0qweh123

human-readable text message
--ha0qweh123
Content-Type: message/delivery-status

per-message delivery-status fields

per-recipient delivery-status fields sets
--ha0qweh123
Content-Type: message/rfc822

message
--ha0qweh123--
```

Appledouble

Section 4.4.3 discussed some of the possible ways native Mac-OS files can be safely transmitted via MIME. The primary issue is that Mac-OS files have a data fork and a resource fork. While the AppleSingle format merges them into a single data file, the AppleDouble format is usually preferable because it allows easy access to the data fork. It can be encapsulated in MIME with the `multipart/appledouble` media type.

This media type contains two body parts. The first is an `application/applefile` entity containing the resource fork. The second contains the data fork. The content type for the second body part should be whatever is appropriate for the data.

```
Content-Type: multipart/appledouble;
              boundary=oi10asdljk123

--oi10asdljk123
Content-Type: application/applefile; name="My Trans-AM"

appledouble header data

--oi10asdljk123
Content-Type: image/png
Content-Transfer-Encoding: base64

contents of data fork

--oi10asdljk123--
```

4.4.6 Other Media Types

New media types can be registered through the IANA registration process. In addition to those described in this chapter, there are numerous media types already registered. Interested readers are strongly encouraged to review the master online list.[5]

Experimental media types can be added without resorting to the registration process by prefixing them with an 'x-'.

4.5 MESSAGE HEADER EXTENSIONS

Up to this point, the emphasis has been on using MIME with message bodies. The ability to encode and encapsulate nonprintable, non-US-ASCII data opens up many possibilities for sending it in message bodies. RFC2047 has a similar mechanism for message headers. It provides the ability to include non-US-ASCII data it in certain portions of a header. Although not as generalized as for message bodies, it is workable for solving many of RFC822's internationalization limitations.

In addition to the internationalization problems it solves, the header encoding defined in RFC2047 provides the ability to encode data in fields so it is more immune to breakage when passing through external gateways.

An encoded word consists of a sequence of initial characters, the name of the charset used, the name of the encoding scheme used, the actual encoded text, and finally a sequence of terminating characters.

```
"=?" charset "?" encoding "?" encoded-text "?="
```

---

[5] http://www.isi.edu/in-notes/iana/assignments/media-types/.

It starts with the character '=?'. The character set used in the encoding, the encoding scheme, and the encoded text come next, with '?' separating each value. The characters '?=' finish the sequence. As with many other places in email, the *charset* and *encoding* values are case-insensitive.

```
=?iso-8859-1?q?J=FCrgen_Mahler?=
```

An encoded word is limited to 75 characters, including the charset, encoding specifier, and delimiter characters, which makes the line more immune to problems with external email gateways. To cope with this limitation, it's possible to use multiple encoded words in sequence. MUAs are allowed to ignore any encoded word longer than 75 characters.

```
Subject: =?us-ascii?q?This_breaks_up_the_line,?=
         =?us-ascii?q?_but_will_annoy_recipients_if_abused.?=
```

In conformant MUAs, the preceding example will be decoded as follows.

```
Subject: This breaks up the line, but will annoy recipients if abused.
```

There is no limit to how many continuation lines can be used with this technique. The most significant issue to be aware of is that it's likely to annoy recipients if misused.

4.5.1 Charsets

The charset used in header encoding can be any allowed in a `text/plain` entity. The ISO-8859 charsets are preferred, since more MUAs are likely to support them.

4.5.2 Encoding

Encoding fields is similar to encoding bodies. There are two modes available, Q and B.

Q Encoding
The Q mode is a variant of `quoted-printable` encoding. It is intended for data consisting primarily of printable text.

```
From: =?iso-8859-1?q?J=FCrgen_Mahler?= <juergen@europe.example.com>
```

Like `quoted-printable`, any individual character can be replaced with its two-digit hexadecimal value and prefixed with a '=' character.

A SPACE character can be replaced with '_' as an alternative to '=20' to improve the readability of Q encoding in MUAs not supporting RFC2047.

Printable US-ASCII characters, except '=', '?', '_', and SPACE, can be left unencoded.

There is one additional restriction when Q encoding is used as a replacement for a *word* token—the set of characters allowed. The alphanumeric characters, '!', '*', '+', '-', '/', '=', and '_' are the only ones permitted in a Q-encoded word. As with the resulting characters in `base64` encoding, this reduces the possibility that an external email gateway will corrupt the data.

B Encoding

The B mode uses `base64` encoding, which, like that used in message bodies, can be used for encoding primarily nonprintable data. It isn't as common as Q mode because binary data is seldom needed in a header.

```
X-Stuff: =?us-ascii?b?SW50ZXJuZXQgRW1haWw=?=
```

As in `base64` encoding, the *encoded-text* portion of a B-encoded word must be a multiple of four characters in length.

4.5.3 Using Encoding

RFC2047 is not a license to encode any and all headers. There are three, and only three, places where it's allowed.

- As a replacement for a *text* token in `Subject`, `Comments`, and extension fields, as well as any MIME field where *text* tokens are allowed.

```
Subject: =?iso-8859-1?q?J=FCrgen's?= favorite food
Subject: Jürgen's favorite food
```

- In a parenthetical comment as a replacement for a *ctext* token.

```
(=?iso-8859-1?q?J=FCrgen's?= favorite dance tune)
(Jürgen's favorite dance tune)
```

A Q-encoded word cannot contain '(', ')', or '"', which isn't a problem with B encoding because, as was shown in Figure 4.2, none of these characters can occur in a B-encoded string.

- In a *phrase* token as a replacement for a *word* token. There are four places where this can occur.
  - In the *display-name* portion of a mailbox.

```
=?iso-8859-1?q?J=FCrgen_Mahler?= <juergen@europe.example.com>
Jürgen Mahler <juergen@europe.example.com>
```

  - In the *group-name* portion of a group address.

```
=?iso-8859-1?q?J=FCrgen's?= Humor List:;
Jürgen's Humor List:;
```

  - In a `Keywords` field.

```
=?iso-8859-1?q?=C6lfred?= xml software
Keywords: Ælfred xml software
```

  - In the older format of the `In-Reply-To` and `References` fields.

```
In-Reply-To: Your question about =?iso-8859-1?q?=C6lfred?=
In-Reply-To: Your question about Ælfred
```

To reinforce the information just given a list of places where encoded words cannot be used is in order. They are explicitly forbidden in any structured field except with a parenthetical *comment* or a *phrase*. They are also not allowed in `Received` fields, including inside a *comment* token. And they are most definitely not allowed inside an *addr-spec* or *quoted-string*.

Interestingly enough, header encoding can be used in messages not containing a `MIME-Version` field. The idea is that requiring the field would require an MUA to scan the entire header looking for it before it could decide whether or not to decode the header. While this might seem like a minor point, it allows MUAs a small performance improvement when processing messages.

Once the data is encoded and safely transmitted, it needs to be decoded by the recipient MUA. The primary thing to remember is that parsing is done before the data is decoded. The following example of a valid RFC822 field illustrates this.

```
From: =?us-ascii?q?=3C?= <tommy@example.com>
```

TABLE 4.9 Sequence of Tokens

Token	Description
From	*field-name*
:	
=?us-ascii?q?=3C?=	*display-name*
<	
tommy@example.com	*addr-spec*
>	

If it were decoded first, the result would be as follows.

```
From: < <tommy@example.com>
```

Clearly, this would be an invalid RFC822 field. However, since the parsing is done before the decoding, a parser interprets it as the sequence of tokens in Table 4.9.

In this encoded form, the information is perfectly valid. To reiterate: Parsing is performed first, then decoding.

4.6 MAILCAP FILES

While some media types, such as the multipart and message major types, are best handled internally by an MUA, many are often better handled by specialized programs designed to deal with specific data formats. It's also considerably easier to add support for new media types if an MUA can use external programs.

Email software on UNIX platforms usually use a series of configuration files called `mailcap` files to associate various media types to corresponding external programs. These are defined by RFC1524 (A User Agent Configuration Mechanism for Multimedia Mail Format Information), which is not a standard but merely an informational document. However, it serves as a example of the issues that need to be taken into account when designing an equivalent mechanism.

Despite the fact that the file format was designed to be usable on a variety of operating systems, it is typically found on UNIX platforms because of UNIX's history of supporting multiple concurrent users, possibly using different MUAs. In fact, the RFC defines the semantics only for UNIX platforms, not for any other operating system. All the examples in this section use the UNIX semantics described in the RFC. Readers not familiar with UNIX, or with no interest in it, should still find this section useful. Readers using UNIX platforms will, of course, find the information directly applicable.

Support for `mailcap` files isn't required for implementing MIME. Non-UNIX MUAs typically provide their own mechanism. Support for `mailcap` files is, however, a de-facto requirement on UNIX platforms.

If support for `mailcap` files is included in an MUA, they are used to determine what external program to launch to handle a particular media type. When an MUA needs to present an entity to the user, it looks at the media type to determine how to do so. If the media type is supported internally, the MUA handles it natively. If not, finding an external program is necessary. It does this by scanning one or more `mailcap` files, using the first matching entry it encounters.

As an example, a common set of `mailcap` files might be a `.mailcap` file in a user's home directory and a system-wide `/etc/mailcap` file. The MUA first scans `.mailcap`. If no match is found, it scans `/etc/mailcap`. In this way a user can override any system-wide entries with personal preferences. Most MUAs allow the list of `mailcap` files to be changed.

4.6.1 General Syntax

A mailcap file consists of a series of lines. Any lines beginning with '#' are considered comments and ignored. Blank lines are also ignored. The remaining lines are *mailcap-entry* records. An individual *mailcap-entry* can span multiple lines using line continuations. If a line ends with a '\' character, it is continued on the next line.

```
# personal mailcap file

single-line mailcap-entry

first line of a multiple-line entry\
continuation of previous line
```

The syntax for an individual mailcap-entry is as follows.

```
mailcap-entry = typefield ";" view-command [";"1#field]
```

Any unknown fields in a *mailcap-entry* should be ignored to prevent the addition of new fields from breaking a mailcap parser.

The *typefield* is a variant of the media type used in `Content-Type` fields. It can take several forms, but the most common is exactly like the `Content-Type` field value, which has a major type and a subtype.

```
image/jpeg
```

The field can also have a '*' wildcard character for the subtype segment, which associates the particular mailcap-entry with all media types in the image major type.

```
image/*
```

This can also be specified without the wildcard by simply identifying the major type. This is equivalent to 'image/*'.

```
image
```

The *view-command* field specifies a command line to execute to handle the given media type. It can contain any US-ASCII character except ';' and nonprintable ones. Any occurrences of '\' characters are considered part of an escaped pair.

The semantics of this field are specific to the operating system the file is used with. The liberal set of characters is allowed so that the command-line notations used by different operating systems can be accommodated.

Here is a simple example mailcap record.

```
image/jpeg; xv %s
```

It states that the XV program should be used for image/jpeg attachments.

Because an entity is embedded in an email message, the MUA extracts the data, decodes it, and places the final result in a temporary file. The '%s' serves as a placeholder for the name of the temporary file. It is replaced with the filename when the MUA launches the program.

Other '%' tokens are available. A '%t' is replaced with the name of the media type. If the type is multipart, a '%n' token is also available to indicate how many parts it holds. A '%F' token is also available for multipart entities which expands to a list of pairs of content-type and filename values for each part. These last two tokens aren't used very frequently because most modern MUAs provide built-in support for multipart entities.

The final form of '%' tokens is for accessing the parameters present in the Content-Type field for an entity. Any parameter can be accessed in a mailcap file using the following notation.

```
%{parameter-name}
```

Thus, '%{charset}' will be replaced with the value of the charset parameter. Since '%' is a magic character in mailcap-entry lines, they must be escaped as '\%' if a literal '%' is wanted.

4.6.2 Fields

In addition to the standard view field, several fields can be added to a mailcap record. Each adds more detail to the record.

Print
A `print` field can be used to specify how to send the file to a printer.

```
application/pdf; acroread %s;\
               print="acroread -toPostScript <%s '| lpr"
```

In this example, a PDF file is converted to PostScript and piped into the default printer, which is presumably PostScript.

Compose
The `compose` field is used to specify a command to create a new file in the specified media type. It is seldom implemented, as most MUAs require a preexisting file when creating an entity.

```
text/html; lynx %s; compose="vi %s"
```

This example illustrates how the vi text editor might be used to create an HTML attachment.

Composetyped
The `composetyped` field is similar to the `compose` type, except that it generates a ready-made MIME entity rather than a raw data file.

The following example shows a hypothetical program being called to create a multipart alternative attachment. This type of record could be used by an MUA that doesn't natively handle that media type.

```
multipart/alternative; showmulti %t %{boundary}; \
               composetyped=makealternative
```

Edit
The `edit` field is used to specify a command line to execute if a user wants to edit an entity. Many MUAs do not implement this field, since few users edit attachments as part of the message composition process.

Test

By default, the first mailcap-entry found with a matching media type is used to process an entity. The `test` field provides the ability to perform an additional test beyond the media type to determine whether the given mailcap-entry is the one to use. If the test fails, the mailcap-entry is not considered a match, and the search continues.

```
text/html; netscape -remote 'openURL(%s, newwindow)'; \
        test=test -n "$DISPLAY"
text/html; lynx %s
```

In this example, the first entry uses the UNIX `test` command to determine whether the `$DISPLAY` environment variable is populated. If it is, the user is running under the X Window system and therefore the entry matches. If the test fails, the entry is skipped and the next matching entry is used, which in this case is a text-based Web Browser.

Description

The `description` field provides a way to add a description to a mailcap-entry.

```
application/octet-stream; od; copiousoutput; \
                    description="Fallback to octal dump"
```

Here it is used to relate information that might not be intuitively obvious to some users—namely, that the interpretation of the data is a raw dump.

Textualnewlines

The `textualnewlines` field alters how end-of-line processing is handled for `base64` encoded data.

When set to a nonzero value, the field indicates that the data is line-oriented. If `base64` encoding is used, all newlines should be converted to CRLF before encoding.

```
textualnewlines=1
```

This field is seldom used, but it can be helpful in the rare case where the media type is a member of the text media type and the data is not line-oriented. It can also be helpful in cases where the media type is not a member of the text media type, but the data is line-oriented.

Setting the field value to '0' will turn off any newline translation, even for text media types.

x11-Bitmap

The `x11-bitmap` field is used to specify the name of a file that contains XBM (X11 Bitmap) data. For graphical user interfaces, this allows a graphic icon to be associated with an attachment.

```
application/postscript; gv %s; x11-bitmap="/var/icons/ghost.xbm"
```

An XBM image is monochrome. Since most graphical interfaces are now color, this field isn't used very much.

Nametemplate

The `nametemplate` field allows a filename template to be associated with the entry. The template is used when generating a temporary filename to pass to the viewer. This field is particularly useful with viewer software that uses a filename extension to determine the file-type.

```
text/html; lynx %s; \
          nametemplate=%s.html
```

In this example, the Lynx Web browser program requires that HTML files have a `.html` extension. The `nametemplate` field causes the temporary filename to be created with that extension, thus allowing the browser to correctly interpret the file.

Notes

The `notes` field isn't part of the RFC1524 specification, but is understood by the Metamail package as an uninterpreted field. It is used as a place to indicate the name of the person who installed a particular mailcap-entry and can also be used for general comments about a particular entry. It is rarely used.

```
image/tiff; tiffviewer %s; \
          notes="Joe Doubloon"
```

4.6.3 Flags

In addition to the fields described in the previous section, a few flags are available for mailcap-entries. Unlike other fields, flags are not set to a particular value. Instead, the presence of a particular flag enables its assigned behavior.

Needsterminal

By default, external programs are launched in the background, with no terminal window. This is usually the preferred way to handle most view programs, since they normally get any required input via graphical input forms. Occasionally, however, a program requires interactive terminal input. To handle this, a `needsterminal` flag is provided. When present, it launches the external program in a terminal window. For the X Window System, this usually means some type of Xterm window. For character-based interfaces, this usually means waiting for input from the user when the external program exits, so the user has a chance to view the output before screen control reverts to the MUA.

```
application/atomicmail; atomicmail %s; needsterminal
```

Copiousoutput

Some external programs present their output as a continuous stream of data with no pagination to help the user navigate it. To handle these programs, a `copiousoutput` flag is available that pipes the output from the external program into a screen paginater.

```
application/pgp-keys; pgp -f < %s; copiousoutput
```

Extensions (x-)

As with many areas of email, additional nonstandard fields can be used if they start with 'x-', since no standard mailcap field will be defined starting with these characters.

4.7 SUMMARY

Under most circumstances, RFC822 messages can contain only 7-bit US-ASCII information. However, since email is a convenient communication mechanism, people want to use it to send and receive other types of information. MIME was created to accomplish this.

MIME defines a set of fields that specify the nature of the enclosed data. The primary fields are `MIME-Version`, `Content-Type`, and `Content-Transfer-Encoding`. The `MIME-Version` field identifies what version of MIME was used. The `Content-Type` field specifies what type of data is enclosed, including files from specific applications, generic data types, email messages, and multipart entities. The `Content-Transfer-Encoding` field indicates what encoding was used to coerce the data into 7-bit US-ASCII. Several other fields enhance these core capabilities.

In addition to encoding message bodies, it's also possible to encode certain field values. This provides the ability to include international information in those fields.

MIME is a very rich extension to RFC822. The core specification spans several RFCs, and many other RFCs have been written that extend its capabilities. This chapter provides a general description of the extensions, as well as several important enhancements. It is impossible to cover the entire topic in one chapter. Readers, especially developers, are strongly encouraged to read the RFCs directly. There is just too much information to be covered here.

This is not the last that will be seen of MIME in this book. MIME has become an integral part of modern email, and several subsequent chapters illustrate this by showing various elements of MIME in the context of other email mechanisms.

Chapter 5

POP

As described so far, a message ultimately is deposited in a mail folder on a destination machine. In many environments, an MUA can be used to directly access the folder on the machine where it resides, but that is not always an optimal solution.

In the early days of email, users logged on to the machine where their email was delivered to read messages. This was seldom an inconvenience, since users typically received email on the machine on which they did their other work.

As personal computers made their entrance into the networking world, many users didn't want to have to process email on a remote server. If, for example, a user received a piece of email he or she wanted to save and use, the message needed to be copied from the server to the PC.

Unfortunately, most personal computers didn't have the resources to act as a full-fledged MTA. Even with the advent of more powerful PCs, many didn't run continuously. The problem was further compounded in the case of dial-up networking, where a personal computer is only sporadically connected to the network. Although the store-and-forward mechanism of SMTP is tolerant of machines occasionally not being connected to the network, it wasn't designed to handle these types of uses. Also, most users don't have the expertise, or desire, to administrate an email server.

POP was created to solve these problems. A user's email is delivered to an intermediate machine, called a POP server. POP clients connect to the server, retrieve messages, and delete them. This avoids using a personal computer as an email server and eliminates the need for an MUA on the server to read email.

The first POP RFC was published in 1984 as RFC918 (Post Office Protocol). It described a basic experimental POP implementation. In 1985, RFC937 (Post Office Protocol—Version 2) was published. It added several new features and became widely deployed.

A third version, RFC1081 (Post Office Protocol—Version 3), was published in 1988. This version has been revised several times, resulting in the following RFCs.

- RFC1225 (Post Office Protocol—Version 3)
- RFC1460 (Post Office Protocol—Version 3)
- RFC1725 (Post Office Protocol—Version 3)
- RFC1939 (Post Office Protocol—Version 3)

RFC1939, published in 1996, is the current POP standard.

Since the introduction of POP version 3, a few extension mechanisms have been proposed. RFC1082 (Post Office Protocol—Version 3: Extented Service Offerings) was published in 1988 as an adjunct to RFC1081. It provides an extension mechanism as well as a simple bulletin board interface and is described in Section 5.4.1. In 1998, RFC2449 (POP3 Extension Mechanism) was published. It defines an extension mechanism for POP, as well as an extended response code syntax, and is described in Section 5.4.2.

This chapter describes version 3 of POP, as well as various extensions. While a few version 2 implementations are in use, the older version is obsolete. The vast majority of implementations use version 3, which, as a general rule, all references to POP in this book refer to.

5.1 INTERFACE MODEL

At the highest level, POP, like SMTP, is implemented as a communication protocol between two machines: a client and a server. It has several similarities to SMTP—it deals with moving mail messages from one location to another, uses a command and reply dialog mechanism, and uses CRLF to terminate lines. On closer examination, however, the similarities quickly fade.

Figure 5.1 illustrates the high-level relationship between a POP client, a POP server, and the other components in an email architecture.

Mail messages are delivered to the server via SMTP. They are stored in a *maildrop,* which provides storage for the messages until the POP client retrieves them. On most POP servers, this is simply a standard mail folder.

A client POP process connects to a POP server via TCP port 110. Upon accepting the incoming connection, the server issues a one-line connection greeting. The line starts with '+OK', which indicates that the server is ready for a conversation.

```
+OK POP3 server ready
```

The client then parses the connection greeting. If the greeting starts with '+OK', it can proceed with the dialog; otherwise, it disconnects from the server.

Assuming it's able to proceed, the client then authenticates to the server. Once authenticated, it issues a series of commands to transfer the messages from the maildrop to the local machine. Usually the client then issues a series of commands to delete messages on the server, although this is not always the case, as will be

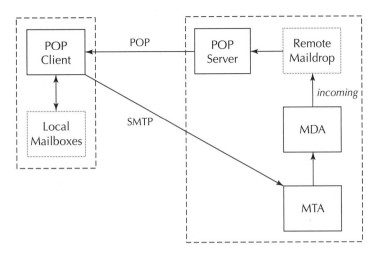

FIGURE 5.1 POP Interface Model

shown later in the chapter. When the necessary transfers are complete, the client terminates the session.

The POP interface model does not provide a way to send mail messages. Normally, if a POP-based MUA needs to send a message, it will submit it to an SMTP relay server, described in Section 3.3.2. However, most POP-based MUAs use SMTP.

There are several reasons for not including a way to send messages in POP. The same is true for IMAP, described in Chapter 6. For one thing, providing message submission in POP complicates the development of the protocol. The various email protocols are handled by separate Working Groups in the IETF, allowing their modular development with minimal dependencies on other protocols. If message submission were included in POP, it would have to track developments in two Working Groups, and since the protocols evolve at different rates, this would present a significant burden on POP development.

Including message submission in POP also makes the assumption that messages should be submitted to the same machine providing POP services. This is undesirable at many sites, particularly large ones where the services are provided on separate machines to balance the load. While the user base might be evenly spread across multiple machines providing both services, it can be difficult to balance the load evenly across them. It's usually easier to provide separate machines for the different tasks, sizing them according to their separate workloads.

Another reason to not include message submission in the protocol is the protocols transaction interface. The POP connection would be tied up while a message was being submitted to the server. With separate protocols, it would be possible to interact with both a POP server and an SMTP server at the same time. While multiple POP channels could be used for this, at that point you might as well use

SMTP for the second communication channel, since the only purpose of the second channel would be to send messages.

Not everyone agrees with this. In fact, an extension command available that allows POP to transmit messages, `xmit`, is described in Section 5.4.1. The most significant reason for providing a way to submit messages via POP is to reduce the amount of code in an MUA. On smaller architectures, this can be an important issue. Enough server implementers, however, disagree with providing message submission in POP, that most POP servers don't support it. This means that most, if not all, POP clients need to support SMTP message submission anyway, so no savings in code size is realized.

5.1.1 Commands and Replies

As mentioned earlier, POP has many similarities to SMTP. It is a text-oriented, command/reply protocol. Each line transmitted, in either direction, is terminated with a CRLF.

The POP client issues commands, and the POP server acts on them and sends replies to the client. By default, the command/reply sequence is synchronous, as illustrated in Figure 5.2. However, the extension mechanism described in

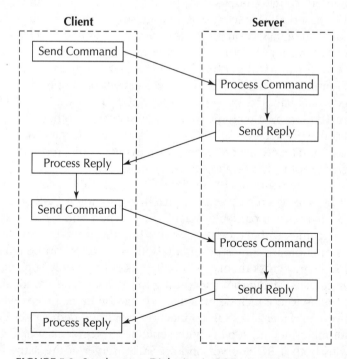

FIGURE 5.2 Synchronous Dialoging in POP

Section 5.4.2 provides a pipelining extension, which loosens this requirement to send one command at a time.

The set of commands for POP is small, approximately the same as for SMTP. They are case-insensitive, and several accept or require parameters. If present, each parameter is separated by a single space, and none can be longer than 40 characters. Table 5.1 lists the standard POP commands in RFC1939 and whether they are required.

A POP reply is much simpler than a SMTP reply. Rather than multiple-digit numeric codes, success and failure are indicated with '+OK' and '-ERR'.

There are two types of replies in POP, single and multiline. A single-line reply consists of a line of text containing a status indicator and optional text. The status indicator '+OK' conveys success; the status indicator '-ERR' conveys failure. The status indicator must be upper-case. A single-line response must be no longer than 512 characters.

```
+OK retr command accepted
```

The syntax of a single-line reply is as follows:

```
single-line-reply = status [SP optional-text]
status            = "+OK" / "-ERR"
```

The contents of the optional text depend upon the command. Some commands have a specific format while others allow arbitrary text. In many reply lines, the

TABLE 5.1 POP Command Summary

Command	Required?	Description
user		Identify user for authentication
pass		Send password for authentication
apop		Alternate authentication mechanism
quit	Yes	Terminate the session
noop	Yes	No operation
stat	Yes	Provide size information about the maildrop
list	Yes	Provide size information about messages
retr	Yes	Retrieve a message from the server
top		Retrieve header and first N lines of a message
dele	Yes	Mark a message for deletion
rset	Yes	Reset the POP session
uidl		Retrieve the unique identifier for a message

optional-text is free-form, not intended to be machine-parsable. Other reply lines have specific formats. POP developers should avoid parsing replies that have no defined format in *optional-text*.

A multiline reply consists of a single-line reply, followed by zero or more additional dot-stuffed lines of text, terminated by a line containing a single period character.

```
+OK
1 58493
2 8492
3 15392
4 2546
.
```

The syntax is as follows.

```
multi-line-response = single-line-response *dot-stuffed "."
dot-stuffed         = *CHAR ; must be dot stuffed
```

5.1.2 Protocol States

A POP session can be in one of three states, each of which represents a specific stage in the session's lifetime. A session starts in the *authorization* state, in which no commands are valid except authentication commands and `quit`.

Once a client has authenticated, the server locks the maildrop. The lock is to prevent multiple POP connections, IMAP connections, or MUAs from modifying the maildrop out from underneath the POP server, while still allowing new messages to be appended to it. Once the mailbox is locked, the server issues a success reply and the session changes to the *transaction* state. Most of the POP dialog is performed in this state.

The session remains in the *transaction* state until either the `quit` command is issued or the session is abnormally terminated. If the `quit` command is issued, the state changes to *update,* in which the server deletes all messages marked for deletion.

POP servers are allowed to implement an *auto-logout timer,* where idle sessions are disconnected after a predetermined amount of time. If implemented, the timer must be at least 10 minutes in duration. The receipt of any command resets the timer. If the session is abnormally terminated—for example, because the client or the server lost its connection or because an auto-logout timer expired—the session bypasses the *update* state. Regardless of whether the session was terminated correctly, the lock on the maildrop is released when the session terminates.

Figure 5.3 illustrates the sequence of state transitions, minus the possibility of closing the connection at any time. Table 5.2 lists the standard commands and which states they can be issued in. If the auto-logout timer expires, the server does

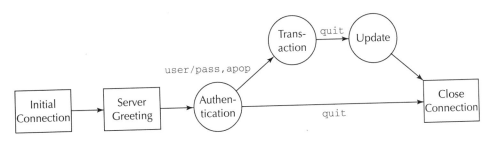

FIGURE 5.3 POP Session States

TABLE 5.2 Which Commands Can Be Issued in Which State

Command	Authorization	Transaction
user	●	
pass	●	
apop	●	
quit	●	●
stat		●
list		●
retr		●
dele		●
noop		●
rset		●
top		●
uidl		●

not enter the *update* state, even if there are pending deletes. The reason is that, since the user did not initiate the end of the session, there is no way of telling whether he or she would have reset it, which would cancel any pending deletes.

5.2 STANDARD COMMANDS

This section describes the standard commands provided in RFC1939. Like the commands in Chapter 3, they are presented in an order intended to introduce the reader to the protocol in an incremental fashion.

As with SMTP, the telnet protocol can be used to interact with a POP server, providing an excellent opportunity to experiment with it. Refer to Section 3.2 for a description of how to use telnet to connect to a server. Instead of connecting to TCP port 25, connect to port 110.

5.2.1 User

```
"user" SP maildrop
```

The `user` command authenticates to the server and specifies the desired maildrop. The name of the maildrop is significant only to the server; for example, it could be the account name of a user or a special maildrop not associated with a specific user.

```
user joe
+OK
```

RFC1939 states that the `user` command is valid only in the *authorization* state after the connection greeting or after an unsuccessful `user` or `pass` command. This is conceptually correct but incomplete. The `user` command can be issued after any unsuccessful authentication command, including `apop`. A better way of looking at `user` is to look at what successful authentication commands it cannot follow. By definition, a complete and successful authentication results in the session transitioning to the *transaction* state. On the other hand, some servers will consider it an error to issue a second `user` command prior to issuing a `pass` command. A review of existing implementations reinforces this interpretation.

If an error is encountered processing the command, the server responds with an error reply.

```
user
-ERR missing user name argument
```

There is one subtlety worth mentioning about the error reply with the `user` command. A cursory analysis might lead to the conclusion that an invalid user name should result in an error reply from the server. However, there is a good reason for not doing this. A server that rejects an invalid user name provides a convenient way for would-be attackers to probe it for valid account names. If the server responds with a positive reply regardless of the account name, the client must submit a `pass` command to complete the validation of the user name. In the event of an authentication failure, most POP servers hide which of the two commands is the problem. While this can cause some difficulties for users trying to determine why they can't authenticate, it reduces the amount of information provided to would-be attackers.

Alert readers might have noticed that Table 5.1 lists the `user` command as optional. This is true, but there is wrinkle—the POP server must implement at least one authentication mechanism, whether `user`, `apop`, or one provided in a POP extension.

5.2.2 Password

```
"pass" SP password
```

The `pass` command is used to provide the password for the maildrop given with the `user` command. It is valid only in the *authorization* state immediately after a `user` command.

```
user joe
+OK
pass 91j.aj!0
+OK
```

The argument to `pass` can contain spaces. This is because the command accepts exactly one argument. Any spaces after the initial space separating the command and argument are interpreted as part of the argument.

If the authentication is successful, the session changes to the *transaction* state. If the authentication fails, the server responds with an error and stays in the *authorization* state.

```
user toor
+OK
pass logmein
-ERR authentication failure
```

The server also responds with an error and stays in the *authorization* state if it fails to acquire the exclusive access lock on the maildrop.

```
pass 91j.aj!0
-ERR maildrop is already locked
```

The preceding examples of authentication failure are not the only ones. In general, a server can perform any type of check as an adjunct to the authentication process. Some servers validate additional types of account information, such as whether the user is allowed to use POP. Some also implement restrictions on how frequently a user may connect to the POP server.

If the pass command fails, the client is not allowed to simply issue another one. It must reissue the user command in order to send another pass command.

5.2.3 APOP

```
"apop" SP mailbox SP md5-digest-string
```

The apop command is an alternative to the user and pass commands. It authenticates without transmitting a password in plain text across a network, by using the algorithm defined in RFC1321. Like the user and pass commands, apop is optional; however, servers must implement at least one authentication mechanism.

Also, as with the user command, RFC1939 states that the apop command is valid only in the *authorization* state after the connection greeting or after an unsuccessful user or pass command. The same issue with the wording for user holds for apop.

Servers that support this command add a timestamp to the connection greeting. This timestamp is styled after the *msg-id* and must be different each time a POP greeting is issued. Many POP server implementations use the following syntax.

```
<process-id.clock@hostname>
```

The *process-id* subfield is an integer containing the unique identifier of the POP server process. The *clock* subfield is an integer containing the system clock time on the server. Lastly, the *hostname* is the FQDN of the POP server.

```
+OK POP3 server starting <14728.896851446@pop.example.com>
```

If the client supports the apop command and plans to use it, it notes the timestamp string provided in the connection greeting.

To issue an apop command, the client generates an *md5-digest-string*. It starts by combining the timestamp, received from the server, and a *shared secret*. The shared secret is known only by the client and the server and acts as a password.

```
<14728.896851446@pop.example.com>ourlittlesecret
```

The client then takes the combined string and applies the MD5 algorithm from RFC1321. Since the output of the algorithm is a 128-bit binary value, the value is split into 16 octets, each converted to its 2-digit US-ASCII hexadecimal equivalent. This is then concatenated to provide the value's 32-character printable version.

```
b9632793b52082679afaff33d17c3ffa
```

This results in a suitable md5-digest-string for the `apop` command. Including the timestamp protects against replay attacks, which are attempts to gain unauthorized access by replaying authentication dialogs. Applying the MD5 algorithm creates a *digest,* or fingerprint, of the timestamp and shared secret. The original information is difficult to derive from the digest, so this avoids transmitting authentication information as plain text across a network. Since the server knows the timestamp and shared secret, it can apply the same algorithm to generate a MD5 digest. If the two MD5 digests are the same, the authentication succeeds.

```
apop joe b9632793b52082679afaff33d17c3ffa
+OK
```

Most of the failure modes possible with the other authentication commands are possible with `apop`. As with those other commands, if `apop` fails, the session stays in the *authorization* state.

There is one very significant negative aspect to the `apop` command—the shared secret must be stored in plain-text form or a method for encrypting the shared secret must be used. This can be very difficult to do well, and it shifts the burden of protecting the password from the network to the server.

5.2.4 Quit

```
"quit"
```

The `quit` command terminates the session and disconnects the client from the server. If the session is in the *authorization* state, `quit` causes the server to close the connection. If the session is in the *transaction* state, the POP server enters the *update* state. In this case, it deletes any messages marked for deletion before closing the connection.

```
quit
+OK
```

If an error is encountered while deleting messages, the server replies with an error response. In this case, it's possible that not all messages marked for deletion were deleted.

```
quit
-ERR exceeded quota rebuilding maildrop
```

Regardless of the success or failure of the command, the lock on the maildrop is released and the connection is closed.

5.2.5 No Operation

```
"noop"
```

The noop command does nothing. A client can use it to prevent an auto-logout timer from expiring or to test whether the client is still connected to the server.

```
noop
+OK
```

This command is valid only in the *transaction* state.

5.2.6 Status

```
"stat"
```

The stat command provides size information about the maildrop, not including messages marked for deletion. It is valid only in the *transaction* state.

```
stat
+OK 4 84923
```

The reply from the server contains the number of messages in the maildrop and the size, in octets, of the maildrop. The format of the reply line is as follows.

```
"+OK" SP number-of-messages SP maildrop-size
```

The size should be calculated based on the canonical RFC822 representation of the messages in the maildrop, including the CRLF line terminators. Some servers store messages in an internal format designed to optimize performance and minimize storage requirements. Some have a bug in which the reported size is based on the internal storage format, which makes it possible for the size value to be reported incorrectly.

5.2.7 List

```
"list" [SP message-number]
```

The list command provides size information, about either a specific message or the entire set of messages not marked for deletion in the maildrop. It is valid only in the *transaction* state.

If the *message-number* argument is provided with the command, the server responds with a single-line reply containing the size information for the specified message.

```
list 3
+OK 3 15392
```

The reply from the server contains the *message-number* and the size, in octets, of the messages. The format of the reply line is as follows.

```
"+OK" SP message-number SP message-size
```

As with the list command, the size should be calculated based on the canonical RFC822 representation of the message.

An error results if *message-number* refers to a message marked for deletion.

```
dele 3
+OK
list 3
-ERR message 3 has been deleted
```

Likewise, an error results if the specified message number doesn't exist or if the parameter isn't a integer greater than zero.

```
list 49123
-ERR message 49123 does not exist
```

If no argument is given with the command, the server sends a multiline response. After the '+OK' line, one line is sent for each message not marked for deletion in the maildrop.

```
list
+OK
1 58493
2 8492
3 15392
4 2546
.
```

Each line contains a message number and the size, in octets, of the associated message.

```
message-number SP message-size
```

If no messages are present, the server still responds with a successful multiline response, with no lines of data between the initial status line and the termination line.

```
list
+OK
.
```

5.2.8 Retrieve

```
"retr" SP message-number
```

The retr command retrieves the message specified in *message-number*. It is valid only in the *transaction* state.

If the specified message exists, the server sends an RFC822 message to the client.

```
retr 4
+OK
Return-Path: <bob@flugelhorn.example.com>
Received: from flugelhorn.example.com by tuba.example.com
         with SMTP id HAA19482
         for <joe@tuba.example.com>; Sat, 4 Oct 1997 08:33:48 -0700
```

```
Received: by flugelhorn.example.com (8.8.8/8.8.8) with smtp
         id CAA17583; Sat, 4 Oct 1997 08:33:47 -0700
Date: 4 Oct 1997 08:33:45 -0700
Message-ID: <19971004083345.18492.1@flugelhorn.example.com>
From: bob@flugelhorn.example.com
To: joe@tuba.example.com
Subject: another question
X-Mailer: MondoMail v42.86

Why is the frobnazoid gefargled again?


--
thx,
bob
.
```

Since it's a multiline response, a period is used to indicate the end of the message. To prevent a sole period from causing the client to finish reading the message prematurely, the same dot-stuffing used with the SMTP data command, described in Section 3.2.9, is used with retr.

As with the list command, an error results if *message-number* refers to a message marked for deletion, if the message doesn't exist, or if the parameter isn't an integer greater than zero.

```
dele 4
+OK
retr 4
-ERR message 4 is deleted
```

Since the *message-number* parameter is required, an error also results if the parameter isn't specified.

```
retr
-ERR missing required message number parameter
```

A few header fields require special mention with the retr command. It's a good idea for clients to strip Content-Length fields from retrieved messages. If the folder format used by the client uses the field, a new value should be calculated to avoid corrupting the maildrop with an incorrect value. It's also a good idea for servers to strip this field when sending the data to the client. If stripped, it should be ignored when calculating the size of the message. RFC1939 doesn't mention the field; however, stripping it reduces the likelihood that an incorrect value will be passed to a naïve client that doesn't recalculate the value.

The `Status` field, if used, is a little more complicated. As with `Content-Length`, RFC1939 doesn't mention it should be processed. Some POP servers use this field to indicate whether the particular message has been retrieved. Some clients might want to have this information when messages are retrieved, so if they access a message with a different MUA, the fact that the message was read is retained. This allows the client to indicate that fact to the user. It also allows the client to decide not to retrieve the message for that reason. On the other hand, some utilities that notify the user of new incoming mail will ignore incoming messages marked as having been read, possibly resulting in delayed notification of incoming messages. The correct behavior depends on the situation. It's not uncommon to find this choice as a configurable option in MUAs.

5.2.9 Top

```
"top" SP message-number SP number-of-lines
```

The `top` command retrieves the header and specified number of lines the message specified in *message-number*. It's valid only in the *transaction* state.

The *number-of-lines* argument must be a non-negative number. The entire message is sent if the number of body lines in the message is fewer than the number in *number-of-lines*.

```
top 2 4
+OK
Return-Path: <bob@flugelhorn.example.com>
Received: from flugelhorn.example.com by tuba.example.com
         with SMTP id HAA19482
         for <joe@tuba.example.com>; Sat,  4 Oct 1997 08:33:48 -0700
Received: by flugelhorn.example.com (8.8.8/8.8.8) with smtp
         id CAA17583; Sat, 4 Oct 1997 08:33:47 -0700
Date: 4 Oct 1997 08:33:45 -0700
Message-ID: <19971004083345.18492.1@flugelhorn.example.com>
From: bob@flugelhorn.example.com
To: joe@tuba.example.com
Subject: another question
X-Mailer: MondoMail v42.86

Why is the frobnazoid gefargled again?

--
thx,
.
```

In this case, the header was retrieved, as were the first four lines of the message. The client could present these lines to the user as a preview.

If *number-of-lines* is 0, then only the header and blank line separator are sent. This provides a way for the client to retrieve just the header, as the following example illustrates.

```
top 2 0
+OK
Return-Path: <bob@flugelhorn.example.com>
Received: from flugelhorn.example.com by tuba.example.com
         with SMTP id HAA19482
         for <joe@tuba.example.com>; Sat, 4 Oct 1997 08:33:48 -0700
Received: by flugelhorn.example.com (8.8.8/8.8.8) with smtp
         id CAA17583; Sat, 4 Oct 1997 08:33:47 -0700
Date: 4 Oct 1997 08:33:45 -0700
Message-ID: <19971004083345.18492.1@flugelhorn.example.com>
From: bob@flugelhorn.example.com
To: joe@tuba.example.com
Subject: another question
X-Mailer: MondoMail v42.86

.
```

As with other commands where a message number is specified, `top` will fail if the message number refers to a deleted message or to a nonexistent message, if it isn't an integer greater than zero, or if the message number isn't specified.

This command is optional; however, server developers are encouraged to implement it. Some POP clients require `top`. Implementing it allows more clients to work with the server.

5.2.10 Delete

```
"dele" SP message-number
```

The `dele` command marks the specified message for deletion and is valid only in the *transaction* state. As described in Section 5.2.4, the message is not actually deleted until the `quit` command is issued.

```
dele 4
+OK
```

Like other commands that specify a message number, `dele` will fail if the message number refers to a deleted message or to a nonexistent message, if it isn't an integer greater than zero, or if it isn't specified.

```
dele 4
-ERR message 4 already deleted
```

5.2.11 Reset

```
"rset"
```

The `rset` command resets the POP session. It's valid only in the *transaction* state. Any messages marked for deletion are unmarked, and a subsequent `quit` command will not delete any messages previously marked. Unlike the corresponding SMTP command, it does not affect the state of the session.

```
rset
+OK
```

5.2.12 Unique-ID Listing

```
"uidl" [SP message-number]
```

The `uidl` command outputs the unique identifier for the given message. Valid only in the *transaction* state, it provides a way to identify unambiguously the same message across multiple POP sessions. At first glance, it might be tempting to consider using the `Message-ID` field; however, `Message-ID` is not a required field and has had a dubious history as a unique identifier of a message.

A unique identifier can be from 1 to 70 characters long, each of which can be any graphic US-ASCII character. It must remain constant between POP sessions so that clients know that the UIDL value for a particular message on the server will be the same the next time it connects. Section 5.3.3 describes a mechanism that uses this UIDL persistence.

Clients need to be able to tolerate duplicate UIDLs so that, if a bug is present in UIDL generation software, they will be less likely to break if a duplicate is encountered.

Like the `top` command, this command is optional; however, server developers are encouraged to implement it since there are POP clients that require it.

If the optional *message-number* argument is not specified, `uidl` lists the unique identifiers for all messages not marked for deletion.

In the following example, the client asks for the UIDL for a specific message number. The server responds with a line containing an '+OK' followed by the requested message number and the associated unique identifier. Each field is separated by a single SPACE character.

```
uidl 3
+OK 3 oghej25qoiw92oqihr934
```

The `uidl` command will fail if the *message-number* refers to a message marked for deletion or is otherwise invalid.

If the client doesn't specify the optional *message-number* argument, the server responds with a multiline reply containing a list of all messages not marked for deletion and their associated unique identifiers.

```
uidl
+OK
1 qofis90asjh23dfkjh234
2 otekj21hfjj42asdjh131
3 oghej25qoiw92oqihr934
4 aoiwh92heeh58frfue528
.
```

5.3 EXAMPLE POP DIALOGS

Perhaps the best way to illustrate the POP commands and their usage is with actual POP dialogs. Despite its simplicity, the command set is capable of a wide variety of tasks. Several of which this section describes.

In the examples, *optional-text* for '+OK' replies is only shown when a specific command requires it. However, the examples do provide *optional-text* for '-ERR' replies, since these are typically presented to the user.

5.3.1 Basic Dialog

The first example to look at is a simple combination of retrieving and deleting messages. It represents the prototypical POP dialog.

```
+OK POP3 server ready
user joe
+OK
pass f02jf!ajds
+OK
stat
+OK 2 7045
retr 1
+OK
server sends message 1
.
dele 1
+OK
retr 2
+OK
server sends message 2
.
dele 2
+OK
quit
+OK
```

Here the server issues the connection greeting, and the client responds by authenticating itself. Another authentication mechanism could have been used—apop, for example—but `user` and `pass` are sufficient for this example.

After authenticating, the client issues the `stat` command to get the number of messages in the maildrop as well as their total size. The `list` command could have been used if more detail was desired for each message.

With the number of messages in hand, the client proceeds to retrieve each message. After a particular message is retrieved, the client issues the `dele` command to mark it for deletion.

After the client has retrieved and deleted the messages, it issues the `quit` command, which causes the server to delete the messages marked for deletion and disconnect. This concludes the dialog. The messages are now located on the client.

5.3.2 Maildrop Summary

The previous example is oriented toward automated transfer of messages from a POP server, where an MUA connects to a POP server and automatically retrieves messages, without user interaction. It's also possible to use POP while interacting with a user, allowing him or her more control over the dialog. As an example, say a client wants to provide a summary of the messages in the remote maildrop and allow the user to select actions to perform on them. To give a feel for what the desired result might be, Table 5.3 shows sample screen output for a fictitious maildrop summary.

TABLE 5.3 Fictitious Maildrop Summary

#	Flags	Date Sent	From	Size	Subject
1		02/15 15:55	joe@tuba.example.com	3K	Announcement
2		02/16 07:19	larry@ictus.example.com	8K	Problem w/ freight forwarder
3		02/16 12:20	harry@gong.example.com	13M	Vacation pictures

The list of messages and their sizes are available from the `list` command.

```
list
+OK
1 3265
2 8250
3 10493894
.
```

The remainder of the information must be gleaned from a succession of `top` commands, one for each message in the folder.

```
top 1 0
+OK
server sends header 1
.
top 2 0
+OK
server sends header 2
.
top 3 0
+OK
server sends header 3
.
```

The client then parses the headers of the three messages, extracts the information to go into the maildrop summary, and presents the summary to the user. The client is now ready for the user to request actions to be performed on the messages in the maildrop.

As far as POP is concerned, there are four things a user can do to a message in the maildrop: delete it, view its header, download it, or ignore it.

In this example, the user has already heard the announcement from Joe and decides to delete the message without viewing it. The POP client issues a `dele` command.

```
dele 1
+OK
```

If the user decides to view the second message, the POP client issues a `retr` command to download the message and presents it to the user.

```
retr 2
+OK
servers sends message 2
.
```

If the user decides to delete the message, the client issues the `dele` command.

```
dele 2
+OK
```

For the third message, the user notices the size and is curious as to whether it's really from Harry, so he or she decides to view the message header.

```
top 3 0
+OK
server sends header of message 3
.
```

In this case, the user decides that the message should be kept and chooses not to delete it.

At this point, the fictitious maildrop summary would look something like Table 5.4. The second column shows the updated status of the messages, where 'D' indicates that a message is marked for delete and 'S' indicates that the message has been seen.

Now the user decides to quit, so the client issues a `quit` command, causing the two messages marked for deletion to be expunged from the maildrop.

```
quit
+OK
```

The connection is then closed.

TABLE 5.4   Second Maildrop Summary

#	Flags	Date Sent	From	Size	Subject
1	D	02/15 15:55	joe@tuba.example.com	3K	Announcement
2	D S	02/16 07:19	larry@ictus.example.com	8K	Problem w/ freight forwarder
3		02/16 12:20	harry@gong.example.com	13M	Vacation pictures

5.3.3 Keeping Recent Messages on the Server

Some POP clients provide the ability to keep recent messages on the server, deleting only those that are older than a certain expiration period. POP doesn't have a direct mechanism for this, but it's possible to synthesize one using a combination of standard POP commands and some bookkeeping on the part of the client.

The key to this technique is the `uidl` command. Since it provides unique identifiers for mail messages, a POP client can use the information in a local cache. The cache typically contains a list of retrieved messages. Showing their UIDL and the date they were retrieved.

To understand this mechanism, assume that the date is July 15, 1999, and that the local cache contains four entries, each one consisting of a UIDL field and a date field.[1]

```
091014a72733866122893c67fb822428 07/05/1999
3535111717v24neb1b124fdi423n1a81 07/01/1999
972594889992526445624796561633313 07/06/1999
cf581c5a565efab81a30f1132e0d892e 07/01/1999
```

When the POP client connects to the server and authenticates, it issues a `uidl` command for the entire set of messages on the server.

```
stat
+OK 6 231483
uidl
+OK
1 cf581c5a565efab81a30f1132e0d892e
2 3535111717v24neb1b124fdi423n1a81
3 091014a72733866122893c67fb822428
4 972594889992526445624796561633313
5 5a28108abbe922971ea65eab2db84c96
6 814006a1005cb7350efd87a696f6f760
.
```

---

[1] The date would typically be represented as an integer, but the example is easier to understand as a human-readable.

Since messages 5 and 6 are not in the local cache, it retrieves them.

```
retr 5
+OK
server sends message 5
.
retr 6
+OK
server sends message 6
.
```

The current date is July 15, 1999, so the client notices that messages 1 and 2 are more than two weeks old. It marks these for deletion and issues a `quit` command to finish the session.

```
dele 1
+OK
dele 2
+OK
quit
+OK
```

Entries in the cache for messages deleted on the server are no longer needed, so they can be removed. The end result is that messages on the server will not be deleted until at least two weeks after they are downloaded by the client.

5.4 POP EXTENSIONS

Since standard POP doesn't provide a way to add new features to the protocol, two extension mechanisms have been created. The first one, defined in RFC1082, was published in 1988. The second, defined in RFC2449, was published in 1998. This section describes these two mechanisms.

5.4.1 Extended Service Offerings

RFC1082 provides an extension to add new commands, as well as several new commands for use with it. Several of the commands are oriented toward providing access, via POP, to discussion groups such as Usenet newsgroups or mailing list archives.

XTND

The extensions added in RFC1082 are provided with one common POP command—xtnd. They are implemented this way to prevent the extension names from colliding with future additions to the core POP command set.

```
"xtnd" SP extension-name [SP arguments]
```

The extensions are valid only in the *transaction* state. In addition, they all issue multiline responses.

BBOARDS

```
"xtnd" SP "bboards" [SP discussion-group]
```

The bboards extension command lists bulletin boards or discussion groups available on the server. These often act as gateways to mailing lists or newsgroups.

```
xtnd bboards
+OK
bug-reports 3
meeting-minutes 1
gripes 103
.
```

If a discussion group is specified, the output is limited to that group.

```
xtnd bboards bug-reports
+OK
bug-reports 3
.
```

ARCHIVE

```
"xtnd" SP "archive" SP discussion-group
```

The archive extension command closes the current maildrop and opens the one specified in *discussion-group*. The server outputs the same information as the corresponding bboards command. Once the maildrop is open, regular POP commands can be used to retrieve information in the discussion group.

```
xtnd archive bug-reports
+OK
bug-reports 2
.
```

TABLE 5.5   Data Returned by `x-bboards` Extension

Line	Description
1	Discussion Group Name
2	Aliases (space separated)
3	Maildrop (system specific)
4	Archive Maildrop (system specific)
5	Information (system specific)
6	Maildrop Map (system specific)
7	Encrypted Password (system specific)
8	Local Leaders (space separated)
9	Discussion Group Email Address
10	Request Address
11	Incoming Feed (system specific)
12	Outgoing Feeds (system specific)
13	Flags '␣' Maxima
14	Last Date

X-BBOARDS

```
"xtnd" SP "x-bboards" SP discussion-group
```

The `x-bboards` extension command is similar to the `archive` command, but provides more detailed information. The output is a multiline response containing the information described in Table 5.5. The items marked as system-specific differ depending upon the underlying mechanism used to populate the bulletin board. An empty line is output for any item that contains no information.

The following example illustrates the `x-bboards` extension. In this case, the bulletin board is a mirror of a `bug-reports` mailing list.

```
xtnd x-bboards bug-reports
+OK
bug-reports
```

```
/usr/bboards/bug-reports
/usr/bboards/archive/bug-reports
/usr/bboards/.system.cnt
/usr/bboards/.system.map

bug-reports@example.com
bug-report-request@example.com

01 452
Thu, 22 Jul 1999 10:31:04 -0700
.
```

XLST

The `xlst` command is a nonstandard extension command available in the Qpopper POP server package, from Qualcomm.

```
"xtnd" SP "xlst" SP field-name [SP message-number]
```

It retrieves a specific header field, in which the *field-name* argument identifies the field of interest. The *message-number* argument identifies which message to search.

```
xtnd xlst content-type 2
2 Content-Type: message/external-body;
            access-type=mail-server;
            server="lists@example.com"
.
```

If the field in the maildrop is folded, as described in Section 2.2.5, it is also folded in the output of the `xlst` command. If no *message-number* is specified, the output consists of a multiline response with the information for every message in the maildrop.

```
xtnd xlst subject
1 Subject: mondomail randomly core dumps
2 Subject: bug: transient window doesn't autoraise
3 Subject: content-language implementation doesn't support x-klingon
4 Subject: another cache corruption bug
.
```

If available, this command can sometimes be used as an alternative to `top` if the number of fields requested is small. The trade-off is the amount of data transferred versus the RTT (Round-Trip Time) latency of performing multiple `xlst` commands.

XMIT

The `xmit` command is another nonstandard extension command available in the Qpopper POP server package.

```
"xtnd" SP "xmit"
```

This command submits an email message to the POP server for subsequent delivery via an MTA. It is an alternative to the client using SMTP to send the message.

```
xtnd xmit
+OK
Date: 4 Oct 1997 08:33:45 -0700
From: bob@flugelhorn.example.com
To: joe@tuba.example.com
Subject: another question
Message-ID: <19971004083345.18492.1@flugelhorn.example.com>
X-Mailer: MondoMail v42.86

Why is the frobnazoid gefargled again?

--
thx,
bob
.
+OK
```

The extension mechanism in RFC1082 isn't ubiquitous. In fact, no additional RFCs have been written to add commands to it. It's use is gradually decreasing, giving way to the extension mechanism described in the following section.

5.4.2 POP3 Extension Mechanism

One of the limitations of RFC1082 is that it has no way to determine which extension commands are supported by a particular server. In addition, several core POP commands are optional, and neither RFC1939 nor RFC1082 provide a way to specify which of them or other behavioral quirks exist on a server. RFC2449 addresses these issues and provides additional machine-parsable detail in status replies.

CAPA

```
"capa"
```

The `capa` command outputs a list of server capabilities. The result is a multiline reply with one capability per line.

```
capa
+OK
top
user
uidl
resp-codes
sasl cram-md5
login-delay 600
pipelining
expire 60
implementation MondoPop-v4.2
.
```

The top, user, uidl capabilities indicate the server's support for the corresponding POP commands. Since these commands are optional, a client can determine whether the server supports them, without having to execute them.

There is no apop capability defined in RFC2449, despite the fact that apop is optional. Clients can discover whether a server supports the command by looking for the initial challenge in the connection greeting.

The resp-codes capability indicates that the server uses extended response codes, which are described later in this section.

In addition to the capabilities already mentioned, RFC2449 makes available additional commands, features, and performance characteristics.

The sasl capability indicates that the server supports the SASL (Simple Authentication and Security Layer) mechanism via the auth command.

```
"sasl" *(SP mechanisms)
```

The parameters are a space-separated list of SASL mechanisms. SASL is described in Section 9.4.2.

The login-delay capability indicates how many seconds must elapse between logins.

```
"login-delay" SP seconds
```

Most POP clients permit periodic checking for new mail. On large servers, small periods of time between checks can present a significant burden. Servers can counter this problem by establishing a minimum amount of time that must elapse before a POP client can reconnect. With login-delay way the server can advertise what that duration is.

The pipelining capability indicates that the server is capable of accepting multiple commands at one time.

```
"pipelining"
```

It is similar to the SMTP pipelining extension described in Section 3.5.2. The client is allowed to send multiple commands to the server before reading the corresponding responses.

```
dele 1
dele 2
dele 3
+OK 1
+OK 2
+OK 3
```

Unlike with SMTP pipelining, there are no commands that require a POP client to wait for a server response before sending subsequent commands. However, if using nonblocking writes, the client must ensure that the window size of the underlying transport layer is not exceeded; otherwise, the dialog could deadlock.

The `expire` capability indicates how many days the server can be expected to retain messages.

```
"expire" SP days
```

Leaving messages on the server can create disk space problems, since some users never delete their messages. To combat this problem, some servers automatically delete mail that has been retrieved and is older than a configurable amount of time. If the server specifies 'never' in the *days* parameter, no expiration policy is in place. If the server specifies 0 in the *days* parameter, it might delete messages when the session ends.

Unlike some of the other capabilities, this one can give a different answer depending on whether the user has authenticated. Prior to authentication, the server responds with a server-wide default. Once the user has authenticated, the server can respond with a user-specific expiration value.

Finally, the `implementation` capability lists the server's package name and version number.

```
"implementation" SP value
```

Many sites consider providing this information a security problem, so it's not uncommon for them to choose not to convey it.

The extension mechanism also allows the use of experimental capabilities by stating that no standard extension will ever start with the letter 'x'. However, a problematic history with this type of mechanism in other email standards, discourages its use.

Extended Response Codes

Sometimes it is helpful to differentiate between POP error responses. For example, a `pass` command will fail if the password is invalid or if the server cannot acquire a lock on the maildrop. POP clients typically present the text associated with the error response to the user for an explanation. There are times, however, when the client can provide a better user interface if it can determine the cause of the error programmatically. Some clients attempt to parse output from some of the more widely deployed servers, but this is problematic.

To address this, RFC2449 adds a mechanism that extends the response code with a machine-parsable section that provides specific information to POP clients.

```
multi-line  = single-line *dot-stuffed-line "."
single-line = status [SP text]
status      = "+OK" / "-ERR"
text        = *schar / [resp-code] *CHAR
resp-code   = '[' resp-level *("/" resp-level) ]"
resp-level  = 1*rchar
rchar       = %x21-2e / %x30-5C / %x5E-7F ; excludes "/" and "]"
schar       = %x21-5A / %x5C-7F          ; excludes "["
```

This is the same as the standard format except that a *resp-code* can occur after the status indicator string.

In addition to the following syntax change, the RFC also extends the connection greeting to a maximum length of 512 octets.

There is a small error in the syntax description in RFC2449. It specifies the syntax as follows.

```
greeting = "+OK" [resp-code] *gchar [timestamp] *gchar
gchar    = %x21-3b / %x3d-7f
```

The ABNF notation defined in RFC2234 requires that all whitespace be explicitly specified. RFC2449, which uses an older ABNF specification, allowed implicit whitespace. Prior to publication as an RFC, it was updated to use RFC2234, but this item was missed. The correct syntax is as follows.

```
greeting = "+OK" [SP resp-code] *gchar [SP timestamp] *gchar
gchar    := %x20-3b / %x3d-7f
```

There are two extended response codes defined in RFC2449. The first, `login-delay`, can be provided with an `auth`, `user`, `pass`, or `apop` command. It indicates that the login delay timer from a previous session has not expired. This allows the client to explain the problem to the user rather than merely indicate that the login failed.

```
user joe
+OK
pass 91j.aj!0
+ERR [LOGIN-DELAY] Login delay timer activated.
```

The other response code, `in-use`, can be provided with an `auth`, `apop`, or `pass` command. It indicates that the login was successful but the session cannot proceed because the user's maildrop is currently in use. This error is more likely caused by another POP client accessing the maildrop.

```
user joe
-ERR [IN-USE] Maildrop already in use.
```

Additional response codes can be added through the IANA registration mechanism.

5.5 SUMMARY

POP gives an MUA the ability to download incoming messages from an intermediate maildrop server. It addresses situations where the final delivery destination for a user's email is not always connected to the network, such as dial-up connections to the Internet.

Designed to be simple and easy to implement, POP is a command-oriented protocol with a small number of commands. Like SMTP, it is text-based, with the client sending commands and the server responding to them. Most of the commands are related to authentication, determining the status of messages in the remote maildrop, retrieving those messages, and deleting them from the maildrop.

There are several extensions available for POP. As with SMTP, these extensions provide additional capabilities not in the core protocol.

This chapter, while smaller than most of the others in this book, serves as important preparatory material for the protocol described in the next chapter—IMAP.

Chapter 6

IMAP

POP works well for what it is supposed to do—provide clients with intermediate storage for incoming email—but it does have limitations. For one thing, it can't handle multiple mailboxes easily, since it was designed to handle a user's incoming email in one folder. For another thing, while it can keep messages on the server, it was designed to download them to the client. IMAP solves these problems by providing both access to multiple remote mailboxes and the ability to keep any or all messages on a remote server.

POP also doesn't handle multiple-client access to the same mailbox very well. This is an increasing problem as more users have personal computers at home and at work, as well as a laptop for business travel. IMAP was specifically designed to support this scenario. It also supports multiple users accessing the same folders as different identities.

Not only does IMAP overcome some of the limitations of POP, it brings several interesting features of its own to the table. Because it allows mailboxes to reside completely on a server, it keeps network traffic to a minimum. It natively supports message and MIME structures, so clients don't need to do complicated parsing of message structures.

IMAP is a relatively recent addition to the world of email, but it is gaining widespread acceptance. Despite its youth, it has undergone several incarnations since its inception, which have resulted in a rapidly maturing email protocol.

The first IMAP RFC was published in 1988, as RFC1064 (Interactive Mail Access Protocol—Version 1). In 1990, it was updated by RFC1176 (Interactive Mail Access Protocol—Version 2). In 1991, RFC1203 (Interactive Mail Access Protocol —Version 3) was published. It defined a so-called "version 3" of the protocol, but this was not accepted by the IMAP development community and was never implemented.

Version 4 was published in 1994 as RFC1730 (Internet Message Access Protocol—Version 4). A companion document, RFC1732 (IMAP4 Compatibility with

IMAP2 and IMAP2bis) was published to aid in the migration from version 2 to version 4. RFC1733 (Distributed Electronic Mail Models in IMAP4) was published in 1994 as well. It outlines a conceptual model for classifying the various types of client/server access to email. RFC1733 is important for an understanding of the capabilities of IMAP compared to POP.

Version 4 was updated in 1996 with RFC2060 (Internet Message Access Protocol, Version 4rev1). RFC2061 (IMAP4 Compatibility with IMAP2bis) was published as well, to update RFC1732.

To further assist the migration from IMAP2 to IMAP4, RFC2062 (Internet Message Access Protocol—Obsolete Syntax) was also published in 1996. It provides a summary of older commands not implemented in IMAP4rev1. Like RFC1732, its primary purpose is to provide information for developers who want backward compatibility with older versions of the protocol.

In addition to the core IMAP standard, several extensions have been defined. Section 6.7 describes them. Also, the author of RFC2060, Mark Crispin, maintains errata documents for RFC2060 and RFC2061.[1]

This chapter describes IMAP4rev1, as specified in RFC2060. While a significant amount of the information in this chapter applies to the older versions of the protocol, references to IMAP generally mean IMAP4rev1.

6.1 INTERFACE MODEL

The interface model is the key to understanding IMAP. While it borrows heavily from earlier standards, it is significantly different from SMTP and POP.

At the highest level, an IMAP session, like SMTP and POP, is a communication dialog between two machines—a client and a server. The client connects to a server via TCP port 143 and sends commands to the server; the server sends data to the client. This continues until one of the two terminates the session.

Figure 6.1 illustrates the relationship between the various components in an IMAP dialog.

As with POP, an MTA receives incoming email and hands it off to an MDA, which delivers it to an incoming mailbox. An IMAP client manages its local mailboxes and communicates with an IMAP server to manage its remote mailboxes. An IMAP server provides the interface between a remote client and mailboxes that are stored on the server. Since IMAP, like POP, doesn't provide a method for sending out-bound messages, the IMAP client talks to an MTA to do this.

Unlike POP and SMTP, where server responses always correspond directly to a given command from the client, IMAP allows the server to send information that doesn't correspond to the current command. In effect, IMAP provides two protocols—one for client commands and the corresponding status responses, the

---

[1] ftp://ftp.cac.washington.edu/mail/rfc206[01]-errata

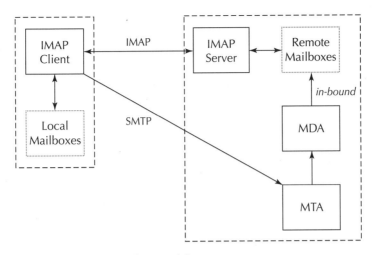

FIGURE 6.1 IMAP Interface Model

other for data sent from the server to the client. It is analogous to the use of two channels for control and data information in FTP, except that it is done with only one channel.

At first this might seem like a complicated way to do things. The main benefit is flexibility. For example, IMAP was designed to support multiple clients accessing a mailbox simultaneously. If another client deletes a message from the mailbox a client has selected, the IMAP server can notify the client of the change, as illustrated in Figure 6.2. This notification is sent without the client explicitly asking for it, using the data protocol. If the notification were to be sent as part of a command sequence,

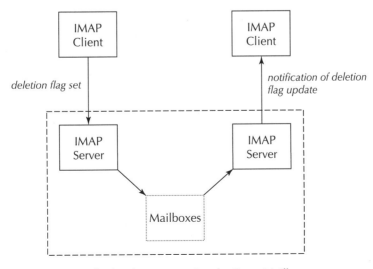

FIGURE 6.2 Multiple Clients Accessing the Same Mailbox

the server would need to wait until the client issued a command in order to notify it of the updated information.

Another interesting difference in IMAP is its handling of multiple pending commands. As with pipelining in SMTP and POP, an IMAP client can send multiple pending commands to a server. However, IMAP allows the server to process the commands simultaneously, possibly even returning the results in a different order than the commands were received in. While not widely used, if at all, this capability presents some interesting possibilities, such as performing long-running search commands in parallel with other commands. Multiple pending commands are discussed in greater length in Section 6.3.4.

Another interesting characteristic of IMAP is that traffic between the client and server can be minimized. IMAP understands the structure of messages and MIME entities. Instead of merely retrieving a message or a certain number of lines of a message, IMAP allows clients to retrieve information about the message structure and subsets of the message, including the individual entities within a MIME message. Clients can use this information to retrieve portions of the data as necessary, which can be very useful over low bandwidth communication links. For example, a client can retrieve the text portions of a message, leaving larger MIME attachments on the server unless the user requests the larger attachments.

One final capability worth mentioning is disconnected mode. IMAP can handle disconnected interactions between a client and a server. In this mode, the client synchronizes with a server and disconnects; the user then processes mail with the disconnected client. When the client reconnects, it resynchronizes with the server. Unfortunately, this use of IMAP isn't well understood, or well explored, yet, although it's expected to evolve.

6.2 PROTOCOL STATES

Like SMTP and POP, IMAP defines several session states, each with its own purpose and limitations. Figure 6.3 shows the various states and the flow between them.

Once a client connects to a server, the server outputs a connection greeting. Clients use the greeting to determine whether the server is willing to carry on a conversation and to what state the server is starting in.

Sessions usually start in the *nonauthenticated* state unless the session has been preauthenticated. Only a small number of commands necessary for authenticating are available in this state.

Once the client has confirmed the identity of its user to the server, the session moves to the *authenticated* state, at which point a larger set of commands is available.

To act on specific mailboxes, the client must enter the *selected* state, by issuing a `select` or `examine` command. The session remains in the *selected* state if the command fails. Once in the *authenticated* state, it remains there until the session is ready to be terminated or until a `close` command is issued.

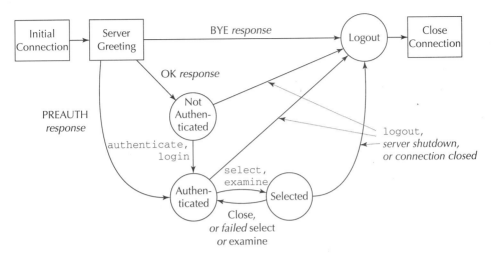

FIGURE 6.3 IMAP Session States

The final state is *logout,* which is preparation for the termination of the connection. This state is entered when the client issues the `logout` command or when the server decides to close down the connection.

6.3 COMMANDS AND RESPONSES

On the surface, IMAP is line-oriented. That is, data is sent in both directions as lines of text and each line is terminated with CRLF. However, IMAP provides the ability to send literals, which can contain arbitrary binary data. Literals are described in Section 6.4.4.

RFC2060 doesn't place any specific line-length limitations on data sent in either direction. As a matter of practicality, message data should adhere to the length limitations required by SMTP. In addition, strings should be kept less than 1K characters in length and literals should be used for larger pieces of data, particularly if the data is longer than 2K to 4K. Quoted strings are described in Section 6.4.3, and literals are described in Section 6.4.4. The primary factor to take into account is that some implementations might have problems processing long lines or long quoted strings; literals can help reduce the likelihood of triggering bugs.

IMAP specifies only one timeout value, an inactivity auto-logout timer, which imposes a limit on the amount of idle time a client can consume. The duration must be at least 30 minutes. Receipt of any command is sufficient to reset the timer. IMAP sessions tend to last much longer than SMTP or POP sessions, often for several days. Because of this, there are no timeouts related to overall session duration except for the auto-logout timer.

The client sends a command; the server processes it and then sends the client zero or more untagged response lines and a completion status response line. For the most part, command lines and response lines are case-insensitive. Any exceptions to this will be noted as they are encountered.

So far, the commands and responses seem conceptually similar to those of SMTP and POP, but there's one very significant difference at this level of the protocol—multiple pending commands. While the pipelining extensions in SMTP and POP allow multiple commands to be sent without waiting for the responses, the commands are processed in order and the responses are sent back in the same order. Not only does IMAP allow multiple commands to be sent before responses are received, but those commands can be processed in any order the server see fit as long as there is no ambiguity in the results. This is one of the primary factors shaping the syntax of IMAP commands and responses. It is described in Section 6.3.4.

A command line consists of multiple fields: a tag followed by an IMAP command and optional command-specific arguments. Each field is separated by a single SPACE character.

```
tag SP command *(SP command-arguments)
```

The following example is a simple command, containing each of the elements just mentioned.

```
d1321 copy 1:3 monthly-archive
```

The tag is `d1321`, the command is `copy`, and the rest of the line contains the arguments for the command.

The tag uniquely identifies the command line. When the server sends the corresponding status response, the client can use that information to associate the status with the original command line.

The syntax for tag is as follows.

```
tag = 1*<any atom-char except "+">
```

The syntax for *atom-char* is described in Section 6.4.2.

Despite the liberal set of characters allowed in a tag, they are frequently just ascending sequences of alphanumeric strings.

Following the tag is the command and any optional arguments. Table 6.1 summarizes the commands. They will be described in detail in Section 6.5.

For each command issued by a client, the server needs to return information to the client. The three types of information returned are status responses, server data, and command continuation requests. Status responses, as the name implies, provide status information. Server data provides information about data maintained

TABLE 6.1 IMAP Commands

Command	N	A	S	Description
capability	•	•	•	List the server's capabilities
noop	•	•	•	No operation
logout	•	•	•	Log off of the server
authenticate	•			Authenticate with the server
login	•			Log into the server
select		•	•	Open a mailbox
examine		•	•	Open a mailbox read-only
create		•	•	Create a mailbox
delete		•	•	Delete a mailbox
rename		•	•	Rename a mailbox
subscribe		•	•	Subscribe to a mailbox
unsubscribe		•	•	Unsubscribe to a mailbox
list		•	•	List mailboxes
lsub		•	•	List subscribed mailboxes
status		•	•	Get the status of a mailbox
append		•	•	Append a message to a mailbox
check			•	Checkpoint the current mailbox
close			•	Close the current mailbox
expunge			•	Expunge the current mailbox
search			•	Search the current mailbox
fetch			•	Retrieve data from a set of messages
store			•	Set flags for a set of messages
copy			•	Copy a set of messages to a mailbox
uid			•	Copy, fetch, store, and search based on UID

by the server. Continuation requests occur when a client sends a command that requires multiple lines; they indicate that the server is ready to receive the rest of the command.

6.3.1 Status Responses

Status responses are the primary way a server communicates command or session state to a client. The syntax is as follows.

```
tag-or-star SP status [SP "["response-code"]"] SP text
```

There are two types of status responses, tagged and untagged. Tagged responses, also referred to as completion status responses, contain a tag in the first field of the line. They indicate whether a particular command succeeded, failed, or had some type of protocol error. The tag matches the tag sent with the corresponding command.

Untagged responses contain a '*' character in the first field of the line. They convey information that isn't directly associated with a specific command, including status responses and server data.

The second field, *status,* indicates whether the command succeeded, failed, or had some type of protocol error. It contains either OK, NO, BAD, PREAUTH, or BYE.

The response code is an optional piece of information for the client beyond a simple success, failure, and error status.

The text portion is human-readable information for users. It normally contains one or more 7-bit characters, except US-ASCII 0, CR, or LF. RFC2060 allows the text to be encoded with the format in RFC2047, described in Section 4.5, but in practice this feature isn't used much, if at all. The problem is that it requires clients to know about charsets merely to display human-readable messages from the server. According to the author of RFC2060, it will be removed in a future version of IMAP, so it's a good idea to avoid it.

OK Response

There are two uses of OK. When used in a tagged response, it indicates successful completion of the command identified by the tag.

```
a042 noop
a042 ok noop completed
```

When used in an untagged response, it is an information message from the server and can be any of several flavors. The first type encountered in an IMAP session is the initial greeting from the server. This is seen if the server is willing to carry on a dialog with the client.

```
connection is established
* ok imap.example.com server ready
```

The second type is used to send optional response codes to the client.

```
* ok [unseen 5] Message 5 is first unseen
```

It can also be used to send diagnostic information for debugging problems.

NO Response

Like OK responses, NO responses can be either tagged or untagged. When tagged, they indicate that the associated command failed.

```
a030 create team-notes
a030 no mailbox already exists
```

When untagged, they indicate some type of warning, without necessarily indicating that the command failed. These are typically sent with response codes.

```
* no [alert] Mailbox is at 95% quota
```

BAD Response

Like OK and NO responses, BAD responses can be either tagged or untagged. When tagged, they indicate a protocol error with the associated command, typically a syntax error.

```
a1035 noop blurp
a1035 bad invalid argument
```

When untagged, they indicate a problem at the protocol level but not associated with a specific command.

```
client sends blank line
* bad missing tag
```

PREAUTH Response

The PREAUTH status response is seen only at the start of a session and is sent only as an untagged response. The server uses it instead of OK if the client has already been authenticated by some other means.

In addition to being used as a network server, some UNIX implementations allow the IMAP server program to be invoked directly by a client on the same machine. In this case, since the user has already been authenticated by the operating system, the IMAP server doesn't need authentication. It signals this by providing an alternate connection greeting.

```
client invokes IMAP server program
* preauth localhost server ready
```

BYE Response

The BYE response indicates that the server is about to close the connection. Like the PREAUTH response, it is always untagged.

When a client sends a logout command, the server sends a BYE response.

```
a152 logout
* bye server logging out
a152 ok logout completed
```

A server will also send this response to announce its imminent shutdown.

```
connection is established
* bye [alert] system shutting down now
connection is closed
```

It is also used as a connection greeting to indicate that the server is unwilling to start a session.

```
* bye access denied
connection is closed
```

Finally, if the auto-logout timer expires, the server will issue a BYE response and immediately close the connection.

```
* bye auto-logout - idle for too long
connection is closed
```

Response Codes

A status response can include an optional *response code,* which informs the client of a specific action it can take. They are enclosed in a pair of '[]' characters. Some codes provide additional arguments inside the brackets.

Alert The alert code indicates that the human-readable text contains a special message that must be presented to the user.

```
* ok [alert] System shutting down in 5 minutes
```

Newname The newname code is used in response to a select or examine command. It indicates that the command is failing because the mailbox was renamed, and the mailbox given in the command no longer exists. This is a hint to the client that the command might succeed if the new name is used. Two arguments are provided: the old mailbox name and the new one.

```
a513 select puns
a513 no [newname puns humor-puns] mailbox has been renamed
a514 select humor-puns
a514 ok select completed
```

Parse If a server encounters an error in parsing an email header or the MIME structure of a message, it can issue a parse response code.

```
b312 fetch 4 envelope
* ok [parse] Warning: message has unknown MIME version
server sends envelope data
b312 ok fetch completed
```

Permanentflags The permanentflags code, returned by the select and examine commands, lists the flags that the client can change permanently. A parenthetical list of flags is returned with the code.

```
* ok [permanentflags (\deleted \seen \*)]
```

The '*' flag is a special token indicating that the server allows new keywords to be created. Flags and keywords are described in Section 6.4.11. Any flags not listed with the `permanentflags` response code are temporary. If the client attempts to store a flag that isn't permanent, the server should accept the flag and forget the change at the end of the session.

Read-Only The `read-only` response code indicates that a mailbox cannot be modified. It is used with the `select` and `examine` commands, and it is always issued if `examine` was used to open the mailbox.

```
b482 ok [read-only] examine completed
```

In many situations, users cannot alter messages in folders marked read-only. If, however, a folder is marked as read-only and `permanentflags` isn't an empty list, the client may alter the permanent flags for the individual user, rather than on a global basis. The most common example of this is with newsgroups, where the user is not allowed to delete the message but is allowed to mark the message as read.

The `read-only` code can also be issued if the status of the mailbox changes from read-write to read-only while the client has it selected. This can be seen with some IMAP implementations that don't allow multiple clients to access a mailbox in read-write mode. In this case the first client might have its read-write access downgraded to read-only, the thought being that the same user is using another client to access his or her mail. It might also be done when the access permissions on the mailbox have changed.

Read-Write The `read-write` code indicates that a mailbox can be modified. It is used only with the `select` command, never `examine`. This is the default, so if neither `read-write` nor `read-only` are sent, the mailbox can be modified.

```
b483 ok [read-write] select completed
```

This code can also be issued if the status of a selected mailbox changes from read-only to read-write. In the scenario described above, the IMAP server might upgrade the access rights back to read-write once the other client closes the mailbox.

Trycreate If an `append` or `copy` command fails because the mailbox doesn't exist, the server can issue a `trycreate` code if it thinks the operation will succeed if the mailbox is created first.

```
d1321 copy 1:2 monthly-archive
d1321 no [trycreate] mailbox doesn't exist
d1322 create monthly-archive
d1322 ok create completed
```

Unseen The unseen code provides the number of the first message in the mailbox without the \seen flag set. This number is provided as an argument inside the brackets. As with several other response codes, the select and examine commands generate this in an untagged response.

```
* ok [unseen 50] 50 is first unseen message in mailbox
```

UIDvalidity The uidvalidity code is sent in response to a select or examine command and contains an argument that provides the *unique identity validity* value for the mailbox. It is described in greater detail in Section 6.4.10.

```
* ok [uidvalidity 901188081] UID validity status
```

UIDnext The uidnext code indicates the server's prediction for the UID value to be assigned to the next message added to the mailbox. When combined with the uidvalidity value, it can be used by clients to detect whether any new messages have been added. The actual value isn't important; only the fact that it changed should be noted. This code is not included in RFC2060, but has become a de-facto standard.

In addition to the codes just described, experimental codes can be created by prefixing them with 'x'. As with most experimental extensions, this should be used sparingly, if at all.

The possibility of experimental code brings up one last point—clients should ignore any response codes they don't understand to prevent unknown ones from breaking implementations.

6.3.2 Server Data

In addition to status responses, the server can also send *server data,* that is, any information maintained by the server not considered status information. This

TABLE 6.2   Server Data

Server Data	Must Save	Commands	Description
capability		capability	List of server capabilities
exists	•	select, examine, *unsolicited*	Number of messages in the mailbox
expunge	•	expunge, *unsolicited*	A message has just been expunged
fetch		fetch, uid fetch, store	Requested data about a message
flags	•	select, examine, *unsolicited*	Flags applicable to a mailbox
list		list	Mailbox information sent after a list command
lsub		lsub	Mailbox information sent after a lsub command
recent	•	select, examine, *unsolicited*	Number of recent messages in the mailbox
search		search, uid search	Search results sent after a search or uid search command
status		status	Status information

includes, but is not limited to, message text, message flags, mailbox lists, search results, and server capabilities.

Server data is always untagged. Clients should record it for later use to avoid requesting it again. In fact, some server data types must be recorded by the client. Table 6.2 summarizes these, each of which will be discussed in detail in Section 6.5 with their associated commands.

6.3.3   Command Continuation Request Responses

A client can sometimes send an incomplete command. When the server receives such a line, it sends a command continuation request response to the client, indicating it is ready to accept the remainder. These responses are used primarily with fields sent as literals, which are described in Section 6.4.4, and authentication dialogs.

When a command continuation response is called for, the server sends a single line starting with a '+' character followed by a SPACE character and optional human-readable text.

```
+ go ahead
```

The client then sends the remainder of the data expected at this point in the dialog. Multiple continuation requests can be sent. In this case, the dialog is repeated as necessary. The server can send a BAD response if it needs to abort a continuation request.

This mechanism is used only inside a command. The client must complete the command before initiating another one.

6.3.4 More on Multiple Pending Commands

As mentioned earlier, IMAP allows multiple pending commands, which, on the surface, are similar to the pipelining extensions for SMTP and POP. There is, however, one very important difference—while SMTP and POP pipelining requires that the commands be executed in the order they are received, IMAP allows multiple pending commands to be processed in any order, including simultaneously. This feature isn't used much, if at all, but it bears scrutiny, particularly for threaded IMAP servers. With multiple pending commands, it's possible to run multiple commands in parallel.

The primary issue with this feature is that the multiple commands must not introduce any ambiguities, in which the results depend on the order of processing. As a simple example, say a rename command and a create command are issued together. If the commands are executed in order, the results will be as follows.

```
b285 rename status-reports status-reports-old
b286 create status-reports
b285 ok rename completed
b286 ok create completed
```

If, on the other hand, they are executed in reverse order, the following will result.

```
b285 rename status-reports status-reports-old
b286 create status-reports
b286 no mailbox already exists
b285 ok rename completed
```

In addition to the obvious interactions between commands, there are also situations where specific uses of a set of commands could result in an ambiguity. As an example, issuing a `fetch` and a simultaneous `store` of the same message's flags might be ambiguous, depending on whether the `.silent` option is used with `store`. To illustrate this, the following example uses the option.

```
b393 store 6 flags.silent (\answered)
b392 ok store completed
b394 store 6 flags.silent (\deleted)
b395 fetch 6 (flags)
b394 ok store completed
* 395 6 fetch (flags \deleted)
b395 ok fetch completed
```

If the commands were executed in reverse order, the results would be as follows.

```
* 6 fetch (flags \answered)
b395 ok fetch completed
b394 ok store completed
```

The previous example used the `.silent` option to the `store` command. If it were not used, the results would be unambiguous because the server would send untagged responses accounting for each flag change, allowing the client to keep accurate records.

```
b393 store 6 flags.silent (\answered)
b392 ok store completed
b394 store 6 flags (\deleted)
b395 fetch 6 (flags)
* 6 fetch (flags \deleted)
b395 ok fetch completed
* 6 fetch (flags \deleted)
b394 ok store completed
```

The results processed in the opposite order would be

```
* 6 fetch (flags \answered)
b384 ok store completed
* 6 fetch (flags \deleted)
b395 ok fetch completed
```

In this case, the outcome is the same. Care is required, however, when choosing which form of the `store` command to use.

Another possible ambiguity is related to `expunge` responses. If a client sends any command other than `fetch`, `store`, or `search`, it must wait for a response before sending any command that uses message numbers because of the effect `expunge` has on them. Message numbers are described in detail in Section 6.4.9. To illustrate the ambiguity, take the following example.

```
b436 copy 7 status-reports
b437 copy 10 presentations
```

Remember that multiple IMAP clients can have the same folder selected. Thus, if another client were to issue an `expunge` command on the folder between the two `copy` commands, the message number could be incorrect.

For example, if the other client marks message 8 for deletion and then expunges the folder, message 10 becomes message 9. This is because the server can send `expunge` responses when responding to any command other than `fetch`, `store`, or `search`. Depending on which order the multiple pending commands are processed in, the expunge responses will invalidate message numbers. This isn't a problem for the three commands just mentioned because a server is not allowed to send an `expunge` response while any of them are in process.

If the client waits for the first `copy` to complete, it will receive the `expunge` response from the server, allowing the client to update its message numbers. Once this is done, it can issue the second `copy` command, specifying message 9 instead of 10.

```
b436 copy 7 status-reports
* 8 expunge
b436 ok copy completed
b437 copy 9 presentations
b437 ok copy completed
```

If the second command is, say, `delete`, no ambiguity will result.

```
b436 copy 7 status-reports
b437 delete junk
* 8 expunge
b436 ok copy completed
b437 ok delete completed
```

It's also possible to introduce ambiguity with opening and closing folders. For example, the results of a `store` command and a `select` command are dependent on the order in which they are processed.

```
b391 select folder1
server sends data for folder 1
b391 ok select completed
b392 store 6 +flags.silent (\deleted)
b393 select folder2
b391 ok select completed
b392 ok select completed
```

In this case, the `store` command was processed before the second `select` command, so message 6 in `folder1` was marked for deletion. If the order were reversed, the results would be significantly different.

```
b391 select folder1
server sends data for folder 1
b391 ok select completed
b392 store 6 +flags.silent (\deleted)
b393 select folder2
b392 ok select completed
b391 ok store completed
```

Here message 6 in `folder2` would be marked for deletion, which means the results are different depending on processing order.

While the limitations just mentioned might seem restrictive, this doesn't mean that multiple pending commands are useless. As an example, it's possible to issue a series of `create` commands in one fell swoop without incurring the RTT waiting for the status responses.

```
b592 create meeting-archives
b593 create status-archives
b594 create review-archives
b595 create film-archives
b592 ok create completed
b593 ok create completed
b594 ok create completed
b595 ok create completed
```

As another, more interesting example, imagine issuing a long-running `search` command while still being able to issue other commands.

```
b625 search text "the test results"
b626 fetch 4892 (bodystructure)
* 4892 fetch (bodystructure bodystructure-data)
b626 ok fetch completed
b627 store 4892 +flags.silent (\deleted)
b628 fetch 4893 (bodystructure)
b627 ok store completed
* 4893 fetch (bodystructure bodystructure-data)
b628 ok fetch completed
* search 3115 3117
b625 ok search completed
```

The key to understanding why this example is valid is to remember that servers are not allowed to send `expunge` responses while a `fetch`, `store`, or `search` command is being processed. Therefore, the message numbers are not invalidated, and none of the commands conflict with each other.

Few, if any, IMAP server implementations process multiple pending commands simultaneously. As a result, few, if any, IMAP clients take advantage of them, although they are still an important concept. As IMAP implementations mature, and developers gain a better understanding of the protocol, it's quite possible that this feature will be more widely implemented.

6.4 DATA OBJECTS

Unlike SMTP and POP, which both have a relatively simple syntax, IMAP's syntax is rather complicated. This is particularly evident in the several types of data communicated between the client and server. These require special discussion.

6.4.1 NIL

One of the simplest data objects is `NIL`, a token used in places where the nonexistence of a value needs to be represented. There are several such places, as will be seen as this section unfolds.

6.4.2 Atoms

IMAP has many terms in its syntax, many of which are based on the *atom* token. Because of this, a detailed look at their definition is called for.

```
atom            = 1*atom-char
atom-char       = <any char except atom-specials>
char            = 0x01-7f
atom-specials   = "(" / ")" / "{" / SP / CTL /
                  list-wildcards / quoted-specials
list-wildcards  = "%" / "*"
quoted-specials = DQUOTE / "\"
```

An *atom-specials* token consists of characters used in other syntax items in the protocol. In other words, an *atom* cannot contain any character used for other purposes in the IMAP syntax. Readers familiar with language parsers might think that this restriction is unnecessary, since parsers can be created to handle *atom* tokens containing other characters. As it turns out, however, this definition simplifies the parsing considerably. When a parser looks for an *atom,* it simply collects a consecutive sequence of characters that aren't contained in *atom-specials* without concerning itself with special quoting rules.

6.4.3 Quoted Strings

Atoms are fairly restrictive in what they can contain. To address this, a *quoted-string* is defined that is similar to the *quoted-strings* found in other languages.

A *quoted-string* is a sequence of zero or more 7-bit characters, contained in a pair of '"' characters. Any 7-bit character except US-ASCII 0, CR, or LF is permitted. Because '"' is used to contain the string, it must be escaped with '\' if it occurs in the string. Any '\' characters not used to escape double-quote characters must also be escaped.

6.4.4 Literals

Quoted-strings are a convenient alternative when *atoms* are too restrictive, but they, too, have restrictions. For example, they are limited to a single line of data and require parsing to handle escaped characters. To address this, IMAP defines a construct with even fewer restrictions—a *literal.*

A literal consists of an octet count field, a CRLF, and the data payload. The octet count consists of a non-negative integer inside a pair of '{}' characters.

The data in a literal can contain any 8-bit character except US-ASCII 0. However, this doesn't mean that 8-bit data is acceptable in all places. In the case of mail messages, the data must follow the normal rules for content transfer encoding. Thus, if an 8-bit message is transmitted, it must have the appropriate value in a `Content-Transfer-Encoding` field as well as the appropriate `charset` value in the `Content-Type` field.

To illustrate how a literal is used, the following example shows a server sending three fields of data, with the second field being a literal.

```
field1 {13}
ab%"\q921!$yz  field3
```

When the client encounters the literal, it reads past the CRLF and then reads in the *exact* number of characters specified in the literal count, including CRLFs in the data. When this is done, the client is ready to parse the next field.

If a client sends a literal to a server, it must wait for the server to send a continuation request response before sending the literal data.

```
field1 {13}
+ go ahead
ab%"\q921!$yz  field3
```

There is a nonsynchronizing literals extension that doesn't require the server to send a continuation request before the client sends the literal data. It is described in Section 6.7.1.

Syntactically, only one place requires a literal—the append command. Other places allow it as an alternative to other notations. IMAP defines the following constructs containing literals.

```
string  = quoted-string / literal
astring = string / atom
nstring = string / "nil"
```

These are used in many places in the IMAP syntax. With each there is a choice of using a literal or one of the other types. The general guideline is that the simplest device that expresses the data should be used. For example, in the case of an *astring*, an *atom* should be used if the data value can be expressed as an *atom*. Otherwise, it should be expressed as a *quoted-string* if that works. A literal should be used as a fall-back if neither *atom* nor *quoted-string* is acceptable. That said, it's not unusual to find data sent as a literal that could have been sent as a *quoted-string*. There's nothing wrong with this; it's simply an implementation decision made by the developer of the package. In fact, at times a literal is more desirable than the other two representations. If a *quoted-string* is larger than 1 kilobyte or so, it should probably be sent as a literal. This will reduce the likelihood of triggering a data-length bug in the software on the other end of the connection.

6.4.5 Parenthesized Lists

There are several places in IMAP where data structures need to be communicated between client and server. IMAP uses parenthetical lists to notate them. These parenthetical lists are the kind most programmers encounter on a regular basis. They consist of a sequence of data items wrapped in parentheses. The data items are delimited by a single SPACE character.

The following example shows a list being used in a response to a `status` command.

```
* status monthly-archives (messages 5 recent 1 unseen 2)
```

The list syntax also allows lists to contain other lists, which means that arbitrarily nested data structures can be represented as lists. At this point, we have what Lisp and Scheme programmers will recognize as an *s-expression*.

This example shows a nested list being used in a `fetch` response.

```
* 1 fetch (envelope
         ("Wed, 10 Feb 1999 14:22:36 -0700"
          "Re: another question"
          ((NIL NIL "joe" "tuba.example.com"))
          ((NIL NIL "joe" "tuba.example.com"))
          ((NIL NIL "joe" "tuba.example.com"))
          ((NIL NIL "bob" "flugelhorn.example.com"))
          NIL NIL NIL
          "<19990210142237.9823.1@tuba.example.com>"))
```

The contents of lists have specific structures, based on how they are used in IMAP. These structures will be described in detail as they are encountered in this chapter.

There's one small, but important, item to mention at this point. The previous example shows the list spanning several lines, with indentation matching the levels of nesting in the s-expression. This is *not* how IMAP uses them. IMAP parenthetical lists are contained on a single line, without wrapping. Line-wrapping is used in this chapter for ease of reading and layout. Be sure to keep this in mind when viewing the examples.

Also note that IMAP is very strict about whitespace. Where a SPACE character is required there must be one, and only one. If no SPACE character is required, none should be present.

6.4.6 Mailbox Names

In addition to the syntax objects just described, IMAP has several types of data with specific semantic meaning. One of the most fundamental objects is, unsurprisingly, the mailbox. This acts as a container for a collection of messages. While IMAP insulates the client from the mailbox format, it must cope with referencing it. Specifically, what is its name?

Mailbox names are fairly liberal in IMAP, and as a result an *astring* is used as the syntax element. Despite this fact, they should be limited to 7-bit data. RFC2060 doesn't include this stipulation, but the next update will reserve 8-bit data for future use as UTF-8 mailbox names. The problem with 8-bit mailbox names is the charset. Without charset information, the client has no way to determine which charset to use when rendering the 8-bit data.

From a protocol perspective, there is only one special mailbox name—`inbox`. This refers to the primary mailbox used to store incoming email. `Inbox` is case-insensitive, with any combination of upper- or lower-case versions referring to the same incoming mailbox.

The case sensitivity of other mailbox names is a little more complicated. A server can implement them as sensitive or insensitive. In fact, there is nothing in the protocol that stops a server from having both.

Some clients use special mailbox names for special purposes, such as storing copies of sent, draft, or deleted messages. There is no standard for these, which can cause some confusion for users if they use clients from more than one vendor. For example, one client might use 'Sent Mail' to store copies of all out-bound messages, while another might use 'sent-mail'. If the user is lucky, the clients provide the ability to configure the names of these special mailboxes.

Hierarchical Mailbox Names

IMAP allows mailbox names to reflect a tree structure, like directory trees. These hierarchical names provide users the ability to organize their mailboxes into categories. Servers are not required to support hierarchical folders, but most, if not all, do.

Figure 6.4 illustrates a hierarchy of mailbox names. The hierarchy is interpreted from left to right, with a single character used to separate the levels. As with directories on UNIX, MS-DOS, and OS/2, the same delimiter character is used at each level of the tree.

The following example shows a resulting mailbox name, assuming the hierarchy delimiter is '/'.

```
mailing-lists/security/bugtraq
```

FIGURE 6.4 Hierarchical Mailbox Names

Other characters can be used as the separator. One common alternative is '.', often seen with newsgroups made available via IMAP.

The other common alternative is '\', since this is the directory separator used on MS-DOS and OS/2. Something worth mentioning is that since this is a special character in IMAP syntax, it cannot be used in an *atom* and must be escaped if used in a *quoted-string*.

```
"C:\\mailing-lists\\security\\bugtraq"
```

The separator character used for a particular folder is determined by the server, not the client. Also, there is no requirement that a separator be used. Some clients assume a certain separator or that a separator character is used. This can cause problems when they communicate with servers that haven't made the same choice. Clients should use the separators chosen by the server, since different namespaces can have different separators, even on the same server.

Namespaces

IMAP allows interfacing to multiple message repositories on the server—for example, newsgroups. This kind of environment can cause name collisions between mailboxes in the different repositories. In other words, how can a mailbox name in one repository be prevented from duplicating a mailbox name in another? In IMAP, the answer is *namespaces*. A namespace is a prefix to a mailbox name that indicates in which repository the mailbox resides.

RFC2060 describes a convention for naming namespaces. If the first segment starts with a '#' character, a mailbox is in a particular namespace. For example, '#news.comp.mail.headers' could specify a comp.mail.headers newsgroup in a news repository, whereas a mailbox without a namespace could indicate that a user created it to save messages from the newsgroup.

Different kinds of namespaces are possible. For example, a server might implement a '#shared' namespace to provide access to a repository of shared mailboxes, or a '#public' namespace to provide access to a publicly accessible repository.

There is no requirement for servers to implement namespaces, and RFC2060 isn't very detailed about their use. Consequently, there are a variety of implementations. In fact, since the use of '#' is not a requirement, some servers use other conventions.

RFC2342 (IMAP4 Namespace) describes an IMAP extension that allows clients to query a server for information on available namespaces. This extension is described in Section 6.7.3.

International Mailbox Names

To handle international mailbox names, a modified version of UTF-7 is used. The modifications are necessary because of conflicts between UTF-7 and several aspects of mailbox names on current operating systems.

The use of '+' and '/' in UTF-7 conflicts with their common use in mailbox names. Furthermore, UTF-7 doesn't allow the unencoded use of '\' or '~'. Since these are popular characters in mailbox names, it would be cumbersome to encode them. Finally, UTF-7 allows printable US-ASCII characters to be represented in encoded form.

In *modified UTF-7*, all printable US-ASCII characters, except '&' are unencoded. The '&' character is represented as '&-'. All other characters are represented in a modified version of `base64`. In modified `base64`, the '=' padding character is not used because it conflicts with its use as an `escape` character in `quoted-printable` content transfer encoding. In addition, the ',' character is used instead of '/' when performing the `base64` encoding.

The following example shows a few unencoded strings and the associated mailbox name encoded in modified UTF-7.

```
Meat&Potatoes
Meat&-Potatoes

Conversations with Jürgen
Conversations with J&APw-rgen
```

6.4.7 Internal Date

When a message is appended to a mailbox, it is assigned an *internal date*—the date and time the message was received, as opposed to the date contained in the `Date` field. This is the IMAP equivalent of the date contained in the message's final `Received` field, and might, in fact, be the same value in many implementations.

6.4.8 Size

Several places in IMAP refer to the size of a message, that is, the *exact* number of octets. This seems simple enough, but it bears special attention.

This value is defined in IMAP as the size of a message when it is in RFC822 format. Some servers store messages in an internal format designed to optimize performance and minimize storage requirements, which can be problematic. Servers can have a bug that uses the size of the internal data structures, rather than the canonical RFC822 size, when reporting message size. As a result, it's possible for the size attribute to be incorrect on some servers. Client software should be wary of the information if preallocating disk space or memory buffers based on it. Over time, this problem should go away as bugs such as this are fixed, but it's something for developers to be wary of.

This bug presents tangible problems for users when searching by size, since, if the attribute is incorrectly calculated, the search results will be incorrect. It also can also prevent partial fetches if the server doesn't know the correct size.

6.4.9 Message Numbers

There are two numbering systems used to reference messages in a mailbox. The simplest one is message sequence numbers, or message numbers, which indicate the ordinal position of a message in a mailbox. For example, message 5 is the fifth message. As a convenience, '*' is provided to refer to the highest message number in the mailbox. Message numbers are always ascending and always contiguous.

IMAP has several places where a collection of message numbers can be referenced. These are called *message sets*. The syntax is as follows.

```
message-set   = sequence-num /
                (low-sequence-num ":" high-sequence-num) /
                (message-set "," message-set)
sequence-num = non-zero-number / "*"
```

A pair of numbers separated by a ':' character indicates a contiguous set of messages ranging from the first message number to the second. IMAP also allows a set of noncontiguous numbers to be specified with the ',' character. This provides the ability to specify a comma-list of arbitrary message numbers that can also contain message ranges. A few examples are in order. Table 6.3 lists several message sets and their associated members. The examples are based on a mailbox with eight messages.

The primary difficulty with message sequence numbers is that they change when messages are expunged. For example, message 5 becomes message 4 after message 2 is expunged. Figure 6.5 illustrates this graphically. The arrows track a particular message as messages are added to and deleted from the mailbox.

Another difficulty with message numbers is that they are valid only for the length of a session. Say a client is interested in message 5. If that client disconnects and another one expunges message 2, when the first client reconnects, message 5 will be message 4, but the client has no way of knowing that. Clearly, message numbers have their limitations, which lead us to the second numbering system used by IMAP.

TABLE 6.3 Message Sets

Message Set	Members
3	3
3,5	3 5
3:5	3 4 5
5:*	5 6 7 8
1,3,5,7	1 3 5 7
1,3:5,7	1 3 4 5 7
1:3,5:7	1 2 3 5 6 7
1,3:5,6:*	1 3 4 5 6 7 8

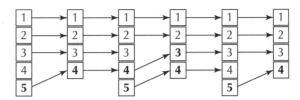

FIGURE 6.5 Message Numbers as Messages Are Added and Expunged

6.4.10 Unique Identifiers

IMAP assigns an unique identifier to every message while it is in a mailbox. This 32-bit integer uniquely identifies each message in a particular instance of a mailbox, regardless of whether any messages have been added or expunged.

Unique identifiers are assigned in ascending order, but there is no requirement for them to be contiguous. The numbers *must* be in ascending order because IMAP allows the message set notation to be used with them.

Figure 6.6 illustrates how unique identifiers are affected as messages are added and expunged.

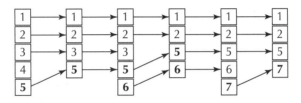

FIGURE 6.6 Unique Identifiers as Messages Are Added and Expunged

Since it is persistent data, a unique identifier can be used in a caching mechanism, similar to the one shown for POP messages in Chapter 5. This allows a client to maintain a cache of messages and summary information about them, reducing the amount of data that needs to be transferred to the client. There's only one minor snag to work out.

Because unique identifiers must be ascending numbers in a mailbox, a physical reordering of the mailbox would cause them to be out of sequence. In this case, a new set of unique identifiers must be recalculated, invalidating those referenced in a client's cache. To handle this, each mailbox is assigned a `UID-validity`, or *unique identifier validity,* value—is a 32-bit integer that identifies a specific instance of a mailbox. If a mailbox is physically reordered, or if messages are inserted into the middle of folders, the unique identifiers are recalculated and a new validity value is assigned that is greater than the previous one. A new one is also assigned if a mailbox is deleted and recreated, since the client needs to know that the messages in the recreated mailbox can be totally different.

The combination of unique identifiers and the associated validity number allows a client to cache information with a mechanism for determining if the cache is valid. In essence, the combination provides a 64-bit unique value for a message that is tolerant of structural changes to a mailbox.

6.4.11 Message Flags

As was seen in Chapter 2, messages often have status information associated with them, including such things as whether a message is new, whether it's been seen, or whether it's marked for deletion. IMAP provides a protocol-level interface to this type of information through the use of *message flags*. It also allows more status information to be tracked than what is normally tracked in the `Status` field commonly found in UNIX mailboxes.

There are two types of flag: system flags and keywords. System flags are analogous to the `Status` field described in Section 2.3.6. In fact, some UNIX IMAP servers use this field to store IMAP flag information. The flags provide a small set of standard attributes that most clients will need. Keywords provide a looser set of attributes that can be associated with a message.

All system flags are prefixed with the '\' character to distinguish them from keywords. Table 6.4 lists the available system flags.

The `\answered` flag is set on a message by a client when it sends a reply. A client must explicitly set this flag. The server sets the `\deleted` flag on a message when a client issues a `store` command for that message.

When users are composing a message or replying to one, they might want to suspend editing temporarily. IMAP allows the client to store the message on the IMAP server with the `\draft` flag set. This allows the client to identify the message as a draft for later editing.

TABLE 6.4   System Flags

Flag	Description
\answered	Message has been replied to
\deleted	Message is marked for deletion
\draft	Message is an incomplete composition
\flagged	Message is flagged as important
\recent	Message has recently arrive in the mailbox
\seen	Message has been read

A client can mark a message as "important" with the \flagged flag. Actually, users can assign their own meaning to this flag, since, unlike some of the other flags, it has no special semantics.

The final system flag is \recent, which is slightly more complicated than the others. When a new message arrives, the server will set the \recent flag for the first client to see it. This is similar to the *New* flag in a Status field. When an *Old* flag is in a Status field, the \recent flag means *Old* is not set. Servers set it as a side effect of processing incoming messages.

Keywords provide a way to define new flags outside of the standard set. While the set of system flags is small and predefined, there are no predefined keywords and no limit to how many can be available. A keyword can be any *atom* that doesn't start with a '\' character.

```
c481 store 42 flags (todo-list)
* 42 fetch (flags (todo-list))
c481 ok store completed
```

The implementation of keywords depends on the server. A server might define its own or it might also allow clients to define them.

System flags and keywords can be permanent, persisting between IMAP sessions, or session-only, ceasing to exist after a connection is closed. IMAP identifies the permanent flags through the permanentflags response code, described in Section 6.3.1.

If a client encounters a system flag is doesn't understand, it *must* accept it. The client must not reject the message or fail in any way.

On a similar note, there is no 'x' prefix available to allow experimental system flags to be created. This isn't a problem, since keywords can be used as an alternative. System flags can be added only by standards-track extensions to IMAP.

6.4.12 Envelope Structure

IMAP flags provide a good example of how the protocol has simplified, and at the same time extended, an existing functionality for client developers. Developers don't need to concern themselves with the various ways flags are implemented in email folders, but can focus on providing an interface for these items to the user.

Envelope structures are another good example of this simplification. An envelope structure is a parsed representation of the originator fields, recipient fields, and the `Date`, `Subject`, `In-Reply-To`, and `Message-ID` fields. This is not the same thing as the envelope discussed in Chapter 3. An IMAP envelope structure is a subset of the message header that provides a convenient subset of the message for folder summaries.

The fields are presented in the following order.

- `Date`
- `Subject`
- `From`
- `Sender`
- `Reply-To`
- `To`
- `Cc`
- `Bcc`
- `In-Reply-To`
- `Message-ID`

Any fields in this list that aren't present in the message are set to default values as necessary. If the `Reply-To` field isn't present, it is populated with the contents of the `From` field. The same is true for the `Sender` field. Any other fields in the envelope not present in the message header are set to `NIL`.

The `Date`, `Subject`, `In-Reply-To`, and `Message-ID` fields are represented with *quoted-strings*. The other fields, `From`, `Sender`, `Reply-To`, `To`, `Cc`, and `Bcc`, are each represented with a parenthetical list of address structures.

An address structure is a parenthetical list that contains the parsed elements of an email address. The elements of the list are, in order, personal name, SMTP source route, mailbox name, and domain name. As an example, the address 'Joe Doubloon <joe@tuba.example.com>' would be represented as follows.

```
("Joe Doubloon" NIL "joe" "tuba.example.com")
```

Any fields in an address structure with no applicable information are populated with NIL, as in the previous example, where there is no source route information.

Since the fields in an envelope structure can contain multiple addresses, the envelope structure uses a list of address structures to represent the address header fields. To illustrate this, the following address header field will be converted to an IMAP address structure list.

```
To: Joe Doubloon <joe@tuba.example.com>,
    Mary Quintessence <mary@glockenspiel.example.com>
```

This field is represented by the following address list.

```
(("Joe Doubloon" NIL "joe" "tuba.example.com")
 ("Mary Quintessence" NIL "mary" "glockenspiel.example.com"))
```

The outer parentheses are always used, even for address fields that contain only one address. This simplifies the parsing because the client doesn't need to differentiate between single and multiple address values.

```
(("Joe Doubloon" NIL "joe" "tuba.example.com"))
```

To show how this looks when put together, the following header fields will be converted to an envelope structure.

```
From: joe@tuba.example.com
To: bob@flugelhorn.example.com
Subject: Re: another question
Date: Mon, 5 Oct 1998 14:22:36 -0700
Message-ID: <19981005142235.18492.1@tuba.example.com>
In-Reply-To: <19981003072313.947.2@flugelhorn.example.com>
```

Here is the result.

```
("Mon, 5 Oct 1998 14:22:36 -0700"                         Date
 "Re: another question"                                    Subject
 ((NIL NIL "joe" "tuba.example.com"))                      From
 ((NIL NIL "joe" "tuba.example.com"))                      Sender
 ((NIL NIL "joe" "tuba.example.com"))                      Reply-To
 ((NIL NIL "bob" "flugelhorn.example.com"))                To
 NIL                                                       Cc
 NIL                                                       Bcc
 "<19981003072313.947.2@flugelhorn.example.com>"           In-Reply-To
 "<19981005142235.18492.1@tuba.example.com>"               Message-ID
)
```

RFC822 group lists, described in Section 2.5.2, require special treatment. A list of address structures is used, but special ones represent the list name and the marker indicating the end of the list. The first address structure contains the group list name in the mailbox field and has the hostname set to NIL. This works because a regular email address will never have a NIL hostname. Additional records are added for each list member. The end of the list is represented by an address structure containing a NIL mailbox and a NIL hostname. This works because no other address will have these fields set to NIL.

Consider the following group list.

```
To: Tiger Team: joe@tuba.example.com,
                mary@glockenspiel.example.com;
```

This list is represented as follows.

```
((NIL NIL "Tiger Team" NIL)
 (NIL NIL "joe" "tuba.example.com")
 (NIL NIL "mary" "glockenspiel.example.com")
 (NIL NIL NIL NIL))
```

The first two fields of each address structure are NIL because no display names were used in the group list.

As can be seen, the envelope structure minimizes the amount of parsing a client needs to perform in order to handle the fields provided in the structure.

6.4.13 Body Structure

There is another data structure that IMAP provides in a parenthetical list—the body structure, a parsed representation of a message's MIME structure. Compared to envelope structures, body structures are relatively sophisticated, but the preparsed MIME structure simplifies the amount of work a client needs to do.

There are two types of body structures—non-multipart and multipart. These correspond to the two major structures for MIME entities.

Non-Multipart

A non-multipart body structure contains three field categories: common, type-specific, and extension.

Common fields are those associated with all MIME entities.

- MIME media type
- MIME subtype
- `Content-Type` parameter list
- `Content-ID`
- `Content-Description`
- `Content-Transfer-Encoding`
- size

The following examples show all these pieces of information in the initial part of a body structure. Messages with no MIME fields are treated as non-multipart MIME entities, with the fields set to default values if necessary.

```
"text"
"plain"
("charset" "us-ascii")
"<1998041562071534.2@example.com>"
"system logs from last week"
"7bit"
2112
```

All of the fields are represented as strings, except the `Content-Type` parameter list and the size information. The parameter list contains the attributes in the `Content-Type` field. This is a parenthetical list containing attribute/value pairs for each attribute. The size field is an integer containing the total number of octets in the corresponding text for the MIME entity.

The next item in the structure is type-specific information for certain fields. Two types of MIME entity require type-specific information to be included in the body structure: `text` and `message/rfc822`.

For text entities, a field containing the number of lines in the body is added—that is, the number in encoded format, not the number after decoding. This eliminates the need for clients to calculate this information, which is particularly useful, since, in the case of readable text, users often consider the number of lines more interesting than the number of octets. It's also useful for developers of GUI-based clients, since they can use the information when creating a scrollbar in a scrollable panel for displaying the text.

The added fields are more complicated for a `message/rfc822` entity. In this case, the basic fields—envelope structure, body structure, and size in text lines of the encapsulated message—are added to the body structure.

The final set of fields in a body structure is the extension fields. Since new MIME fields can be defined in future RFCs, IMAP makes it possible for them to be represented in body structures without breaking existing implementations. RFC2060 defines three additional fields for non-multipart entities.

- `Content-MD5`
- `Content-Disposition`
- `Content-Language`

These are added to the end of the body structure in the order shown above.

```
("text" "plain"
 ("charset" "us-ascii")
 "<1998041562071534.2@example.com>"
 "system logs from last week"
 "7bit"
 2112
 42
 NIL
 ("inline" NIL)
 ("en" "de")
)
```

Clients should ignore any unrecognized extension fields, since it allows additional fields to be defined in the future, without breaking older clients. New fields can consist of zero or more instances of NIL, strings, numbers, or nested parenthetical lists.

Multipart

Body structures for multipart MIME entities are somewhat more complicated than those for non-multipart entities because multipart entities are more complex.

Multipart entities are represented in body structures as nested parenthetical lists. The body parts for a multipart entity are represented as a list of IMAP body structures with an extra element following it to indicate the multipart entity subtype.

To illustrate this, the following MIME entity will be converted to an IMAP body structure.

```
Content-Type: multipart/mixed; boundary=qvz412

--qvz412

inner body part 1
--qvz412
Content-Type: image/png
Content-Transfer-Encoding: base64

inner body part 2
--qvz412--
```

This entity results in the following body structure.

```
(("text" "plain" ("charset" "us-ascii") NIL NIL "7bit" 2112 42)
 ("image" "png" () NIL NIL "base64" 123829)
 "mixed" ("boundary" "qvz412") NIL NIL)
```

One important quirk worth mentioning here is that, unlike in other places in list structures, no space separates these body part lists. Thus, the output from a server looks more like the following.

```
((list-1-data)(list-2-data) "mixed" ("boundary" "qvz412") NIL NIL)
```

The remainder of the body structure provides information about the multipart entity. This consists of the subtype followed by extension data. The extension data defined in RFC2060 includes, in order, the parameters in the `Content-Type` field, the contents of the `Content-Disposition` field, and the contents of the `Content-Language` field.

Since body parts of multipart entities can themselves contain multipart entities, body structures can nest to accommodate them.

```
(("text" "plain" ("charset" "us-ascii") NIL NIL "7bit" 2112 42)
 (("text" "plain" ("charset" "us-ascii") NIL NIL "7bit" 49283 782)
  ("text" "plain" ("charset" "us-ascii") NIL NIL "7bit" 78132 1100)
  "mixed" ("boundary" "f71hodj1") NIL NIL)
 ("mixed" ("boundary" "a9gh1j42") NIL NIL))
```

In this case, the nested entities are directly represented as nested lists in the body structure.

6.5 STANDARD COMMANDS

With the preparatory material addressed, it's time to review the commands available in IMAP. This section describes the standard commands in RFC2060. As in previous chapters, the commands are presented in an order that introduces them to the reader incrementally.

As with SMTP and POP, telnet can be used to interact with an IMAP server. IMAP requires a little more work because of its complexity, but it's still possible. Refer to Section 3.2 for a description of how to connect to a server using telnet. Instead of TCP port 25, connect to port 143.

6.5.1 Capability

```
tag SP "capability"
```

The `capability` command returns a list of server capabilities. The response from the server includes revision information as well as supported authentication mechanisms and extensions.

The server response is a space-separated list of capabilities.

```
"*" SP "capability" 1*(SP capability-item)
```

A *capability-item* consists of an *atom*.

Clients typically issue this command first in an IMAP session. In processing the list of capabilities, they make note of any that affect their interactions with the server. Any unknown capabilities are ignored.

Servers supporting IMAP4rev1 include an 'imap4rev1' item in the list of capabilities. Those supporting the older IMAP4 include an 'imap4'. Both of these strings are case-insensitive. The original protocol required the version to be the first item in the list, but IMAP4rev1 loosened this restriction. If a server supports both versions, both will be included.

```
* capability imap4 imap4rev1
```

Since the protocol can support multiple authentication mechanisms, the server lists each one, prefixing it with the string 'auth='.

```
* capability imap4rev1 auth=CRAM-MD5 auth=ANONYMOUS
```

This identifies a server capable of supporting the CRAM-MD5 and ANONYMOUS authentication mechanisms.

The capability response also includes a list of the extensions supported by the server, each of which has a defined capability string. The more common extensions are described in Section 6.7.

The following example shows a typical response from a server, including revision strings, supported IMAP extensions, and available authentication mechanisms.

```
a001 capability
* capability imap4 imap4rev1 acl quota literal+ auth=CRAM-MD5
a001 ok capability completed
```

With the exception of 'imap4', which must be listed first if present, capability items can occur in any order.

Any item in an auth= field that starts with 'x' identifies an experimental authentication mechanism. As with many experimental additions to other email protocols, its use is discouraged.

There's one final subtlety worth mentioning about capability. Some authentication mechanisms provide the ability to protect the communication channel from outside attacks. However, the capability command must be issued to determine which authentication mechanisms are supported. If the client uses an authentication mechanism that has data integrity protection, it should reissue the capability command after negotiating the protection. This will ensure that the capability data is valid and has not been corrupted by an attacker altering the data between the client and server.

6.5.2 Noop

```
tag SP "noop"
```

The `noop` command does nothing and always succeeds.

```
a042 noop
a042 ok noop completed
```

Because the server can send status updates at any time, this command can be used to periodically poll for updates if the client has no other commands it needs to send. Since `noop` causes activity between the client and server, it can also be used to reset the inactivity auto-logout timer.

```
a142 noop
* 2 expunge
* 4 expunge
* 5 exists
* 1 recent
a142 ok noop completed
```

In this example, the server notifies the client that two messages were removed from the mailbox and one was added. The updated number of messages is also provided as a convenience. The client should cache the information to avoid asking the server for the same information in the future.

Some developers might wonder why the client needs to poll the server for updates—after all, the client can just perform a nonblocking read to see if there is any data pending from the server. The reason is flow control. RFC2060 states that if servers send untagged responses when there is no command in progress, they must either verify that the data size does not exceed the underlying transport's window size or use nonblocking writes. Failure to take one of these actions could result in the server being blocked, waiting for the client to read the pending data, possibly preventing it from reading the next client command. Thus, the only time a server knows a client is willing to accept an arbitrary amount of data is when the server is sending data in response to a command.

6.5.3 Logout

```
tag SP "logout"
```

The `logout` command is used to quit the IMAP session. The session proceeds to the *logout* state, the server sends a `BYE` response line, followed by the status line, and then closes the connection.

If a mailbox is currently selected when the `logout` command is issued, it is closed without expunging messages marked for deletion. Those messages will still be marked for deletion in the next session.

```
a523 logout
* bye server logging out
a523 ok logout completed
client and server close the connection
```

6.5.4 Login

```
tag SP "login" SP user-name SP password
```

The `login` command authenticates the client to the server. It's analogous to the POP `user` and `pass` commands, except that the two commands are combined into one. As with the POP `pass` command, the *password* field is a plain-text string.

```
a001 login joe g42one86!
a001 ok login completed
```

If the command succeeds, the session state advances to *authenticated*. If, for whatever reason, the login fails, the server sends a 'NO' response and remains in the *nonauthenticated* state.

```
a001 login joe lemmein
a001 no login failed
```

6.5.5 Authenticate

```
tag SP "authenticate" SP mechanism
```

The `authenticate` command authenticates the client to the server. The *mechanism* parameter specifies what authentication mechanism to use. Unlike the `login` command, this command is extensible, meaning that new authentication protocols can be added in the future.

Each authentication protocol is implemented as a series of server challenges and client responses to those challenges. Each challenge is in the form of a continuation request, followed by a string encoded in `base64`. The client responds with a string also encoded in `base64`. This encoding is not done to improve security, but to allow the challenge and response to include binary data. The requirements for these exchanges by the client and server are specific to a particular authentication mechanism.

If the client wants to cancel the authentication dialog, it sends a line containing a single '`*`' character. The server will reject the authentication and issue a BAD response.

In addition to providing a more secure way to authenticate, some IMAP authentication mechanisms also permit the client and server to negotiate integrity checking and encryption of data transmitted during a session.

If a protection mechanism is negotiated, it takes effect immediately following the authentication exchange. The command and response data is processed in cipher-text buffers, each of which is transferred as a stream of octets prepended with a 4-octet field, in network byte order, that indicates the length of the data being transferred in it. The maximum buffer length is a function of the authentication mechanism used.

RFC2060 doesn't require any authentication mechanism. In fact, it doesn't mention any mechanisms at all. All mechanisms are added as extensions to IMAP. If the one the client requests isn't supported by the server, the server replies with a NO completion status response.

Like the `login` command, the session state advances to *authenticated* if the command succeeds and otherwise stays in the *nonauthenticated* state.

The authentication mechanism used in IMAP has been turned into a generalized authentication framework, SASL. This framework and its use with IMAP are described in Section 9.4.2.

6.5.6 List

```
tag SP "list" SP reference-name SP wildcard-mailbox
```

The `list` command returns a subset of the list of mailboxes available to the client. The parameters given to the command determine the desired subset.

The *reference-name* parameter is analogous to a 'cd', or change directory, command in many operating systems. It provides a context for interpreting the *wildcard-mailbox* parameter. It can be the name of a mailbox or a level in a mailbox tree, or it can be an empty string, "", in which case *wildcard-mailbox* refers to the exact mailbox pattern desired.

The *wildcard-mailbox* parameter specifies a mailbox name, with optional wildcards, that is interpreted in the context of *reference-name*.

Two wildcard characters are available for use. The '*' character matches zero or more characters and crosses hierarchy delimiters, potentially causing an entire tree of mailboxes to match. The '%' character is similar to '*', except that it doesn't cross hierarchy delimiters. The matching will be confined to a particular level in a hierarchy.

The '%' character is almost always the one to use when listing with wildcard characters. Since the '*' doesn't discriminate against hierarchy delimiters, it can generate a huge amount of data if used in the wrong place. Imagine, for example, using it in a listing of newsgroups. The result could be tens of thousands of response lines.

The output of a list command is a series of zero or more untagged list response lines, the syntax of which is as follows.

```
"*" SP "list" SP name-attributes SP hierarchy-delimiter SP mailbox-name
```

The *mailbox-name* contains the name of a mailbox that matches the criteria in the list command. It is made up of a "canonicalized" combination of *reference-name* and *wildcard-mailbox*. The hierarchy character used in the mailbox name is provided in *hierarchy-delimiter*.

The *name-attribute* field is a parenthetical list of attributes associated with the given mailbox. Table 6.5 list the possible values.

The following example illustrates a basic list command and the elements just described.

```
a002 list "~/Mail/" "%"
* list (\noselect) "/" ~/Mail/
* list (\noinferiors \unmarked) "/" ~/Mail/design-notes
* list (\noinferiors \marked) "/" ~/Mail/junk-mail
* list (\noselect) "/" ~/Mail/mlists
a002 ok list completed
```

TABLE 6.5 Attributes in a list Response

Attribute	Description
\noinferiors	Mailbox cannot have any child mailboxes.
\noselect	Mailbox cannot be opened with a select or examine.
\marked	Mailbox might contain messages added since the last time it was opened with a select or examine.
\unmarked	Mailbox doesn't contain any new messages added since the last time it was opened with select or examine.

The client sent a request to list the mailboxes in the '~/Mail' directory, using the '%' wildcard character so as not to retrieve information about an entire tree of mailboxes. The server responded with four items. The first item is the top level. In this case, it has the \noselect attribute and cannot be selected as a mailbox. This is found in implementations that use filesystem directories to hold collections of mailboxes and files to store them, because directories cannot directly contain messages.

The following two items are selectable mailboxes. The \noinferiors attribute indicates that item is only a mailbox and contains no mailboxes underneath. One of the two mailboxes probably has recent mail, while the other does not. The final item, like the first one, appears to be a directory. The client could issue another list command to query the contents of that mailbox if desired. In this case, the command is as follows.

```
a003 list "~/Mail/mlists/" "%"
server sends list responses
a003 ok list completed
```

The client can also move the data from the *reference-name* parameter into the *wildcard-mailbox* parameter. Because of differences in how servers implement *reference-name,* this might even be desirable.

```
a003 list "" "~/Mail/mlists/%"
server sends list responses
a003 ok list completed
```

An empty string for *wildcard-mailbox* is a special case. This is a request for the hierarchy character and the root name of the item specified in *reference-name.* It allows a client to determine the hierarchy character even if no mailboxes exist by that name.

```
a004 list Mail ""
* list (\noselect) "/" ""
a004 ok list completed
```

6.5.7 Create

```
tag SP "create" SP mailbox
```

The `create` command creates the specified mailbox on the server.

```
a029 create team-notes
a029 ok create completed
```

It will fail if the mailbox already exists.

```
a030 create team-notes
a030 no mailbox already exists
```

Creating `inbox` should fail, even if an actual `inbox` doesn't exist. This is because of the special nature of `inbox`.

```
a028 create inbox
a028 no mailbox already exists
```

If a hierarchy character appears in the given mailbox name, servers should create any intermediate mailboxes as necessary.

```
a049 list "" "newstuff/%"
a049 ok list completed
a050 create newstuff/toys
a050 ok create completed
a051 list "" "newstuff/%"
* list (\noselect) "/" newstuff
* list () "/" newstuff/toys
a051 ok list completed
```

If the server doesn't create intermediate mailboxes like this, or if access rights don't permit it, a NO response is returned.

6.5.8 Delete

```
tag SP "delete" SP mailbox
```

The `delete` command deletes the specified mailbox.

```
a030 delete team-notes
a030 ok delete completed
```

Parent names in hierarchical trees can also be deleted. There are two cases to be aware of. If the parent name has the \noselect attribute, it cannot be deleted and the server will generate an appropriate error.

```
a032 list "" "archives/%"
* list (\noselect) "/" archives
* list () "/" archives/1999-01
a032 ok list completed
a033 delete archives
a033 no not allowed
```

If the parent name doesn't have the \noselect attribute, any messages in the mailbox are removed and the mailbox name acquires \noselect.

```
a034 list "" "bounces.%"
* list () "." bounces
* list () "." bounces.resolved
a034 ok list completed
a035 delete bounces
a035 ok delete completed
a036 list "" "bounces.%"
* list (\noselect) "/" bounces
* list () "/" bounces/resolved
a036 ok list completed
```

Neither case causes the inferior mailboxes to be deleted. It isn't possible to delete a name completely if *any* inferior names exist.

As with creating inbox, attempting to delete it will result in an error.

```
a031 delete inbox
a031 no can't delete inbox
```

6.5.9 Rename

```
tag SP "rename" SP old-mailbox SP new-mailbox
```

The rename command changes the name of a mailbox.

```
a152 rename team-notes design-team-notes
a152 ok rename completed
```

The `inbox` mailbox can be renamed, but it has a slightly different behavior from that of a regular mailbox. All the messages in it are moved to the new mailbox, leaving it empty. If the server supports hierarchical mailboxes under `inbox`, they are unaffected by renaming.

```
a0192 list "" "inbox.%"
* list () "." inbox
* list () "." inbox.postmaster
a0192 ok list completed
a0193 rename inbox inbox.1999-01
a0193 ok rename completed
a0194 list "" "inbox.%"
* list () "." inbox
* list () "." inbox.1999-01
* list () "." inbox.postmaster
a0194 ok list completed
```

If a rename fails, the server will respond with a tagged `NO` response.

```
a153 rename notafolder notabene
a153 no notafolder doesn't exist
```

If the mailbox being renamed has inferior mailboxes, they will reside under the new name of the parent mailbox.

```
b192 list "" "mlists/%"
* list (\noselect) "/" mlists
* list () "/" mlists/advisories
b192 ok list completed
b193 rename mlists mailing-lists
b193 ok rename completed
b194 list "" "mailing-lists/%"
* list (\noselect) "/" mailing-lists
* list () "/" mailing-lists/advisories
b194 ok list completed
```

6.5.10 Status

```
tag SP "status" SP mailbox SP data-items
```

The `status` command returns status information about the specified mailbox, without affecting the currently selected mailbox.

The *data-items* argument is a parenthetical list of items of desired information for the given mailbox. The contents can be any combination of the items listed in Table 6.6. If successful, the server responds with an untagged `status` response line.

```
"*" SP "status" mailbox SP status-list
```

The *status-list* field is a parenthetical list of name/value pairs corresponding to the information requested by the client.

```
a016 status design-notes (messages recent unseen)
* status design-notes (messages 15 recent 3 unseen 5)
a016 ok status completed
```

In this example, the client asks for the number of messages in the given mailbox, the number of recent messages, and the number of unseen messages. The server communicates that there are 15 messages, three of them recent and five of them not yet seen. Note that unlike the `unseen` response code, which indicates the message number of the first unseen message, the `unseen` item in the response to a `status` command indicates the quantity of unseen messages.

The `status` command should not be issued against the currently selected mailbox. According to RFC2060, clients must not assume that any command after

TABLE 6.6 Data Items for the `status` Command

Data Item	Description
messages	Number of messages in the mailbox
recent	Number of messages with the `\recent` flag set
uidnext	Next UID that will be assigned to a new message
uidvalidity	The unique validity number for the mailbox
unseen	Number of messages without the `\seen` flag set

a mailbox is selected will return the size of that mailbox. This is so that servers can implement commands on it, particularly `status`, without taking into account any pending updates. For example, `status` could be as a separate program, executed by the IMAP server process. If so, it wouldn't necessarily be synchronized with the selected mailbox. Since updates to the selected mailbox are communicated to the client as needed, the client must make note of them and avoid using `status`.

6.5.11 Select

```
tag SP "select" SP mailbox
```

The `select` command opens the mailbox for read-write access, permitting access to the messages within.

If the session is in the *authenticated* state, successful completion of `select` advances it to the *selected* state. If a mailbox is currently selected and a `select` or `examine` command is issued, it is closed without expunging messages marked for deletion.

Upon opening the mailbox, the server responds with a series of untagged response lines followed by a tagged response. The server must send `flags`, `exists`, `recent`, and `uidvalidity` lines. It should also send `permanentflags` and `unseen` lines—although RFC2060 makes this optional—since clients are likely to need the information.

The tagged response line at the end not only indicates whether the command succeeded, it also indicates whether the mailbox can be modified. If not, it will include a `read-only` response code. If the folder can be modified, it will have either no response code or a `read-write`.

```
a005 select inbox
* 47 exists
* 3 recent
* ok [unseen 41] message 41 is first unseen
* ok [uidvalidity 1938273826] UID validity status
* flags (\answered \flagged \deleted \seen \deleted)
* ok [permanentflags (\answered \deleted \seen \*)] Permanent flags
a005 ok [read-write] select completed
```

In the case of `inbox`, the command always succeeds, even if `inbox` doesn't already exist. Compare this to `create`, which always fails if the client attempts to create `inbox`.

6.5.12 Examine

```
tag SP "examine" SP mailbox
```

The examine command is the same as the select command, except that the mailbox is always opened as read-only, even if it is otherwise writable.

Since the mailbox is opened read-only, the response code in the tagged response line always contains read-only. In addition, permanentflags always contains an empty list, since flags can't be altered in a read-only mailbox.

```
a005 examine inbox
* 47 exists
* 3 recent
* ok [unseen 41] message 41 is first unseen
* ok [uidvalidity 1938273826] UIDs valid
* flags (\answered \flagged \deleted \seen \deleted)
* ok [permanentflags ()] no permanent flags permitted
a005 ok [read-only] examine completed
```

6.5.13 Close

```
tag SP "close"
```

The close command closes the currently selected mailbox and changes the session state from *selected* to *authenticated*. If the mailbox is writable, it also expunges any messages that have the \deleted flag set, without sending any untagged expunge responses.

```
a023 close
a023 ok close completed
```

6.5.14 Subscribe

```
tag SP "subscribe" SP mailbox
```

In some situations, the list command is inappropriate or undesirable for getting lists of mailboxes. For example, there can be many thousands of newsgroups on a server. News reader clients provide the ability to subscribe to and unsubscribe from them, allowing users to avoid viewing newsgroups that don't interest them.

In the case of email, some users have a large number of mailboxes, but only read a subset of them the majority of the time. In addition, some IMAP servers provide access to newsgroups, so subscriptions are doubly important. IMAP provides this feature in the form of the `subscribe`, `unsubscribe`, and `lsub` commands.

The `subscribe` command adds the given mailbox to the user's list of subscribed mailboxes. The most obvious example is subscribing to a newsgroup.

```
a025 subscribe #news.comp.mail.imap
a025 ok subscribe completed
```

As mentioned earlier, the command is not limited to newsgroups.

```
a026 subscribe #public.announcements
a026 ok subscribe completed
```

While a server is allowed to validate the *mailbox* argument, it is not allowed to remove an existing mailbox name from the subscription list, even if it no longer exists. This is because a particular mailbox might not exist at all times. In the case of the announcements subscription, for example, it might be emptied periodically during routine maintenance.

6.5.15 Unsubscribe

```
tag SP "unsubscribe" SP mailbox
```

The `unsubscribe` command removes the specified mailbox from the user's subscription list.

```
a026 unsubscribe #news.alt.fan.oscillating
a026 ok unsubscribe completed
```

6.5.16 Lsub

```
tag SP "lsub" SP reference-name SP wildcard-mailbox
```

The `lsub` command is similar to the `list` command, except that only subscribed mailboxes are listed.

```
a003 lsub "" "#news.comp.mail.*"
* lsub () "." #news.comp.mail.headers
* lsub () "." #news.comp.mail.imap
* lsub () "." #news.comp.mail.mime
* lsub () "." #news.comp.mail.misc
a003 ok lsub completed
```

The lsub command is one place where the '*' wildcard character can be appropriate, since users don't typically subscribe to enough mailboxes to cause problems with it.

6.5.17 Copy

```
tag SP "copy" SP message-set SP mailbox
```

The copy command copies a set of messages to a specified mailbox, preserving their flags and internal dates.

```
a104 copy 13:37 design-notes
a104 ok copy completed
```

The server sends a NO response if the mailbox doesn't exist. The response will have a trycreate response code if the server thinks that the error can be resolved by creating the mailbox.

```
a105 copy 13:37 nonexistentfolder
a105 no [trycreate] no such folder
```

Some older implementations do not preserve the flags and internal date.

6.5.18 Append

```
tag SP "append" SP mailbox
                [SP flag-list]
                [SP date-time]
                SP message-literal
```

The append command appends the message contained in *message-literal* to the specified mailbox. This is not the same as sending a message for subsequent delivery, which IMAP doesn't support.

The optional *flag-list* parameter is a parenthetical list of flags that are set when the message is appended.

If the *date-time* parameter is provided, the internal date of the appended message should be set to the specified value.

The *date-time* parameter for IMAP is formatted slightly different than it is in other places. The syntax is as follows.

```
date-time       = DQUOTE date-day-fixed "-" date-month "-" date-year
                  SP time SP zone DQUOTE
date-day-fixed = (SP DIGIT) / 2DIGIT
date-month      = "Jan" / "Feb" / "Mar" / "Apr" / "May" / "Jun" /
                  "Jul" / "Aug" / "Sep" / "Oct" / "Nov" / "Dec"
date-year       = 4DIGIT
time            = 2DIGIT ":" 2DIGIT ":" 2DIGIT
zone            = ("+" / "-") 4DIGIT
```

The message is provided with the *message-literal* parameter. It should be in RFC822 format. It might be appropriate for some folders to allow messages that aren't strictly compliant, as in the case of a draft folder. Implementers need to evaluate the pros and cons carefully.

```
a124 append draft-mail (\draft) "15-Jun-1999 05:30:05 -0700"{200}
To: bob@flugelhorn.example.com
From: joe@tuba.example.com
Subject: we need a new copy machine

Bob,
I think it's time for a new copy machine.
I've attached a breakdown of the costs involved.
a124 ok append completed
```

If the mailbox doesn't exist, the server will issue a failure response. In this case, if it's possible to create the mailbox, the server adds a `trycreate` code to the failure response.

If the mailbox specified in the `append` command is currently selected, the server should send appropriate `exists` and `recent` untagged response lines, just as if the append had been done by an outside source.

```
a124 append draft-mail (\draft) "15-Jun-1999 05:30:05 -0700"{200}
data to append
* 4 exists
* 1 recent
a124 ok append completed
```

If the server doesn't immediately send this information, the client should issue another command, such as noop, shortly after the append command to cause the server to send it.

```
a124 append draft-mail (\draft) "15-Jun-1999 05:30:05 -0700"{200}
data to append
a124 ok append completed
a125 noop
* 4 exists
* 1 recent
a125 ok noop completed
```

The message can contain 8-bit data if the appropriate MIME fields are present. If unable to process 8-bit messages, the server should convert to 7-bit data and update the Content-Transfer-Encoding field.

```
a124 append drift-mail (\draft) {200}
client sends message data
a124 no [trycreate] mailbox doesn't exist
```

If the append fails, the mailbox is restored to its initial state. In other words, a failed append will not cause a partial message to be appended, which simplifies the error handling a client needs to perform.

6.5.19 Check

```
tag SP "check"
```

While a mailbox is open, a server might defer writing certain types of information to disk. This improves performance, particularly in implementations where flag updates would require an entire mailbox to be recreated. If, however, a mailbox is open for an extended period of time, the number of pending updates can increase to an uncomfortable level. Flushing these pending updates is called *checkpointing,* which most, if not all, servers do periodically.

The check command allows clients to trigger a checkpoint on the currently selected mailbox.

```
a015 check
a015 ok check completed
```

6.5.20 Search

```
tag SP "search" ["charset" SP charset] 1*(SP search-criteria)
```

The `search` command is used to retrieve the message numbers for the set of messages that matches the specified criteria. The optional *charset* parameter allows a charset other than US-ASCII to be used in strings in the search criteria.

If the search finds any matching messages, one or more untagged search response lines are sent. The format of these lines is as follows.

```
"*" SP "search" *(SP message-number)
```

The data returned is one or more message numbers, each separated by a single space.

The *search-criteria* parameter specifies the conditions the messages must match in order to be returned in an untagged search response. If multiple search criteria are specified, the messages must match all of them.

Each search criterion consists of one or more search keys. Since there are a large number of search keys available, they can be separated into categories to make them more digestible.

The first category consists of the keys related to message flags. These are summarized in Table 6.7. The following example illustrates a simple query using one of these flags. In this case, a search for unseen messages is performed.

```
a2192 search unseen
* search 1 2 3 4
a2192 ok search completed
```

The next category of search keys contains the keys related to message contents. These are summarized in Table 6.8. As an example, the following IMAP command matches any messages containing 'example.com' in the Cc field of their envelope structure. In all search keys that have string arguments, the target value is searched to see if the string argument is a substring. This comparison is also case-insensitive.

```
a2193 search cc "example.com"
* search 2 4
a2193 ok search completed
```

TABLE 6.7 Search Keys Related to Message Flags

Search Keys	Description
answered	Messages with the \answered flag set
deleted	Messages with the \deleted flag set
draft	Messages with the \draft flag set
flagged	Messages with the \flagged flag set
keyword *flag*	Messages with the given keyword present
new	Messages with the \recent flag set, but not the \seen flag
old	Messages without the \recent flag set
recent	Messages with the \recent flag set
seen	Messages with the \seen flag set
unanswered	Messages without the \answered flag set
undeleted	Messages without the \deleted flag set
undraft	Messages without the \draft flag set
unflagged	Messages without the \flagged flag set
unkeyword *flag*	Messages without the given keyword present
unseen	Messages without the \seen flag set

TABLE 6.8 Message-Related Keywords for the search Command

Search Key	Description
bcc *string*	Messages containing *string* in envelope structure's Bcc field
body *string*	Messages containing *string* in message body
cc *string*	Messages containing *string* in envelope structure's Cc field
from *string*	Messages containing *string* in envelope structure's From field
header *field-name string*	Messages containing *string* in header field *field-name*
larger *N*	Messages larger than *N* octets
smaller *N*	Messages smaller than *N* octets
subject *string*	Messages containing *string* in envelope structure's Subject field
text *string*	Messages containing *string* in header or body
to *string*	Messages containing *string* in envelope structure's To field

TABLE 6.9 Date-Related Keywords for the `search` Command

Search Key	Description
before *date*	Messages with internal date earlier than *date*
on *date*	Messages with internal date on same day as *date*
since *date*	Messages with internal date later than *date*
sentbefore *date*	Messages with `Date` field earlier than *date*
senton *date*	Messages with `Date` field on same day as *date*
sentsince *date*	Messages with `Date` field later than *date*

Table 6.9 lists the keywords for searching based on date information. Since there are two date types in IMAP, internal date and the `Date` field, there are two keys. The *date* parameter uses a special format, to simplify parsing. It is similar to the format of the *date-time* parameter of the `append` command, described in Section 6.5.18, but without the *time* portion. Thus, searching based on date is limited to a granularity of one day.

```
a2194 search since 15-Jun-2001
* search 2 3
a2194 ok search completed
```

Some search keys are based on message sets. Table 6.10 summarizes these keys.

```
a2195 search 1:3
* search 1 2 3
a2195 ok search completed
```

TABLE 6.10 Miscellaneous Keywords for the `search` Command

Search Key	Description
all	All messages in the mailbox
message-set	Messages contained in *message-set*
uid *message-set*	Messages contained in UID-based *message-set*

TABLE 6.11 Logical Keywords for the `search` Command

Search Key	Description
not *search-key*	Messages not matching *search-key*
or *search-key1 search-key2*	Messages matching either search key
(1#*search-key*)	Group the *search-key* together

TABLE 6.12 Message Attributes for Logic Search Examples

Message Number	answered	cc "example.com"
1		
2		•
3	•	
4	•	•

The utility of the message set search keys might not seem obvious until the next category of search keys is looked at—logical operators. In addition to the ability to join multiple search criteria into a logical *and* clause, IMAP provides search keys for logical negation and logical *or* operations. It also allows the use of parentheses to group sets of search keys. Table 6.11 summarizes this last key set. To illustrate the logical operators, Table 6.12 lists a set of messages with various combinations of the `answered` search key and a specific `Cc` value.

As mentioned earlier, having multiple *search-criteria* parameters is equivalent to a logical *and*ing of all the criteria. In this example, only message 4 matches the criteria.

```
a1052 search cc "example.com" answered
* search 4
a1052 ok search completed
```

The `or` construct is used to select messages matching either of two conditions. In this case, messages 2, 3, and 4 match one or more of the search criteria.

```
a524 search or cc "example.com" answered
* search 2 3 4
a524 ok search completed
```

The not construct negates a search term. Here the search will return the list of messages in which the underlying search term, 'cc "example.com"', is not true.

```
a524 search not cc "example.com"
* search 1 3
a524 ok search completed
```

Parentheses can be used to expand these logical operators into more complex expressions. The following example specifies a search term where either of two search terms is true.

```
a525 search search or (cc "example.com" not answered)
                      (not cc "example.com" answered)
* search 2 3
a525 ok search completed
```

One more thing to mention about the search command is the *charset* parameter. When present, the strings used in search criteria are encoded with the specified charset. The server will return a tagged NO response if it doesn't support this charset.

The following example shows the charset argument to submit an ISO-8859-1 value in a search query.

```
a767 search charset iso-8859-1 from {6}
+ Ready for literal data
Jürgen
* search 8 9 13
a767 ok search completed
```

Notice the use of the literal to send the field. This is required because 8-bit data is outside of the range allowed by an *atom* or *quoted-string*.

One additional issue with the charset option bears mentioning. Some charsets share common characters, but use different values for them. In addition, many charsets don't have the same characters at the same integer positions. It's recommended that servers implementing the charset option normalize the data internally, preferably to UTF-8, prior to searching. This will allow string matches even if the data is in a different charset.

6.5.21 Fetch

```
tag SP "fetch" SP message-set SP data-items
```

The `fetch` command retrieves the specified data items from the currently selected mailbox. It is one of the most complicated commands in IMAP and one of the main tools for minimizing traffic between clients and servers.

The *message-set* parameter limits the request to the specified set of messages. The client requests specific items in the *data-items* parameter, either singly or in a parenthetical list. Table 6.13 summarizes the defined data items.

After a server processes a `fetch` command, it sends back an untagged `fetch` response line for each message specified in the *message-set* parameter. The response lines are formatted as follows.

```
"*" SP "fetch" SP data-item-list
```

The *data-item-list* is specific to the data requested by the client, so descriptions, as shown in Table 6.13, will be provided as each *data-item* is described.

TABLE 6.13 Data Item Names for the `fetch` Command

Data Item	Description
uid	The unique identifier for the message
flags	The flags that are set for the message
internaldate	The internal date of the message
envelope	The envelope structure of the message
bodystructure	The MIME structure of the message
body	Non-extensible form of bodystructure
body[*section*]<*partial*>	A particular section of a message
body.peek[*section*]<*partial*>	A variant of body[] that doesn't set the \seen flag
rfc822	The entire message
rfc822.header	The header of the message
rfc822.size	The size of the message
rfc822.text	The body of the message
fast	Combination of flags, internaldate, and rfc822.size
all	Combination of fast and envelope
full	Combination of all and body

To illustrate the `fetch` command, the data items will be described with examples and presented in an order intended to incrementally introduce them to the reader. To make the examples more tangible, the message shown in Figure 6.7 will be used as a starting point.

```
Return-Path: <joe@tuba.example.com>
Received: from tuba.example.com by flugelhorn.example.com
          with smtp id CAB23718 for <bob@flugelhorn.example.com>
          ; Wed, 6 Oct 1999 14:22:40 -0700
Received: by tuba.example.com (8.8.8/8.8.8) with smtp
          id HAA19984; Wed, 6 Oct 1999 14:22:39 -0700
Date: Wed, 6 Oct 1999 14:22:36 -0700
Message-ID: <19991006142237.9823.1@tuba.example.com>
From: joe@tuba.example.com
To: bob@flugelhorn.example.com
Subject: Re: another question
MIME-Version: 1.0
Content-Type: multipart/mixed; boundary=a9gh1j42
X-Mailer: WaWaPeddleMail v1.0.1.0

--a9gh1j42
Content-Disposition: inline

>> Meet me for lunch tomorrow.
>> We need to discuss the strategy you defined.
>
> I can't. I'm in meetings all day tomorrow.
> Let's shoot for Wednesday.

ok.
Don't forget, we need to deal with the problem Larry found.

--
thx,
joe

--a9gh1j42
Content-Type: message/rfc822
Content-Disposition: attachment

From: larry@ictus.example.com
To: joe@tuba.example.com
Date: Sun, 3 Oct 1999 14:45:51 -0700

We have a problem!
The freight-forwarder lost the truck.

--a9gh1j42--
```

FIGURE 6.7 Sample Email for `fetch` Examples

UID

The uid is one of the simplest data item. It requests the unique identifier for each of the specified messages.

```
a822 fetch 5 uid
* 5 fetch (uid 1952)
a822 ok fetch completed
```

Flags

The flags item returns a parenthetical list containing the flags set for the specified message.

```
a823 fetch 5 flags
* 5 fetch (flags (\recent \seen))
a823 ok fetch completed
```

Internaldate

The internaldate item returns the internal date of the specified message as a *quoted-string*.

```
a824 fetch 5 internaldate
* 5 fetch (internaldate "06-Oct-1999 14:55:57 -0700")
a824 ok fetch completed
```

RFC822.size

The rfc822.size item returns the size of the message in octets.

```
a825 fetch 5 rfc822.size
* 1 fetch (rfc822.size 1150)
a825 ok fetch completed
```

Fast

Since the previous three items are commonly requested in concert, IMAP provides the fast item as a convenience to retrieve them all in one transaction. It is equivalent to '(flags internaldate rfc822.size)'.

```
a826 fetch 5 fast
* 5 fetch (flags (\recent \seen)
          internaldate "06-Oct-1999 14:55:57 -0700"
          rfc822.size 1150)
a826 ok fetch completed
```

Some readers might wonder why the `fetch` data is returned in a parenthetical list. If the client requests a single piece of data, why not just return it without the parentheses? Providing it as a list simplifies the parsing required. The client knows that in all cases the data is contained in a list. It simply needs to traverse the list and extract any data contained in it.

Envelope

The `envelope` item returns a message's envelope structure, which is described in Section 6.4.12.

```
a826 fetch 5 envelope
* 1 fetch (envelope
          ("Wed, 6 Oct 1999 14:22:36 -0700"
           "Re: another question"
           ((NIL NIL "joe" "tuba.example.com"))
           ((NIL NIL "joe" "tuba.example.com"))
           ((NIL NIL "joe" "tuba.example.com"))
           ((NIL NIL "bob" "flugelhorn.example.com"))
           NIL NIL NIL
           "<19991006142237.9823.1@tuba.example.com>"))
a826 ok fetch completed
```

All

As with `fast`, since the envelope is a common data item to retrieve in combination with the `flags`, `internaldate`, `rfc822.size`, IMAP provides an `all` data item as a convenience to retrieve all four at once.

```
a827 fetch 5 all
* 1 fetch (flags (\recent \seen)
          internaldate "06-Oct-1999 14:55:57 -0700"
          rfc822.size 1150
          envelope ("Wed, 6 Oct 1999 14:22:36 -0700"
                    "Re: another question"
                    ((NIL NIL "joe" "tuba.example.com"))
                    ((NIL NIL "joe" "tuba.example.com"))
```

```
                   ((NIL NIL "joe" "tuba.example.com"))
                   ((NIL NIL "bob" "flugelhorn.example.com"))
                   NIL NIL NIL
                   "<19991006142237.9823.1@tuba.example.com>"))
  a827 ok fetch completed
```

Bodystructure

The `bodystructure` item returns a message's body structure, which is described in Section 6.4.13.

```
a828 fetch 5 bodystructure
* 5 fetch (bodystructure
              (("text" "plain"
                ("charset" "us-ascii") NIL NIL "7bit" 250
                12 NIL ("inline" NIL) NIL)
               ("message" "rfc822" NIL NIL NIL "7bit" 160
                ("Sun, 3 Oct 1999 14:45:51 -0700" NIL
                 ((NIL NIL "larry" "ictus.example.com"))
                 ((NIL NIL "larry" "ictus.example.com"))
                 ((NIL NIL "larry" "ictus.example.com"))
                 ((NIL NIL "joe" "tuba.example.com"))
                 NIL NIL NIL NIL)
                ("text" "plain"
                 ("charset" "us-ascii") NIL NIL "7bit" 53 2
                 NIL NIL NIL)
                 6 NIL ("attachment" NIL) NIL)
                "mixed" ("boundary" "a9gh1j42") NIL NIL))
a828 ok fetch completed
```

Body

The previous example shows some extra italicized areas. These indicate the extension portions of the body structure. IMAP also provides a `body` item that allows clients to retrieve the body structure information without the extension data. The output lacks the extension data; it is provided for compatibility with older IMAP versions.

Full

The `full` item is a combination of `flags`, `internaldate`, `rfc822.size`, `envelope`, and `body`. As with `fast` and `all`, this item is provided for programmer convenience. Its output is similar to that of the `all` item, with the addition of the `body` data.

RFC822.header

The data items encountered so far return values derived from the messages, but none return actual messages without parsing or interpretation. The rest of the data items do this.

The `rfc822.header` item returns the complete header for the specified messages. The blank line following the header is included in the output.

```
a829 fetch 5 rfc822.header
* 5 fetch (rfc822.header {608}
Return-Path: <joe@tuba.example.com>
Received: from tuba.example.com by flugelhorn.example.com
        with smtp id CAB23718 for <bob@flugelhorn.example.com>
        ; Wed, 6 Oct 1999 14:22:40 -0700
Received: by tuba.example.com (8.8.8/8.8.8) with smtp
        id HAA19984; Wed, 6 Oct 1999 14:22:39 -0700
Date: Wed, 6 Oct 1999 14:22:36 -0700
Message-ID: <19991006142237.9823.1@tuba.example.com>
From: joe@tuba.example.com
To: bob@flugelhorn.example.com
Subject: Re: another question
MIME-Version: 1.0
Content-Type: multipart/mixed; boundary=a9gh1j42
X-Mailer: WaWaPeddleMail v1.0.1.0

)
a829 ok fetch completed
```

Notice the use of a literal in the first line sent by the server. Literals are frequently encountered with the output of `fetch` commands.

This item is functionally equivalent to `body.peek[header]`, which is described in a subsequent section. The latter is preferred, since it provides more functionality.

RFC822.text

The `rfc822.text` item retrieves the body of a message without the message header. It also causes the `\seen` flag to be set.

```
a830 fetch 5 rfc822.text
* 5 fetch (rfc822.text {542}
message body
)
a830 ok fetch completed
```

This item is functionally equivalent to body[text], which is described in a subsequent section. Again, the latter is preferred, since it provides more functionality.

RFC822

The rfc822 item retrieves the entire message. As with rfc822.text, this item causes the \seen flag to be set.

```
a830 fetch 5 rfc822
* 5 fetch (rfc822 {1150}
entire message
)
a830 ok fetch completed
```

Notice that the size in the literal matches the size returned with the rfc822.size example.

This item is functionally equivalent to body[], which is described in the next section. The latter version here, too, is preferred, since it provides more features.

Body[*section*]<*partial*>

Of all the data items available from fetch, this one is the most complicated. It provides nonstructured data output, but gives the client access to the elements of the body structure. Essentially any element of a message can be retrieved with it.

One side effect should be noted before walking through examples—this data item sets the \seen flag when used on a message. An alternative, body.peek, which does not set the \seen flag, is described at the end of the section.

The first variation of this command to look at is body[*section*]. The *section* parameter can contain zero or more part specifiers. A part specifier can be a part number, header, header.fields, header.fields.not, mime, or text, or it can be empty. The simplest of these is the empty specifier, which references the entire message.

```
a831 fetch 5 body[]
* 5 fetch (body[] {1150}
entire message
a831 ok fetch completed
```

A part specifier is a dotted sequence of numbers that identifies a particular entity in a MIME structure. It can be viewed as a directory path, navigating down to a particular MIME entity, with the dots as the separators. At any level, an integer is used to indicate a particular body part at that level.

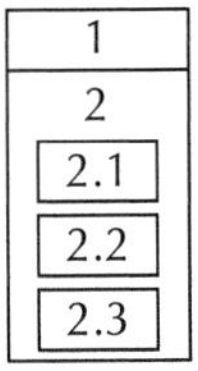

FIGURE 6.8 Body Part Section Notation

By definition, every message has at least one part specifier. Non-MIME messages have only one part specifier, as do non-multipart messages with no encapsulated messages.

The body parts of a multipart entity are assigned consecutive part numbers corresponding to their position in the entity. For example, if a message consisted of a multipart entity containing two body parts, the first would be number 1 and the second one would be number 2.

A dot notation is used to handle nested entities. If the second of the two body parts in the previous example were a multipart entity containing three body parts, the notation would be as shown in Figure 6.8.

Since message/rfc822 entities nest, the notation can be used to reference an entity's child message. If, for example, the first body part in the previous example were a message/rfc822 entity, the encapsulated message in that entity would be '1.1'.

The following fetch command illustrates retrieving the second body part of the multipart entity of the example message.

```
a831 fetch 5 body[2]
* 5 fetch (body[2] {157}
From: larry@ictus.example.com
To: joe@tuba.example.com
Date: Sun, 3 Oct 1999 14:45:51 -0700

We have a problem!
The freight-forwarder lost the truck.
)
a831 ok fetch completed
```

Since the previous example was the contents of a message/rfc822 entity, the pieces of the entity structure can be accessed by adding a period followed by the number of the desired subpart.

```
a831 fetch 5 body[2.1]
* 5 fetch (body[2.1] {59}
We have a problem!
```

```
The freight-forwarder lost the truck.
)
a831 ok fetch completed
```

This process of adding a period followed by a part specifier can be repeated to access an entity at any depth in a MIME structure. It also works for multipart entities.

In addition to the part specifier notation, there are symbolic names to reference specific pieces of a body: header, header.fields, header.fields. not, and text. These retrieve what one would expect, with one extra feature—they can be used at the end of a dotted part specifier sequence.

```
a833 fetch 5 body[2.header]
* 5 fetch (body[2.header] {98}
From: larry@ictus.example.com
To: joe@tuba.example.com
Date: Sun, 3 Oct 1999 14:45:51 -0700
)
a833 ok fetch completed
```

The header.fields and header.fields.not items take a required list of field names.

```
a834 fetch 5 body[header.fields (return-path received)]
* 5 fetch (body[header.fields ("return-path" "received")] {320}
Return-Path: <joe@tuba.example.com>
Received: from tuba.example.com by flugelhorn.example.com
        with smtp id CAB23718 for <bob@flugelhorn.example.com>
        ; Wed, 6 Oct 1999 14:22:40 -0700
Received: by tuba.example.com (8.8.8/8.8.8) with smtp
        id HAA19984; Wed, 6 Oct 1999 14:22:39 -0700
)
a834 ok fetch completed
```

The entire field name must match. The field matching is case-insensitive. Also, note the blank line following the header subset; the output is a true header, blank line and all. Header.fields.not returns the set of fields not matching any of the specified list of fields.

The last symbolic name to show is mime. This returns the MIME headers for a specified message. It must be used with a part number specifier.

```
a837 fetch 5 body[2.mime]
* 5 fetch (body[2.mime] {65}
Content-Type: message/rfc822
Content-Disposition: attachment
)
a837 ok fetch completed
```

In addition to those just described, there is one more variation—partials. IMAP provides the ability to extract a portion of the associated body[] item.

A partial is enclosed in a pair of '<>' characters. It contains two integers separated by a period. The first integer specifies how many characters into the string to start reading; the second, how many characters to read.

```
a839 fetch 5 body[2.text]<8.23>
* 5 fetch (body[2.text]<8> {23}
a problem!
The freight)
a839 ok fetch completed
```

Notice the '<8>' in the response. The period and the second integer aren't needed because the subsequent literal includes the size.

If a partial fetch attempts to read beyond the end of the data being retrieved, it is truncated appropriately.

Body.peek[*section*]<*partial*>

As mentioned earlier, the body[] item sets the \seen flag for the message in question. This item is an alternative that doesn't set that flag. Except for this difference, the syntax and behavior for the two are the same.

6.5.22 Store

```
tag SP "store" SP message-set SP data-item SP data-value
```

The store command alters message flags for the given set of messages. It's possible that it will support changing other data in the future. The *data-item* parameter specifies the way in which the flag will be altered. The *data-value* specifies the flag to alter, which can be a system flag, a keyword, or a list of these items.

The syntax for *data-value* is as follows.

```
data-value = flag-list / #flag
flag-list  = "(" #flag ")"
```

RFC2060 has an error in the definition of *data-value*. The syntax allows the value to be empty, since '#flag' includes zero instances of *flag*. The only valid way to indicate "no flags" is to use an empty *flag-list,* that is, '()'. As a matter of fact, it is probably better to use *flag-list* in all cases.

There are three components to a *data-item* parameter and six possible combinations for them.

```
 flags
+flags
-flags
 flags.silent
+flags.silent
-flags.silent
```

The first version is a simple `flags` item, which causes the flags for the specified messages to be replaced with the given flags. The server sends back a `fetch` response for every message specified in the `store` command.

```
a194 fetch 6 (flags)
* 6 fetch flags (\deleted \seen)
a194 ok fetch completed
a195 store 6 flags (\answered)
* 6 fetch flags (\answered)
a195 ok store completed
```

The `flags` item can optionally be prefixed with a '+' or '–' character. The '+' adds the flags to the message's set of flags rather than replacing them. The '–' removes the flags.

```
a196 store 6 +flags (commitments)
* 6 fetch flags (\answered commitments)
a196 ok store completed
a197 store 6 -flags (\answered)
* 6 fetch flags (commitments)
a197 ok store completed
```

There can also be a `.silent` token appended to the `flags` token. This prevents the server from sending the flag responses.

```
a196 store 6 +flags.silent (commitments)
a196 ok store completed
a197 store 6 -flags.silent (\answered)
a197 ok store completed
```

6.5.23 Expunge

```
tag SP "expunge"
```

The expunge command permanently removes any messages in the currently selected mailbox that have the '\deleted' flag set. If successful, the server sends zero or more expunge response lines. The syntax for these lines is as follows.

```
"*" SP message-number SP "expunged"
```

The *message-number* field contains the message number of the expunged message. As was mentioned in Section 6.4.9, these numbers can change as messages are deleted. From a client's perspective, this takes effect immediately when the expunge response is sent to the client, even for a cluster of expunge responses coming from a single expunge command. For example—if messages 3, 5, and 7 are expunged from a mailbox—the resulting expunge output would be as follows.

```
a104 expunge
* 3 expunged
* 4 expunged
* 5 expunged
a104 ok expunge completed
```

Remembering that expunge responses take effect immediately, once the first is received, messages 5 and 7 become messages 4 and 6. Thus, the second expunge response references message 4. After this one is received, message 6 becomes message 5. Thus, the third expunge response references message 5.

6.5.24 UID

```
tag SP "uid" SP command SP command-arguments
```

There's one final standard command to discuss—uid. This provides an interface to several commands that uses unique identifiers instead of message numbers.

The uid command takes as its arguments an entire copy, fetch, or store command. Instead of message numbers for the *message-set* parameters for these commands, it uses unique identifiers.

```
a1320 fetch 1:3 (uid)
* 1 fetch (uid 148293)
* 2 fetch (uid 148297)
* 3 fetch (uid 148325)
a1320 ok fetch completed
a1321 uid copy 148293:148325 monthly-archives
a1321 ok uid copy completed
```

The uid command also provides an interface for the search command, but in this case the search responses contain unique identifiers instead of message numbers. The search parameters are unaffected, since they permit both message numbers and unique identifiers.

```
a1322 search answered
* search 1 2 3
a1322 ok search completed
a1323 uid search answered
* search 148293 148297 148325
a1323 ok uid search completed
```

6.5.25 Experimental Commands

Before this section is complete, there's one final type of command to discuss. Like most email protocols, IMAP provides the ability to add nonstandard commands for experimentation.

Any command starting with an 'x' is considered experimental. Associated untagged response lines can also be prefixed this way. A client should not issue an experimental command unless an associated capability is listed in the server's capability response. Likewise, servers should not send experimental responses unless the client acknowledges its acceptance of the experiment by sending an associated experimental command.

6.6 EXAMPLE IMAP DIALOGS

With that rather long section about standard commands out of the way, it's time to put some of the information presented there into practice with some example IMAP dialogs.

There's one point worth mentioning about the dialogs in this section—they do not take into account unsolicited responses from the server. This shouldn't be a problem, since the important thing at this stage is to understand how the commands fit together to do something useful. Keep in mind, however, that unsolicited data can crop up at any time.

6.6.1 Replacing POP

The first dialog provides an IMAP equivalent to the POP dialog presented in Section 5.3.1. Although IMAP does much more than simply emulate POP, this example provides a simple introduction to the basics of IMAP dialogs.

The client starts by making a TCP connection to port 143 on the server. Once connected, the server responds with a connection greeting.

```
client connects to port 143 on server machine
* ok imap.example.com IMAP4rev1 server MondoIMAP version 4.2
```

At this point, the session is in the *nonauthenticated* state, which means the client needs to authenticate. If the client supports multiple authentication extensions, it needs to issue a `capability` command to determine what mechanisms the server supports.

```
1 capability
* capability imap4rev1 namespace idle auth=CRAM-MD5
1 ok capability completed
```

In this case, the server supports the `CRAM-MD5` authentication extension, but the client can fall back to the `login` command if it doesn't support any of those listed. Since authentication extensions aren't described until Chapter 9, this example will use `login`.

```
a001 login joe g42one86!
a001 ok login completed
```

Assuming that the authentication is successful, the session state changes to *authenticated.*

The client can now select the mailbox. POP's maildrop folder is equivalent to IMAP's `inbox`.

```
a005 select inbox
* 3 exists
* 3 recent
* ok [unseen 1] message 1 is first unseen
* ok [uidvalidity 1938273826] UID validity status
* flags (\answered \deleted \draft \flagged \seen)
* ok [permanentflags (\answered \deleted \seen \*)] Permanent flags
a005 ok [read-write] select completed
```

The information worth noting in the example is the number of messages in the mailbox. In this example the `exists` response indicates that the mailbox contains three.

To emulate the POP dialog, each message needs to be retrieved from the server and then deleted on the server.

```
a002 fetch 1 rfc822
server sends message 1
a002 ok fetch completed
a003 store 1 flags.silent (\deleted)
a003 ok fetch completed
```

This example uses the `flags.silent` option with the `store` command because the message is being marked for deletion. This avoids the server having to send back the updated flags.

One small point to notice here—since the messages are going to be deleted, there's no need to retain the previous flags on the message, so `+flags` is not used as the argument to `store`. The `.silent` string is used for the same reason—there's no need to see the updated flags.

The client then does the same thing for the rest of the messages.

```
a004 fetch 2 rfc822
server sends message 2
a004 ok fetch completed
a005 store 2 flags.silent (\deleted)
a005 ok fetch completed
a006 fetch 3 rfc822
server sends message 3
a006 ok fetch completed
a007 store 3 flags.silent (\deleted)
a007 ok fetch completed
```

Since both the `fetch` and `store` commands accept a message set as the first argument, it's possible to collapse the previous series of `fetch` and `store` commands into one pair. This can improve performance, particularly on dial-up links; since fewer commands are issued, fewer command round-trips result.

```
a002 fetch 1:3 rfc822
server sends message 1
server sends message 2
server sends message 3
a002 ok fetch command completed
a003 store 1:3 flags.silent (\deleted)
a003 ok store completed
```

The main concern with sending one pair of commands is the amount of data that can be retrieved with the `fetch` command. With a large number of messages or with large messages, this can mean in a significant amount of uninterruptible retrieval time.

The best approach is probably a combination of the two extremes—batching up multiple messages into single commands when size permits and fetching individual pieces if messages are large.

With all the messages retrieved and marked for deletion, regardless of which approach is used, the client is now ready to expunge the mailbox and log out.

In many situations where a mailbox needs to be expunged, the client issues an `expunge` command. This gives it the opportunity to update its message numbers. However, given the nature of the dialog, this client isn't concerned with updating. In this case, a `close` is sufficient. It's also much faster than an `expunge`, since the server doesn't have to send the expunge responses.

```
a008 close
a008 ok close completed
a009 logout
* bye server logging out
a009 ok logout completed
client and server then close the connection
```

With the completion of this sequence of commands, the dialog is finished. It should be noted that IMAP is also capable of emulating the dialog in Section 5.3.3 as well. It's simply a matter of using unique identifiers.

6.6.2 Folder Summary

Most, if not all, MUAs present a summary of the currently selected mailbox to the user. This summary typically includes information about the entire mailbox, such as the name, the number of messages, and information about each message.

The information about each message typically includes who sent it, the date it was received, its size, and the subject. It might also include what flags are set on the message or whether it has MIME attachments. It could even provide a threaded view of a folder, where messages are arranged in a tree structure based on the `Message-ID`, `In-Reply-To`, and `References` fields.

This section walks through an example dialog where the information is retrieved to allow an MUA to display one of these mailbox summaries to a user. As it turns out, IMAP provides several features that make this relatively easy to do.

To give a feel for the desired result, Table 6.14 is a sample screen output for a fictitious mailbox summary. The first two pieces of information needed are the quantity of messages in the folder and the list of flags defined for the folder. This information is available in the responses from the `select` command.

```
a002 select inbox
* 3 exists
* 1 recent
* ok [unseen 2] message 2 is first unseen
* ok [uidvalidity 900188081] UID validity status
* ok [uidnext 417232] Predicted next UID
* flags (\answered \flagged \deleted \seen \deleted)
* ok [permanentflags (\answered \deleted \seen \*)] Permanent flags
a002 ok [read-write] select completed
```

The next step is to retrieve the summary information for each message in the folder. As it turns out, the envelope structure described in Section 6.4.12 contains some of it: `From` and `Subject`. While this information could be retrieved as individual pieces, the envelope structure presents it as parsed data, saving the MUA that task.

TABLE 6.14 Sample Screen Output

#	Flags	Date Received	From	Size	Subject
1	SDA	02/15 15:57	joe@tuba.example.com	3K	Announcement
2	S AF	02/16 07:20	larry@ictus.example.com	8K	Problem with freight forwarder
3	R	02/16 12:23	harry@gong.example.com	13M	Vacation pictures

The MUA also needs `flags`, `internaldate`, and `rfc822.size` to complete the information to retrieve with the `fetch` command. As luck would have it, there is a data item for `fetch` that includes these as well as the envelope structure—`all`.

```
a003 fetch 1:3 all
* 1 fetch (flags (\answered \deleted \seen)
          internaldate "02-Feb-1999 15:57:23 -0700"
          rfc822.size 3265   .
          envelope ("Wed, 2 Feb 1999 15:56:54 -0700"
                    "Announcement"
                    ((NIL NIL "joe" "tuba.example.com"))
                    ((NIL NIL "joe" "tuba.example.com"))
                    ((NIL NIL "joe" "tuba.example.com"))
                    ((NIL NIL "mary" "glockenspiel.example.com"))
                    NIL NIL NIL
                    "<19990202155654.1582.2@glockenspiel.example.com>")
                    )
remainder of fetch responses
a003 ok fetch completed
```

With the data retrieved, all that's left to do is to reformat it as human-readable.

Like the example POP emulation dialog in Section 6.6.1, the message sets given to `fetch` should be carefully crafted in order to prevent excessive uninterruptible transfer times. In fact, this folder summary dialog is a prime candidate for fetching the data a screenful at a time instead of the entire set. This is also considerably faster than fetching the data one item at a time.

6.7 IMAP EXTENSIONS

Like SMTP and POP, IMAP has an extension mechanism. Unlike the other two protocols, however, which are older, RFC2060 defines the extension mechanism as part of the core protocol through the `capability` command.

This section describes several important extensions available in some IMAP implementations.

6.7.1 Nonsynchronizing Literals

The core IMAP standard requires the server to issue a continuation request response when the client sends a literal.

```
field1 {13}
+ go ahead
ab%"\q921!$yz field3
```

This introduces a turnaround between the time when the client sends the literal braces, the server sends the continuation response, and the client sends the remainder of the data for the literal. On low-bandwidth connections, such as dial-up lines, this can translate to a noticeable lag in the dialog.

As an optimization, RFC2088 (IMAP4 Nonsynchronizing Literals) defines an extension that eliminates the need for the continuation request response from the server. Servers supporting this extension include a 'literal+' token in their capability response line.

If this extension is available, the client can append a '+' to the integer of the *size* field and the server will not issue the continuation request response.

```
field1 {13+}
ab%"\q921!$yz field3
```

The primary drawback of nonsynchronizing literals is that they do not provide the server the opportunity to reject the literal data before the client sends it. If, for example, the size of the literal data is unacceptable, the server must read in the entire data chunk and then reject the command it was sent with.

6.7.2 Idle

```
tag SP "idle"
```

Clients normally uses the noop command to check for updates on the currently selected mailbox. Some software designs can benefit if the updates are received in real-time rather than having to be polled for. RFC2177 (IMAP4 Idle Command) provides an extension to do just that.

A server announces its support for the extension by including an idle argument in the capability response. The client issues the idle command to the server. The server responds with a continuation request. Until the client completes the continuation request, the server will send updates as they occur. The client ends the idle mode by sending done in response to the continuation request. Clients are not allowed to send any commands while the idle mode is in effect.

```
a132 idle
+ Ready for argument
... time passes
* 3 expunge
* 6 exists
... time passes
```

```
* 7 exists
done
a132 ok idle completed
```

The inactivity auto-logout timer is still in effect when the server is in the middle of an `idle` command. To avoid triggering the timer, clients need to complete the `idle` command and reissue it before the timer expires.

6.7.3 Namespace

As mentioned in Section 6.4.6, RFC2060 doesn't define a default set of namespaces; server developers are free to implement whatever ones they see fit. This presents a dilemma for clients, since there is no way to discover the namespaces a server provides. RFC2342 offers a solution to this problem. Servers announce their support for this extension by including `namespace` in the capability response.

RFC2342 defines three types of namespaces. Those the server considers within the personal space of an authenticated user are called *personal namespaces*. This includes a user's inbox as well as any mailboxes he or she owns.

Personal namespaces are typically only accessible by their owners; however, there are times when it's handy for a user to have access to somebody else's. This might include a development team, a secretary handling a manager's email, or even an administrator managing a collection of email accounts. For this, RFC2342 provides the *other users' namespace.*

Lastly, *shared namespaces* contain mailboxes intended to be shared among users as opposed to those in a user's personal namespace.

Since RFC2060 doesn't provide a way to query a server for its list of available namespaces, the namespace extension defines a `namespace` command to do this. The command takes no arguments. It returns a response line in the following format.

```
"*" SP "namespace" SP personal-namespace
                   SP other-user-namespace
                   SP shared-namespace
```

The three namespace description lists can be `NIL` or parenthetical. `NIL` means there is no namespace of that particular type.

```
namespace = "nil" /
            "(" 1*(namespace-desc) ")"
```

Each list contains a string specifying a namespace prefix, the delimiter string for that namespace, and optionally a set of namespace response extensions.

```
namespace-desc        = "(" namespace-prefix
                            SP delimiter
                            *(namespace-resp-ext) ")"
namespace-prefix      = string
delimiter             = <"> quoted-char <"> /
                            "nil"
quoted-char           = <any CHAR except CR, LF, and quoted-specials> /
                            "\" quoted-specials
quoted-specials       = <"> / "\"
namespace-resp-ext    = SP string SP "(" string *(SP string) ")"
```

The namespace response extension portion allows extra flags to be specified for a particular namespace. None are defined at this time.

As an example, the following list describes two namespaces: a news namespace, which uses '.' for its hierarchy delimiter, and an FTP namespace, which uses '/'.

```
(("#news." ".") ("#ftp/" "/"))
```

By convention, namespaces start with the '#' character as a way to identify them. However, the namespace extension provides a way for them to be identified without it. This turns out to be a valuable feature with IMAP URLs, since '#' must be encoded as '%23' when used in URLs.

6.7.4 Access Control Lists

IMAP offers commands for managing and accessing folders, but it doesn't provide the means to configure who can perform these actions. In nearly all email environments, default folder permissions are fairly strict, allowing only the creator of a folder to access or modify it. Implementing shared folders requires using some mechanism outside of IMAP to alter the folder permissions. While this is workable in some environments, it can be cumbersome in others, particularly when end-users aren't familiar with the operating system on a machine running an IMAP service, or on architectures where end-users can access only the machine running the IMAP service via IMAP.

RFC2086 (IMAP4 ACL Extension), published in 1997, was created to address this problem. It defines an IMAP extension that allows users to manipulate the ACL (Access Control List) configuration of folders via the IMAP protocol.

In RFC2086, an ACL is a collection of identifier/rights pairs. The identifier names the entity being granted a particular set of access rights to a given folder. The access rights determine which actions the entity can perform on it.

Identifiers are US-ASCII strings. They typically represent user accounts, but it's possible for them to represent groups of users or administrative accounts. In addition, the special identifier 'anyone' represents all users, including anonymous ones.

TABLE 6.15 IMAP ACL Rights

Right	Char.	Affected Commands and Flags
Lookup	l	`list` and `lsub`
Read	r	`select`, `check`, `fetch`, `search`, and `copy`
Seen	s	`\seen` flag
Write	w	`store` flags other than `\seen` and `\deleted`
Insert	i	`append` and `copy`
Post	p	not used by IMAP
Create	c	`create`
Delete	d	`\deleted` flag and `expunge`
Administer	a	`setacl`

To represent revoking rights, the identifier can be prefixed with a dash character. This last feature is optional; servers are not required to implement it.

A given user can be a member of multiple identifiers in an ACL. When this occurs, it's possible, even likely, that the multiple identifiers' rights will be different. The RFC doesn't specify which rights apply in this situation; implementations are free to resolve this conflict in whichever manner seems appropriate or feasible.

A set of rights is represented by a string of alphanumeric characters. Each character represents a particular type of operation. Letters are reserved for standard rights, defined in standards-track documents. Digits can be used as extension rights, much like the 'x' prefix character is used for experimental commands in the various email protocols. The set of standard rights can be amended only by a standards-track document.

The current standards rights are listed in Table 6.15. This is a relatively large list. Not all operating systems provide the complete set at the granularity in the ACL extension, so the extension allows rights to be tied together to force particular combinations to be on or off in concert. For example, some UNIX IMAP implementations will tie the write and insert rights together, since appending a message typically requires the ability to write to a folder, which typically implies the ability to append to it. The `listrights` command, described later in this section, determines which rights are tied.

SetACL

```
tag SP "setacl" SP mailbox SP identifier SP ["+" / "-"] rights
```

The `setacl` command changes the ACL for the specified mailbox. With no '+' or '–' character preceding the *rights* parameter, the command sets the access rights for the entity specified in *identifier* to the parameter contents. If *rights* is prefixed with '+', the rights are added to any existing rights associated with *identifier*. If it is prefixed with '–', the specified rights are removed. There are no untagged responses specific to the `setacl` command.

The following example gives read and lookup rights to Joe for the `status-reports` folder.

```
b481 setacl status-reports joe +rl
b481 ok setacl completed
```

DeleteACL

```
tag SP "deleteacl" SP mailbox SP identifier
```

The `deleteacl` command removes any ACLs for *identifier* in the specified mailbox. There are no untagged responses specific to this command.

```
b482 deleteacl status-reports joe
b482 ok deleteacl completed
```

GetACL

```
tag SP "getacl" SP mailbox
```

The `getacl` command retrieves the ACL for the specified mailbox. The ACL information is returned in zero or more untagged `acl` responses, the syntax for which is as follows.

```
"*" SP "acl" SP mailbox *(SP identifier SP rights)
```

The following example shows a mailbox with an ACL containing two items, one for Larry and one for Mary.

```
b483 getacl status-reports
* acl status-reports larry lrswid mary lr
b483 ok getacl completed
```

Listrights

```
tag SP "listrights" SP mailbox SP identifier
```

The listrights command indicates which rights may be granted to *identifier* for the specified mailbox. The information is returned in an untagged listrights response, the syntax for which is as follows.

```
"*" SP "listrights" SP mailbox SP identifier
                SP rights *(SP rights)
```

The *mailbox* and *identifier* fields correspond to the parameters provided with the listrights command. The first *rights* field contains the set of rights that will always be granted in the mailbox. This value can be an empty string, indicating that there are no rights always granted. The remaining *rights* fields are sets of rights the specified *identifier* may be granted. Rights mentioned in the same field are tied together, meaning that either all the rights must be granted at the some time or none of them can be granted. A specific access right can only be listed once.

The following example illustrates the listrights command and the associated listrights untagged response.

```
b484 listrights status-reports joe
* listrights status-reports joe "" l r swid
b484 ok listrights completed
```

Myrights

```
tag SP "myrights" SP mailbox
```

The myrights command returns the set of rights the current user has to the specified mailbox. The information is sent in an untagged myrights response.

```
"*" SP "myrights" SP mailbox SP rights
```

The following example illustrates the use of the myrights command and the associated myrights untagged response.

```
b485 myrights status-reports
* myrights status-reports lrswicda
b485 ok myrights completed
```

6.8 SUMMARY

IMAP is a client-server protocol that allows a client to manage email on a remote server. It is rich and sophisticated, and has many areas that are relatively complicated. This complexity, however, provides several features useful in a modern email environment, including access to collections of remote folders, access to those folders via multiple clients, and the ability to minimize network traffic between a client and server.

Like SMTP and POP, IMAP is a text-based protocol, with the client sending commands to the server and the server sending data to the client. However, IMAP uses a much more sophisticated interaction model, allowing the server to send the client unsolicited data. This gives a server the ability to notify a client of changes caused by other clients.

The commands available in IMAP manage mail folders, manipulate their contents, and extract various pieces of information from them. The protocol provides a full-featured interface to email, including the ability to optimize the dialog for minimal network traffic. In addition, the data sent from a server to a client is designed to minimize the complex parsing necessary for email data.

IMAP provides built-in support for adding extensions to the protocol. Several extensions are in wide use today. As with the extension mechanisms available for SMTP and POP, IMAP's extension mechanism has proven very useful in adapting the protocol as messaging requirements change.

With only a few exceptions, this chapter concludes the discussion of core email protocols and standards in this book. The remaining chapters focus on using this information to enhance the inherent capabilities of these protocols and standards. This is particularly true for the following chapter—Filtering—where information from the earlier chapters will be put to the proverbial test.

Chapter 7

Filtering

Filtering adds another dimension to email delivery: control over the flow of email. In general, the standards and extensions presented thus far focus on the mechanics of free-flowing email. Very little emphasis is on restricting or controlling the flow.

For example, some users go through a little ritual when processing newly received email; certain messages are refiled into auxiliary mailboxes for later perusal, some are automatically deleted as uninteresting, and others are forwarded to other people. Occasionally, a message is saved to a file and processed with some type of program that is capable of acting on its contents.

For modest amounts of incoming email, this procedure is seldom a problem. However, as the volume increases, frequent repetition of processing tasks can become tedious and time-consuming. Filtering provides a way to automate those tasks.

Standards and guidelines for filtering email have evolved more slowly than other areas of email. This is because filtering has traditionally been considered an application-specific facility, outside the scope of protocol standards. There is, however, some work being done in the IETF standards community. In 1999, RFC2505 (Anti-Spam Recommendations for SMTP MTAs) was published. This is a BCP (Best Current Practice) RFC that provides recommendations for MTA implementations to improve their handling of unsolicited bulk email. Also, work has started on SIEVE, a standard filtering language, whose goal is a portable way to describe email filters. Because little work has been done on filtering in the IETF standards process, this chapter will focus on reinforcing our knowledge of how email works by walking through various aspects of filtering.

Many readers are already familiar with filtering to some degree, for example, filtering junk mail. While this is an important application, there are other significant uses of the technology. Filtering is used for such varied tasks as sifting incoming email into categories, redistributing messages to other recipients, and auto-responding to certain messages. And this is by no means the entire scope of its capabilities. A goal of this chapter is to provide a model for filtering that will trigger thought on new uses for it.

7.1 A MODEL FOR FILTERING

To understand the larger picture, it's helpful to view filters as they pertain to all areas of an email architecture. Several places in the architecture are filtering candidates. Figure 7.1 illustrates email's major components, with the channels in which filtering is often applied represented as arrows with thick lines.

Borrowing a model from the world of security, the filter points shown in Figure 7.1 can be viewed as a set of concentric rings, as shown in Figure 7.2. Each layer provides additional protection, relieving inner layers of some of the filtering burden.

This chapter focuses on MTA, MDA, and MUA filtering. A description of router filtering would require detailed information about TCP that is outside of the scope of this book.

Filters are typically implemented as a series of rules, each of which is a conditional test and a set of associated actions. Each test checks for matches between available input data and the criteria specified in the test. If the conditions are met, the associated actions are performed. Rules are processed in a variety of ways, typically involving checking each of them until an action indicates that the processing is complete or until there are no more rules to check.

The conditions, input data, and actions available in a filter depend on the type of filtering performed. These are described later in the chapter.

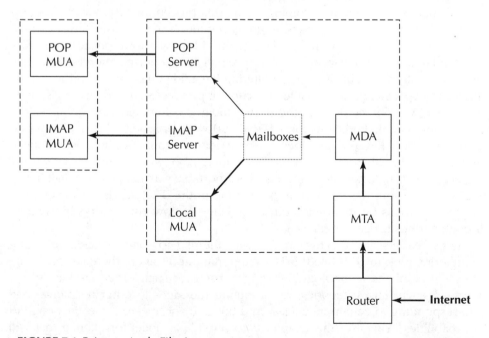

FIGURE 7.1 Points to Apply Filtering

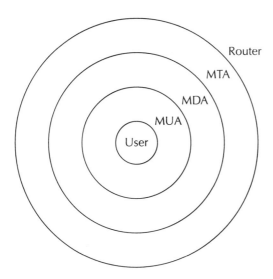

FIGURE 7.2 Filtering in Layers

7.1.1 Available Inputs

Several types of input data can be checked in filters. Some are available at all filter layers, others are not. This has an impact on what checks can be implemented in a particular filter type.

For a process communicating over the network, the FQDN and IP address of the remote machine available. These can be used to check whether a specific machine, or range of them, should be allowed to communicate with the local machine.

SMTP provides, among other things, an envelope that includes sender and recipient information. If used, DSN, described in Section 3.5.6, provides the original recipient, envelope identifier, and delivery notification parameters. MTA and MDA filters are typically the only ones with access to the envelope data, and some MDA filters don't have access to the newer DSN envelope information.

The availability of system resources can provide input data, including system load, free disk space, and current number of messages being processed. Similarly, the size of the message being processed can be input to a filter, as can configuration and historical data. For example, a filter may adjust its behavior based upon information in a configuration file or use derivatives of log information to control how messages are processed.

Last, but not least, the textual content of the email message can provide a wealth of information to use in filter tests. Messages are, arguably, the most complex input data.

MIME presents several complications to filter implementations. The first one is providing convenient access to body parts of potentially nested MIME entities, optionally decoding them as needed. The MIME access model used in IMAP is a good starting point for filter developers desiring this level of functionality. Just as IMAP gives its clients the ability to extract information about a particular element of a MIME message, it can help these implementations achieve the same level of detail when providing data to filter rules.

Another complication related to MIME is encoded header fields, described in Section 4.5. The intuitive thing is to provide the decoded version of the data, but this can complicate the specification of filter rules. The first problem is that it's difficult for developers to enable users to input data for arbitrary charsets. Another problem is that some data can be represented in multiple ways, with different encodings, and still be equivalent. In this case, the data should be decoded and compared in the decoded form. In other instances, it's useful to match against an exact string of encoded characters, but here the comparison needs to be done without decoding the data. It is a complicated user interface problem, with no universal solution.

Message Parsing

The subject of MIME provides a good lead-in to a more general topic—message parsing. There are several levels of detail a parser can provide in a filter, ranging from high-level parsing down to detailed parsing of structured fields and MIME entities.

Several major components can be extracted in a high-level parse: the header, the fields in the header, the field name and value in a field, and the message body.

To split a message into a header and body, the parser searches for its delimiting blank line. It then separates the message into these two pieces. Using a fictitious filter language, the following example shows how a rule is applied to an element parsed at this level.

```
if header contains "make money fast"
```

Separating the fields is slightly more complicated, but not difficult. The result is a list of fields, each of which can be split into field name and field value, allowing a more precise filter rule to be specified.

```
if field "Subject" contains "make money fast"
```

Some filter implementations allow specific instances of a multiple occurrence field to be referenced.

```
if first field "Received" contains "example.com"
```

Sometimes it's useful to check a set of fields.

```
if fields! "To!Cc!Bcc!Resent-To!Resent-Cc!Resent-Bcc" contains "joe@"
```

This can be cumbersome, so some filters allow a set of related fields to be referenced with one logical name.

```
if field recipients contains "joe@"
```

High-level parsing is limited in its ability to handle complicated field structures, because it doesn't delve into the contents of a field. Received fields, dates, and addresses are the most obvious examples of data that is cumbersome to match in all instances.

A low-level parser analyzes the field values and builds a representation of the data structure in memory. For example, a To field value consists of a comma-delimited list of addresses, as shown in Figure 7.3. IMAP provides a good example of a low-level parse. IMAP envelope structures, described in Section 6.4.12, are an excellent example of data that can be extracted from an address (see Figure 7.4).

A filter program that implements this technique has access to these low-level components. Using the fictitious filter language, the following example illustrates matching against the domain name of an address in a To field.

```
if any address in field "To" has domain "tuba.example.com"
```

For Received fields, a low-level parser can extract the subfields, as shown in Figure 7.5. The following example shows the detail possible.

```
if first field "Received" has for with mailbox "joe"
```

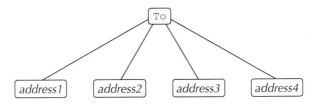

FIGURE 7.3 To Field Value

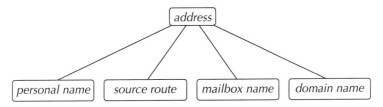

FIGURE 7.4 Data Extracted from an Address

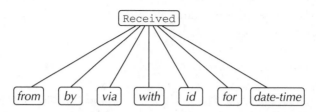

FIGURE 7.5 Data Extracted from a `Received` Field

Low-level parsing has two notable limitations. The first one is that syntax errors in fields can be difficult to handle. The most common solution is to be very liberal in what the parser will accept. This works well, but there are frequent instances where the field contents are so malformed that they cannot be parsed. This can be handled by falling back to high-level parsing so that a filter rule can still be applied.

The other limitation with low-level parsing is caused by parenthetical comments. While notations for most subfields can be provided, comments are problematic since they can occur just about anywhere. It's difficult to provide a notation for accessing arbitrary parenthetical comments. As with syntax errors, falling back to high-level parsing is a workable solution.

Many filter packages provide, to some degree, a combination of parsing levels. This allows the most appropriate notation to be used for the problem at hand.

7.1.2 Condition Matching

Condition matching is the basis for deciding which actions to perform on target messages. There are several types of condition matches, including numeric comparisons and strict string comparisons, as well as *substring, glob,* and *regular expression.* In practice, filter programs usually provide some combination of these.

When numeric data is being checked, the most efficient match is usually a true numeric comparison. However, many filter programs do not have this capability.

```
if system-load > 5
```

If the original format of the data was text, it is sometimes necessary, or cheaper, to do a string comparison.

```
if field "Sender" is "mary@glockenspiel.example.com"
```

A commonly found condition operator is the *substring* match, which checks to see whether a given string occurs within a target string. It is limited in what it can test, but is relatively efficient.

```
if field "Subject" contains "make money fast"
```

Another type of string comparison is a *glob.*[1] This provides a couple of meta-characters, or *wildcards,* that have special meaning. Most implementations provide at least two meta-characters: an '*' for matching zero or more arbitrary characters, and a '?' for matching any single character. As an example, the glob 'tuba*com' will match 'tuba.example.com', 'tuba.com', and 'tubacom'. The glob 'b?b' will match 'bob' and 'bub', but not 'bulb'. The glob pattern is compared to the entire target string starting at the beginning. This type of matching operator is very common in command shells on many operating systems.

In a filter rule, the following test will match any string where the word "make" occurs before the word "fast," with any amount of text separating, preceding, or succeeding the two words.

```
if field "Subject" contains "*make*fast*"
```

The glob matches 'makefast'. Under the right circumstances, this can yield surprising results, so care is necessary when crafting globs.

Glob matching is very common in filter implementations, since it is easy to use and easy to understand. It is, however, very limited in what it can match. A more powerful alternative is a regular expression. Like globs, regular expressions provide a notation for matching, but they are capable of matching much more sophisticated patterns. Table 7.1 summarizes some of the more common meta-characters available.

As a brief example of a regular expression, the following rule checks for an email address in a Sender field for an address of 'joe' in any subdomain of 'example.com'.

```
if field "Sender" matches /^joe@.*\.example\.com$/
```

Note that the preceding regular expression will not match 'joe@example.com'. To include this address, the regular expression can be rewritten as follows.

```
/^joe@(.*\.)?example\.com$/
```

Often multiple patterns will obtain the same results.

```
/^joe@(.*\.e|e)example\.com$/
```

---

[1] For those curious readers, the term *glob* came from the name of a program used to expand wildcards prior to the availability of the Bourne shell in UNIX.

TABLE 7.1 Common Regular Expression Operators

Operator	Description
.	Match a single character
?	The preceding item is optional
*	Match the preceding item zero or more times
+	Match the preceding item one or more times
^	Match the start of the line
$	Match the end of the line
[*range*]	Match a character specified in *range*
[^*range*]	Match a character not specified in *range*
(*pattern*)	Group the specified pattern as one item
a|b	Match *a* or *b*
char	Escape a meta-character

The '.' meta-character bears special mention when matching email addresses. Unlike other meta-characters, '–' is ubiquitous in email addresses. This can result in some rather ugly regular expressions. As it turns out, however, it is often possible to dispense with escaping them, without seriously affecting the quality of a regular expression.

Although regular expressions are more powerful than the other types of matching described in this section, they have their limits. In particular, it is impossible to match arbitrarily nested parentheses, which presents a problem for parenthetical comments in fields. Also, they can be difficult to write, difficult to understand, and difficult to maintain—all aggravated in the case of email because the syntax of fields is relatively complex. Most of the time these limitations aren't too serious, since it is often possible to craft a regular expression that gets the job done without worrying about all the subtleties found in email data.

A difficulty with regular expressions is that each implementation is slightly different. For example, the meta-characters available often vary. In addition, some programs implement enhancements to regular expressions tailored to their needs. A program might implement regular expressions with an implied '^' character to anchor searches to the start of the string being matched. Or it might have case-insensitive matching, which is particularly useful for information in email fields.

A person new to regular expressions might think that they are very complicated. Well, they can be. They do, however, provide a powerful notation for describing pattern matching that is not possible with globs. In many cases, they can be worth the extra effort required to learn them.

7.1.3 Filter Actions

The ultimate goal of a filter is to trigger actions. There are several types of actions worth investigating.

The obvious default action is to do nothing to the message or, more accurately, to pass it through to its default destination. In the case of MTAs, this means to a delivery agent; with MDAs, it means to a recipient's inbox; with MUAs, it means leaving the message alone, letting the user decide how to process it.

Another common action is to discard the message. In an MTA, this means accepting a message but not delivering it. This is very seldom done, since throwing away a message violates the rules of SMTP. On the other hand, MDAs and MUAs are allowed to discard messages and are often used to do so. Discarding presents an interesting dilemma when DSN is used. If the DSN `notify` parameter is present, the sender wants to know the delivery status of a message. How should a notification be handled when a message is discarded? If one is sent at all, it should only be to notify the originator of a success, not a failure. Since it's unlikely that a sender of junk mail will want notification of successful deliveries, it's probably not a problem if the discard results in this. A notification of success also avoids situations where a recipient doesn't want a local user, maybe a manager, to know that his or her email is being thrown out.

For MTA filters, a more appropriate alternative to discarding a message is to reject it. This can be done with a temporary or permanent reply code, depending on the desired result. Some MDA filters can also reject a message, since an MTA can report a delivery failure based on the MDA's exit status. MUA filters cannot reject a message, since the message has already been delivered by the time the MUA filter processes it.

MDAs and MUAs usually can save a message to an alternative folder. This is useful for categorizing messages before they are read by a user. MTAs cannot do this because they do not access mail folders.

Another type of action commonly available is to send the message to another destination. This includes redistributing it, forwarding it by rewriting the envelope recipient information, forwarding it by encapsulating it in a new message, or replying to it.

Some filters have the ability to alter messages by adding, changing, or deleting fields, as well as manipulating the message body. One common use for this type of action is to pass information to a subsequent filter by adding a header field. For example, an MTA can add a header field, which is then checked by an MDA or MUA filter.

Modifying header fields is relatively safe and easy to do if care is taken not to break the headers. Modifying message bodies is another story. Some filters do things such as remove unwanted body parts from multipart MIME entities or compensate for missing features in an MUA. It is relatively easy, however, to break a MIME structure if these modifications are not done correctly.

MIME presents several opportunities for useful filter actions. One such action is automatically decoding an entity and saving it to a file. Other content types providing these opportunities include the following:

- `message/partial`
- `message/external-body`
- `multipart/digest`

One final area of MIME technology is worth mentioning—DSN. If a filter provides sufficient ability to process MIME entities, it's also possible to process `multipart/report` entities.

Designing filter actions is not always an easy task. For example, what if a user creates a filter rule that redistributes an incoming message to thousands, or tens of thousands, of users? In some environments, this can create a significant problem. Some filter implementations prevent users from doing such disruptive things.

Another issue is the design of the user interface. While it's possible to design a filter package that provides arbitrary complexity, it's very difficult to design one that provides that complexity in a convenient user interface.

Another issue is the design of the filter when handling combinations of actions. Some combinations make a lot of sense—for example, saving a message and then forwarding it. Others make less sense—for example, discarding a message and then saving it. Some readers may not consider those to be serious problems, but they present interesting challenges to designers, particularly when designing filters for end-users who are not technically savvy.

7.2 FILTERING IN MAIL AGENTS

As mentioned earlier, there are several types of filters. This section describes them, starting with MTA filters, proceeding to MDA filters, and finishing with MUA filters.

The filter at each layer takes advantage of the strengths of that particular filter type. For example, an MTA filter is well suited for filtering based on SMTP envelope information.

Some filter mechanisms are incapable of performing certain types of tests. For example, not all MDAs and MUAs have access to the envelope sender and recipient information. MTA filtering minimizes this problem. As another example, an MDA filter for a site that only handles POP for MUA access to mailboxes cannot refile, since POP doesn't normally support accessing multiple mail folders.

Some types of filtering present performance problems in certain layers. For example, filtering on message content can, under certain circumstances, severely impact the performance of an MTA filter, and so it is often best done in an MDA or MUA.

TABLE 7.2 Information Sources

	MTA	MDA	MUA
Envelope data	●	●	
Message header data	●	●	●
Message body data	P	P	●
Filtering per user	P	●	●

TABLE 7.3 Mail Agent Action Capabilities

	MTA	MDA	MUA
Discard	●	●	D
File		●	●
Forward	●	●	●
Modify	P	●	●
Resend	●	●	S
Reject	●	●	
Reply	●	●	●

Table 7.2 provides a summary of filtering types possible with MTA, MDA, and MUA filters. A 'P' indicates that a performance penalty is incurred with this particular combination of filter and mail agent. The last item in the table, filtering per user, means using different filter rules for different end-users.

There are also issues related to particular mail agents with various filter actions. Table 7.3 summarizes which actions are possible with MTA, MDA, and MUA filters. A 'D' indicates that the combination presents issues with the DSN extension. An 'S' indicates that the combination presents issues when used with MSAs.

The discard action can be problematic with delivery notifications. The resend action can be problematic if used with an MSA that imposes a policy on the contents of the envelope sender. Having an MTA modify incoming messages can impede performance.

The remainder of this section walks through each of the three mail agent filters, providing specifics about each one.

7.2.1 MTA Filtering

Most, if not all, MTAs provide some filtering, since they are near the frontline of email management. MTA filters are frequently used to control incoming mail.

One of the first things an MTA filters on is incoming connections, checking the address of the incoming connection and deciding whether to accept it. Perhaps one of the most obvious ways to use MTA filtering is against the information provided in the SMTP dialog. This includes the initial protocol greeting and the mail transactions.

Connection Greeting

The SMTP `helo` and `ehlo` commands provide one of the first pieces of information available in an SMTP dialog. Filter writers may be tempted to verify that the value provided with `helo` or `ehlo` corresponds to the host actually connecting to the receiving SMTP server. On the surface, it seems like a good idea, but it has some problems.

RFC1123 states that the SMTP receiver may verify that the domain name in `ehlo` or `helo` actually corresponds to the IP address of the SMTP sending machine, but the receiver must not refuse to accept the message even if the verification fails.

On the surface, this seems like an unreasonable requirement. After all, if the two values don't match, the sending machine may be attempting to spoof the message. In practice, however, an improperly configured server, which is an extremely common problem, can cause the same symptom. In order to keep the lines of communication open, the RFCs forbid this type of check.

There is one type of value given in the `helo` and `ehlo` commands that servers *are* allowed to reject—syntax errors. If the value isn't in the proper syntax, the server can issue a `501` error reply to the sending machine.

```
ehlo somewhere.example.net..
501 Syntax error
```

Envelope Data

The SMTP `mail` command can be checked to see if the envelope sender is permitted to send email to the machine.

```
mail from:<larry@ictus.example.com>
550 access denied
```

A couple of envelope sender values must be handled carefully when applying filter rules. Failure to do so may result in loss of important mail. The most important value is '<>', which is used in error replies. Users won't get notification of delivery failures if this envelope sender is filtered out.

The other situation requiring special attention is where the envelope sender appears to be on the local domain but the message is coming from an external domain. This can occur where the owner of a mailing list is local but the list is hosted remotely. If any of the list members are also local, the filter will see a transaction in which the envelope sender points to an internal mailbox but the IP address of the sending machine will be remote.

In addition to the envelope sender, there are several possibilities for crafting filter rules based on the message recipient. One is frequently used to prevent relaying on Internet email servers. This is discussed in greater detail in Section 7.4.1.

```
rcpt to:<mary@glockenspiel.example.com>
550 access denied
```

Along with the standard data provided in `mail` and `rcpt` commands, the DSN parameters, described in Section 3.5.6, are useful in some situations. For example, if the value of the `notify` parameter is available, it can be used in filter rules to implement automated processing of delivery notifications.

Message Size

Most MTAs can be configured to reject large messages as well as do checks against the envelope. This is important since it's very easy to send extremely large messages via email, making it easy to attack a site by sending such messages in large quantities.

If a server doesn't implement the SMTP Size Declaration extension, described in Section 3.5.1, it must issue the failure reply after reading the entire message.

```
data
354 Start mail input; end with <CRLF>.<CRLF>
the message
.
552 Message is too large
```

This technique requires the receiving MTA to read the entire message and the sending MTA to send it. The SMTP size extension allows the sending MTA to declare the size of the message before sending it, so that the receiving MTA can reject the message before the SMTP `data` command is issued.

```
mail from:<joe@tuba.example.com> size=17283982
552 Request mail action aborted: Message is too large
```

System Load

One of the oldest uses of MTA filtering is based on the system load of the machine running the MTA. If the load is too high, accepting more incoming email will probably make the situation worse. In this case, the receiving MTA can refuse to accept the incoming TCP connection. If there are other hosts listed as mail exchangers for the destination, the sending MTA can try those, otherwise, it can defer sending the message.

The same technique can be used for other system resources the receiving SMTP expects to need, such as free disk space and various kernel resources.

```
mail from:<joe@tuba.example.com>
452 insufficient system storage
```

Reply codes aren't the only tools available for MTA filtering. A receiving MTA also can throttle the throughput of the data coming across an SMTP connection by adding a delay before each attempt to read data from the peer machine.

Because the data will take longer to be transmitted, it will also slow down the rate at which the sending machine can dequeue the data to the receiving machine. If the sending machine is transmitting a large amount of email to the receiving machine, this can provide some relief to the receiver.

Message Contents

Some MTAs provide the ability to filter on message content, which can be useful when implementing server-wide policies for incoming email. Extra care is needed, however. Most MTA filters don't differentiate between users, resulting in filter rules being applied to all incoming messages. On servers with high email traffic loads, this can cause significant performance problems.

In addition, it's possible for improperly configured MTA filters to prevent any incoming email from being accepted, which is particularly frustrating because it prevents sending email to the postmaster of a server to notify he or she of the problem.

Despite these limitations, MTA filters are useful if care is taken when managing filter rules and the performance impact of each filter rule is understood.

There is one place where aggressive MTA filtering is often appropriate—MSA servers, described in Section 3.5.8, since they are allowed greater latitude when imposing local message submission policies. In addition, since MSAs are typically not required to process the same incoming load that an MTA must handle, they are less prone to the problems aggressive filtering can cause.

7.2.2   MDA Filtering

Even though the contents of a message pass through an MTA, most MTA filters do not provide checks based on them. This type of filtering is typically reserved for

MDAs. The most common MDA filter package is Procmail, but there are several others available. As with the rest of this book, these packages are not discussed. Instead, this section provides a conceptual overview of MDA filtering.

When the MTA hands an message over to an MDA for final delivery, the MDA applies filter rules for additional processing. Some of the most sophisticated filtering is done with MDA filters.

The disadvantage MDA filters have compared to MTA filters is that they don't have direct access to the SMTP dialog. Once an MDA filter starts processing a message, the message has already been transferred to the local MTA.

Despite this limitation, MDA filters are one of the most widely used filter types. In fact, MDAs are often the optimal place for local filters, as shown in Tables 7.2 and 7.3. In addition to their flexibility, their popularity is also due, in part, to the history of email on the Internet. Prior to the introduction of personal computers, MUAs typically resided on the machines where final delivery of email was performed. Rather than provide their own, most relied on MDA filters. The lack of built-in filtering was seldom considered a problem, since users had ready access to their MDA filtering configuration files, which also allowed them to switch MUAs without affecting their filter configuration. This history is the primary reason that MDA filters provide some of the most sophisticated filtering available, and explains why MDA filtering is still widely used.

Local mail delivery normally entails appending incoming messages to a user's inbox. MDAs replace this action with a process that reads the messages to be delivered and analyzes the contents to determine what actions to take. The rules are typically defined in a configuration file that is read each time the MDA filter is executed; thus, filter rules are relatively simple to modify.

MDA filter conditions are oriented toward identifying certain types of messages based on the contents of fields. For example, a mailing list may include a certain header field in all out-bound messages. A filter rule that detects that field might include an action to refile the message to a folder dedicated to messages from that mailing list.

Field contents aren't the only conditions available, however. A size condition may detect large messages and automatically delete them. A filter also may detect certain contents in the message body as well as the existence of specific message fields.

To extend their capabilities, MDA filters often have some type of extension mechanism. This can be a simple escape out to a command shell or a built-in programming language for adding new features. Extension mechanisms are an instance in which MDA filters shine. No matter how limited the native features are in a filter program, an extension mechanism can add a desired one.

There are generally two types of interface to external programs. One type hands the message to an external program and expects a modified version of the file in return. A possible use for this type is as an interface to a program that scans for computer viruses. The virus checker scans the message and flags any suspects. Since virus checking is not something most filters provide internally, this is a way to add it.

Another type of extension mechanism is one in which the filter hands a message off to an external program for processing. Instead of expecting a modified version of the message, the filter expects an indication of success or failure from the external program to determine whether the message was processed successfully. This extension mechanism is often used to add support for folder formats not otherwise understood by a filter program. For example, say a user doesn't like the default folder format used on a machine. There are several alternative formats available, a few of which are described in Appendix A. If a particular filter implementation doesn't support the desired format, the user can use an auxiliary program to append the message to the folder wanted.

There are several variations on these types of external interface. Most are associated with running programs to return information from the operating system.

In addition to external program interfaces, some MDA filters have built-in programming languages for programming additional functionality into the filter program, limited only by the resources accessible from the programming language and the ability of the programmer.

7.2.3 MUA Filtering

MDA filters present several problems for end-users. Primarily, they reside on the email server, but end-users generally want the convenience of managing personal filter rules from their primary email interface—their MUA.

MUA filters are familiar to most personal computer users. These users often don't have access to email servers, so their filtering is limited to the MUA's capabilities.

While MUA filtering is more convenient for most users, there is a trade-off. As a general rule, MDA filters are more powerful, but harder to learn. Most MUA filters provide convenience at the expense of power. For example, many MUA filters are limited to filtering on a small set of field names.

Another negative characteristic of MUA filtering is that actions are performed at the final step in delivering mail—when the user tries to access his or her mailboxes. This means greater disk storage requirements and message handling overhead.

An unfortunate side effect of most delivery processes is that envelope data is usually not passed to the MUA. This prevents an MUA filter from using it in rules. The envelope recipient is sometimes found in the most recent `Received` field, and some MTAs add a `Return-Path` field to indicate the envelope sender. However, few, if any, provide the newer information added by DSN services. In addition, since the message has already been delivered, much of the DSN information is of minimal value in an MUA filter.

Another problem occurs if MUA filtering is used in an environment where an MSA is used for out-bound messages. If the MSA imposes limits on acceptable envelope sender values, the MUA filter may not be able to redistribute certain incoming messages, since it could violate local policy rules designed to prevent improperly configured clients or unsolicited bulk email.

Despite these limitations, MUA filters are a convenient way for users to control filtering without having to manage MDA filters on a remote server.

POP Filtering

Most modern MUAs provide support for POP and IMAP, which adds another dimension to MUA filtering. It may not be obvious, but the POP command set provides enough functionality for simple filtering. The key is the `top` command. Since `top` can be used to retrieve a message header, a POP client can use it to analyze messages for filtering rules without retrieving the entire message.

As an example, the following set of filter rules will be implemented in a POP dialog.

```
if field "Subject" contains "make money fast"
then discard
else if size > 1000000
then keep
else retrieve
```

After the POP client authenticates, it issues a `list` command to get the list of messages and their associated sizes.

```
client authenticates
list
+OK
1 3913
2 2781921
3 23132
.
```

The client then iterates through the list, applying the filter rules to each message. This example requires the filter to check the contents of the `Subject` field and the message size. The client issues a `top` command to retrieve the header, and the filter then checks the contents of `Subject` for a match. If it matches, the POP client issues a `dele` command to discard the message.

```
top 1 0
+OK
server sends header for message 1
.
dele 1
+OK
```

At this point, the processing for message 1 is complete, so the filter moves to message 2. It once again issues a `top` command, but in this case the `Subject` field doesn't contain a match. The message is large enough, however, to match the next filter rule, so the filter keeps the message on the server, and no additional processing is done to it.

```
top 2 0
+OK
server sends header for message 2
.
```

The filter then moves to the third message. Say the first rule doesn't match, and the size doesn't trigger the second rule. In this case, the POP client retrieves the message, then deletes it from the server.

```
top 3 0
+OK
server sends header for message 3
.
retr 3
+OK
server sends message 3
.
dele 3
+OK
```

This concludes the filter processing for the messages on the POP server.

IMAP Filtering

In general, filtering in POP requires retrieving the entire header of each message to determine how the message should be handled. IMAP, on the other hand, allows specific fields to be retrieved with the `fetch` command, so the client only needs to retrieve the information needed for the filter rules.

Although the finer granularity available from IMAP is enough to make efficient filtering possible, there is an even better way—the `search` command. Using `search` lets the server do the searching rather than the client having to retrieve the data involved in the filtering rules. The client submits search criteria, the server responds with a list of messages that match, and the client submits commands to the server to process those messages.

This section describes, in general terms, how to do filtering in IMAP. A small note is in order—this example doesn't represent IMAP-based filtering exactly. In particular, it has several limitations, which are mentioned at the end of this section. Here we merely give examples of various components of such a filter. Since filtering is typically done only on incoming email, we assume that `inbox` is selected. The examples pick up at that point.

One simple example involves using `search` to identify messages with a certain subject line which should be automatically deleted.

```
if field "Subject" contains "get rich quick"
then discard
```

This filter rule could be implemented in IMAP as follows.

```
a030 search unseen undeleted subject "get rich quick"
* search 3 24
a030 ok search completed
a031 store 3,24 +flags.silent (\Deleted)
a031 ok search completed
```

Filtering should be done only on unseen and undeleted messages. This reduces the chances of reapplying a filter to a particular message. Thus, the `search` command has additional parameters to narrow the search appropriately.

In this example, messages 3 and 24 match the search criteria. This information is used to create a message set for a `store` command, which marks the messages for deletion.

Another example entails identifying messages from a specific destination so they can be automatically moved to a related mailbox.

```
if field "header" contains "mondomail-bugs@"
then refile to bug-reports
```

This is similar to automatically deleting the messages, except that they are copied to another folder before being marked for deletion.

```
a032 search unseen undeleted header sender "mondomail-bugs@"
* search 4 5 6 7 8 15
a032 ok search completed
a032 copy 4:8,15 bug-reports
a032 ok search completed
a033 store 4:8,15 +flags.silent (\Deleted)
a033 ok store completed
```

One thing to note about the IMAP `search` command is that it provides only substring matching. In addition, while the command can search MIME fields for specified substrings in the top-level header, it does not provide a convenient way to search for messages based on the MIME fields in lower-level entities. To implement more sophisticated string matching, the filter needs to iterate through the messages, retrieving the necessary information and performing the matching on the client side of the connection. This is similar to the technique described for the POP command. Depending on the complexity of the filters, the amount of data they need to retrieve from IMAP, and the level of sophistication when interacting with the IMAP server, this technique can impose a significant performance penalty.

Using IMAP to filter email messages has other limitations. The technique described here only works well with filters that delete messages that match once they are processed. If they aren't deleted, there needs to be a way to prevent the filters from being reapplied to messages already scanned, such as setting a keyword in the messages to indicate that they have been filtered. Otherwise, they could be refiled multiple times. The \recent and \seen flags may be helpful, but these also have limitations.

This leads to another difficulty—multiple clients. The filtering described here does not cope with the possibility of multiple clients triggering filters at the same time. Several race conditions arise that it is unable to handle. There are ways to avoid the race conditions, but they are relatively complex and beyond the scope of this book.

There's another limitation worth mentioning. If there are a lot of filter rules to apply, or if the server doesn't implement an efficient search mechanism, the user could experience a significant delay while the filtering process is under way. It is often more efficient to filter the messages with an MDA filter as they are delivered into the user's `inbox`. This is true for the other MUA filters, as well.

7.3 BASIC FILTERING

So far, the discussion on filtering has focused on the overall architecture and the various types of filtering available. Very little has been said about specific filtering tasks. This section describes some of the simpler uses of filtering.

7.3.1 Simple Personal Filtering

As with the layers of filters shown in Figure 7.2, it's helpful to use layers when developing filter rules within a particular filter type. Personal filter rules are no exception. One of the most effective ways to manage them is to view them as making multiple passes over the data. On each pass, the filter scans for a particular type of message. As each type is identified, subsequent passes have fewer messages to examine.

Just about everyone has a small set of people they correspond with on a regular basis. Moving messages from frequent correspondents to another folder early in the filtering process helps prevent important messages from being inadvertently deleted by an improperly configured filter.

```
if field originators contains any of my-friends
or field originators contains any of my co-workers
```

System administrators, particularly email administrators, usually receive a significant amount of email from system services. This type of email is a prime candidate for filtering.

```
if field senders contains any of administrative-accounts
```

Mailing lists are another common category of messages to filter. Each mailing list has particular characteristics that can be detected. These are described in Chapter 8. As with messages from frequent personal correspondents, refiling mailing list mail helps keep an inbox free of clutter and reduces the possibility of inadvertently deleting important email.

This process of refiling important messages to separate folders can greatly simplify filtering. After all the important messages are refiled, what remains is the junk, at least in theory. In practice, it also includes important messages that haven't been filtered. This brings us to another important topic in filtering—unsolicited bulk email. This has not been forgotten. It is discussed in detail in Section 7.4.

Personal filters with an MDA or an MUA are a good place to start learning about filtering. These help to gain the requisite experience needed to deal with other filter types.

7.3.2 Vacation

With the right features implemented in a filter package, some very interesting uses are possible. An example is a vacation auto-responder. Unlike the telephone, email doesn't normally provide a way for a sender to tell if a recipient is available to answer a question. If the recipient is on vacation, a question will go unanswered, with no way for a sender to know.

A vacation filter processes each incoming message and sends a reply to the sender stating that the recipient is on vacation, possibly with some indication of when the recipient is expected back, much like an answering machine.

```
To: larry@ictus.example.com
Subject: Vacation reply to (Subject: let's do lunch)
From: mary@glockenspiel.example.com
```

```
X-Loop: mary+vacation@glockenspiel.example.com

Hello,

I'm away on vacation. This is an automatic reply to your message.

I'll be back next week. Your message has been saved, so I can
review it when I get back.

--
regards,
Mary
```

A crude vacation filter can be crafted with the following rule.

```
if on_vacation
then reply with "vacation-message.txt"
```

The first problem with this rule is that it will send a vacation reply to every message received. Thus, the first improvement is to prevent the filter from responding to senders that have already received a vacation reply. This is done by keeping a list of senders that the filter has replied to and only responding if the sender is not in that list.

```
if on_vacation
    and sender not in sent-list
then
    reply with "vacation-message.txt"
    add sender to sent-list
```

This is a start, but there are certain senders that should never receive a vacation reply. One example is administrative accounts managed programmatically, because replying to them is a waste of time. They are detected by checking the originator fields in the original message. Unfortunately, a list of administrative accounts that shouldn't be sent vacation replies is rather large and open-ended. One source of information on such addresses is available in RFC2142 (Mailbox Names for Common Services, Roles and Functions), which enumerates recommended email addresses for various operational roles and business functions in an organization. While not directly related to filtering technologies, most of the addresses it mentions should not receive vacation auto-replies.

- abuse
- ftp
- hostmaster
- info

- marketing
- news
- noc
- postmaster
- sales
- security
- support
- trouble
- usenet
- uucp
- webmaster
- www
- *-request

The list provided in RFC2142 is not exhaustive; there are several others that should not be sent vacation auto-replies.

- daemon
- listserv
- mailer-daemon
- majordomo
- newsmaster
- nobody
- root

In addition to administrative accounts, some senders don't need to be notified when a recipient is on vacation. Both of these situations can be handled by having the vacation filter check a list of recipients that shouldn't receive vacation responses.

```
if on_vacation
    and sender not in sent-list
    and sender not in dont-respond-list
then
    reply with "vacation-message.txt"
    add sender to sent-list
```

Mailing list messages are another type of message that should not receive a response from a vacation auto-responder. Members of mailing lists generally frown on it, and it's a good way to get a large amount of hate mail.

Some mailing lists add a `Precedence` field containing the word `list` to all out-bound messages. This is a nonstandard field designed to indicate what level of importance should be placed on the message. It is sometimes used for bulk announcements and the like, in which case it can have the value `bulk` or `junk`. Thus, the auto-responder should not reply to messages in which this field has one of these values.

```
if on_vacation
    and sender not in sent-list
    and sender not in dont-respond-list
    and field "Precedence" is not "list" or "bulk" or "junk"
then
    reply with "vacation-message.txt"
    add sender to sent-list
```

Unfortunately, in the general case there is no direct way to prevent a vacation reply from being sent to a list short of identifying all of the lists a person belongs to. However, there is an indirect way to handle this. Mailing lists don't generally put the name of the recipient in any of the recipient fields; the address of the mailing list is used instead. A vacation auto-responder won't reply to a mailing list if it doesn't reply to any message in which the owner's address is not in a recipient field, so this should be part of its filtering rules. Since many users have multiple addresses, the rule needs to check the recipient fields for all of them.

```
if on_vacation
    and sender not in sent-list
    and sender not in dont-respond-list
    and field "Precedence" is not "list" or "bulk" or "junk"
    and recipient-fields contain one of my-addresses
then
    reply with "vacation-message.txt"
    add sender to sent-list
```

There's one more thing a vacation auto-responder should check for—mail loops. A vacation auto-response being sent to another vacation auto-responder could cause a mail loop. To prevent this, most implementations add a field to detect loops. The use of `X-Loop` is common, but there is no requirement to use this name.

```
X-Loop: mary+vacation@glockenspiel.example.com
```

A filter rule is added so the auto-responder will not reply to a message in which this field already exists. This prevents a loop.

```
if on_vacation
   and sender not in sent-list
   and sender not in dont-respond-list
   and field "Precedence" is not "list" or "bulk" or "junk"
   and recipient-fields contain one of my-addresses
   and field "X-Loop" is not loop-address
then
   add field "X-Loop" with loop-address
   reply with "vacation-message.txt"
   add sender to sent-list
```

This completes a simple vacation auto-responder that won't result in large volumes of hate mail.

7.3.3 Email Robots

Another useful application that can be implemented with filters is an email robot, which detects messages matching a certain format and replies with information. In fact, a vacation auto-responder can be viewed as a type of email robot.

The capabilities of an email robot are limited only by the imagination. For example, it can be used to create email-based file servers, status monitors, or remote job processors.

```
if field "Subject" contains "send status report"
then reply with "status-report.txt"
else if field "Subject" contains "show mail queue"
then reply with command "mailq"
```

Security can be a major concern with mail robots. If commands can be executed based on the contents of a message, serious security breaches can result. Chapter 9 describes several technologies that can be used to reduce such exposure.

Many of the same rules that apply to vacation auto-responders apply to email robots. In addition, care needs to be taken with validating the addresses to which a robot will send a reply.

Email robots were common prior to the wide availability of WWW, when many companies had limited connectivity to the Internet.

7.4 UNSOLICITED EMAIL

Email was designed for the free flow of messages from person to person. Filesystems on multi-user operating systems have the ability to control who can or cannot update the information in them, but Internet email has no such mechanism. As far as the standards are concerned, there's nothing to prevent a person from sending email to a valid destination. This being the case, it's inevitable that some people will use the medium to send unsolicited and unwanted messages.

Unsolicited email can take many forms, ranging from legitimate commercial advertisements, to dubious business ventures, to illegal chain letters, to pornography. The response to this type of email can vary just as much.

Some might consider unsolicited email a recent problem. RFC706 (On the Junk Mail Problem), dated 1975, shows that it was a problem in the early days of ARPANET. As a result, mechanisms to filter unsolicited email have been around nearly as long as the problem has.

Most unsolicited email is sent in bulk to large numbers of recipients. It is referred to as UBE (Unsolicited Bulk Email). Another frequently used term is UCE (Unsolicited Commercial Email), which designates commercial UBE. In general, most people refer to UBE and UCE as *spam*. This term derives from a Monty Python comedy sketch, which takes place in a restaurant that only serves dishes containing SPAM™. The main character in the sketch does not want a meal containing SPAM. The sketch culminates with a boisterous chorus of "SPAM, SPAM, SPAM ...", drowning out all conversations.

UBE is a source of frustration for many people. Large ISP (Internet Service Provider) sites are affected because the large amounts of bulk email consume valuable resources. End-users are affected because many pay money for bandwidth, disk space, and online time consumed when connected to the Internet. Besides its added cost much of UBE is offensive material that most people don't want to see.

Filtering provides a way to reduce the amount of unsolicited email a user sees. This section describes some of the filtering techniques that combat UBE. In addition to being useful, it provides an opportunity to exercise knowledge gained about email from earlier chapters.

Filtering UBE is a difficult problem. At the risk of overdramatizing, it's a war of escalation. As new techniques are developed to counter the problem, UBE techniques mutate to adapt.

There are few RFCs that deal directly with UBE issues. RFC2505 provides guidelines for developers and administrators in using MTAs to cope with UBE, contained in a BCP published in 1999. RFC2476 also provides useful guidelines for implementing MSAs that support message submission policies not normally acceptable in a general MTA.

One last note before the details—technology isn't the only solution to unsolicited bulk email. There are legislative approaches to the problem as well. However, this section does not cover the socio-political issues but only the technical aspects.

7.4.1 Relaying

Section 3.3.2 described how an MTA relays messages. Unfortunately, relaying can also be used by junk mailers to hide their tracks. Figure 7.6 illustrates how a junk mailer uses a relay host to send to other destinations.

Relaying also helps UBE engines on low-speed Internet links send much more email than would normally be possible. A UBE engine can connect to the Internet

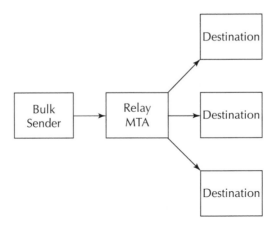

FIGURE 7.6 Relaying UBE

via a dial-up link, send its payload to a server on a fast link that allows relaying, and transmit over one million messages in a single night.

One of the first ways to combat this problem is to disable the relaying feature on all MTAs accessible from the Internet, as some of the anti-UBE techniques are nearly useless if relaying is allowed. It doesn't necessarily need to be disabled on internal machines, but at the very least it should be disabled on external servers.

Most modern MTAs provide a way to disable relaying. The mechanics at the protocol level are relatively simple. The value provided with the SMTP `rcpt` command is checked. If it is in the set of domains the server will accept, then the transaction is permitted. For example, an incoming email hub on an Internet firewall might be configured to accept messages being sent to the domain. It's also possible for a particular site to accept email for several other domains. This is common when an organization has more than one domain name or acts as a service provider for other organizations.

If an envelope recipient doesn't meet the criteria, the next step is to refuse the email. The receiving SMTP server can accomplish this by issuing a permanent failure reply, with appropriate text, to the sending machine.

```
rcpt to:<frank@dorm-13.example.edu>
550 Access denied. Relaying not permitted.
```

Under certain circumstances, some SMTP servers need to accept relaying. For example, local POP and IMAP clients may need a server to deliver out-bound email messages. In this case, checking the value with an SMTP `rcpt` command is inadequate, since the criteria need to be based on the sending machine.

This can be solved by checking the source IP address of the incoming SMTP connection. If the IP address or domain name of the machine connecting to the server is authorized to use the server for relaying, the operation is permitted.

Under certain circumstances, it's also possible to use an SMTP authentication extension requiring clients to authenticate with the server before they can perform mail transactions. Authentication is described in further detail in Chapter 9.

7.4.2 Known Offenders

Some sites exist specifically to send unsolicited email. In fact, some sites do only that. These *known offenders* are responsible for a significant amount of the problem.

After relaying is disabled, it's possible to filter out known offenders. This technique can be applied to several points in the filter model. It's commonly used in MTA filters, but router filters can be used at the outer perimeter to prevent MTAs from even seeing the connections.

Known offenders are detected by checking all incoming connections against a list of known offenders, affectionately referred to as *blacklists*. A current and accurate list is the key to making this an effective technique for filtering UBE. The first implementations used a flat file. Various sites on the Internet maintained lists that other people could reuse at their own sites.

MAPS RBL

Blacklists are difficult for any one person to maintain. Not only is the process time-consuming, but administrators must periodically retrieve any updates.

The MAPS (Mail Abuse Prevention System) RBL (Realtime Blackhole List) addresses those problems.[2] It provides a database accessible via DNS for MTAs to check for blacklisted sites.

To use the service, an MTA performs a DNS query of the following format.

```
n4.n3.n2.n1.rbl.maps.vix.com.
```

The first four segments of the domain name correspond to the octets of the IP address in reverse order. If the given site is in the blacklist, the query answer will contain an address record pointing to `127.0.0.2`. The decision to use this address was arbitrary, but will not change.

This technique is becoming increasingly popular on the Internet. Most MTAs have built it into their code.

ORBS

As mentioned earlier, relaying reduces the effectiveness of UBE filtering. To aggravate the problem, there are sites that openly allow relaying, and large-scale

---

[2] `http://maps.vix.com/rbl/`

unsolicited email operations use them to reduce detection. To address this problem, the ORBS (Open Relay Blocking System) service is available for filtering out sites that allow open relaying.[3] It provides an online database available via DNS which can be queried to determine whether a particular site is a known open relayer.

Using the service is similar to using RBL. An MTA performs a DNS query looking for a domain name with the following format.

```
n4.n3.n2.n1.relays.orbs.org
```

If the given machine is a known open relayer, the DNS query will return an A record.

An MDA filter can implement this technique by extracting the appropriate information from the `Received` fields. This is a little more complicated, but still possible. In fact, the same is true for RBL.

MAPS DUL

MAPS DUL (Dial-up User List)[4] is another variation on the RBL design. It provides a list of known dial-up or dynamically assigned pools of IP addresses. Since dial-up lines are frequently used by UBE engines, this service can be used to block mail coming directly from those sources.

The DNS query is similar to that used with MAPS RBL and ORBS. The MTA performs a DNS query looking for an A record for a hostname of the following format.

```
n4.n3.n2.n1.dul.maps.vix.com
```

If the DNS query returns an A record, the IP address is in the DUL.

DSSL

DSSL (DynamicIP Spam Sources List)[5] is a variant of the RBL mechanism. It provides a list of sites originating UBE from dial-up or cable-modem connections to the Internet. MTAs use the same process for DSSL as for RBL, employing the following format for queries.

```
n4.n3.n2.n1.dssl.imrss.org
```

RBL, ORBS, DUL, and DSSL are useful tools for implementing blacklist filtering. Since the information is provided via DNS, it doesn't have to be downloaded periodically. In addition, each service has a process for keeping the information up to date, which is more efficient than the original manual process.

---

[3] http://www.orbs.com/

[4] http://maps.vix.com/dul/

[5] http://www.imrss.org/dssl/

All the previous mechanisms work by attempting to identify incoming sites that are UBE sources, independent of the material being sent. Another possibility is to identify UBE independent of the source. For example, Christopher Lindsey, of NCSA (National Computational Science Alliance), has been experimenting with a service he calls ASID (Algorithms for Spam Identification and Destruction), in which a "footprint" is calculated for each incoming message. Using a DNS mechanism similar to the one used for other RBLs, each footprint is checked against a master list of footprints for message bodies of known UBE. The design supports several techniques for generating the footprint, such as simple checksums, MD5 checksums, or advanced pattern analysis. This is an interesting area of research. While not a replacement for other RBL services, it could be useful for those wanting even more protection from UBE.

The primary concern with any external blacklist mechanism is the possibility of blocking sites that have a legitimate need to transfer a message. Readers should review their requirements and scrutinize the process used by each of these services before implementing blocking based on any of them.

7.4.3 Originator and Recipient Fields

Up to this point, the focus has been on techniques that can be implemented in MTAs. Blacklisting is intended to block sites that send only unsolicited email or those that allow large-scale UBE services to be relayed through their servers. Other techniques are needed to catch UBE coming from legitimate sites or from sites that are not on a blacklist.

These techniques are based upon analyzing the contents of a message for telltale signs of unsolicited email. One place to look is in the recipient and originator fields. It's not unusual for senders of UBE to put easily detected strings in these fields.

As an example, say a piece of unsolicited email is received that has the following field.

```
To: Friend@example.org
```

Sometimes it's easy to tell whether a field contains something that can be used in a filter rule. In this case, it could go either way, but it's safe to add it if you know you'll never receive a valid piece of email that contains this address. If you're not sure, some additional investigation is required.

Since a rule with wider scope will catch more offenders, the first thing to look at is the domain name. Is 'example.org' an appropriate item to filter on? The first step is to check whether this name is registered. The easiest way is to perform a DNS query for the domain.

```
$ nslookup -q=any example.org
```

If the domain doesn't exist, the DNS query program will output an appropriate error message; otherwise, it will provide DNS information about the domain.

Sometimes more detailed analysis is required, which can be done by checking the **whois** databases on the Internet. These provide domain registration information. Several databases are available. Each handles a specific segment of the domain space.

Since the address we are interested in ends with '.org', the Internic database needs to be queried.[6] Its web site has pointers to the other sites if needed.

There are several ways to query the database. Many UNIX operating systems have a command to query a **whois** server. Web interfaces are also available. In this example, the command-line interface is used.

```
$ whois example.org
[rs.internic.net]

Registrant:
data

    Domain Name: EXAMPLE.ORG

    Administrative Contact, Technical Contact, Zone Contact:
        contact information
    Billing Contact:
        contact information

    miscellaneous update information

    Domain servers in listed order:

    domain server list

pointers to other whois servers
```

If the response from the server indicates that the domain doesn't exist, the domain name may be a candidate for a filter rule.

If the query returns domain registration information, the domain is allocated. At this point a decision must be made. If the domain is valid, it's possible that filtering on it will cause valid email to be rejected. In some cases this is appropriate, but it often isn't.

If the decision is not to filter on the domain name, the next step is to determine whether the *local-part* portion of the address is a good candidate for a filter rule. In this example, *local-part* is friend, which on the surface sounds dubious. It's possible that this can be used in a filter rule, but some care is required. For example, friend may be a valid mailbox name,[7] and personal filters may be able to use

---

[6] http://www.internic.net/.

[7] In fact, it is the surname of at least one well-known Internet software developer.

it without serious risk of false hits. Central filter mechanisms might not want to implement it because of the likelihood of filtering out legitimate mail.

The final question to ask is whether the entire address, `friend@example.org`, should be used in a filter rule. As with `friend`, it is quite possible that this is a candidate for a personal filter, but it may or may not be a good candidate for a centralized server; a judgment call is necessary.

One of the best ways to determine whether an address, or any field for that matter, is a good candidate for a filter is to check an existing collection of messages. Many people delete unsolicited email, which isn't always the best thing to do. If the junk mail is refiled into a separate folder, the data can be analyzed to help create filter rules. If a particular email address is found only in unsolicited email, it quite possibly could be a safe thing to filter.

7.4.4 Field Contents

Originator and recipient fields aren't the only place to look for information to filter. Many other fields contain information useful for detecting unsolicited email, and the same techniques can be used with them.

One example is the `X-Mailer` field. Some unsolicited bulk email developers put the name of their product in the field, making it particularly easy to detect them.

Some UBE engines add information to the `Subject` field to identify a message as UBE.

```
Subject: ADV: Career Opportunities

Subject: Come on over (adv;adlt)
```

Most UBEs don't contain these strings in `Subject` field, but there are other strings that can be detected. Many sites maintain a list of word phrases commonly found in `Subject` fields, some of which are quite long.

`Received` fields are another fertile source of information for filters. The same techniques used with originator and recipient fields can be used with `Received` fields. Examples range from poorly implemented spoofs of other packages to outright structural defects in the field contents.

Care must be taken when analyzing the field contents, as it's very easy to misinterpret the data. As an example, some UBE engines use the Bulk_mailer program, designed to help mailing list processors speed up distribution. It adds a `Received` field to messages it processes, which some email administrators notice and add to their UBE filter. Unfortunately, messages from valid mailing lists can also contain this field, and deleting messages based on its presence can result in users not getting messages from a subscribed mailing list.

The lesson to be learned is that it's important not to be too zealous when crafting filter rules. Careful research and a cool head can help avoid unpleasant accidents.

7.4.5 Telltale Fields

When looking at a piece of unsolicited email to determine what filter to apply, the names of the fields should be analyzed. Some unsolicited email contains fields some people might want to filter on. For example, a `X-Advertisement` field in a header is a sign that the message is unsolicited.

Care is required when doing this. There are a lot of email packages in use on the Internet, and many insert extra fields in the header. As when interpreting the contents of fields, it's very easy to misinterpret what the existence of a field means. There is a highly visible example of this—the `X-PMFLAGS` field, used by Pegasus Mail for internal bookkeeping. Newer versions of the program strip the field when sending a message, but older versions don't. Unfortunately, some UBE generation software adds it to messages. As a result, many filtering rules include a check for it, making it quite possible that legitimate mail will be lost.

7.4.6 Header Errors

Many of the headers generated by UBE engines contain errors. Some of these errors are good candidates for filter rules.

`Received` fields often contain errors. A common one is an invalid IP address in the parenthetical comments, which is a strong indication that the field was generated by a UBE engine; it's unlikely to be a bug in a legitimate MTA.

```
Received: from tuba.example.com (tuba.example.com [300.300.300.300])
          by example.com with ESMTP id QPR10321
          ; Sat, 3 Jan 1998 16:03:04 -0800 (PST)
```

In this case, 300 is not a valid value for a segment of an IP address, since no segment can have a value larger than 254.

The *date* subfield can also be checked for a valid value. For example, the following invalid time-zone information has been found in UBE messages.

```
-400 (EDT)
```

The numeric time-zone is missing the leading 0. If it were correctly formed, it would be '`-0400`'.

Some UBE engines attempt to spoof a legitimate MTA and get it wrong.

```
Received: from hub.example.net
          by dorm.example.edu (8.8.5/8.6.5) with SMTP id GAA08839
          ; Wed, 3 Feb 1999 17:56:25 -0500 (EST)
```

In this example, the parenthetical comment is supposed to make it appear that the field was added by the Sendmail program. However that queue identifier is invalid for this Sendmail version, indicating that a UBE package is generating the errant field. Because this type of error could be a bug in a legitimate program, it's important to check other messages to determine whether it's a good candidate for a filter rule.

Another common field error can be found in X-UIDL fields. Normally these are removed from outbound messages, but they leak out occasionally. In a message this field isn't necessarily an indication of UBE, but UBE messages often use malformed versions of it. The value should be 32 characters in length. If it's not, it's a sign that the message is UBE.

```
X-UIDL: a
```

Sometimes the field has the correct length, but is still obviously UBE.

```
X-UIDL: 1212121212121212121212121212121212
```

The Message-ID field is another source of field errors. It's well worth a careful look when analyzing UBE messages. A common example is a null address in the field.

```
Message-ID: <>
```

Other obviously bogus values are also found.

```
Message-ID: <xxxxxxxxxxxxxxxxxxxx>

Message-ID: <guaranteedcredit@card.com>

Message-ID: <youd like to know heh ? >
```

Sometimes it tells you directly.

```
Message-Id: <199808233352CAA18232@spam.is.good.crsc.k12.ar.us>
```

Again, caution is called for. The following `Message-ID` field was found in a UBE message.

```
Message-ID: <a51d67c4.35ea7efe@aol.com>>
```

The duplicate '>>' characters at the end of the *msg-id* value are invalid. Yes, the message was UBE. Unfortunately, a version of email software from AOL (America Online) has a bug that generates this error.

Careful scrutiny of large samples of email will uncover one more fact of life regarding header errors in legitimate messages. They are more common than one might think. This is particularly true with features that have been recently added to a software package or with implementations of newer protocol extensions, such as DSN. Filtering on errors in headers could result in losing legitimate email.

7.4.7 Message Bodies

The message body can also be searched for indications of UBE. Many of the same pattern matches for `Subject` also apply to it. The primary problem with checking message bodies is that it can take considerably longer, since they can be quite large. One optimization is to check a relatively small number of lines at the start and end.

7.4.8 Opt-Out Lists

Some unsolicited email offers recipients the option to be removed from the mailing list. This is called an *opt-out list*.

On the surface, this seems like a good thing—send email to the given address and never get email from that site again. Unfortunately, opt-out lists are generally useless. Not only do they not result in removal, but responding results in being added to another list—a list of people that respond to opt-out lists, bringing even more unsolicited email.

On the other hand, messages with opt-out options provide information for creating new filters for deleting UBE.

```
If you wish to be removed from our mailing list, write us
at remove@example.net.
```

The problem is that this type of text comes in many forms. Sometimes it's found in an `X-Advertisement` field, but most often it's somewhere in the body of the message. To complicate the problem, there is no common format for the text, so crafting filter rules is problematic.

7.4.9 Whitelists

The techniques presented so far have erred on the conservative side. They are based on the idea that it's better to let a piece of UBE go through than to filter out a piece of legitimate mail. Some users prefer a more aggressive approach.

Instead of filtering out UBE, why not filter out all messages not sent by a select list of senders? This is referred to as a *whitelist,* and for some people it's an effective way to avoid ever seeing a piece of UBE.

The idea is that as a message is received, the originator information is analyzed. If the filter has no record of the originator, it sends the originator a message explaining that a whitelist is being used, with instructions on how to be added to it.

7.4.10 Prevention

One way to handle UBE is to avoid getting on a UBE distribution list in the first place. This requires an understanding of how such lists are created.

Many lists are created by *harvesting* addresses, which involves scanning Web sites, newsgroups, and public mailing lists. This is an extremely effective tool for populating UBE lists, as people generally like to provide their email address so that other people can send them mail.

When scanning Web pages, harvesters can find email addresses by looking for 'mailto' URLs.

```
<a href="mailto:joe@tuba.example.com">Joe's Places</a>
```

Usenet postings are also a rich source for email addresses, since news messages contain email addresses to allow readers to reply to them.

```
From: Larry Ictus <larry@ictus.example.com>
```

Harvesting is not limited to Internet services. Programs exist to extract addresses from discussion groups provided by online services such as America Online and CompuServe.

To avoid being put on a UBE list, some users *cloak* their address when posting news or publishing their address on a Web page, then provide instructions in the message or page so humans know how to decloak it.

```
larry@NO-SPAM.ictus.example.com
```

This has mixed results. It can significantly reduce the amount of UBE received, but some people find it annoying to have to decloak an address in order to send a person a mail message and simply don't bother. This is especially true in the case of technical mailing lists and newsgroups. Cloaking also impedes technical support and is a violation of many site policies. Another problem is that harvesting programs have started to detect some of the more common cloaking strings and compensate accordingly.

Some people use subaddressing when providing their address in various places.

```
larry+news@ictus.example.com
```

While this technique doesn't stop UBE, it indicates how a UBE engine got the address.

Another technique being researched is random one-time addresses, a variation of the subaddress technique. Here, a random address is generated for a single use, such as posting an article to a newsgroup. If the address ends up on a UBE list, the user can disable it, thus preventing it from being used by UBE engines.

If you've been left with the impression that UBE is a difficult problem, you're right. Unsolicited bulk email is a big problem for some people. Unfortunately, there's no silver bullet. Coping with it requires a variety of techniques and a willingness to adapt as UBE software developers come up with ways to circumvent filters.

Businesses contemplating the use of UBE for bulk advertising should consider the fact that many users think that no legitimate business would send it. While bulk advertising can be effective in other mediums, it is a very bad idea to try it with email. Contrary to what some people might believe, it is not the same as sending junk mail through the postal system. Bulk advertising by otherwise legitimate businesses is likely to be met with an aggressive response from the Internet community.

7.5 ADVANCED FILTERING

Information filtering has been a research topic for many years. The filters described so far are fairly simple: A person creates a filter rule with a condition that yields a true or false result when evaluated. There are several interesting variations on this model, and this section describes a few: scoring, collaborative filtering, and dynamic addresses.

7.5.1 Scoring

All the example conditions presented up to this point have been Boolean tests that have simple true or false results. Sometimes, a more sophisticated answer is desired.

Scoring is a technique where, instead of applying a Boolean true or false, a numeric value is assigned to a message. A sequence of conditions is tested on the message that either increase or decrease its score. Once a score is calculated, additional filter rules are applied, based on it.

This has been used in some news readers, like Gnus, for several years and is found in some traditional filter programs, like Procmail.

7.5.2 Collaborative Filtering

Two heads are better than one, yet most filters are designed to be maintained by one person. While some filtering programs provide the ability to incorporate rules from other locations, they aren't designed to take into account rules from more than one user.

What if filtering input could be taken from a large number of users? This is precisely what was done with the GroupLens project,[8] a study that investigated collaborative filtering with newsgroups. Users would rate individual articles, and the results would be visible to other readers.

As of the date this book was written, collaborative filters hadn't become very common, but they show promise for some types of problems, such as filtering unsolicited email.

7.5.3 Dynamic Email Addresses

Email addresses are generally static pieces of information, which most people view as something that needs to be valid for an extended period of time. Research has been done on the use of dynamic email addresses, which were mentioned in Section 7.4.10.

With this technology, a user can generate a dynamic email address for a specific purpose, amassing a large collection of addresses for various purposes. If one of the addresses gets on a UBE mailing list, the user can revoke it and generate a new one. The dynamic portion is generated in such a way that it is computationally infeasible to guess what a valid value would be.

Dynamic addresses can be implemented using subaddresses, where some portion of the address is dynamically generated. Since subaddresses support a subset of the *local-part* of an email address, the dynamically generated portion can be directed into an appropriate filter for processing.

```
joe+1831782738@tuba.example.com
```

In this example, the normal destination, 'joe', is filtered so only a small set of senders is allowed to send directly to that address.

---

[8] http://www.cs.umn.edu/Research/GroupLens/.

7.6 SUMMARY

Filters are a valuable addition to an email architecture. They extend its capabilities from a simple way to send messages from one location to another to a tool for managing information.

Filtering provides the ability to programmatically delete, refile, and reroute messages. They are implemented as a series of rules tested against the information in question. Each rule has a set of conditions and associated actions to take if the conditions are met.

There are several types of filters available and several places where they are used. Each has particular strengths and weaknesses that make it more or less suited for certain filtering situations.

Filters are primarily used for two things. People use them to programmatically organize or act on incoming email, which eliminates some of the day-to-day drudgery of these tasks. They are also used to detect unsolicited bulk email. Of the two, bulk email is the most difficult problem to solve. It is a serious issue for some organizations and people, and, unfortunately, there is no simple solution. It is one of the most complicated applications of filtering.

The uses for filtering are limited only by the imagination. The next chapter provides a good example—mailing list processing. As the chapter is being read, keep in mind the role filters can play.

Email allows a message to be sent to multiple recipients. Typing in recipients works relatively well for small lists, but it becomes unwieldy when the list becomes large or needs to be typed in repeatedly. Imagine, for example, a To field with thousands or tens of thousands of recipients, or typing in the same set of recipients for an extended email conversation with a group.

The solution to typing in the addresses each time is a facility that lets a user store a list of addresses and reference that name instead of the individuals in the list. Such a facility could be a personal address book, an MTA group alias, or a dedicated mailing list processor. This chapter focuses on mailing list processing, but reviews the other two techniques as precursors to mailing lists. The emphasis is on how mailing list processors work, what features many of them provide, and how those features might be implemented using the standards and protocols presented in this book. It is not an exhaustive survey of the capabilities of the various list processors that exist today; it is an overview of what is possible. The topic also provides the opportunity to exercise some of the knowledge gained from earlier chapters.

Mailing lists are analogous to Usenet newsgroups, in that groups of people can participate in conversations. Each member of a list sees all the messages sent to that list.

Lists have been used with Internet email since the earliest days of ARPANET. In fact, one of the first mailing lists on ARPANET was MSGGROUP, a forum on the various developments in email. It also provided a vehicle for early email developers to explore email for group communications. Early mailing lists were not limited to technical topics. Another one of the earliest mailing lists was SF-LOVERS for fans of science fiction.

The early users of mailing lists encountered many of the same problems seen today, including threats of legal action for statements made on a list, unsolicited bulk email, and aggressive debates called "flame wars."

Many of the features in modern mailing lists have been around for a long time. In 1980, list digests were devised to reduce the amount of messages received from a list. A message digest is a collection of messages bundled into one message. Also, 1980 saw the introduction of moderated mailing lists, to which only certain individuals are allowed to post messages.

As the Internet grows, mailing lists' popularity grows due, in part, to the fact that it is relatively easy to create and manage a modest one. People without the technical skills to manage a list can even use one of the many mailing list services available on the Internet. The growth of mailing lists, both in number and size, presents interesting challenges, but they show no sign of losing steam.

Interestingly enough, there are very few standards directly related to mailing lists. Instead, one must rely on an understanding of the other email standards and how they can be combined to provide mailing list services.

8.1 PRECURSORS TO MAILING LISTS

One of the best ways to learn about how mailing lists work is by reviewing the various techniques for distributing email to a list of recipients. This section walks through the precursors to full-scale mailing list processing.

8.1.1 Personal Address Lists

Most MUAs have personal address books that assign a virtual name to a set of one or more email addresses. The primary purpose is to provide a convenient interface for commonly used recipient addresses, or sets of addresses. Instead of typing in all the recipients, the user selects the corresponding address book entry and the MUA expands the contents into the message field being populated.

```
To: joe@tuba.example.com,
    bob@flugelhorn.example.com,
    larry@ictus.example.com
```

There are limitations to personal address lists. For one thing, they are difficult to share with other people as they are available only to the user who created them. In order to use them, another user needs to get a copy of a list from the person who created it, or have that person send the message.

List maintenance is another problem. If a person is included in several lists, and that person's email address changes, the address book might need to be changed in several entries. One solution to this problem is to add personal address list entries for all individuals referenced in an address book, then refer to these entries when creating new lists. This approach improves the maintenance of the lists, but most users don't use it.

Another limitation is privacy. Since the contents of a list are expanded into the header of the message, all recipients see them. There are situations where this is undesirable.

Scalability is a big problem with address book lists. A recipient list containing hundreds or thousands of entries results in a very large message header. Most recipients consider such headers obnoxious, and in practice they can also cause serious problems. For example, older versions of Sendmail truncate long fields, often making them syntactically invalid.

8.1.2 Group Lists

Group lists, described in Section 2.5.2, alleviate some of the limitations just mentioned. On one level, they are very similar to personal address lists. In fact, some MUAs present personal address lists as group lists.

```
To: Golf Club: joe@tuba.example.com,
               bob@flugelhorn.example.com,
               larry@ictus.example.com;
```

Maintenance requirements are the same as for personal address lists. Scalability issues are the same as well.

Some MUAs provide the ability to suppress the contents of a group list when populating the recipient fields in a message keeps the identity of the membership private, but it makes it impossible to reply to the list. Sometimes this is desirable, sometimes not.

```
To: Golf Club:;
```

When populated, group lists are slightly easier to share if MUAs permit extracting a group list from a message header into an address book. Maintaining accurate copies of the list is still a problem, however, since copies of the data are distributed across multiple address books and mailing list memberships do tend to change over time.

8.1.3 MTA Alias Lists

Centralization is the most common solution to the problem of sharing address lists. One of the most common techniques for centralizing is MTA distribution lists.

Most MTAs provide some sort of aliasing mechanism, which allows virtual destinations, or *aliases,* to be created. These aliases can contain lists of recipients much like the personal address book lists. The primary difference is that the list is expanded into envelopes, not into the messages.

```
To: golf-club@lists.example.com
```

When an incoming message is received for one of these aliases, the MTA generates the expanded list internally and uses it to send one or more SMTP transactions, with separate envelopes.

This technique provides the foundation for a simple centralized mailing list. An originator sends to the alias; the receiving MTA expands the alias internally and sends the message to each member of the list.

The first problem here is error handling. Where should the MTA send the failure notification if a delivery problem is encountered? Since failure notifications are sent to the envelope sender, the notification will be sent to the person who originally sent the message to the list. If the sender doesn't have control over the contents of the list, he or she can't do anything about the error. While the sender might want to know if a particular recipient didn't get the message, it's quite likely he or she can't correct the problem.

The de-facto technique for solving this type of problem is to create an adjunct alias that points to the maintainer of the list.

```
owner-golf-club@lists.example.com
```

If the MTA encounters a delivery problem, it sends the bounce message to the maintainer. When performing the SMTP transactions for redistributing a message, the MTA sets the envelope sender to the address of the list owner.

```
mail from:<owner-golf-club@lists.example.com>
```

If a subsequent MTA encounters an error after it has accepted responsibility for a message, it has the necessary information to notify the correct person. At this point, we have a simple mailing list with basic error handling.

There's one more problem to work out. How do people ask to be added to the list and taken off? This is usually done by providing a separate address users can email to for administrative requests. The de-facto standard is for the address to be the name of the list with '-request' appended to it. In fact, it has become so common, it should be available for all lists; too many people expect it to be there.

```
golf-club-request@lists.example.com
```

Readers might wonder why the owner address prepends and the request address appends. Actually, either combination can be used for either address—it varies from list to list. The convention described here is a result of history, and old habits die hard. In early MTAs, when request addresses were added, they were appended because it made more sense to read.

In practice, various combinations are used, but there are a few things to be aware of when contemplating variations. Most people are used to the '*-request' form for request addresses. Deviating from this will probably be confusing. Staying with the convention with owner aliases isn't as crucial, since this is used in message envelopes, which most users don't deal with.

At first, one might be tempted to use the owner of the list all the time, and in many cases this is reasonable. However, as will be shown later in the chapter, the owner and request addresses can be automated, and it's easier to automate them if they are kept separate. In fact, it's possible to have various addresses for all manner of programmatic processing.

```
golf-club-help@lists.example.com
golf-club-info@lists.example.com
golf-club-subscribe@lists.example.com
golf-club-unsubscribe@lists.example.com
```

Another benefit of the `request` address is that administrative requests can be kept away from the primary list traffic. If a user wants to be removed from a list, he or she can send an appropriate message to the request address without disturbing the other members.

MTA aliases solve most of the problems that address books and group lists have. The lists are sharable because an email address is associated with them. They are centralized, so users don't have to worry about keeping multiple copies up to date. The list members aren't expanded into message fields, so MTA aliases also offer more privacy and scalability.

8.2 BASIC LIST PROCESSING

MTA aliases are workable for many situations. In particular, many lists internal to an organization can be implemented quite nicely.

The next leap forward is true mailing list processing. It's actually a variation of the MTA aliases technique with the primary difference that several elements are replaced with components designed to improve list performance and maintenance. These components include an exploder for redistributing incoming messages to list members, a bounce handler for automating the handling of delivery problems, and an interface for performing various administrative tasks.

8.2.1 Exploders

The heart of a mailing list processor is the software that processes incoming messages and redistributes them to the members. These are often referred to as *exploders,* since they explode a single message into multiple messages.

As mentioned earlier, simple mailing list processing can be accomplished by redistributing a message to a list of recipients; the local MTA is used to distribute the messages, with the envelope sender pointing to the bounce handler. There are, however, several useful improvements that can be made to this technique.

Queue Optimizations

For small lists, the process for redistributing is relatively unimportant. Large lists, however, are another story. The overhead for sending a message to a remote destination is high enough that care should be taken to reduce the number of times a list processor needs to connect to a particular machine when sending out-bound messages. The problem is particularly important with high-volume lists or those with a large number of recipients.

As incoming messages are exploded, the destination machine is determined and they are deposited in the out-bound queue. This queue is handled by another process in one of several ways. The simplest is to process the messages in the order they were received. This is acceptable as long as the rate of incoming messages isn't too high or the rate of processing isn't too low. If either of these is true, the queue will keep getting larger, until manual intervention is necessary. It could, for example, fill up a disk.

The rate of incoming messages in some lists may be high enough that the list cannot cycle through all the destinations before another message is received. If this persists, the out-bound queue will not be able to empty the queue fast enough. However, queuing optimizations can improve the situation.

The most common optimization is to sort destinations. Most MTAs do this to varying degrees. In this case, the MTA sorts the recipients based on the domain name or MX information gathered while determining the destination machines. Instead of processing each piece of mail individually, the MTA scans the entire list, determines the real destinations for all the email addresses, then sorts the recipients based on destination. It then cycles through the destination machines, attempting to deliver all the messages for each one. This reduces the quantity of connection attempts required to redistribute a message to the smallest number possible.

Of the several ways to sort the messages, the simplest is by the domain name in the recipient addresses. Another way is to perform MX queries. All destinations with the same query results are processed in one SMTP session. The sorting must not be done based on partial overlaps of MX information. In other words, if two destinations have a command MX record, but the other MX records differ, email for the two destinations should not be sent together. This is because, if the first MX destination fails, the queue processor should try the next one, and the only way this works is if the MX records match completely.

This last technique is more complicated and requires careful planning to implement correctly. It can, however, provide a significant improvement over simple sorting based on domain name, particularly if large numbers of recipients get routed through a common gateway or firewall.

Another way to speed up queue processing is to aggregate messages going to the same destination into a single SMTP session. This reduces the amount of time the queue processor spends establishing connections to destination machines. It also reduces the amount of data sent over the network. All of the recipients with the matching domain names get sent in one SMTP transaction, with one SMTP `mail` command, multiple `rcpt` commands, and one `data` command.

Since most MTAs provide some amount of destination sorting and transaction aggregation, many mailing list processors rely on the MTA resident on the machine where the processor resides. Many MTAs, however, are not designed for large volumes of recipients or may not implement very sophisticated optimizations. As a result, their sorting features are often not optimal for large lists.

To address this problem, some mailing list processors do their own distribution, with the queue processing tuned for handling large volumes of SMTP traffic. Integrating it into the list processor also allows optimizing some of the bounce processing.

Access Control

The mailing list mechanisms described thus far assume every received message is automatically redistributed to the members. There are many situations where it's desirable to limit who can post a message to a list.

One of the most common limits on incoming email is a *closed list,* in which only members can post messages. The simplest way to implement a closed list is to check the originator information on incoming messages and compare it to the members in the list. If the originator is not a member, it is bounced back to the sender with a suitable explanation.

```
extract address from field "From"
if address is not in subscription-list
then reply to sender with rejection-message
```

This technique is commonly used, but it has a couple of shortcomings. For one, it's relatively easy to spoof a message so it appears to be coming from a list member. While most lists can tolerate a certain amount of spoofing, it would present a significant problem for some. As an example, a security alert list might receive a spoofed false alarm, causing time and money to be spent on a nonexistent problem. Or worse, a message could be spoofed saying a real problem was, in fact, a false alarm. Combating this is nearly impossible without resorting to some of the security extensions available for email detailed in Chapter 9. For the most part, however, most lists just tolerate the problem, since it's not a common occurrence.

Some lists are moderated, meaning only a small set of people are allowed to post to it. This is called a *moderators list.* People not in the moderators list send a proposed message to the moderators, who then approve or disapprove its posting.

The technique is similar to that for a generic closed list, except the list of people allowed to post is smaller.

```
extract address from field "From"
if address is not in moderators-list
then reply to message with explanation-message
```

Filtering also can be used to prevent certain originators from submitting to the list. This is similar to creating a closed list, except the list of addresses is used to determine who is not allowed to post rather than who is allowed to post.

```
extract address from field "From"
if address is in blacklist
then if address is not in notified-list
    then send notification to sender
        add address to notified-list
    delete message
```

Filtering Incoming Messages

The previous examples of screening submitted messages are specific uses of filtering. It's not unusual to find mailing lists that use some amount of filtering. In fact, much of the information in Chapter 7 can be applied to mailing lists, particularly filtering for extremely large messages and unsolicited bulk email. Open lists find this extremely useful in keeping down the noise level.

Message Manipulation

In addition to filtering incoming messages to determine whether they should be redistributed to a list, it's also possible, and quite common, to alter them. The alterations can be roughly divided into two categories: to headers and to bodies. Altering headers includes deleting undesirable fields, adding new ones, and manipulating existing ones.

Deleting undesirable fields not only can reduce some of the clutter in message headers, but it can also avoid some annoying problems. One example includes removing nonstandard fields that should never be seen in transmitted messages or that can cause problems for list members. The following list contains example of such fields.

- `Content-Length`
- `Disposition-Notification-To`
- `Precedence`
- `Priority`
- `Return-Path`
- `Return-Receipt-To`

- Status
- X-Ack
- X-Confirm-Reading-To
- X-UIDL

Some list processors can modify existing fields. One of the most visible examples is Subject. To aid in filtering, some processors prepend a string containing the name of the list to the subject.

```
Subject: [golf-club] tourney next week
```

One set of fields commonly modified should be left alone—the originator fields. Of these, the most commonly modified field is Reply-To. The idea is that setting the field to the list address will cause replies to go to the list. As an example, say the following addresses are involved in a message submission.

```
To: golf-club@lists.example.com
From: larry@ictus.example.com
```

MUAs generally provide two replies. One is to the originator. The other is to all recipients listed in the message, commonly referred to as a *group reply*. In the example above, if Joe wants to reply to the message, he can have his MUA reply to Larry or he can do a group reply. The group reply will result in some variation of the following.

```
To: larry@ictus.example.com
Cc: golf-club@lists.example.com
From: joe@tuba.example.com
```

Since Larry is already on the list, he should be removed from the reply message. In this case, the contents of the To field need to be deleted and golf-club@lists.example.com should be moved to the To field. Most users find this tedious and generally leave the original as is, resulting in a duplicate message for Larry. Although there are techniques to minimize this problem, such as duplicate message detection in an MUA, the problem is generally frustrating for many users.

Setting the `Reply-To` field to the list address allows users to use the MUA's normal reply function to reply to the list, instead of having to use a group reply.

```
To: golf-club@lists.example.com
From: joe@tuba.example.com
Reply-To: golf-club@lists.example.com
```

The problem occurs when Joe wants to reply to Larry instead of to the entire list. Since the MUA is using the `Reply-To` field to override the recipient value, Joe must edit the field so it contains the correct value.

Not everyone agrees that this is bad. Some people argue that replying to an individual is relatively rare in a mailing list, so the inconvenience of having to hand-edit the field is minor. As a general rule, opinions are strongly polarized in either direction.

Regardless of your opinion of altering originator fields, there is one that should never be altered—`From`. Modifying this field can erase any indication of who sent the original message.

The desire to alter the originator fields is prompted by two issues. First, the semantics of originator fields don't support some of the transactions people want to perform with mailing list messages. Second, most MUAs don't provide interfaces well suited for interacting with mailing lists. Mailing lists are similar to newsgroups. News reader programs provide a way to post a reply to the newsgroups and a way to reply, via email, to the person who posted a message. Most MUAs do not provide a convenient way to perform the equivalent to a posting with mailing lists. This is due, in large part, to the difficulty in determining the correct mailing list address.

One way to handle this problem is to use a `Mail-Followup-To` field, which, while not part of a published RFC as of the writing of this book, is gaining acceptance in many circles. It may very well be documented in an RFC in the not-too-distant future.

The field is used as an alternative to modifying the `Reply-To` field.

```
Mail-Followup-To: golf-club@lists.example.com
```

The idea is to have MUAs detect the field and provide an alternative reply, so users can send the reply directly to the list. This is similar to what is provided in news readers, where there is a distinct difference between posting a follow-up article to a newsgroup and replying to the originator of a message.

Modifying the `Sender` field is problematic for similar reasons. If it is replaced, the original sender information is no longer available.

In general, the following fields should not be modified or added by the mailing list software, since doing so circumvents the purpose of the fields.

- `To`
- `Cc`
- `Sender`
- `From`
- `Reply-To`
- `Message-ID`
- `In-Reply-To`
- `References`
- `Date`
- `Received`
- `Resent-*`

Fields can also be added to messages. A list processor might, for example, add an extension field to identify the list, making it easy for users to refile the list messages to a separate folder.

```
X-List: golf-club
```

There is, however, an even better set of fields to add to messages. The answer lies in RFC2369 (The Use of URLs as Meta-Syntax for Core Mail List Commands), which defines fields that provide several pieces of helpful information about a list. They are illustrated in Table 8.1. All the fields are optional, but `List-Help` and `List-Unsubscribe` are extremely useful to users and should be considered for all mailing lists.

TABLE 8.1 Set of Fields

Field	Description
`List-Archive`	Location of archived messages
`List-Help`	Request help for the list
`List-Owner`	Human contact for list
`List-Post`	Message submission address
`List-Subscribe`	Subscribe to the list
`List-Unsubscribe`	Unsubscribe from the list

Each of the fields contains a command list of URLs. Each URL points to a location where the corresponding information can be found. Since one of the URL types available is `mailto`, the fields can even be used to generate a mail message for interacting with the mailing list software.

The `List-Help` field provides a pointer to a location where help information can be found. Since the content is a URL, it can take several forms.

```
List-Help: <mailto:golf-club-request@lists.example.com?subject=help>

List-Help: <http://www.example.com/lists/>

List-Help: <ftp://ftp.example.com/lists/>
```

Because the field can contain a comma-list of URLs, multiple sources can be provided, allowing the user to choose a preferred method for retrieving the information.

```
List-Help: <mailto:golf-club-info@lists.example.com>,
           <http://www.example.com/lists/>
```

The `List-Unsubscribe` field provides information on how to unsubscribe from a list.

```
List-Unsubscribe:
   <mailto:golf-club-request@lists.example.com?subject=unsubscribe>

List-Unsubscribe:
   <http://www.example.com/lists.cgi?cmd=unsubscribe?list=golf-club>
```

As a complement to `List-Unsubscribe`, `List-Subscribe` provides information on how to subscribe to a list. This might seem like a silly thing to include in a list message, since all the recipients in the list are already subscribed. It is useful, however, if someone wants to provide the information to a friend or co-worker.

The `List-Post` field provides a way to specify the address to use when submitting messages to a list. If the list is unmoderated, the field contains its address. This can be used by an MUA to implement a reply function for posting to the list. If the list is moderated, it provides the email address of the moderator.

```
List-Post: <mailto:golf-club@lists.example.com>

List-Post: <mailto:golf-club-moderator@lists.example.com>

List-Post: NO
```

The last example shows how the field can be used to indicate that no submissions are allowed. This is useful for announcement lists.

Another useful field is `List-Owner`, which indicates a human contact for the list.

```
List-Owner: <mailto:larry@ictus.example.com>

List-Owner: <mailto:larry@ictus.example.com?Subject=golf-club>
```

The final field is `List-Archive`, which provides the location of message archives for the list.

```
List-Archive:
    <mailto:golf-club-request@lists.example.com?Subject=index>

List-Archive: <http://www.example.com/lists/golf-club/archive/>
```

This section has focused on altering message headers. As mentioned earlier, it's also possible to alter message bodies. One of the simplest, and most common, forms of manipulation is prepending or appending additional text, which is often used to tell users how they can unsubscribe from the list. This is a perennial problem. One of the ways some list maintainers address it is to include text at the beginning or end of the message body of every out-bound message. While it isn't a complete solution, for some audiences it can make all the difference in the world.

```
--
To unsubscribe from this list send a message to
golf-club-request@example.com with the following subject line.
    Subject: unsubscribe
```

This type of alteration has one serious drawback—it can damage MIME entities. As an example, imagine a single-part MIME mail message containing a `base64` encoded body. If text is indiscriminately added to it, the resulting decoded information will be different. While there are ways to safely add the text, the problem is not solvable in the general case.

On a similar note, some MUAs add proprietary MIME attachments to messages, which can be annoying. List administrators often remove the offending attachments. It's possible to safely do this in some instances, but extreme care is required to avoid damaging the MIME structure of the document.

8.3 ADVANCED LIST PROCESSING

The functions described in Section 8.2 are by no means the only features available in list processors. The long history of mailing lists on the Internet means they have had many years to evolve. This section describes some of the more advanced features some list processors provide.

8.3.1 Bounce Handling

There are three basic problems to solve when processing bounces: correlating a bounce message with the address in the recipient list that caused the bounce, determining the cause of a bounce, and determining what actions to take because of a bounce. These problems are at the heart of any activity related to bounces, particularly automated bounce handlers.

Correlating Bounces

One of the problems with bounce messages is that sometimes the address being reported in the message is different from the address in the list. If the address in a list is forwarded to another address, even another mailing list, a delivery failure will often not refer to the subscription address.

So, how can a list administrator determine the list member address associated with the bounce message? With a small list, or familiarity with the membership, a simple visual scan can uncover the offending address, but the goal here is to automate the handling of bounces. While it is impossible in the general case, it can be achieved for certain types of address differences.

Subscription addresses often contain the FQDN of the machine used for final delivery. For example, our user Joe might subscribe to a list as `joe@tuba.example.com`, where `tuba.example.com` is the machine used for final delivery of his email. If he moves to another machine, say `oboe.example.com`, and forwards his email to it, errors in final delivery will reflect the new address instead of the one in the subscription list.

Since the primary difference between the two addresses is the left-most segment of the domain name, a bounce processor can search, taking advantage of this similarity. If the bouncing address is `joe@oboe.example.com`, the bounce handler first looks for that address. If that address isn't found in the subscription list, the program can then look for any addresses matching the user name and the trailing portion of the domain name. In this example, the two addresses would be good candidates for searching:

```
joe@example.com
joe@*.example.com
```

This approach won't catch all address changes, but it can catch a noticeable percentage. It does suffer from a small problem—it doesn't prevent a mismatch. In other words, it's possible to match an address that is not causing a bounce. This problem can be minimized with bounce probing, discussed later in this section, but this isn't always a workable solution.

Other types of address changes can be handled with pattern matching, but it doesn't take much to cause this technique to fail. In extreme cases, pattern matching fails completely. For example, our user Joe might move to another domain and use a different *local-part,* such as `joe.doubloon@example.net`. In this case, both sides of the address are different. Pattern matching cannot hope to solve this type of address change.

Another technique for correlating subscription addresses to bounce addresses is to alter the envelope sender to include the return path of the recipient. The VERP (Variable Envelope Return Path) mechanism provides this. The envelope sender is not simply the address of the list owner; it is modified to include the recipient in the return path.

```
mail from:<owner-golf-club-joe.doubloon=example.com@lists.example.com>
```

This is essentially a subaddress, as described in Section 2.5.1. The '@' character is encoded as a '=' to avoid problems with the address format. If a bounce occurs, it will be sent to `owner-golf-club`. The additional information allows the bounce handler to identify which recipient address was involved without the risk of mismatches.

VERPs provides a one-to-one mapping between a message sent and a bounce received, but they suffer from one significant problem—a separate copy of the message must be sent for every member in the subscription list. Remembering the queue optimizations described in Section 8.2, it can be extremely important to process the out-bound queue as fast as possible. Coalescing multiple recipients destined for the same machine into one SMTP transaction can be an important optimization. Since VERPs require the envelope sender to be unique for each recipient, transaction coalescing cannot be used with them. While this might not be a problem for small to medium lists, it can be a severe one for large lists.

Generating separate messages for each recipient can cause another problem. Some email environments store a single copy of a message sent to multiple recipients on the same machine. In other words, if a mail transaction delivers to 100 recipients on the same machine, there might be only one copy of the message stored on disk, with those 100 recipients able to view it. In this way significant savings in disk consumption can be achieved. Since VERPs cause a separate message to be sent for each recipient, separate messages will be stored for each recipient, reducing the ability of an email server to optimize disk space consumption.

Another problem with VERPs is that they don't do a good job handling bounces from subscription list members that are actually sublists. If a bounce is caused by an address in a sublist, the bounce message will be associated with that address. This is probably not the desired behavior for a bounce handler.

While the techniques just mentioned can be useful, there is another one that can be used to correlate bounce addresses to subscription addresses—DSN, described in Section 3.5.6. The `orcpt` parameter allows the original recipient address to be propagated as a message is transferred through a set of MTAs, even if the envelope recipient is changed along the way.

```
rcpt to:<joe@oboe.example.com> orcpt=rfc822;joe@tuba.example.com
```

If all the MTAs support the DSN SMTP extension, the bounce message will include the value of the `orcpt` parameter in the `Original-Recipient` field of a `message/delivery-status` MIME entity, described in Section 4.4.4. In this case, the address causing the bounce and the address in the subscription list are provided in the entity.

```
Original-Recipient: rfc822; joe@tuba.example.com
Final-Recipient: rfc822; joe@oboe.example.com
```

This allows a bounce handler to easily correlate the two addresses. When processing incoming bounce messages, if it detects a message containing the `message/delivery-status` entity, it simply parses the entity and extracts the appropriate information.

One problem with DSN is that it isn't ubiquitous. The DSN delivery status will be generated only if the reporting MTA supports the DSN extension. Also, the original recipient information will not always match the offending subscription list address. If, for example, an intermediate machine doesn't support the DSN extension, it will not propagate the original recipient information. If a subsequent MTA does support the extension, the original recipient information might be different, since an SMTP server is allowed to populate the field with existing information if a client SMTP server doesn't provide any. Thankfully, the vast majority of them do support the extension. With the ability to correlate addresses, as well as several other features mentioned later in this section, the DSN extension has become an important tool for the automated management of mailing lists.

Determining the Cause

The second problem to solve with bounce handling is determining what caused a bounce. There are many causes. While this, by itself, is not a serious problem, it is aggravated by a more serious one—the large number of formats used in bounce messages. RFC1211 (Problems with the Maintenance of Large Mailing Lists) illustrates this vividly. It contains general descriptions of common problems, as well as many examples of failed message deliveries.

One way to programmatically determine the cause of a bounce message is to parse the message and extract the necessary information. Despite the apparent impossibility of this task, it has been done successfully by many bounce handlers. How? As it turns out, a relatively small number of MTA implementations account for the vast majority of MTAs in use. Since a particular implementation will tend to provide a predictable format in bounce messages, it's possible to parse a small number of formats, resulting in the ability to programmatically process a large percentage of bounce messages.

Just as the DSN extension helps with correlating addresses, it also helps when trying to determine why a message bounced. If a `message/delivery-status` entity is present in the bounce message, it will contain several pieces of information useful for an automated bounce handler.

The first area where the DSN extension is useful for determining the reason for a bounce message is in controlling the size and type of bounce messages received. The `ret` parameter can be used with the SMTP `mail` command to control what portion of the original message to include in the bounce. Since a bounce handler isn't interested in the message, this parameter should be set to `hdrs` to tell servers to send only the header in the delivery report.

```
mail from:<golf-club-owner@lists.example.com> ret=hdrs
```

The `notify` parameter can be used with SMTP `rcpt` commands to control what type of delivery reports the bounce handler should receive. Four possible keywords can be used with `notify`: `delay`, `failure`, `never`, and `success`. Since the bounce handler is interested only in delivery failures, a value of `failure` should be used.

```
rcpt to:<joe@tuba.example.com> notify=failure
```

In addition to the additional DSN parameters in the SMTP transactions, there are several fields present in a delivery report that are very useful for automated bounce handling.

The `Action` field, which is required, can contain one of five possible values: `delayed`, `delivered`, `expanded`, `failed`, or `relayed`. Since the `notify` parameter was used, the only value the bounce handler should see is the `failed` value, which is precisely the one it is interested in.

```
Action: failed
```

The `Status` field contains the 3-segment enhanced status code associated with the failure. It can be used to identify well-known failures for subsequent processing.

```
Status: 5.1.1 (bad destination mailbox address)
```

Finally, the `Diagnostic-Code` field will contain the SMTP reply returned to the reporting MTA. While not necessarily usable by an automated bounce handler, it can provide useful information to a human administrator if the bounce handler can't process the error. It can also provide information for log entries.

```
Diagnostic-Code: smtp; 550 mailbox "vera" does not exist
```

These fields are capable of providing enough information to determine the cause of a significant percentage of bounce messages. Not only are they more reliable than parsing unformatted bounce messages, but they are easier to parse, resulting in less computing resources being spent handling bounces.

Determining the Action

After a bounce has been correlated with an associated address in a subscription list, and its cause has been determined, it's time to take action based on this information. There are several things a bounce handler can do to disposition a bounce message.

Since all bounce messages sent to the bounce handler should have a null envelope sender, messages from other senders should probably be sent to a human to be dispositioned. This is also the case if the bounce handler either can't correlate the address or can't determine the cause of the bounce.

The bounce handler can decide not to do anything with a bounce message. For example, if an errant DSN implementation mistakenly sends a delivery report with an `Action` field set to `delivered`, the message should probably be ignored or maybe logged.

Other actions require a little more thought. For example, if a delivery problem is temporary, it might be acceptable to ignore the error, but excessive temporary failures to a specific location might be an indication of another problem. On a high-volume list, it might be useful to suspend out-bound messages to that location until the problem can be investigated.

Permanent delivery problems require even more thought. The issue here is the definition of "permanent." If an address is stale, it should probably be removed. For example, the enhanced status code 5.1.1 is a good indication that the address should be removed from the subscription list. On the other hand, a 5.7.1, which indicates that the delivery is unauthorized, might actually be a configuration error on the remote machine, particularly if previous messages were successfully delivered.

If a problem is temporary, there's a reasonable chance it will be fixed in the not-too-distant future. This includes problems identified as temporary as well as seemingly permanent problems that are actually temporary. The most common technique for resolving the issue is to use bounce probing. When a delivery failure report is received, the recipient address is added to a probe list, and messages sent to the list are suspended until the matter can be resolved. Each recipient on the probe list is periodically sent a probe message to determine if the address is still having delivery problems. If delivery to a recipient starts working, it is removed from the probe list, and pending messages are transmitted to the recipient.

If, however, the address continues to have delivery problems, it is removed from the subscription list. Typically, probe handlers are configured to remove a recipient after a specified number of days or a specified number of delivery attempts. Because a problem may occur over a holiday weekend or may take several days for administrators to correct, retry limits of 5 days or so are common.

Automated bounce handling can significantly reduce the administrative burden placed on a list maintainer. While there are no RFCs that directly dictate how mailing list bounce processing should be performed, the existing standards provide information that can help. This is particularly true for the DSN extensions, which, as shown in this section, can make the job of automated bounce handling considerably easier and more reliable.

8.3.2 Administrative Commands

Managing bounce messages isn't the only thing in mailing list processors that can benefit from automation. The '-request' interface, allowing administrative requests such as adding and removing users, is an excellent candidate.

The typical interface for automated administrative interfaces is a command interface. The user can send a message to the request address with a command in the Subject field or in the message body. A program on the receiving side processes the command and sends a reply to the requester.

As an example, if the commands are implemented in the Subject line, a user can unsubscribe from a list as follows.

```
To: golf-club-request@lists.example.com
Subject: unsubscribe
```

Several other tasks can be automated. Since there are no standards related to administrating mailing lists, interfaces vary widely. Table 8.2 lists common commands available via these interfaces, but not all list processors implement all of

TABLE 8.2 Administrative Commands

Command	Description
send *filename*	Retrieve a specific file from the archive
help	Overview of available commands
index [*list*]	List of available files in archive
info	Summary information about a list
lists	List of available lists
subscribe	Subscribe to a list
unsubscribe	Unsubscribe to a list
which [*address*]	Lists containing *address*
who [*list*]	List of members in *list*

them, and many others are possible. The commands listed in the table are not available in all list processors. The sets of commands available in each list processor vary widely.

One very productive way of looking at administrative interfaces is as email filter rules. To illustrate this, the examples of this section will use the fictitious filtering language used in Chapter 7.

Some interfaces allow the requester to specify an address to be added to the list. This is useful if, for whatever reason, the values in the From and Reply-To fields don't contain the desired contents. In particular, this is how a user employs a subaddress when subscribing to a list.

```
Subject: subscribe mary+golf@glockenspiel.example.com
```

Using our fictitious filtering language, the following rules provide the basis for a subscription command.

```
split field "Subject" into command and arguments
if command is "subscribe"
then if arguments is empty
    then extract address from "Reply-To" or "From"
    else extract address from first argument
    add address to subscription-list
```

Subscribing to and unsubscribing from lists deserve special attention. Since it is easy to spoof standard email, some lists take special precautions with these actions. It's not uncommon to find harassment attacks, where a victim is subscribed to many mailing lists. One of the most common ways to cope with them is to send a confirmation message to the requester. Rather than automatically adding the address to the subscription list, the confirmation is sent and the address is added to a list of pending subscriptions.

```
split field "Subject" into command and arguments
if command is "subscribe"
then if arguments is empty
     then extract address from "Reply-To" or "From"
     else extract address from first argument
     send confirmation-message to address
     add address to pending-subscription-list
```

The message contains an explanation for itself and instructions for confirming the subscription request. This typically entails replying to the confirmation message. There is, however, one small issue to resolve. If the original subscription request was spoofed, it's possible for a confirmation request to be spoofed. What is needed is a way to know that the confirmation actually comes from the person being sent the confirmation message. The most common way to do this is to add a string to the message that cannot be known unless a person reads the message, similar to a one-time password. A random series of characters will do nicely, since it will be difficult to guess the contents of the string. To implement this, the confirmation filter rule needs to be altered slightly.

```
split field "Subject" into command and arguments
if command is "subscribe"
then if arguments is empty
     then extract address from "Reply-To" or "From"
     else extract address from first argument
     generate confirmation key string
     generate confirmation message with confirmation key
     send confirmation-message to address
     add address and confirmation-key to pending-subscription-list
```

Instead of simply sending a confirmation message and adding the address to a pending subscription list, a confirmation key is generated. A confirmation message is then generated, with the key added, and sent. Once this is done, the address and confirmation key are added to the pending subscription list.

This technique works reasonably well because, while spoofing email is relatively easy, intercepting email sent to a mailbox is relatively difficult.

The following example shows the general flavor of a confirmation message with a subscription confirmation key included.

```
To: mary@glockenspiel.example.com
From golf-club-request@lists.example.com
Subject: subscription confirmation
```

```
I received a request to subscribe your email address to the golf-
club mailing list. To confirm this request, simply reply to this
message and include the contents of this message in the reply. You
will be added to the list.

If the subscription request is erroneous, simply ignore this
message, or contact <larry@ictus.example.com>

Subscription Confirmation Key: 19as1ioasdj12390asd98poiwdqkjkhqwe


--
The Golf Club
```

Assuming the subscription request was legitimate, the recipient simply replies to the message. The administrative interface filter can identify these replies and complete the processing of the subscription request.

```
if field "Subject" contains "subscription confirmation"
then extract confirmation-key from message body
     if confirmation-key is in pending-subscription-list
     then add address to subscription-list
          delete entry from pending-subscription-list
     send list-greeting-message to address
```

Unsubscribing from a list can be done in a similar manner. Several of the other administrative commands are even easier to implement using filter rules. The following illustrates some of the more obvious ones.

```
if field "subject" starts with "help"
then send help-file
     exit
if field "subject" starts with "index"
then send archive-index
     exit
if field "subject" starts with "get"
then extract filename from field "subject"
     if ok to send
     then send filename
     else send rejection-message
     exit
```

These examples illustrate one way to perform these tasks. There are many variations, but the concept is the same in nearly all cases.

One common problem found in mailing lists is that some users attempt to send administrative requests to the main list rather than to the administrative address—for example, sending a request to golf-club instead of golf-club-request. To minimize this problem, some list processors scan incoming messages for patterns that look like administrative requests.

So far, all the discussion of administrative functions has focused on email-based interfaces. This is partially for historical reasons. Prior to the introduction of WWW, email interfaces were the most convenient way to provide list management, but this doesn't mean that other interfaces are not possible. Command-line interfaces are popular in situations where a list administrator has access to a command line on the machine serving the list. In recent years, Web-based interfaces have become increasingly popular. Dedicated administrative protocols, which provide a non-email, network-based command interface, are also found in a few list processors.

8.3.3 Digests

Some lists have a very high volume of traffic, and it's not unusual for them to receive hundreds of messages a day. In addition, some lists have a large number of subscribers. A combination of high volume and large subscription bases equates to a large burden on the mailing list processor. It's also a burden on the receiving side, where each individual message must be delivered.

One of the earliest ways to combat these problems was message digests. Instead of receiving each message separately, the members of the list received a bundle of several. This considerably reduced the overhead required for distribution.

RFC934 describes an early format for encapsulating messages into a digest. The simple message encapsulation described in Section 2.4.3 provides the basis for this. The encapsulating message is a standard RFC822 message, the body of which contains three sections: an initial text section, the encapsulated messages, and the final text section. The sections are separated by an encapsulation boundary, as described in Section 2.4.3.

The initial text section contains arbitrary information. It is generally used to hold a table of contents or a brief introduction. The final text section usually provides some sort of sign-off banner, such as

```
End of golf-club digest
```

The encapsulated message section contains all the messages separated by encapsulation boundary strings. RFC934 also recommends preceding each encapsulation boundary string with a blank line for compatibility with older digest parsers.

An encapsulated message consists of a header and a body, just like a standard email message, but the header can be stripped down to save space. At the very least, each header must have `Date` and `From` fields. No others are required, although a `Subject` field is common. The following example shows the body of an RFC934 digest message.

```
------- start of digest (3 messages) (RFC 934 encapsulation) -------
Date: Fri, 1 Oct 1999 12:23:16 -0700
From: larry@ictus.example.com
Subject: tee time

6am - be there or be square...

----------------
Date: Fri, 1 Oct 1999 12:23:16 -0700
From: mary@glockenspiel.example.com
Subject: Re: tee time

excellent - I'll be there.

----------------
Date: Fri, 1 Oct 1999 12:23:16 -0700
From: bob@flugelhorn.example.com,
Subject: Re: tee time

count me in

------- end -------
End of golf-club digest
```

Another format available for encapsulating message digests is the MIME `multipart/digest` media type, which is described in Section 4.4.5.

Some MUAs include the ability to burst MIME digests. This is a particularly useful feature for digested mailing lists. Users receive one message but like to be able to navigate the encapsulated messages conveniently.

Mailing list digests are relatively easy to implement. Each user who wants to receive digests is identified, either in a separated list or with an attribute in the main subscription list. A copy of each incoming message is saved in a queue. When the number of messages in the queue exceeds a certain threshold, when the total size of the messages exceeds a certain threshold, or when a certain time limit has expired, the list processor encapsulates the messages into a digest, which is distributed to those users in the digest list.

8.3.4 Archives

Most mailing list processors provide the ability to keep archives of the messages posted to a list. This allows users to retrieve old messages sent to the list, thus reducing the need to save local copies.

For many years, the most common interface for list archives was, surprisingly enough, email, typically through the request address.

```
To: golf-club-request@lists.example.com
Subject: send 523
```

Upon receiving the request, the list processor retrieves the specified message and sends it to the requester. The first obstacle for a user to overcome is knowing which message number to ask for. This is usually provided with an `index` command, which provides a summary of the messages in the archive. Because there can be quite a few messages, some implementations provide an optional parameter to specify a number range for the index request.

```
To: golf-club-request@lists.example.com
Subject: index 1-200
```

The processor replies with the list of messages in that range.

```
 1 kickoff
 2 Re: kickoff
 3 tap-tap
 4 tourney next week
 5 Re: tourney next week
 6 unsubscribe
 7 Re: unsubscribe
 8 Re: unsubscribe
 9 list instructions
10 Re: tourney next week
```

There is no standard format. Some processors provide a minimal amount of information; some provide a detailed summary reminiscent of an MUA folder summary.

Searching is often provided for situations where the index has insufficient information for finding a message.

```
To: golf-club-request@lists.example.com
Subject: search tourney
```

As expected, the processor replies with a list of messages matching the search criteria.

```
 4 tourney next week
 5 Re: tourney next week
10 Re: tourney next week
```

Prior to WWW, this style of email interface was common. However, the Web changed everything. An email interface is cumbersome and time-consuming. Web interfaces are easy to use and can be navigated quickly. Most also take advantage of hypertext links by linking message threads together with HTML. Web interfaces to list archives have become so popular that email interfaces are seldom used. Newer users may not even be aware that an email interface exists.

There are several aspects of mailing lists and their messages to factor in when implementing a Web interface. In addition to the threading just mentioned, some messages use charsets other than US-ASCII in both the headers and bodies. MIME, in general, presents several interesting challenges. Many users find a Web interface that doesn't decode MIME, and converts the entities appropriately, frustrating to use. While it's understandable why Web interfaces have been developed, fashioning a well-designed one for mailing list archives is difficult.

One interesting solution to the problem of providing access to mailing list archives comes from the email community—IMAP. In this case, a copy of every incoming message is saved in a mail folder, which is available to an IMAP server. If a user's MUA supports IMAP, it can use it to connect to the server and navigate the archive. This approach uses the best of both worlds—it's integrated into the MUA and it's easy to navigate.

8.3.5   Distributed List Processors

As mentioned earlier, large lists present unique performance problems. Everything must be tuned for maximum performance; otherwise, the list runs the risk of clogging up. One technique for solving this problem is to break a list into chunks and distribute the processing across multiple servers.

There are two common ways to accomplish this. The easiest way is to use special recipients in the member list that forward a message to another list processor. This is useful with lists that send to a large number of recipients at large sites, such as universities or large corporations. The master list contains only the address for the satellite site, which redistributes each message to the recipients at that site.

The first problem to solve with this type of architecture is how to handle administrative requests. Error handling isn't a problem because the satellite processor can provide its own information for out-bound messages. Administrative requests are another story, as many of them are specific to the processor. For instance, a subscription request for a satellite site needs to be directed to that site.

One technique is to provide the users at a satellite site with a different address for administrative requests. This can be very effective, but users often send requests to the master processor instead. This can be avoided if the processor software is configured to forward all pertinent administrative requests to the satellite site as necessary.

Another technique is to process all administrative requests at the central site and forward requests to satellites when necessary. This has the advantage of not confusing users.

Another problem to overcome with distributed servers is monitoring the health of a distribution list. A central administrator needs to be able to check the status of remote machines in case a remote administrator is unaware of some problem at that site.

While this can be done with an email interface, it may not always be possible to query the processor via email. One solution is to provide a dedicated administrative interface outside of the normal email channels of communication. Each list processor runs a daemon capable of processing administrative requests, including, but not limited to, help, status information, subscription management, and server control. This type of interface is very useful for large lists, since it reduces the turnaround time needed to resolve a problem.

As an alternative to using a single address to redistribute to a satellite site, it's also possible to spread the load by using multiple servers to distribute out-bound messages. All administrative commands and all incoming messages are processed on a central server. Slave servers process the out-bound messages, which spreads the load across multiple machines for the most time-intensive part of list processing—distribution. This technique is also useful if reliability is a concern. If a server goes down, the master configuration can be adjusted to redistribute the load across the remaining servers. The result is a very scalable architecture capable of processing high volumes of list traffic.

8.4 SUMMARY

Mailing lists are almost as old as email itself. They grew out of the desire of groups of people to communicate via email and have become an essential part of email and its use on the Internet. While there are very few RFCs directly related to mailing lists, many of the email RFCs provide information to control how they operate.

Mailing lists evolved from personal address books and group lists. Once the envelope sender is set to an owner of a list, a mailing list is born.

The primary components of a modern mailing list are an exploder, which redistributes incoming messages to a set of recipients, an administrative interface for performing various actions on the list, and a bounce handler for processing the inevitable delivery failures encountered by an exploder.

Filters can play an important role in managing mailing lists, including preventing unwanted submissions to a list, altering the message in various ways, managing administrative requests, and processing bounce messages. Other than those described in Chapter 7, mailing list processors are one of the most significant filtering applications.

The major challenge facing modern mailing list processors is scalability. As the population on the Internet increases, lists become larger. Several techniques keep the performance at an acceptable level, including optimizing the processing of out-bound queues and distributed list processors.

Despite the availability of other means of group communication on the Internet, mailing lists show no sign of losing ground. They continue to play a major role in Internet communications.

Chapter 9

Security

Preceding chapters have paid very little attention to security. There are two reasons for this. First, many earlier email protocols didn't provide any built-in security features. This has changed in recent years. Second, most of the information about security applies to all of the protocols. This is particularly true with encryption and authentication, where common algorithms are used for several email protocols.

The earliest versions of email provided little or no security provisions. Some readers might find this odd, but its important to remember that the Internet started as an environment for researchers investigating inter-machine communications, with the initial priority getting a disparate set of machines talking to each other. Security mechanisms can hinder communications if improperly designed or implemented. In a research environment, free-flowing communication is often a higher priority than security. This does not mean that early email developers and users were ignorant of security issues. In fact, RFC644 (On the Problem of Signature Authentication for Network Mail), published in 1974, demonstrates that early researchers were concerned about them.

As more users have joined the Internet, security has become a major priority for the Internet standards committees. In fact, a strong focus is on adding high-grade security features to most Internet protocols, particularly the core protocols.

In 1997, the IAB held a security architecture workshop, the goal of which was to design a security architecture for the Internet, or at least to understand what the current state of Internet security was and what direction to steer it in. RFC2316 (Report of the IAB Security Architecture Workshop) reports some of the findings of the workshop and provides guidance to Internet protocol designers and implementers. It should be considered required reading for designers, developers, and system administrators until a future document supersedes it.

At the highest level, the workshop concluded that end-to-end security is superior to the alternative. For example, encrypting a MIME entity is more effective than encrypting the SMTP links between a sender and a recipient. In particular, link encryption would require that each link be encrypted to have any assurance of a piece of data arriving securely. Even if this were accomplished, an email message would still reside on intermediate servers in an unencrypted form. Encrypting the data at its source, so it can be decrypted only by an intended recipient, minimizes reliance on an infrastructure not capable of guaranteeing security at every step along a message's path.

The workshop identified a set of core security protocols, which should be given preference when designing and implementing security services for Internet protocols. These include the following.

- IPsec
- ISAKMP/Oakley, for key negotiation in IPsec
- DNSsec
- Signed keys in DNS
- Security multiparts, for securing data using MIME
- X.509v3 for certificates
- TLS (Transport Layer Security)

The first two items provide security at the IP layer. In particular, IPsec can be used to create VPN (Virtual Private Network) architectures, in which collections of machines can communicate in private over public networks.

The third item, DNSsec, provides protection for DNS information. Like core SMTP, the security of core DNS is, at best, tenuous. Secure of DNS information is becoming increasingly important as the Internet is used more and more for public communication and commerce. DNSsec is intended to provide an additional layer of security for DNS data, allowing more trust to be placed in the information.

The fourth item, signed keys in DNS, involves using DNS for the delivery of public key information. Public keys are discussed later in this chapter. For the purposes of this book, the last items, X.509v3 and TLS, are of particular interest. They are described later in this chapter.

Several protocols were identified in RFC2316 as being useful, but not part of the core set because they were too new or duplicated features of the core protocols. Some of these are described in this chapter: CRAM (Challenge-Response Authentication Mechanism), GSS-API (Generic Security Service Application Program Interface), Kerberos, OTP (One-Time Password), PGP (Pretty Good Privacy), PGP-MIME, SASL, and S/MIME (Secure/Multipurpose Internet Mail Extensions). Any of the protocols in this category could be promoted to core protocols, or they could be demoted.

The workshop determined that some protocols should not be used because they have failed to gain widespread acceptance, despite being available for many years. These include PEM (Privacy Enhanced Mail) and MOSS (MIME Object Security Services).

The workshop found one type of security service to be unacceptable—plaintext passwords, for which new protocols are required to provide an alternative by either replacing them or encrypting the channels used to transmit them. The increased incidents of security breaches caused by monitoring network packets has shown unprotected plain-text passwords to be inadequate and, at times, dangerous.

The workshop identified three areas where security components could use the most improvement: object security, secure email, and route security.

Object security means securing data objects rather than network connections. This can include such things as MIME entities or DNS packets. Route security includes whatever devices are created to add security to the packet routing infrastructure on the Internet. Since routing is outside the scope of this book, the focus will be on the mechanisms in use, and being developed, for securing email.

This chapter describes various security aspects related to Internet email, including what type of security problems are found in protocols and implementations, what security services and extensions are available, and how these services are implemented in the protocols.

One final note before we begin—a single chapter in a book cannot hope to do justice to the topic of security. The best that can be hoped for is a reasonable overview. Even narrowing the topic down to Internet email security doesn't help. Therefore, readers are encouraged to read additional material on security and not simply rely on the information here.

9.1 SECURITY ISSUES

Before reviewing the various technologies available for email security, an overview of some of the related issues is in order. These issues distill down to four broad topics: eavesdropping, impersonation, denial of service, and system integrity, none of which is isolated from the others. In fact, there are strong interactions between them, as will be seen.

First, some explanation is in order. The fact is that email services are the target of many system attackers. They are a tempting target because email is one of the most ubiquitous services on the Internet—even the most conservative firewall architectures allow email to traverse the firewall. As a result, it is imperative that email developers take extra care to avoid any a weakness in their software that attackers can exploit.

The problem is aggravated by the complexity of email services: They are non-trivial to develop, require care when deployed, and are used by end-users who often have no understanding of the underlying security issues.

9.1.1 Eavesdropping

Since email typically travels over the network, it is subject to eavesdropping. This can be very easy to do, depending on the networking environment. Many network interface cards provide the ability to view all network packets on a network segment, not just the packets going to and from the machine in question. This eavesdropping is sometimes called *snooping,* or *sniffing,* and any data transmitted in plain text is subject to it. Network switches can minimize the problem, since they only send packets to the devices they are addressed to, but this can be circumvented by network administrators.

The problem of eavesdropping is not limited to a local network. The potential exists at all points between the client and server.

The most effective way to prevent eavesdropping is to use encryption, either of communication links between machines or of the data before it is even sent over the network. Subject sections in this chapter describe various encryption technologies.

Sometimes protecting data is not sufficient. Often it's desirable to protect the identity of a sender or recipient—sometimes from each other. With email, this can be done with anonymous remailers, servers that cloak the identity of a sender or recipient. This is discussed in further detail in Section 9.7.

9.1.2 Impersonation

Nearly all computer users are familiar with authentication. It provides some amount of assurance that users are who they say they are. If the identity of a user can be forged, the forger can perform any tasks the real user can.

Since core SMTP doesn't provide any authentication, it is easy to forge email. It's simply a matter of supplying the appropriate envelope information to the SMTP server and populating the associated email message with the desired data. Section 9.5.3 describes how authentication can be added to SMTP.

One of the simplest authentication mechanisms available involves the use of an identity string, or account name, and a password. To authenticate, the user provides his or her account name and password to a server. The server checks the two values; if they are correct, the user is considered authenticated. This is a workable solution unless the data needs to be transmitted over a network. If someone is snooping a network, they can see the account name and password information moving along. They can then use this information to impersonate the user. Most older protocols that implement authentication transmit the password as plain text across the network. This has been a significant problem for several years, so much so that the IETF now requires all new protocols to support a more secure means of communicating user credentials. There are several ways to avoid sending plain text passwords over a network. The more common ones are described later in this chapter.

Assuming that passwords are no longer transmitted in the clear doesn't mean the problem is solved. There are two more problems to address. The first is that it's still possible to use a *dictionary attack,* in which an attacker repeatedly tries different passwords in an attempt to gain access to a system. This type of attack is relatively common on the Internet. Protecting a password sent over the network doesn't necessarily protect against dictionary attacks, since it may still be possible to guess correctly. At a minimum, using passwords unlikely to be found with a dictionary attack will help, but most users aren't good about this. Even if they were, there is still the problem of a brute-force combinatorial attack on the password. There are several techniques used to solve this problem, but at the least, using long sequences of truly random data for passwords can make a dictionary attack computationally infeasible. One-time passwords can also provide protection.

The second problem once passwords are no longer transmitted in the clear is *man in the middle* attacks, which involve a person or program insinuating itself between two communicating parties. The communication channel is subverted in such a way that the third party can intercept data sent between two people, manipulate it, and send it to the recipient. Many authentication mechanisms are susceptible to this type of attack to one degree or another.

There is one final concept to mention related to impersonation—*nonrepudiation*. This is the ability to protect against a sender or a recipient denying he or she sent or received a message. Some authentication mechanisms are strong enough to provide nonrepudiation, which is very important for legally binding transactions. These are described later in this chapter.

9.1.3 Denial of Service Attacks

Another issue to deal with is *denial of service* attacks, which include anything that will prevent a service from being operational. They are used primarily for two purposes: to prevent a service from being used and to coerce a vulnerability in a system. It can be difficult to test a design under all adverse conditions. As a result, some systems develop weaknesses when stressed that under the proper circumstances, can be exploited to gain unauthorized access.

There are several common denial of service attacks, broadly categorized as network-based and machine-based. The network-based attacks attempt to disrupt the network communications for a machine. This includes consuming all available TCP connections into the machine, thus preventing it from accepting connections from other machines; disrupting the connection between two machines by sending network packets designed to cause one of them to close the connection; or flooding a network connection so that other traffic times out or takes an inordinately long time to complete.

Some of these attacks, such as disrupting connections, can only be prevented or minimized in the operating system. The higher-level protocols can minimize some of the other attacks by implementing, for example, idle timeouts and constraints on the number of connections a server is willing to accept from a client.

The other type of denial of service attack is machine-based. One technique is consuming a resource on the machine such as disk space, memory, or processor cycles. If not controlled, attacks on any of these resources can severely cripple a machine, sometimes to the point where it is unusable. Most protocol servers and operating systems provide the ability to constrain the amount of system resources a process consumes.

9.1.4 System Integrity

Email is communication. In general terms, communication channels must have three characteristics in order to be useful: they need to be available, they need to be trusted, and they sometimes need to be private. In order to provide these capabilities, the channels and the systems implementing them must have integrity. This means that unauthorized access, disruption of service, or corruption of the message needs to be minimized.

Most operating systems provide various types of security. These are critical to a reliable and trustworthy email environment. Even with system security, however, email services can be disrupted, corrupted, or otherwise subverted. There are several places were this has traditionally been a problem. The remainder of this section describes some of those areas and mentions some of the things that can be done about them.

Permissions and Ownership

By default, most UNIX MTAs deliver email for all local users to a central maildrop directory. There are some shortcomings to this approach. Since the MUA must pick up incoming mail from this central directory, it needs the ability to modify a user's inbox. This presents a problem in that the inbox must be protected from other users accessing it. On SystemV flavors of UNIX, this is accomplished by having the setgid bit on the MUA turned on and the group ownership of the MUA set to the `mail` account. The permissions are on the inboxes and on the directory and are set such that the `mail` group has permission to alter them. It is up to the MUA to prevent users from accessing each other's inbox. Since root privileges are required to enable the setgid bit on a program, this technique works reasonably well, except for one thing—it is not always easy to write a setgid program that is immune to security attacks.

BSD flavors of UNIX solve the central maildrop problem in a different way. They set the permissions on the directory so that it is world-writable, but they also set a bit in the directory permissions that prevents users from deleting a file they don't own. This eliminates the need for the setgid bit, but presents another problem—traditional dot-locking, described in Appendix B's Section B.2, isn't secure, since any users can create a lock on an inbox, even if they don't own it. If kernel locking is used instead, the dot-locking problem is avoided; however, every piece of software that accesses the maildrop directory must use the same locking type.

One solution to the problems associated with central maildrop locking is to deposit incoming email into a directory the user owns, typically the user's home directory. Many MDAs and MUAs provide a way to configure where incoming email is located. This solution is highly recommended, particularly on any system where users don't have a vested interest in each other's privacy.

Since personal email is just that, personal, the permissions on email folders are typically set to allow only the user to read their contents. On UNIX, the file permissions are set to 0600, meaning that only the owner of the file, and the root account, can read or write to it. Many MUAs provide the ability to configure the default permissions for newly created folders. The only rational "out of the box" default is 0600. Anything less is a security flaw, since many users never alter the default settings in software packages.

Buffer Overruns

Because email can be the target of attackers, many input sources should be considered hostile. This means email software needs to take extra precautions when processing data from the outside world. This is true for all stages of email processing.

One place where hostile input has been a problem for email software is *buffer overruns*—attempting to write more data into a buffer than will fit. Depending on where the buffer is located in memory, and what is adjacent to it, buffer overruns can, under certain circumstances, be exploited by attackers to gain unauthorized access or to disrupt operations.

This is, arguably, less of a problem than it used to be, but developers must always code in a such a way that buffer overruns are prevented, including always doing boundary checks when populating data and avoiding library routines that don't check for overflow conditions. One of the most common instances of this is the **sprintf(3)** C library routine. This routine provides a way to build a string from multiple pieces of data, but, unfortunately, it doesn't provide any boundary checks. An alternative, **snprintf(3),** available on most platforms, limits the amount of data that will be written into the target buffer. While **sprintf(3)** is probably the most notorious example, there are other string C library routines with potential problems, for example, **strcat(3)** and **strcpy(3).** The lack of boundary checking means that developers need to be particularly careful when processing strings in C.

Temporary Files

Temporary files can also be a source of problems. Actually, this applies to files in general, but temporary files often are not treated very rigorously.

Email software often uses temporary files to store intermediate data. *Race conditions* are one of the most common problems encountered with them. A race condition can occur where an action is made up of two or more atomic steps. The period of time between the steps can be exploited by attackers if proper precautions aren't taken. As a side note, folder locking, described in Appendix B, can also be subject to race conditions.

The race condition most frequently encountered occurs with file creation. For example, if a piece of software creates a file by first performing a test for its existence, a window of opportunity is available for a race condition. The proper way to create a file is usually to do so if, and only if, the file doesn't already exist, but atomically. In the UNIX world, this is done with a call to **open(2),** giving it the O_CREAT and O_EXCL flags.

Another race condition can arise if a file is created, closed, and then reopened at a later time. Software needs to perform sanity checks when it reopens the file to make sure it hasn't been subverted, for example, making sure that it's not a symbolic link to another file, that the owner and permissions are valid, and that the contents are rational before writing to the file.

Privileged Access

Most operating systems only allow a privileged account to accept incoming connections from TCP ports below 1024.[1] This includes all of the network protocols for email.

There are some places, such as mail delivery, where a program needs to run under the identity of an end-user. While the program might be able to do so as the privileged user, this opens up another opportunity for exploiting any program weakness. As a general rule, the exposure as a privileged user should be kept to a minimum. To further complicate things, extra care needs to be taken when switching to and from the privileged account or end-user. The design of a program has a big impact on how difficult this is. Developers need to pay close attention to this area of their code.

One technique some MTA developers use to solve, or at least minimize, the problems associated with privileged access is to implement the MTA as a collection of small components, each with a specific task and scope of access. This minimizes the need to switch between privileged and nonprivileged access. It also minimizes damage, since a security problem in one component might not affect the security of the entire system.

Trojan Horses

One particularly difficult problem in email is that of *Trojan horses,* in which an attacker gets a user to execute code that subsequently allows the attacker to gain access. Since email can be used to send programs to people, special care is required when processing those programs. It's not difficult to write and send one to an email recipient and get that recipient to extract it and execute it. In nearly all environments, the program can perform any actions permitted to the user.

The problem is not limited to programs designed to run on the recipient's native operating system. It includes Postscript code, as mentioned in the discussion of `application/postscript` entities in Section 4.4.3. It also includes macro viruses written for word processors and spreadsheet programs, since most modern office applications include one or more ways to extend the capabilities of the application through an extension language.

The risk of Trojan horses is not limited to programs transmitted in message bodies, by the way. In general, any breach in security could be used to introduce one.

---

[1] This is root on UNIX.

Message Integrity

The discussion has, so far, focused on the integrity of machines. There's one more type of integrity to look at—that of a message. By default, the core protocol definitions for SMTP, POP, IMAP, and email messages provide no indication of the integrity of the data being transmitted. However, there are ways to verify this. The more common ones are described later in this chapter.

9.2 CORE SECURITY TECHNOLOGIES

Most networking technologies are designed as layers, from the protocols that allow network cards to talk on a wire all the way up to applications that use protocols which run on the network. Security is no exception. At the lowest level are the core security technologies. These provide fundamental services such as encryption and cryptographic hash functions and are typically integrated into higher-level services, such as software packages or security services independent of the protocols using them. At the top levels are frameworks to integrate the security services into protocols. The boundaries between the layers are by no means cast in concrete. For example, it's possible for a core security technology to be implemented as a stand-alone computer program, but viewing the elements as part of a multilayer environment helps sift through their complexities.

There are a lot of algorithms for cryptographic applications, too many to cover in this book. This section describes the technologies, in general terms, and some of the algorithms commonly used in network and email security.

Four types of algorithm are at the core of most security mechanisms: pseudo-random number generators, cryptographic hash functions, symmetric encryption, and asymmetric encryption. These are combined, in one form or another, to create two additional core security technologies: digital signatures and messages authentication codes.

There's one additional comment to make about the core security technologies before going any further. Many countries regulate their import and export. Some of the regulations are severe, and readers are strongly encouraged to research the regulations that affect them.

9.2.1 Pseudo-Random Number Generation

Many security algorithms rely on random numbers as part of their process. There's one slight problem with this. Technically speaking, computers can't programmatically generate numbers that are truly random. Hardware can help, but a pure software solution can only generate what is called a *pseudo-random* number. The better the quality of a PRNG (Pseudo-Random Number Generator), the less likely an encryption function using it will be compromised.

RFC1750 (Randomness Recommendations for Security) provides useful information for developers implementing or using a PRNG. The computer science and mathematics behind PRNGs are beyond the scope of this book; however, several key points are worth mentioning.

One common technique for generating a random number is to seed a PRNG with the system clock time or with some other system counter. This might be acceptable where an apparently random number is needed, but the requirements in cryptography are much stronger. If attackers can determine what time a PRNG value was generated, they can narrow their search space considerably.

Another common fallacy is that a sufficiently obtuse algorithm reduces the likelihood of its being attacked. Cryptologists don't necessarily approach an algorithm square on; they often approach it obliquely. If the quality of the random numbers is low, no matter how obtuse the algorithm, it will probably become evident to a cryptologist.

As this book was being written, Intel was announcing plans to provide hardware-based RNG (Random Number Generator) capabilities for its Pentium-III line of microprocessors. This is good news for the security world, since hardware is generally superior to software in generating random numbers.

9.2.2 Cryptographic Hash Functions

A *hash function* is an algorithm that takes input data and generates a shorter-length piece of it based on some function. A special variant is a *cryptographic hash function,* which has specific requirements, making it suitable for certain uses in cryptography. In general, the input data can be any length. This is important, since it might be necessary to generate a cryptographic hash value for large files. The output is usually a fixed length. The hash function should be relatively easy to compute for any given input. It should be *strongly collision-free,* meaning that finding two input values that generate the same hash value is computationally infeasible. Lastly, the hash function should be one-way, meaning that it should be computationally infeasible to determine the input data based on the resulting hash value.

As will be seen later in this chapter, cryptographic hash functions are used in many email security mechanisms.

MD4

MD4 (Message Digest Algorithm 4), documented in RFC1320 (The MD4 Message-Digest Algorithm), was developed by RSA Data Security. It provides a cryptographic hash function designed for speed, generating a 128-bit hash value from an arbitrary amount of input data. MD4 has been shown to be unacceptably weak for many applications and should be avoided if possible.

MD5

MD5, also developed by RSA Data Security, is one of the most common cryptographic hash functions. It uses a more conservative algorithm than MD4, at the expense of speed. It generates a 128-bit hash value from an arbitrary amount of input data. It is documented in RFC1321.

SHA

In 1994, the U.S. government published a Federal Information Processing Standard, FIPS-180-1, which defines SHA (Secure Hash Algorithm). SHA generates a 160-bit value from an arbitrary amount of input data. In 1994, SHA-1 was published, to correct a flaw in SHA.

There are many cryptographic hash functions available. MD4, MD5, and SHA are simply a few of the most common in email security.

9.2.3 Symmetric Encryption

Symmetric encryption involves taking a piece of data and a key, and encrypting them in such a way that the same key can be used to decrypt the data. This is a very common type of encryption.

There are two types of symmetric encryption: block ciphers and stream ciphers. A block cipher transforms blocks of unencrypted data into blocks of encrypted data. Some of the common block cipher algorithms include DES (Data Encryption Standard), IDEA (International Data Encryption Algorithm), and Blowfish. Several block cipher modes can be used with the cipher algorithms: ECB (Electronic Code Book), CBC (Cipher Chaining Block), CFB (Cipher Feedback), OFB (Output Feedback), and PCBC (Propagating Cipher Block Chaining). The simplest mode is ECB, in which two blocks containing the same data will result in the same encrypted result. This duplication can sometimes be used by cryptographers to decipher the encrypted data. The other modes use more complicated algorithms to ensure that duplicate input blocks do not result in duplicate output blocks.

In contrast, stream ciphers are typically used to process smaller pieces of data, often individual bits. While block ciphers generate the same encrypted data given the same input data and encryption key, stream ciphers can generate different output depending on when in the encryption process the data is encountered. The most common stream cipher in Internet security is RC4. As a side note, block ciphers can be used to synthesize stream ciphers.

DES

DES has been the workhorse of the encryption world. One of the most widely deployed encryption algorithms, it was created by IBM, which patented the algorithm in 1976 but later placed it in the public domain, with the stipulation that implementations adhere to the original specification. The patent expired in 1993. The algorithm is defined in FIPS-46-1.

DES uses a 64-bit block size and a 56-bit key. It is considered unacceptably weak for many applications because of its small key size and increases in computer performance in recent years. Several variations most notably triple-DES, shore up some of DES' weaknesses.

In 1997, NIST (National Institute of Standards and Technology) announced a call for candidate algorithms for a new encryption standard to replace DES. Several companies and individuals submitted entries for the new standard, which will be called AES (Advanced Encryption Standard). A final decision is scheduled for the latter half of 1999 or the year 2000.

IDEA

The IDEA algorithm was developed by Dr. Zuejia Lai and Prof. James Massey as part of a joint project of Swiss Federal Institute of Technology in Zürich and Ascom Systex Ltd. It uses 64-bit blocks and a 128-bit key, and is found in, among other places, PGP and OpenPGP. It is patented by Ascom, and commercial use requires a license.

RC2

RC2, developed by Prof. Ronald L. Rivest for RSA Data Security, is a block cipher that uses 64-bit blocks and a variable key size. It is designed as a drop-in replacement for DES, with better performance.

RC4

RC4 was also developed by Prof. Rivest for RSA Data Security. It is a stream cipher with a variable key size and operates at a byte level. One of its more notable uses is in the SSL (Secure Socket Layer) and TLS protocols. RC4 is not patented by RSA, but is protected as a trade secret. In 1994, a functional equivalent, if not the exact source code, was published anonymously.

Blowfish

Blowfish was designed in 1993 by Bruce Schneier of Counterpane Systems. It uses a variable-length key from 32 to 448 bits. Unlike many other algorithms, it is not encumbered by any patents or licensing restrictions and is finding its way into many security implementations.

9.2.4 Asymmetric Encryption

Symmetric encryption uses the same key for both encrypting and decrypting a message. Its primary difficulty is that the key must be communicated between two parties involved in secure communications. In 1976, Whitfield Diffie and Martin Hellman devised an alternative called *asymmetric,* or *public-key,* encryption.

With public-key encryption, each person uses a pair of keys: a public one and a private one. All communications use the public key, but the private key is only available to the user and is never transmitted. This means that the communication channel used to transmit the public-key information doesn't need to be trusted.

There is a wrinkle: the source of the public-key information does need to be trusted, which means that there needs to be a way to verify the identity of someone providing a key, and that person has to be trusted to provide valid key data. It would appear, at first glance, that this problem is circular, but two techniques for key management have evolved that address this. One is a so-called *web of trust,* which is used by PGP. The other is a centralized certificate authority, which is used by other public-key packages.

A web of trust is distributed, with no one central authority for valid keys. A user can collect public keys from a variety of other users, who can digitally sign a key as being valid. Thus, if person A trusts person B's process for verifying key validity and protecting the key information, A can choose to trust that all the keys signed by B are valid.

On the other hand, distributed key management can be difficult for large organizations to manage predictably. For them, a more attractive solution is to rely on centralized agencies to provide the public-key data.

Ironically, trust is at the core of each of the two techniques. Some people don't trust centralized institutions to provide public keys, preferring to use a more decentralized key management architecture. On the other hand, some organizations don't trust decentralized key trust systems and prefer a centralized authority. Both techniques, however, address the same fundamental problem—confirming that a given public key is valid.

To illustrate how a public key retrieved from a remote source can be validated, a brief overview of certificates will be provided. The most common format for structuring certificates is X.509v3, published by the ITU. X.509v3 certificates contain the following information.

- Version
- Serial number
- Signature algorithm
- Issuer name
- Validity duration
- Subject name
- Subject public-key data
- Issuer unique identifier
- Subject unique identifier
- Extensions

One last piece of information is provided—a digital signature for the certificate, created by the issuer.

This structure addresses how the data is represented, but it doesn't address the infrastructure necessary to support it. What is needed is a PKI (Public-Key

Infrastructure) for managing public-key information over the Internet. The scale and distributed nature of the Internet pose interesting problems for such an infrastructure. In 1995, an IETF working group, PKIX (Public-Key Infrastructure (X.509)), was created to develop standards to support an X.509-based PKI. It has published several RFCs related to this effort, with several more expected in the future.

- RFC2459 (Internet X.509 Public Key Infrastructure Certificate and CRL Profile)
- RFC2510 (Internet X.509 Public Key Infrastructure Certificate Management Protocols)
- RFC2511 (Internet X.509 Certificate Request Message Format)
- RFC2527 (Internet X.509 Public Key Infrastructure Certificate Policy and Certificate Practices)
- RFC2528 (Internet X.509 Public Key Infrastructure Representation of Key Exchange Algorithm (KEA) Keys in Internet X.509 Public Key Infrastructure Certificates)

RSA

The RSA algorithm was invented by Ronald L. Rivest, Adi Shamir, and Leonard Adleman, in 1977, and has become the most popular public-key encryption algorithm in use. It employs several different key sizes, including 512, 768, and, 1,024. RSA is patented in the United States and free in other countries. The patent expires in the year 2000.

9.2.5 ElGamal

The ElGamal algorithm, created by Tather ElGamal in 1985, is a public-key encryption system based on the Diffie-Hellman key exchange protocol. Unlike the RSA algorithm, it is not encumbered by a patent.

9.3 SECURITY SERVICES

Several security services are available, that are independent of any email protocol. These include IP security services, secure DNS, and several authentication and encryption techniques. IP and DNS are outside of the scope of this book, but the authentication and encryption techniques are not. This section describes some of the security services that use the algorithms listed in Section 9.2. These services are also important because they are used by the email security extensions described later.

9.3.1 CRAM

CRAM is an authentication mechanism designed as an alternative to transmitting plain-text passwords over the network. The `apop` POP command is the precursor to CRAM. It is defined in RFC2195 (IMAP/POP AUTHorize Extension for Simple Challenge/Response) as part of an authentication extension for POP and IMAP, which is described in Section 9.4.2.

To authenticate, a client and server need a shared secret. The server issues a challenge to the client containing an arbitrary string of random digits, a timestamp, and the FQDN of the server. This information is formatted as a *msg-id* token.

The client responds to the challenge with the name of the user, followed by a space and a digest value. The digest value is computed by applying the keyed MD5 algorithm described in RFC2104 (HMAC: Keyed-Hashing for Message Authentication), using a shared secret for the key and the *msg-id* as the text to digest. The keyed MD5 is a variation on the MD5 algorithm described in RFC1321.

To compute the keyed MD5 digest, a 64 octet value is needed. If the shared secret is not longer than this, it is used, and nulll-padded to 64 octets. If it is longer than 64 octets, the MD5 digest of the shared secret is used instead. Since an MD5 digest is 16 octets long, it is null-padded to 64 octets. The 64-octet value is then exclusive-ored with a sequence of 64 consecutive octets having the hexadecimal value `0x36`.

The *msg-id* token is then appended to this value, and the MD5 digest algorithm is performed on the resulting data. Next the 64-octet version of the shared secret is exclusive-ored with a 64-octet sequence of `0x5c` octets, and the MD5 digest value just computed is appended to the result.

The MD5 algorithm is applied to the value just created, resulting in a keyed MD5 digest. When the server receives the response, it verifies the digest value. If the verification succeeds, the user is considered authenticated.

9.3.2 OTP

OTP is a derivative of S/Key, which was originally developed by BellCore. It provides the same type of single-use password lists for authentication. The first RFC describing OTP was RFC1938 (A One-Time Password System), published in 1996. An update was published in 1998 as RFC2289 (A One-Time Password System).

In OTP, a secret pass-phrase is used to generate a list of single-use passwords. Each time a successful authentication is performed, the current password is expired. The next time the user needs to authenticate, he or she use the next password in the list.

OTP is well suited for environments using public access terminals or for any environment where the security of the input terminal cannot be completely trusted, since no secrets need to be provided through the terminal.

At the highest level, there are two elements involved in an OTP mechanism: a generator and a server. The generator is the client. It generates the one-time passwords as needed. The server is the entity that the user is attempting to authenticate to.

Password Generation

A secret pass-phrase is used when generating passwords. Visible only to the generator, it must be at least 10 characters in length. Implementations must support pass-phrases at least 63 characters in length. Longer lengths are allowed, but at the risk of interoperability problems with implementations that support shorter lengths.

To generate a series of one-time passwords, the OTP client concatenates the user's pass-phrase and the seed value sent from the server. The concatenated string is then passed through a cryptographic hash function and reduced to 64 bits. RFC2289 lists MD4, MD5, and SHA as valid algorithms. Implementations are required to support MD5, support for SHA is optional but recommended, and support for MD4 is optional. The algorithm used to reduce the result to 64 bits depends on which hash algorithm is used. RFC2289 defines the reduction algorithms for MD4, MD5, and SHA. Other algorithms can be added through the IETF standards process.

To generate a sequence of one-time passwords, the initial 64-bit value is processed through the hash function multiple times. For each subsequent password, the number of interactions is decremented by one. Thus, to generate three one-time passwords, the first is hashed three times, the second is hashed twice, and the third is hashed once. The result is a series of 64-bit one-time passwords.

Authentication Dialog

To perform an authentication, the server sends a challenge to the client containing a sequence number and a seed value. This challenge is in a standard format so that automated generators can programmatically extract the necessary information. The syntax for the challenge is as follows.

```
"otp-" algorithm-identifier 1*WSP sequence-number 1*WSP seed
```

The challenge is terminated with either a space or an LF character. The `otp-` string must be lower-case, and the *algorithm-identifier* parameter is case-sensitive. RFC2289 specifies `md4`, `md5`, and `sha` as valid parameter values.

```
otp-md5 52 9ah19fhdj452
```

The client uses this information to calculate the next one-time password, which it then sends. The sequence number is an integer that tells the client which password is expected. The seed value used by the client to generate the password is a case-insensitive sequence of alphanumeric characters, from 1 to 16 characters in length.

Because 64-bit binary data is difficult for users to enter, and some protocols allow only printable US-ASCII characters, a hexadecimal string format or a *6-word* format can be used to encode the data.

The hexadecimal string format is typically chosen by automated clients, where the user doesn't have to input the data. The characters in it are case-insensitive. Also, the generator is allowed to insert whitespace at arbitrary points in the string which servers must ignore.

```
23EFC01D3928B379
23 EF C0 1D 39 28 B3 79
23ef c01d 3928 b379
2 3ef c0 1 d39 28 b 379
```

The 6-word format splits the 64 bits into six 11-bit values, after a 2-bit checksum is added; then it converts the 11-bit values into words from a lookup table.

The checksum is calculated by splitting the 64-bit value into pairs of bits, which are then added together. The two least significant bits of the summed number are then used as a checksum for the 64-bit value.

```
00100011 11101111 11000000 00011101 00111001 00101000 10110011 01111001

00 10 00 11 11 10 11 11 11 00 00 00 00 01 11 01 00 11 ...
```

The sum of these 2-bit pairs is 49 or, in binary, `00110001`. The two least significant bits are extracted and appended to the 64-bit value, which is then split into six 11-bit segments.

```
00100011111 01111110000 00000111010 01110010010 10001011001 10111100011
```

The resulting 11-bit numbers are used as index values to look up words in an array of 2,048 strings. The strings are designed to be short, common words, which are easy to remember while typing them in. Appendix D of RFC2289 contains the list of words used for the conversion.

The following six words are the final result of this example.

```
LEG FAST BIB DENT GIFT MITT
```

All OTP servers must support both the hexadecimal and human-readable formats.

RFC2289 also provides an alternative dictionary algorithm. In this case, a dictionary of 2,048 words is created. The array position for a word is computed by applying a hash algorithm to it and extracting the least significant 11 bits.

To avoid ambiguities with the standard dictionary and the hexadecimal representation, an alternate dictionary must not use words in the standard dictionary or words consisting solely of the letters 'A' through 'F.' Also, unlike the other two representations, words in an alternate dictionary are case-sensitive since a hash is being applied.

The process for verifying a one-time password is simple. The server maintains a database containing the one-time password from the most recent successful authentication, or the first password if this is an initial sequence. The server decodes the password received from the generator into a 64-bit value. It then processes the value through the hash function once. If the results match the value of the previous password, stored in its database, the server stores the current password in the database and considers the authentication successful.

RFC1938 doesn't specify how seeds or sequence numbers should be changed, but only offers guidelines for implementers. In 1997, RFC2243 (OTP Extended Responses) was published. It defines an extended challenge and response syntax for OTP that can provide encoding information and reinitialize a sequence and change parameters.

The extended challenge consists of a standard OTP challenge, a whitespace character, and a list of extended responses the server supports. The capability list starts with the string 'ext' to indicate that the challenge contains extension data. Like the standard challenge, it is terminated with either whitespace or line termination appropriate for the context, such as CRLF for email protocols. The syntax for an extended challenge is as follows.

```
extended-challenge = otp-challenge 1*LWSP capability-list (NL / *LWSP)
capability-list    = "ext" *("," extension-set-id)
extension-set-id   = *<any CHAR except LWSP, CTL, or ",">
```

Extension set identifiers that start with 'x-' are private. All other identifiers should be registered with the IANA, which maintains a list of assigned values.

As an example of an extended challenge, here is a mythical extension, 'mondo'.

```
otp-md5 52 9ah19fhdj452 ext,mondo
```

An extended response consists of a two or more tokens separated by ':' characters. The syntax for an extended response is as follows.

```
extended-response = type 1*(":" argument) end-of-line
type              = token
argument          = token
token             = 1*<any CHAR except ":" or CTL>
end-of-line       = <line terminator appropriate for the context>
```

The following example shows what this looks like when sent by a generator.

```
mondo:arg1:arg2:arg3
```

RFC2243 defines a few extended responses that don't require declaration in the extended challenge. The `hex` and `word` responses allow the generator to indicate which encoding technique was used for the response data. This solves the problem of ambiguity when a standard response could be valid as either a hexadecimal string or a word string. Both `hex` and `word` use one argument to convey the actual response data.

```
hex:23ef c01d 3928 b379
```

Two other responses are defined in RFC2243—`init-hex` and `init-word`, which enable a client to change an OTP parameter on the server. The `init-hex` response is used to send the data in the hexadecimal string format, while the `init-word` is used to send it in 6-word format.

```
init-hex-response = "init-hex:" current-OTP
                        ":" new-params
                        ":" new-OTP end-of-line
new-params        = algorithm SP sequence-number SP seed
algorithm         = "md4" / "md5" / "sha1"
```

The syntax for `init-word` is equivalent, except for the use of `init-word` instead of `init-hex`.

The *current-OTP* field authenticates the request. The *new-params* field sets the algorithm, sequence number, and seed to the specified values. The *new-OTP* field confirms the request. If the reinitialization is successful, the server stores the new OTP in its database as the most recent successful one.

```
init-hex:23efc01d3928b379:sha1 42 8fh72f8ag192:1523ef1d9d1336d0
```

For an example of how OTP can be integrated into email, Section 9.4.2 describes its use in SASL.

9.3.3 Kerberos

Kerberos is a network authentication protocol designed at the Massachusetts Institute of Technology. There are two versions, v4 and v5, available. The latter is described in RFC1510 (The Kerberos Network Authentication Service—V5). Kerberos provides encryption and strong authentication. One of its main features is that information for authenticating users doesn't need to be stored on the machines needing the authentication; servers ask a third-party server for it. This third-party server is the only place where any secret information about a user needs to be stored, allowing a single sign-on for any applications configured to use Kerberos.

At the highest level, there are four components to the Kerberos system: a server running a service, a client wanting to authenticate itself to that service, an

AS (Authentication Server), and a TGS (Ticket Granting Service). Together, the AS and TGS constitute the KDC (Key Distribution Center).

Both the user and the service to which the user needs to connect have keys registered with the AS. A user's key is based on his or her password. A service key is a randomly generated password.

To perform the authentication, the client sends a ticket request to the AS containing the name of the user, a timestamp, and the identity of the service the client wants to communicate with.

The AS creates a session key for communication between client and service. It then creates a ticket containing this session key and the name of the service specified by the client. The ticket is encrypted with the user's key. The AS creates a second ticket containing the session key, a start time and expiration time, and the name of the user. This one is encrypted with the service's key. These two tickets are then sent back to the client.

The client unlocks the first one with the user's key and extracts the session key. It then creates an authenticator packet containing the current time and encrypts it with the session key. It sends the second ticket received from the AS and the authenticator to the service.

The service decrypts the ticket with its key to extract the session key and the identity of the user. It then attempts to decrypt the authenticator packet with the session. If it is successful, the service considers the user authenticated.

To authenticate itself to the client or user, the service creates another ticket containing the timestamp received from the client and the name of the service. (The contents of the ticket were slightly different in version 4 but conceptually similar.) It encrypts the ticket with the session key and sends it to the client. If the client successfully decrypts the ticket with the session key, it considers the service authenticated.

The dialog as presented thus far has a small problem. Every time the user wants to connect to the server, his or her password must be retrieved when the client decrypts its first ticket from the AS. One solution would be to cache the user's key, but that is subject to security breaches. To solve this problem, the TGS is used.

Before accessing any service, the client contacts the AS and requests a ticket to communicate with the TGS. This ticket is called a TGT (Ticket Granting Ticket). After this, any time a client needs to contact a service, it uses its TGT to request a ticket from the TGS instead of the AS. The response from the TGS is not encrypted with the user's secret key but with the session key received from the AS when the client requested the TGT.

The response from the TGS contains the new session key that will be used between the client and service. The TGT is typically valid for a relatively short time, after which the client must request another one. Since the user's key is needed only when a new TGT is received, this provides a more secure alternative to caching it.

The primary difficulty with Kerberos is that, in general, it's an all or nothing solution. To deploy Kerberos in an environment, all the services requiring authentication need to be *kerberized*. This can be a serious impediment in many environments. Despite this limitation, Kerberos has been deployed at many universities to provide strong authentication.

9.3.4 GSS-API

GSS-API is designed to provide security services to applications. It is capable of supporting various underlying mechanisms, but is most commonly used to support version 5 of Kerberos. Several RFCs have been published that define various aspects of the protocol.

- RFC1508 (Generic Security Service Application Program Interface)
- RFC1509 (Generic Security Service API—C-Bindings)
- RFC1511 (Common Authentication Technology Overview)
- RFC1964 (The Kerberos Version 5 GSS-API Mechanism)
- RFC2025 (The Simple Public-Key GSS-API Mechanism)
- RFC2078 (Generic Security Service Appilcation Program Interface—Version 2)

9.3.5 OpenPGP

PGP is a software package that provides digital signatures and encryption. Originally written by Phil Zimmerman, who first released it in 1991, it has since become widely deployed in some Internet user circles.

RFC1991 (PGP Message Exchange Formats) was published as an Informational RFC, documenting features in PGP version 2.6. It was not placed on the standards track because PGP relies on IDEA and RSA (Rivest, Shamir, and Adleman) algorithms that are encumbered with license or patent restrictions. Instead, a Working Group was created to define a version that didn't require those technologies. The result was RFC2440 (OpenPGP Message Format), published in 1998, which builds on RFC1991. This RFC allows use of IDEA or RSA, but requires that OpenPGP implementations implement triple-DES, DSA, and ElGamal as alternatives.

In fact, OpenPGP expanded the number of supported cryptography algorithms significantly. Removing the reliance on encumbered software has allowed it to be placed on the IETF standards track. For the remainder of this chapter, OpenPGP will be discussed, with occasional references to PGP. As a general rule, most information about OpenPGP also applies to PGP, except as noted.

OpenPGP was designed to provide encryption and digital signatures for files and email messages. It uses a combination of conventional and public-key encryption.

Digital Signatures

To generate an OpenPGP digital signature for a file or message, the software first creates a hash string for the data, which it then encrypts using the user's private key. This results in a digital signature for the data that can be prepended to it or stored separately.

To determine whether data originated from a particular person, a recipient uses PGP software to check the digital signature. The software generates a hash string and decrypts the signature using the originator's public key; it then compares its own calculated hash string with the decrypted one. The data was signed by the originator if the two hash strings match.

Encryption

Encrypting a file in OpenPGP is similar to generating a digital signature. The OpenPGP software generates a random number called a *session key,* with which it compresses the data and encrypts it. The session key is then encrypted using the recipient's public key and prepended to the data.

To decrypt the data, the recipient decrypts the session key with its private key. The actual data is then decrypted with the decrypted session key and decompressed.

If the originator wants to both encrypt a message and add a digital signature, it generates the signature first and then encrypts the message and signature.

Compression

As mentioned earlier, OpenPGP optionally compresses the data before it is encrypted, providing a choice of ZIP, ZLIB, or a private algorithm. ZIP is described in RFC1951 (DEFLATE Compressed Data Format Specification version 1.3); ZLIB is described in RFC1950 (ZLIB Compressed Data Format Specification version 3.3). Implementations are required to support uncompressed encryption. Support for all other compression algorithms is optional, but ZIP is recommended for compatibility with PGP.

ASCII Armor

OpenPGP defines an encapsulation scheme for converting binary data into printable US-ASCII characters, called *ASCII armor,* or *Radix-64 encoding.*

The armor scheme consists of a prefix line, several header fields, a blank line, the data encoded using `base64` encoding, a checksum, and a suffix line. The prefix line consists of five dashes, the string 'BEGIN␣', text identifying the type of OpenPGP data being encapsulated, and five more dashes.

RFC1991 defines several types of encapsulated data. RFC2440 added a few more. Table 9.1 summarizes them and indicates which ones were added by OpenPGP.

For this example, an encrypted message will be encapsulated.

```
-----BEGIN PGP MESSAGE-----
```

The header fields are standard RFC822 style. They provide information about the encapsulated data. RFC1991 defines two fields for use here: `Version`, and `Comment`.

TABLE 9.1 OpenPGP Encapsulation Data Types

Data Type String	OpenPGP	Description
PGP MESSAGE		Signed, encrypted, or compressed data
PGP PUBLIC KEY BLOCK		Public key data
PGP PRIVATE KEY BLOCK	•	Private key data
PGP MESSAGE, PART X/Y		Part X of Y multipart messages
PGP MESSAGE, PART X	•	Part X of an unspecified number of multipart messages
PGP SIGNATURE	•	Signature data

```
Version: GnuPG v0.9.5 (GNU/Linux)
Comment: For info see http://www.gnupg.org
```

The `Version` field identifies what version of PGP was used to create the armor. The `Comment` field is a user-defined piece of information. In terms of RFC822, both fields contain unstructured data, so parsing their contents isn't a good idea.

RFC2440 add several more fields. `MessageID` holds a 32-character string of printable characters. If the armor data type is 'PGP MESSAGE PART X', all the corresponding messages must use the same value. The value should be a unique string unlikely to be encountered in another message. It should be present only in multipart messages.

```
MessageID: a0dHa0d91Dh291jF992FahwuQo3hSjaK
```

A `Hash` field is used in clear-signed messages and contains a comma-separated list of hash algorithms used on the message.

```
Hash: MD5
```

A `Charset` field can be provided to indicate what charset the data is in. By default, OpenPGP uses UTF-8.

```
Charset: iso-8859-1
```

If the headers are improperly formatted, a receiving PGP program should consider the entire armor encapsulation to be corrupted. Unknown fields should be reported to the user, but if the formatting is valid, the armored data should be processed.

The next item is a blank line. Like an RFC822 message, it is used to separate the header from the body. Following the blank line is the data encoded in `base64` format.

```
hQEOA63R0LNzn3aPEAP9GvweWc5tqb6gpliJE7jx1LHqZfn5ZkR5nR6s6m9H0Ys5
2jJmAYXqsTxS60vY+KjGDtNVcINBENXhARy0AMT5UCcMsp1NbK8mJPd1R+YNQR8u
AEvwEtfrRGIeETmMi8Wf6ND0bAluaVzEDSM8BC02yi/KZECtINjlBQ9IsGNUJ58D
/Awpau7vyyI7OqRjjwm78TlILZ2SUasCg4SOGRXAkEeRWO2DemifGqtc2OkMXADR
3j31jJ3lWmX0/smVyNnU+qWLgb452pG+xZfM2euoBVHyvDlmwbOk4vrDgZvzodkt
xbrLSH1ybzD4hnZllv38ygJKpeXGW3NTxMik6+UvFzFdpCpi+CEDXQsFkRMw7THj
O5oCwpV8exgzXxgpLRZ7ePSbQ9kRVmsAYN81n1s=
```

The underlying format of the data is described in RFC1991 and RFC2440.

The checksum consists of an '=' character, followed by a 24-bit CRC (Cyclic Redundancy Check) converted to four characters using radix-64 encoding.

```
=+GQc
```

The algorithm for calculating the checksum is provided in Section 6.1 of RFC2440.

The suffix line is in the same format as the prefix line, except the initial 'BEGIN' is replaced with 'END'.

```
-----END PGP MESSAGE-----
```

When combined, the entire encapsulation looks something like this:

```
-----START PGP MESSAGE-----
Version: GnuPG v0.9.5 (GNU/Linux)
Comment: For info see http://www.gnupg.org

hQEOA63R0LNzn3aPEAP9GvweWc5tqb6gpliJE7jx1LHqZfn5ZkR5nR6s6m9H0Ys5
2jJmAYXqsTxS60vY+KjGDtNVcINBENXhARy0AMT5UCcMsp1NbK8mJPd1R+YNQR8u
AEvwEtfrRGIeETmMi8Wf6ND0bAluaVzEDSM8BC02yi/KZECtINjlBQ9IsGNUJ58D
/Awpau7vyyI7OqRjjwm78TlILZ2SUasCg4SOGRXAkEeRWO2DemifGqtc2OkMXADR
3j31jJ3lWmX0/smVyNnU+qWLgb452pG+xZfM2euoBVHyvDlmwbOk4vrDgZvzodkt
xbrLSH1ybzD4hnZllv38ygJKpeXGW3NTxMik6+UvFzFdpCpi+CEDXQsFkRMw7THj
O5oCwpV8exgzXxgpLRZ7ePSbQ9kRVmsAYN81n1s=
=+GQc
-----END PGP MESSAGE-----
```

The encapsulation scheme provided by PGP is simple-minded. RFC2015 (MIME Security with Pretty Good Privacy) describes how to encapsulate PGP data using MIME. This is described in Section 9.6.2.

9.4 SECURITY FRAMEWORKS

None of the algorithms and services in Section 9.2 and Section 9.3 are ubiquitous. Each has particular strong and weak points that prevent it from being appropriate for all situations. OpenPGP is a good example of the trend toward providing a framework for supporting multiple core security technologies, so that whichever algorithms or services are most suitable can be used.

Another advantage of frameworks is that as computing power increases, older security technologies become obsolete, but implementing new technologies can become more and more difficult. In addition, developers supporting multiple protocols must deal with their differences. One solution is security frameworks that support security services as add-on modules and designed with interfaces easy to integrate into various protocols.

Two protocols in particular are becoming increasingly common in Internet email protocols: TLS and SASL. They provide general frameworks not only for various core security technologies but also for current and future protocols.

9.4.1 TLS

TLS provides a way for higher-level protocols to implement public-key and symmetric encryption as well as authentication, in which it serves as an intermediate layer. It is based on version 3.0 of the SSL protocol, created by Netscape, which was originally designed for adding security to Web services. The protocol allows implementations to fall back to SSL 3.0 if necessary.

TLS, published in RFC2246 (The TLS Protocol—Version 1.0), is a recent addition to networking protocols. At the time of writing, the only published RFC defining the use of TLS in a protocol was RFC2487 (SMTP Service Extension for Secure SMTP over TLS), described in Section 9.5.3. RFCs defining how to add it to other protocols, particularly POP and IMAP, are expected in short order.

TLS provides security services for connection-based protocols, like TCP. It consists of multiple channels of data, each with its own protocol, encapsulated in a record protocol. These include the channel to carry the application data, the alert protocol, the change cipher spec protocol, and the handshake protocol.

The application data are the data transmitted by the protocol in which TLS is being used. The alert protocol communicates warning messages and fatal errors between the client and server. The change cipher spec protocol communicates changes in the state of the cipher engines. And the handshake protocol is used by the client and server to authenticate each other and to negotiate which algorithms and encryption keys are used for the session. The negotiation performed in the handshake protocol is designed to be immune to man-in-the-middle attacks.

Additional record types can be supported in the protocol if necessary. To cope with this possibility, TLS implementations should ignore record types they don't understand.

Record Protocol

The record protocol takes messages to be transmitted, fragments or coalesces them into blocks, optionally compresses the data, applies a MAC (Message Authentication

Code) function to the block, encrypts the data, and then transmits the result. The process is reversed when receiving data.

The record layer receives data from higher layers. Message boundaries of the original data are not preserved. Multiple messages of the same type may be coalesced into one TLS record, or a single message may be fragmented into multiple TLS records. The maximum record length is negotiated with the connected peer, with an absolute maximum length of 16,384 octets.

To send a TLS record over the network, a data structure is first created from the data provided by the higher-level protocol. This data structure contains the following information:

- Content type
- Protocol version
- Length
- Data fragment

Since TLS supports compression, the data structure is converted to a TLSCompressed structure, using the negotiated compression algorithm. RFC2246 doesn't define any compression algorithms, but future RFCs should remedy this. A compression algorithm used with TLS should be lossless and should not increase the length of the data by more than 1,024 octets. Also, the decompression must not result in a decompressed buffer larger than 16,384 octets.

The resulting structure with or without compression is as follows.

- Content type
- Protocol version
- Length
- Compressed fragment

The content type and protocol version values are taken from the original plain-text structure.

Once the data has been compressed, they are converted to cipher text using the negotiated parameters for the session. A MAC value is also computed for the data. The final structure contains the following information.

- Content type
- Protocol version
- Length
- Encrypted data
- MAC value

This structure is used for both stream and block ciphers. For block ciphers, the structure also contains padding needed to expand the data to match the block size requirements as well as an octet containing the length of the padding. The numeric value of the padding length is used for the value used to pad the buffer.

The final packet structure is sent over the network. To process it the receiving side simply reverses the process and passes it up to the application program.

Handshake Protocol

The handshake protocol is used by the client and server to negotiate the record protocol session parameters and to authenticate each other.

The session parameters consist of a session identifier, the X.509v3 certificates for the two parties, the compression algorithm, the bulk encryption algorithm, the MAC algorithm, parameters for the cryptographic algorithms, the master secret known only by the client and server, and a flag indicating whether the session can resume a previous session. These parameters are used by the record layer when converting application data for transmission to the connected peer.

There are several steps involved in the handshake protocol. First, the client sends a client *Hello* message, to which the server responds with a server *Hello* message. If this doesn't happen, the dialog fails.

The client *Hello* message includes the client protocol version, a random number, a session identifier, and a list of cryptographic options and a list of compression algorithms supported by the client. The server *Hello* message contains the server protocol version, a random number, the session identifier, and the cipher algorithm and compression method selected by the server.

Once the *Hello* messages have been exchanged, the server sends a list of certificates to the client, if they are required. The first one in the list is the server's certificate. Additional certificates certify the preceding certificate in the chain.

If the session options require it, the server sends a *Key Exchange* message consisting of a set of key exchange parameters as well as a hash value constructed from a combination of the client's random number, the server's random number, and the server's key exchange parameters. If necessary, the server then sends a *Certificate Request* message to the client, which will cause the client to send a certificate later in the handshake sequence.

With the previous messages sent, the server finishes its *Hello* message with a *ServerHelloDone* message, informing the client that the server is done with its initial portion of the handshake. At this point, the client sends its *Hello* message.

If the server requests a certificate from the client, the client sends it and then sends a key exchange message, the contents of which depend on the public-key algorithm chosen earlier in the negotiation. If the client certificate has signing capabilities, the client then sends a *CertificateVerify* message. This consists of a hash calculated for the entire set of client handshake messages sent to the server, not including *CertificateVerify*.

TABLE 9.2 Full TLS Handshake Sequence

Client	Server
ClientHello	
	ServerHello
	(Certificate)
	(ServerKeyExchange)
	(CertificateRequest)
	ServerHelloDone
(Certificate)	
ClientKeyExchange	
(CertificateVerify)	
ChangeCipherSpec	
Finished	
	ChangeCipherSpec
	Finished
Application Data	Application Data

At this point, the client updates its session configuration, based on the negotiated parameters, and sends a *ChangeCipherSpec* message to the server. This informs the server that subsequent communication from the client will be based on the updated parameters.

The client is now done with its portion of the *Hello* handshake, so it sends a *Finished* message to the server. To complete the handshake, the server updates its configuration based on the negotiated parameters and sends a *ChangeCipherSpec* message and a *Finished* message to the client. The client and server can now send application data to each other, with the negotiated TLS layer in effect.

Table 9.2 summarizes the sequence of messages performed in the handshake. The items in parentheses are either optional or sent only in certain circumstances. The italicized items are a separate record type, not actually a handshake record.

The computation and network traffic required to complete a full handshake can have a noticeable impact on the time it takes for the client and server to establish communications. As a performance optimization, the TLS protocol allows an existing session to be reused or duplicated. In this case, the client uses the identifier of the desired session in its portion of the handshake. If the server finds the session identifier and is willing to establish a connection with it, it uses the same session identifier for its portion of the handshake. The client and server then send *ChangeCipherSpec* messages to each other, verifying that each party is valid. At that point, the client and server can exchange application data appropriate for application protocol being used. This abbreviated handshake sequence is summarized in Table 9.3.

TABLE 9.3 TLS Handshake Sequence with Session Reuse

Client	Server
ClientHello	
	ServerHello
	ChangeCipherSpec
	Finished
ChangeCipherSpec	
Finished	
Application Data	Application Data

If the server can't find the requested session identifier, it generates a new one and sends that back to the client instead of the requested one. The client and server must then perform a complete handshake.

9.4.2 SASL

SASL, described in RFC2222 (Simple Authentication and Security Layer), defines an architecture for adding auxiliary authentication mechanisms to connection-based protocols such as SMTP, POP, and IMAP. It also enables integrity and encryption services to be added to the communications channel.

All protocols that use SASL for authentication provide a command for initiating the SASL dialog. This command includes an argument to specify the authentication mechanism to be used. Mechanism names can be from 1 to 20 characters in length, with the allowable characters upper-case letters, digits, hyphens, and underscores. Also, the name must be registered with the IANA.

The basic sequence for authentication consists of a challenge from the server and a subsequent response from the client. This is repeated as necessary, based on whatever the authentication mechanism requires, until the server sends either a successful completion status or a failure status.

The exact nature of this sequence is specific to the SASL mechanism being used. Most, if not all, of the mechanisms use binary data for the challenges and responses. Protocol extensions that add SASL authentication define encoding specific to the protocol to cope with the binary data.

The authentication process not only performs the necessary authentication, but also transmits identity information and negotiates options in the security layer. If a security layer is negotiated, it takes effect immediately after the authentication negotiation is complete, subject to any specific requirements of the protocol using SASL. The security layer is in effect for the remainder of the session.

The data streams between the client and server are processed by the security layer before being handed over to the protocol. A data stream consists of blocks of data starting with a 4-octet field containing the length of the data in the buffer, followed by data itself. The length data is sent in network byte order, that is, a series of bytes from the most significant to the least significant. The buffer length is not allowed to exceed the maximum size negotiated during the SASL authentication dialog.

A few general points about SASL are in order. A SASL mechanism is selected with plain text, which can be subverted by an attacker. It is therefore imperative that any protocol negotiations sensitive to security be renegotiated by the client and server if integrity protection is negotiated in the mechanism. This ensures that those negotiations are secure.

Profiling Requirements

A SASL profile describes how to add SASL to a protocol. The RFC process publishes profiles.

An RFC adding SASL to a protocol provides several pieces of information needed by developers. For one, it identifies the service being extended. The service name must be registered with the IANA, via the GSS-API host-based service name form, described in RFC2078. The defined service names are listed in the IANA repository.

The RFC specifies a command to initiate the authentication dialog. The command must accept a parameter identifying the authentication mechanism used. It should also allow an optional parameter for allowing the client to provide initial data for the authentication dialog. Some authentication mechanisms have the client send data first. If the extension doesn't allow this, this initial data must be synthesized by having the server send a blank challenge, which the client can answer with its initial response.

The RFC also describes how the authentication dialog is carried out. This includes any encoding required, success and failure indications, aborting a dialog, coping with protocol limitations such as line length, and exactly when the negotiated security features take effect.

The remainder of this section describes several of the authentication mechanisms that can be used with SASL.

Anonymous

This is the simplest of the SASL authentication mechanisms. As an analog to anonymous FTP, RFC2245 (Anonymous SASL Mechanisms) provides a definition for an 'ANONYMOUS' SASL mechanism.

The client sends a human-readable sequence of characters to the server for logging. The characters should be an Internet email address, a sequence of characters of significance to the system administrator of the server, or nothing. The information is not authenticated, so, like anonymous FTP, it cannot be trusted for audit purposes. The syntax for the characters is as follows.

```
message        = [email / arbitrary-token]
email          = addr-spec
arbitrary-token = 1*255TCHAR
TCHAR          = %x20-3F / %x41-7E
```

There is one stipulation on the *addr-spec* in the *email* token. It is the same token used in email messages, but without the free insertion of linear whitespace. If the *local-part* of the *addr-spec* contains any spaces, it must be quoted in full.

Like anonymous FTP, the purpose of this authentication mechanism is to provide access to anyone. Given that fact, access should be restricted in a manner similar to that of anonymous FTP, where users accessing a service anonymously are allowed to view only a subset of the data available on the server.

CRAM

RFC2195 defines a POP and IMAP extension that uses the CRAM authentication algorithm, described in Section 9.3.1. Technically speaking, it isn't a SASL mechanism, since it was created before SASL was available. It can be used with SASL, however, and many SASL implementations support it. The mechanism name is CRAM-MD5.

The server's initial challenge contains a string of random digits, a timestamp, and the FQDN of the server. These fields are formated as an *msg-id* token. The client responds with a string containing the user name, followed by a space and a keyed-MD5 digest value.

S/Key

One of the profiles included in RFC2222 is for S/Key, a description of which is provided in RFC1760 (The S/KEY One-Time Password System). The mechanism name for S/Key in SASL is SKEY. S/Key has been replaced by OTP, described in the following section.

The client sends an initial response containing the authorization identity. The server then issues a challenge containing the sequence number followed by a single space and the seed value for the specified authorization identity. The client responds with a one-time password, which is sent either as a 64-bit value, in network byte order, or encoded in the 6-word format. The server then verifies the password, and the client is considered authenticated if the verification succeeds.

OTP

RFC2444 (The One-Time-Password SASL Mechanism) defines how to use OTP in SASL. As mentioned earlier, OTP replaces S/Key. Its mechanism name is OTP.

The OTP profile requires that the client and server use the extended response syntax described in RFC2243. In addition, the client and server are required to support MD5; support for SHA-1 is recommended.

The initial client response contains an authorization identity and an authentication identity. Both of these fields may be up to 255 octets in length, and they must contain printable US-ASCII or printable UTF-8 characters. The two fields are separated by an US-ASCII 0 character. The authorization identity allows the system administrators or proxy servers to authenticate with a different user identity.

The server responds to the client with an OTP challenge, which is in the extended format. If the server is using a hash algorithm the client doesn't understand, the client can prompt for the 6-word format, cancel the authentication sequence and try another SASL mechanism, or close the connection and refuse to authenticate.

Kerberos Version 4

The mechanism name used by SASL for Kerberos version 4 is KERBEROS_V4. This mechanism is described in the main SASL RFC, RFC2222.

The first challenge from the server consists of a 32-bit random number, which, as with most network protocols, is transmitted in network byte order. The client responds with a Kerberos ticket and an authenticator. The authenticator is for the following principle.

```
service.hostname@realm
```

The *service* token is the service name for the protocol's profile. The *hostname* token is the first segment of the FQDN of the server, in lower-case. The *realm* token is the Kerberos realm of the server.

```
imap.tuba@example.com
```

The authenticator contains an encrypted checksum field. This value contains the server's challenge in network byte order.

When the server receives the response from the client, it decrypts it and verifies the ticket and the authenticator. If the verification succeeds, the server increments the checksum, then builds an 8-octet data value. The first four octets contains the incremented checksum in network byte order. The fifth octet contains a bit-mask indicating what security layers are supported by the server. The sixth through eighth octets contain, in network byte order, the maximum cipher-text buffer the server is willing to accept.

The meanings of the bits in the bit-mask are summarized in Table 9.4. Since other bits may be defined in the future, the additional bits should be set to zero. Next, the server encrypts the eight octets in the session key, using the ECB mode of DES. The encrypted data are then issued as a second challenge to the client. The client decrypts the challenge and checks the first four octets of the resulting data. It considers the server authenticated if they are equal to the checksum sent in the previous response plus one.

At this point, the client can determine whether the server is authentic, but it must now prove its own identity by responding to the server's challenge, just issued. To do this, it builds an 8-octet value similar to the one built by the server. The first

TABLE 9.4 Kerberos Security Layer
Bit-Masks

Bit Value	Description
1	No security layer
2	Integrity protection
4	Privacy protection

four octets contain the server's original checksum. The fifth byte contains a bit-mask identifying which security layers the client wishes to use. The sixth through eighth octets contain the maximum cipher-text buffer size the client is willing to accept from the server.

Next the client appends the authorization identity to the eight octets, following by enough zero octets to make the total length a multiple of eight octets. It then encrypts this data with the session key, using the PCBC mode of DES, and sends it to the server as a response to the server's second challenge.

The server decrypts the data and verifies the checksum contained in the data. It then verifies that the principal identified in the Kerberos ticket is authorized to connect as the authorization identity. Assuming the verification succeeds, the client is considered authorized and the authentication process is complete.

GSS-API

RFC2222 also defines a profile for the GSS-API service, mentioned in Section 9.3.4, which is primarily used to provide SASL services for Kerberos version 5. The mechanism name is `GSSAPI`. Like `KERBEROS_V4`, it provides optional integrity and privacy protection.

External

The `EXTERNAL` mechanism, defined in RFC2222, allows information external to SASL to be used to authenticate the client. This can be useful when security services such as IPsec or TLS have already been negotiated. The server queries the additional services to determine whether to allow or deny the authentication. The client uses the authorization identity for the initial response. If it sends an empty string, the server determines the authorization identity from the external authentication mechanism.

This mechanism presents a good opportunity to discuss some of the overlap between the various security frameworks. There is considerable overlap in functionality between SASL and TLS, which raises the question of which one should be used when both are available.

As a general rule, SASL is an authentication framework and it happens to support some mechanisms that also provide encryption. TLS, on the other hand, is primarily an encryption protocol. It provides authentication, but its primary goal is connection security.

Using both frameworks is possible and in many cases even desirable. To do this, the client and server initiate the TLS layer, providing a secure channel for communications. They then use SASL for authentication, knowing that the authentication dialog is secure from eavesdroppers.

9.5 PROTOCOL SECURITY EXTENSIONS

Section 9.4 described the SASL and TLS security frameworks. In combination with the underlying core security technologies, they provide a modular framework to add security services to various Internet protocols. This section describes how these frameworks can be used with SMTP, POP, and IMAP.

As this book was being written, not all of the protocols had associated RFCs for use with SASL and TLS. However, this is expected to change very soon—as fate would have it, probably shortly after this book goes to print.

9.5.1 IMAP Extensions

Although IMAP predates SASL, the IMAP `authenticate` command, described in Section 6.5.5, implements SASL dialogs. RFC1731 (IMAP4 Authentication Mechanisms) documents several authentication mechanisms for IMAP, but it is largely unneeded because of the SASL RFCs.

As of the writing of this book, no RFC had yet been published to specify how to add TLS to IMAP.

The `authenticate` command allows the client to select an authentication algorithm. However, no mechanisms to use with the command are specified. In fact, any SASL mechanism will work if both the client and server support it. The server announces support for a particular authentication extension by providing an appropriate 'auth=' entry in the `capability` response.

Some extensions allow the client and server to negotiate session encryption and integrity protection. Section 6.5.5 described the data structure used if these added layers of protection are enabled.

9.5.2 POP Extensions

POP provides plain-text authentication via the `user` and `pass` commands, and MD5 digest authentication via the `apop` command, but provides no facilities for encryption.

The TLS protocol can be implemented in POP. As of the writing of this book, the POP implementation was only in Internet Draft, but it is expected to be completed soon.

In 1994, RFC1734 (POP3 AUTHentication Command) was published. This was prior to SASL, but like the IMAP `authenticate` command, it implements SASL for the protocol. It also adds an optional `auth` command that performs authentication and selects the authentication mechanism to use.

```
"auth" SP mechanism
```

RFC1734 uses the same interaction model as the one for IMAP. In addition, the authentication services it lists apply to RFC1731.

9.5.3 SMTP Extensions

SMTP provides no facilities for authentication or encryption. However, two extensions are available that add these capabilities, both of which require the SMTP extension mechanism, described in Section 3.5.

Authentication

RFC2554 (SMTP Service Extension for Authentication) defines the use of SASL with SMTP. The extension allows a client to authenticate itself to a server and to negotiate an optional security layer for the SMTP session. Servers supporting the extension add an `auth` keyword to their `ehlo` reply, with a list of supported authentication mechanisms.

```
ehlo tuba.example.com
250-flugelhorn.example.com
250 AUTH CRAM-MD5 KERBEROS_V4 GSSAPI
```

The extension adds `auth` to the list of available commands.

```
"auth" mechanism [initial-response]
```

The *mechanism* parameter specifies the SASL authentication mechanism the client wants. The *initial-response* parameter can be used, depending on the chosen mechanism, to provide the initial part of the authentication negotiation.

To use the extension, a client issues the `auth` command. If the server needs to reject the command, it responds with a `504` error.

```
auth NOTAMECHANISM
504 Unrecognized authentications type
```

If it accepts the command, the two machines proceed with a series of challenges from the server and responses from the client.

```
auth CRAM-MD5
334 PFRGdGdvTWxvckJyeVUwNnJ4cTJOMXdAVEhPUi5JTk5PU09GVC5DT00+
aGV5ISBub3cgZ28gYmFjayB0byByZWFkaW5nIHRoZSBib29rIQ==
235 Authentication successful.
```

The client can send a line containing a single '*' if it wishes to abort the authentication sequence. In this case, the server responds with a 501 reply.

```
auth CRAM-MD5
334 PFRGdGdvTWxvckJyeVUwNnJ4cTJOMXdAVEhPUi5JTk5PU09GVC5DT00+
*
501 Authentication aborted
```

If the authentication fails, the server can issue a 535 reply, unless a more specific reply is appropriate.

```
535 Authentication failed
```

The auth command can be issued only once in an SMTP session. In addition, it cannot be issued while in the middle of a mail transaction. The extension also adds an optional parameter to the mail command.

```
auth=addr-spec
```

The *addr-spec* contains the identity of the person who submitted the message. This value can be encoded using *xtext,* described in Section 3.5.6. The parameter can also contain '<>' to indicate that the identity of the person is unknown.

```
mail from:<joe@tuba.example.com> auth=joe@tuba.example.com
```

The *addr-spec* parameter allows cooperating MTAs in a trusted environment to share authentication. If the server trusts the client, it should supply the same *addr-spec* when relaying a message to another server. If the parameter is not supplied, the client has authenticated, and the server has reason to believe the message is an original submission to the client, the server can supply the parameter when relaying to another MTA.

If the parameter is supplied, but the server does not trust the client, the server must act as if '<>' had been specified in the parameter. If the '<>' is actually there, the server must supply the value when relaying the message to another MTA that supports the extension, assuming the authentication with that server succeeded.

The authentication extension is a significant enhancement to SMTP. It provides a solution to one of the oldest problems with the SMTP protocol—the lack of any authentication. Expect a significant number of software packages to implement the extension.

TLS

SMTP servers normally transmit data in clear text. This means anyone with access to the communication between two servers can view the contents of the dialog. In addition, the core SMTP protocol doesn't provide the ability for a pair of SMTP servers to authenticate themselves to each other, which, as previously mentioned, means spoofing is relatively easy. RFC2487 is a proposed standard that provides this added security. It uses the TLS protocol, described in Section 9.4.1, to provide privacy and authentication services.

TLS enables authentication and privacy between two SMTP processes. It doesn't provide end-to-end security unless the added security is negotiated by each hop.

A server announces its support for TLS by adding the keyword `starttls` to its `ehlo` reply.

```
ehlo tuba.example.com
250-ictus.example.com
250 starttls
```

The extension adds a `starttls` command, which has no parameters, to a client's repertoire.

```
starttls
```

If the server is willing to negotiate TLS for the session, it issues a `220` reply code. The client and server then perform the TLS negotiation.

```
starttls
220 Ready to start TLS
TLS negotiation
remainder of SMTP session
```

There are several failure replies to the command. The server can issue a 454 reply to indicate a temporary problem with initiating the TLS negotiation.

```
starttls
454 TLS temporarily unavailable.
```

If the client provided parameters to the command, the server can issue a 501 reply indicating a syntax error.

```
starttls
501 Syntax Error (no parameters allowed).
```

It's possible, under certain circumstances, that a server will require a TLS negotiation before accepting other commands. In this case, it can issue a 530 reply.

```
mail from:<joe@tuba.example.com>
503 Must issue a STARTTLS command first
```

Not all servers are allowed to require TLS negotiation for delivery requests. Publicly referenced servers may require TLS only when relaying, not for local delivery. Publicly referenced servers are any running on port 25 of an Internet host listed in the MX for the domain name on the right-hand side of an email address. They can also include hosts referenced in an A record if no MX record is present. This stipulation is in place to prevent the extension from damaging the interoperability of Internet email.

Private servers can require TLS negotiation, which makes TLS particularly useful for internal email servers, where security can be mandated by policy. If such negotiations are required, the commands noop, ehlo, starttls, and quit should be exempt from them.

After the TLS negotiation is complete, both the client and the server must immediately decide whether to proceed with the session. Part of the negotiation defines what level of authentication and privacy will be provided. The client or the server can decide if the level is sufficient.

If the client decides to disconnect, it can issue the quit command. If the server decides to disconnect, it should issue a 554 reply to every command except quit.

```
starttls
220 Ready to start TLS
TLS negotiation
mail from:<joe@tuba.example.com>
554 Command refused due to lack of security
```

Assuming that both client and the server agree that the security is sufficient, they are ready to proceed with the session, and the session state is reset to *initial.* Both must forget any knowledge of the other prior to the TLS negotiation, the idea being that after the negotiation both can trust the communication channel. There is no assurance that communication prior to the negotiation can be trusted, so any information gained at that time must be ignored.

The ignored information includes the response to a ehlo command, so the ehlo should be reissued. As it turns out, the response to the command can be different after the client is authenticated. This allows the server to offer a different set of extensions to authenticated clients.

Extensions related to security are a real boon to Internet email. Each one, however, has its strengths and weaknesses, which need to be factored into any architecture that implements it.

9.6 MIME SECURITY

The first RFC describing a structured way to add security to email messages was RFC989 (Privacy Enhancement for Internet Electronic Mail—Part 1: Message Encipherment and Authentication Procedures), or PEM, published in 1987. It used DES for the default encryption algorithm, but provided the ability to add others. The design went through several iterations. It was updated in 1988 by RFC1040 (Privacy Enhancement for Internet Electronic Mail—Part 1: Message Encipherment and Authentication Procedures) and again in 1989 with a series of three RFCs.

- RFC1113 (Privacy Enhancements for Internet Electronic Mail: Part I—Message Encipherment and Authentication Procedures)
- RFC1114 (Privacy Enhancements for Internet Electronic Mail: Part II—Certificate-based Key Management)
- RFC1115 (Privacy Enhancements for Internet Electronic Mail: Part III—Algorithms, Modes, and Identifiers)

Finally, in 1993, it was updated with a series of four RFCs.

- RFC1421 (Privacy Enhancement for Internet Electronic Mail: Part I: Message Encryption and Authentication Procedures)

- RFC1422 (Privacy Enhancement for Internet Electronic Mail: Part II: Certificate-based Key Management)

- RFC1423 (Privacy Enhancement for Internet Electronic Mail: Part III: Algorithms, Modes, and Identifiers)

- RFC1424 (Privacy Enhancement for Internet Electronic Mail: Part IV: Certification and Related Services)

Since PEM predated MIME, it used an older format defined in RFC934. In 1995, RFC1847 (Security Multiparts for MIME: Multipart/Signed and Multipart/Encrypted) was published to define MIME entities to use as a framework for encapsulating digital signatures and encrypted data. As a companion to RFC1847, RFC1848 (MIME Object Security Services) was published to define a MIME descendant of PEM. RFC1847 is the preferred way to provide security services for email messages.

Several other RFCs use the framework defined in RFC1847. RFC2015 uses it for encapsulating PGP data. The S/MIME protocol, described in RFC2311 (S/MIME Version 2 Message Specification) and RFC2312 (S/MIME Version 2 Certificate Handling), uses it for its encapsulation services.

RFC2480 (Gateways and MIME Security Multiparts) was published in 1999 to address several problems related to gatewaying security multiparts in or out of an Internet email environment when the gateways don't support MIME.

POP-before-SMTP

Another technique for providing SMTP authentication is what is called *POP-before-SMTP*. While not technically a protocol extension to SMTP, it can be useful in some environments. The idea is to capitalize on the authentication provided from another protocol, typically POP or IMAP.

To use POP-before-SMTP, the client authenticates with the POP or IMAP server. Then that server provides the IP address of the client to the MTA. If the client connects to the MTA to submit a message, the MTA can use the information provided by the POP or IMAP server to decide whether to allow the connection.

Because POP-before-SMTP authentication requires a companion protocol, it is not usable in all environments. For example, providing POP access merely to connect to a public MTA is not appropriate. MDAs, on the other hand, could benefit if all the users were also POP or IMAP users.

Another limitation of this authentication technique is that both the POP server and the SMTP server must support it, and do so in a compatible way. While this may not be a problem for some administrators, it can be a significant problem for others.

9.6.1 Security Multiparts

RFC1847 defines two content types for security: `multipart/signed` and `multipart/encrypted`. Each type contains two body parts: One contains the protected data; the other, the control information. By itself, RFC1847 doesn't describe how digital signatures or encryption are performed; it deals only the framework for using MIME to encapsulate the data.

Multipart/Signed

The `multipart/signed` media type encapsulates data that has been digitally signed by the originator. The first body which, may be any valid MIME media type, contains the data against which the digital signature was computed. The signature is computed over the entire body part, including the MIME headers. The second body part contains the control information necessary to verify the digital signature.

The `Content-Type` field in the top level of a `multipart/signed` entity requires three parameters: `boundary`, `protocol`, and `micalg`. There are no optional parameters.

The `boundary` parameter is required because it is a multipart entity. The `protocol` parameter contains the value of the `Content-Type` field in the second body part, formatted with the *type/subtype* used in `Content-Type` fields.

```
parameter = "protocol" "=" value
value     = DQUOTE type "/" subtype DQUOTE
```

The `micalg` parameter contains the names of the algorithms used to compute the MIC (Message Integrity Check) for the first body part, given as a comma-separated list of tokens. Its exact meaning is specific to the digital signature mechanism being used. The MIC information can be included in the second body part. When this is true and the two values conflict, the signature should be considered invalid.

In general, the `multipart/signed` entities are generated as follows. The data to be signed is converted into a MIME body part. This includes any required MIME headers. If necessary, a content transfer encoding is applied to the body part, with the appropriate MIME field added. The encoding is very important, since the data must not be altered in transit; otherwise, the digital signature will not match the body part.

With the first body part prepared, a digital signature is calculated for it, which is then used to create the second body part. The final result is something similar to the following example.

```
Content-Type: multipart/signed;
            boundary=8Hajs920Uh191hF;
            protocol=protocol-value;
            micalg=micalg-value

--8Hajs920Uh191hF
Content-Type: text/plain
Content-Transfer-Encoding: quoted-printable
```

```
signed data

--8Hajs920Uh191hF
Content-Type: protocol-value

signature data

--8Hajs920Uh191hF--
```

To verify the contents of a `multipart/signed` entity, the MIME entity is first separated into the two components. Since the `micalg` parameter is available in the top-level `Content-Type` field, the verification software knows what algorithm to use on the first body part. It can calculate the signature for the first body part as it extracts it from the entity. When it is finished reading the first body part, it can then process the second one. It compares its results with the control information contained in the second body part to see if the digital signature matches.

There is one very important point to emphasize about `multipart/signed` entities—an MTA should consider their contents to be opaque, meaning that it must not alter them. Any alteration could invalidate the digital signature.

Multipart/Encrypted

The `multipart/encrypted` media type is used to encapsulate encrypted data. Like `multipart/signed`, its two body parts hold control information and the actual data. However, here the first body part contains the control information while the second contains the encrypted data. The two media types use a different order to simplify one-pass data processing.

The `Content-Type` field in the top level of the entity has two required parameters: `boundary` and `protocol`. The `boundary` parameter is the same one used for all multipart entities. The `protocol` parameter serves the same function as the one used in `multipart/signed` entities, except that it refers to the `Content-Type` of the first body part instead of the second one. There are no optional parameters.

The steps involved in creating a `multipart/encrypted` entity are similar to those used to create a `multipart/signed` entity.

The first body part is created with the appropriate fields. The `Content-Type` field is set to the value of the `protocol` parameter in the `Content-Type` field in the top-level entity. The data to be encrypted is used to create another MIME entity with the appropriate `Content-Type` value. This body part is then encrypted and its data is used to create an `application/octet-stream` entity. Thus, the second body part contains a nested body part.

To decrypt the data, the `protocol` parameter in the top-level `Content-Type` field determines which encryption mechanism was used. The first body part is then parsed to extract the information necessary for decryption. The second body part is then decoded and decrypted. The resulting body part contains the decrypted data and is decoded as necessary to extract the actual data. The following example shows the final result.

```
Content-Type: multipart/encrypted;
              boundary=F91hjAG10913gn61;
              protocol=protocol-value

--F91hjAG10913gn61
Content-Type: protocol-value

control data

--F91hjAG10913gn61
Content-Type: application/octet-stream

encrypted data

--F91hjAG10913gn61--
```

As mentioned earlier, the `multipart/signed` and `multipart/encrypted` media types provide a framework for encapsulating digitally signed or encrypted data in MIME. Now it's time to look at some specific examples: PGP and S/MIME.

9.6.2 PGP

RFC2015 defines how to encapsulate PGP information in security multipart entities using three media types: `application/pgp-encrypted`, `application/pgp-signature`, and `application/pgp-keys`.

Application/PGP-Signature

The `application/pgp-signature` content type encapsulates PGP digital signature data. The `protocol` parameter is set to `application/pgp-signature`, which must be quoted since it contains a '/' character.

The `micalg` parameter contains a value of 'pgp-*hash-symbol*', where *hash-symbol* identifies which MIC was used to generate the signature. RFC2015 defines two values for the MIC algorithm: `md5` and `sha1`.

To generate a signed multipart entity, the top-level `Content-Type` field is populated with the parameters just described. The data to be signed is then converted to a MIME entity with `Content-Type` and `Content-Transfer-Encoding` fields appropriate for the data, the transfer encoding is applied, and each line is terminated with the canonical CRLF.

The digital signature is then calculated for the entire MIME entity just created, and a corresponding MIME entity is created. This entity and the digital signature entity are then used to complete the upper-level `multipart/signed` entity, completing the process.

```
Content-Type: multipart/signed;
             boundary=F0299r90490W723;
             protocol="application/pgp-signature";
             micalg=pgp-md5

--F0299r90490W723
Content-Type: text/plain
Content-Transfer-Encoding: quoted-printable

signed data

--F0299r90490W723
Content-Type: application/pgp-signature

-----BEGIN PGP SIGNATURE-----
Version: GnuPG v0.9.5 (GNU/Linux)
Comment: For info see www.gnupg.org
digital signature
-----END PGP SIGNATURE-----

--F0299r90490W723--
```

To verify a signature, the process is simply reversed, remembering that the signature was calculated over the entire first body part.

Application/PGP-Encrypted

The `application/pgp-encrypted` content type encapsulates PGP encrypted data.

The `protocol` parameter is set to `application/pgp-encrypted`, quoted because of the '/' character. The `Content-Type` field in the first body part is also set to `application/pgp-encrypted` to match the `protocol` parameter in the `Content-Type` field of the top-level entity. The body of the first body part, which contains the control information, consists of a single line indicating the version of the PGP MIME encapsulation.

```
Version: 1
```

Since the PGP data contains all the information necessary for decrypting the data, no other information is needed in the first body part.

The second body part contains the encrypted data in ASCII armor format, with the content type set to `application/octet-stream`.

As an example, the following text will be encapsulated.

```
The latest shipping figures...
```

Since this is regular text, the `text/plain` content type can be used.

```
Content-Type: text/plain

The latest shipping figures...
```

The entire entity is then encrypted with PGP, using ASCII armor encoding. Next the encrypted data is encapsulated into an `application/octet-stream` entity, which is used to create a `multipart/encrypted` entity.

```
Content-Type: multipart/encrypted;
              boundary=g0929g90290w193;
              protocol="application/pgp-encrypted"

--g0929g90290w193
Content-Type: application/pgp-encrypted

Version: 1

--g0929g90290w193
Content-Type: application/octet-stream

-----BEGIN PGP MESSAGE-----
Version: GnuPG v0.9.5 (GNU/Linux)
Comment: For info see www.gnupg.org
encrypted data
-----END PGP MESSAGE-----

--g0929g90290w193--
```

Two techniques can be used for encapsulating data that is both signed and encrypted. The first one is to sign the data and generate a `multipart/signature` entity, then encrypt that entity and create a `multipart/encrypted` entity with the results of the encryption. The other technique is based on the fact that OpenPGP can combine the digital signature and encryption into one final piece of data, which can then be used to populate a `multipart/encrypted` object.

Application/PGP-Keys

This media type encapsulates PGP public-key blocks. There are no required or optional parameters. Unlike the other two PGP media types, this one does not use the RFC1847 multipart entities. It's a plain single-part application media type because the data is completely self-contained and there is no need for MUAs to provide an integrated interface to it. This is unlike regular encrypted or signed information, which MUAs can present to the user after processing it.

```
Content-Type: application/pgp-keys

-----BEGIN PGP PUBLIC KEY BLOCK-----
Version: GnuPG v0.9.5 (GNU/Linux)
Comment: For info see www.gnupg.org
ASCII Armor Key Data
-----END PGP PUBLIC KEY BLOCK-----
```

9.6.3 S/MIME

S/MIME is another technique for encapsulating security services in MIME, via the multipart media types defined in RFC1847. It provides authentication, message integrity, digital signatures, and encryption.

The encryption and signature process in S/MIME is based on PKCS (Public-Key Cryptography Standards), developed by RSA Laboratories. This is a set of standards for RSA encryption, Diffie-Hellman key exchange, and conventional encryption, as well as syntax descriptions for certificates, cryptographic messages, private-key information, and certificate requests. A few RFCs contain the text of some of the PKCS standards related to S/MIME.

- RFC2313 (PKCS #1: RSA Encryption Version 1.5)
- RFC2314 (PKCS #10: Certification Request Syntax Version 1.5)
- RFC2315 (PKCS #7: Cryptographic Message Syntax Version 1.5)
- RFC2437 (PKCS #1: RSA Cryptography Specifications Version 2.0)

Version 2 of the protocol is defined in RFC2311 and RFC2312. It requires the use of the RSA key exchange algorithm, which is patented in the United States, so the RFCs are informational documents rather than standards or proposed standards.

As of the writing of this book, version 3, the focus of this section, is being developed by the IETF S/MIME Working Group in order to allow the use of algorithms not encumbered by proprietary technology. Expect a published RFC to result in the protocol being more widely used.

9.7 ANONYMOUS REMAILERS

The emphasis in this chapter has been on providing security for data, ensuring message integrity, and proving the identity of users. There is one more application of security technology to look at—anonymous remailers. In this case, security services are used to ensure the anonymity of the user.

In general, there are two types of remailers: type I and type II. A type I remailer is very simple. When a message is received, it removes most of the header fields, leaving in the `Subject` field, various MIME fields, and some instruction fields. It then adds enough fields to make the message valid and forwards it to the destination selected by the sender.

Several fields control the behavior of the remailer. Specifically, since the recipient of the original message was the address of the remailer, the user needs a way to specify the intended final recipient.

- `Anon-Send-To`
- `Anon-To`
- `Remail-To`
- `Request-Remailing-To`
- `Send-To`

Other features might also be available. For example, how much latency to add when remailing the message could, be specified with a `Latent-Time` field.

There is a significant problem with a type I remailer—replying to the message doesn't work. Another problem is that the final recipient information is contained in plain text in the message header, so that anyone with access to the message can identify the final recipient.

Type II, or *Mixmaster,* remailers are more sophisticated. They allow messages to be encrypted in such a way that the final recipient information is also encrypted. They even provide the ability to alter the order in which outgoing messages are sent, thereby disassociating out-bound and in-bound traffic. In general, traffic monitors will be unable to use the traffic flow when attempting to determine which users are sending to which destinations.

For additional security, type II remailers provide the ability to route messages through a sequence, or *chain,* of remailers. The message is encrypted with the remailer server's public key and signed with the user's private key. This encrypted message is then used as the body for a new message, with the envelope recipient populated with the address of the first remailer in the chain. This message is encrypted with the first remailer's public key. This sequence of adding a header and encrypting the resulting message is repeated for each remailer in the chain.

Once this is complete, a final message is created, with the body containing the final encrypted message. The `To` field is populated with the email address of the final remailer in the chain and then sent via SMTP.

When a remailer receives a message, it decrypts the data in the message body using its private key. Since the decrypted data is a message destined for another location, the remailer sends it to the destination specified in the header. Each remailer in the chain repeats this process until the final destination receives the original message.

If a recipient replies to the message, it is sent to the first remailer, using an account created for the sender. The server encrypts the message using the original sender's public key. This becomes the body of a new message, which is sent to the next remailer in the user's reply block. The process is repeated until arrival at the final destination—the original sender, who can decrypt the message using his or her private key.

Anonymous remailers have a bad reputation in some circles. They have been used to send spam, to send harassing hate mail, and even to leak confidential information to unauthorized sources. Regardless of this bad reputation, the fact remains that there are some valid uses of anonymous communication.

9.8 SUMMARY

The use of security technologies in Internet email is undergoing significant changes. While the early development of email protocols focused on a workable architecture, the recent growth of the Internet has centered on the importance of integrating strong security features into the protocols.

The several security issues related to email include eavesdropping, impersonation, denial of service attacks, and system integrity. These are the primary problems for any security services used with email protocols and applications.

The core security technologies include cryptographic-quality pseudo-random number generation, cryptographic hash functions, and symmetric and asymmetric encryption. These are combined in various ways to create intermediate security technologies, such as OTP, Kerberos, GSS-API, and OpenPGP.

To make it easier to add security technology to email services, two frameworks are being developed: TLS and SASL. TLS primarily provides transport-level encryption, while SASL primarily provides authentication. There is overlap between the two frameworks, but both provide the ability to add security services to email protocols in a modular fashion. Work is being done to add these frameworks to SMTP, POP, and IMAP.

There is also a framework for adding encryption and digital signatures to MIME entities. It is designed to work with various security technologies. Currently, there are RFCs for using OpenPGP and S/MIME with this MIME framework.

Another area, often overlooked, is anonymity. While there are no RFCs for providing anonymous email, there are a couple techniques in common use.

How security services have been added to email without losing any backward compatibility is a good illustration of the evolution of email standards in such a way that older email programs can still be minimally functional with newer standards. Few areas of computer technology can say the same.

Appendix

A

Example Folder Formats

At some point most email messages are stored in a user email folder. However, while RFC822 specifies the format of messages transferred to SMTP servers, there are no standards for storing messages. Consequently, there are many formats available, and this appendix briefly describes some of them. The emphasis is on their interesting characteristics as well as implications of their design.

A.1 STANDARD UNIX MAILBOX

One of the most common folder formats encountered is the traditional UNIX *mbox* or some variant. This is the default for most UNIX machines. It is simple and designed to be easy to use.

An mbox folder is a text file, to which new messages are appended, resulting in a ordered sequence of messages. Each message starts with a line that contains three of four fields with the following syntax.

```
"From" SP envelope-sender SP date [SP moreinfo]
```

This is frequently referred to as a 'From_' line to differentiate it from a normal From field in a header.

The *envelope-sender* is a single word containing no whitespace. In the case of Internet email, it is usually the envelope sender from the SMTP transaction.

The *date* value is formatted like the output of the **asctime(3)** C library function, without the trailing LF.

```
dow-abbrev SP month-abbrev SP dom SP time SP year
```

The *dow-abbrev* value contains the usual three-letter abbreviation for the day of the week. Likewise, the *month-abbrev* value contains the three-letter abbreviation for the month. The *time* value contains the common colon-separated representation for the time.

```
Tue Nov 21 14:24:53 2000
```

The *moreinfo* value is optional and contains arbitrary information. It is seldom used.

As an example, here is a typical 'From_' line.

```
From joe@tuba.example.com Tue Nov 21 14:24:53 2000
```

The message follows the 'From_' line. On UNIX, this is the delivered message, except that the CRLF line terminators are replaced with a single LF. Some MUA packages on other operating systems retain the CRLF.

Following the message is a blank line. The final result is something similar to the following example.

```
From joe@tuba.example.com Tue Nov 21 14:24:53 2000
message1

From mary@glockenspiel.example.com Tue Nov 21 14:31:41 2000
message2

From larry@ictus.example.com Tue Nov 21 19:04:17 2000
message3
```

Since it's possible for a message to contain lines that looks like message separators, special care must be taken when adding a message to an mbox folder. This is done by prepending a '>' character to any lines starting with zero or more '>' characters followed by 'From_'.

```
>From mary@glockenspiel.example.com Tue Nov 21 14:31:41 2000

>>From larry@ictus.example.com Tue Nov 21 19:04:17 2000
```

In this way the lines cannot be interpreted as message separators. When an MUA reads a message from an mbox folder, it strips the first leading '>' character from any line that starts with one or more '>' characters followed by 'From_'. Some MUAs use a more rigorous comparison to detect 'From_' lines to cope with the possibility that 'From_' lines were not properly escaped when appended to the folder.

Escaping lines that are already escaped allows nested messages to be handled correctly.

The SVR4 flavor of UNIX avoids the problems with 'From␣' lines by adding a `Content-Length` field to each message that is appended to a folder. The field contains the number of bytes in the message so that a program can locate the start of the folder's next message.

To determine whether new mail is present in a folder, two attributes of the file are checked: the modification time and the access time. If the modification time is greater than the access time, the file has been modified since the last time it was accessed. This typically means new mail has arrived.

Status information for individual messages is usually contained in a `Status` field in each message header, as described in Section 2.3.8.

Because of the linear sequence of messages in one file, if any of the message fields need to be updated, the entire folder needs to be rewritten. The same is true when expunging the folder. At first glance, it would appear that the file can be rewritten in place, but to avoid problems such as lack of disk space, it is normally written to a temporary file and then moved into place.

The linear nature of an mbox folder leads to another performance problem. In order to search for information, the entire file must be scanned. Some MUAs speed this up by maintaining indexes of key information in memory. Others add auxiliary index files that can be read to determine the location of information typically used in search commands.

A.2 MH

One alternative to the monolithic design of mbox folders is MH, or Mail Handler. This format was designed in the late 1970s as part of the MH package.

The MH folder design takes advantage of the filesystem to store messages. Each folder is a directory, and each message in a folder is an individual file in the folder directory. The filename of each message file is an integer representing that message's ordinal position in the folder. The message file is an RFC822 message, with LF used for line termination instead of CRLF.

Status information for messages is located in two places. One is in the messages themselves. MH provides the ability to annotate messages with additional fields, via its `anno` command. For each annotation, two fields are added: one containing information date and the other containing the actual annotation.

```
field-name: date
field-name: field-value
```

The user determines the name of the field as well as the annotation text. The *date* value is in the same format as a RFC822 date. The `anno` command also allows an annotation field to be added without the additional date field.

This annotation technique is also used by MH to record when a message is replied to, resent, and forwarded to another recipient. With each of these functions,

TABLE A.1 Internal MH Sequence Names

Name	Description
first	first message in the folder
last	last message in the folder
cur	most recently accessed message
prev	message numerically preceding 'cur'
next	message numerically following 'cur'

an annotation is added to the message with field names corresponding to the action taken. The field value is a list of addresses.

```
Resent: Tue, 21 Nov 2000 14:31:41 -0700
Resent: larry@ictus.example.com
```

MH also maintains status information in a '.mh_sequences' file in each folder directory. Actually, the package allows the file to be named differently, but '.mh_sequences' is the default. An MH sequence is a named list of message numbers that identify a subset of messages in a folder. Many MH commands provide command-line arguments to act on a specified sequence.

```
selected: 1,5-8,13
```

MH maintains several reserved sequence names automatically, summarized in Table A.1.

While MH solves many of the problems inherent in the mbox format, it has some performance problems of its own. For one thing, searching is not particularly fast, since each file in the folder must be opened and scanned to check for data matching the search criteria. For another, UNIX directories suffer performance problems when they contain very large quantities of files, because of how most UNIX filesystems are designed. While an mbox folder containing tens of thousands of messages probably isn't going to perform well, neither is an MH folder with the same number.

Despite these limitations, MH is still used in certain circles, and serves as a good example of one style of folder design.

A.3 MAILDIR

MH suffers from some of the same locking problems mbox does. Maildir, created by Dan Bernstein, is a format reminiscent of MH that doesn't require locks. It is a relatively new, but has some interesting characteristics worth looking at.

As in MH, each mail folder is a directory and each message is an individual file. There are three subdirectories in the folder directory, `new`, `cur`, and `tmp`, where messages are stored rather than immediately underneath the folder directory. The folder directory itself can also contain other files, such as those adding extra functionality not provided by the stock Qmail package.

The `new` directory stores messages that haven't been read by an MUA. When an MUA has seen a new message, it moves it to the `cur` directory. The `tmp` directory stores incoming messages before they are ready to be placed in the `new` directory.

The filenames in `new` have three segments, separated by '`.`' characters. The first segment is the integer time the message was created. The second segment is some value that doesn't repeat within one second on a single host. This can be a simple sequence number. Qmail itself uses the identifier of the process that delivered the message, since it forks a new process for each delivery. The third segment is the name of the machine that deposited the message.

```
919916693.58192.tuba.example.com
```

When a file is moved from `new` to `cur`, a '`:`' character is appended to the filename followed by a status string. This status string is conceptually similar to the `Status` field used in mbox folders.

The first two characters of the status string indicate the semantics of the remainder of the string. The characters '`1,`' are used for experimentation. The characters '`2,`' mean that the remainder of the status string contains a sequence of single-character status indicators.

```
919916693.58192.tuba.example.com:2,RS
```

Table A.2 summarizes these characters. They are sorted in US-ASCII order in the status string.

As in MH, each message file contains an RFC822 message with CRLF line terminators converted to LF. Maildir doesn't use the annotation feature provided by MH, but it does use some extra fields to provide important information. When Qmail delivers a message, it prepends a `Return-Path` field and a `Delivered-To` field.

TABLE A.2 Qmail Status Characters

Character	Description
F	Flagged
R	Replied
S	Seen
T	Trashed

These two fields provide the envelope sender and recipient information from the SMTP transaction that caused the message to be delivered.

The steps necessary to deliver a message are relatively simple but very different from those for other folder formats. After changing to the folder directory, Maildir performs a **stat(2)** system call on the filename 'tmp/*time.pid.fqdn*'. If **stat(2)** returns anything other than ENOENT, the program sleeps for two seconds, updates *time,* and tries again. This step is repeated a limited number of times until it succeeds or exhausts the number of times it is willing to attempt the **stat(2)** operation. Basically, Maildir is trying to identify a unique filename that doesn't yet exist in the tmp directory. If it cannot get an unused temporary filename, the message stays in the MTA's delivery queue. If the message is deferred for more than 24 hours, it is considered undeliverable.

Once it has an available unique filename, Maildir creates the file and proceeds to populate it with the contents of the message being delivered. As each buffer of data is written, the return status of the operation is checked to make sure all the data was written out. The data is also flushed from the disk buffers out to disk using the **fsync(2)** system call and then closed. The return status of each of the system calls is checked for errors.

Once the message is successfully written into the unique filename in the tmp directory, it is linked into new and unlinked from tmp. At this point, the message is delivered.

To process new messages, an MUA checks the new directory. If there are any new messages, the MUA can link them into cur and unlink them in new. MUAs are also expected to check the tmp directory and unlink any temporary files that haven't been accessed in the last 36 hours.

The most interesting things about Maildir are its lack of locking and its ability to safely tolerate NFS (Network File System) environments. For reading messages in a Maildir folder, the performance is comparable to MH.

A.4 CYRUS

The Cyrus IMAP server package, part of the Cyrus Electronic Mail Project at Carnegie Mellon University, uses its own folder format, optimized for IMAP.

As with the MH and Maildir folder formats, Cyrus mail folders are represented as directories. Each message is stored in an individual file in its original RFC822 format. The name of a message file is the IMAP unique identifier value for that message, with a period appended. Messages in a Cyrus folder, unlike the previous folder formats mentioned, retain the CRLF line terminators.

In addition to the message files, Cyrus folders contain four others.

- cyrus.header
- cyrus.index

- `cyrus.cache`

- `cyrus.seen`

The `cyrus.header` file contains information about the mailbox, including a magic string email software can be used to verify that the file is definitely `cyrus.header`. It also includes quota root information for the mailbox, the list of user-defined flags used in the folder, and a redundant copy of the ACL information for the folder.

The `cyrus.index` file contains a header followed by one record for each message in the folder. Tables A.3 and A.4 summarize the information contained in the file.

The `cyrus.cache` file caches information that is frequently needed for messages in a folder. It contains a header and one record for each message. The header contains a sequence number, corresponding to the one in `cyrus.index`. Each individual record contains cached versions of various IMAP data structures designed to improve performance, including IMAP envelope, body structure, and body data optimized for the IMAP `fetch` command, as well as the contents of the To, Cc, and Bcc fields. Each record also contains size, file offsets, charsets, and encodings of the MIME elements in the message.

TABLE A.3 `cyrus.index` Header Structure

Field	Description
generation number	incremented each time cyrus.index is rewritten by an expunge operation
format	nonzero if mailbox is in netnews format
minor version	mailbox format minor version number
start offset	offset of first per-message record
record size	size of per-message records
exists	number of messages in mailbox
last date	UNIX time of the last insertion of a message into the mailbox
last uid	UID of the last message appended to the mailbox
quota used	size quota usage for the mailbox
pop3 last	UID of last message accessed via POP3
uidvalidity	UIDvalidity value

TABLE A.4   `cyrus.index` Per-Message Structure

Field	Description
uid	UID
internaldate	IMAP internaldate, in UNIX date format
sentdate	parsed `Date` field, in UNIX date format
rfc822.size	
header size	size of message header
body offset	offset in file of message body
cache offset	offset in `cyrus.cache` file
last updated	UNIX date of last modification of flags
system flags	bit-vector of system flags
user flags	bit-vector of user-defined flags

The `cyrus.seen` file contains IMAP \seen and \recent flag information. It contains one record per user, sorted by user.

- Userid
- Time when last message was not \recent
- Time \seen state last changed
- UID sequence of \seen messages
- Optional padding

The optional padding is used to avoid rewriting the entire file when it's updated.

Cyrus is interesting as a way to optimize a format for IMAP. It uses one file per message, but maintains additional information to improve the performance. While typically only found on sites using the Cyrus IMAP server, it is an interesting format to study for high-performance email services.

Obviously, there is a lot variance between the folder formats described in this appendix. Each one has strength and weaknesses. The mbox format, while not particularly efficient, is simple and widely available. The MH format provides an improvement over the monolithic mbox format, but doesn't improve searching. The Maildir format avoids the use of locks and is specifically designed to be safe over NFS, but it is relatively new and not widely supported by email packages. Cyrus provides high performance, optimized for IMAP, but requires considerably more bookkeeping.

Appendix B

UNIX Folder Locking

Since MDAs and MUAs are usually implemented as separate processes, it's possible that they will need to access a folder at the same time. As seen in Appendix A, this presents a problem since most folder formats have some aspect that can't tolerate access by multiple processes simultaneously. The solution usually is to use locking to prevent the processes from interfering with each other and corrupting the data in a folder.

This appendix describes some of the issues related to file locking on UNIX systems.

B.1 PROTOTYPICAL LOCKING

One way to implement locking is to use a variable, which is shared among the processes, or threads, needing a lock. A process executes an atomic "*test and set*" machine instruction that will test the variable and set it to a specified value. When used with locking, the variable is set to 1 if, and only if, the value is zero. Most, if not all, modern processors provide a machine instruction capable of performing this task. The primary requirement is that the instruction be atomic. If it isn't, it's possible that the process will be interrupted in the middle of the operation by another process wanting to perform the same operation.

If the process obtains the lock, it can perform the section of code that needs exclusive access to a resource. It then sets the lock variable to zero when its' done.

If the process can't set the lock, it typically retries some predetermined number of times before giving up. It sleeps for a short amount of time between retries.

This type of locking is usually found inside operating systems and amounts to an exclusive lock on a resource. A typical pseudo-code is as follows.

```
max_retries = 5
retries = 0
until lock is obtained or retries > max_retries
      increment retries
      take a short nap
if locked
      perform critical code
      unlock
else
      couldn't perform critical code
```

This example illustrates a simple locking mechanism that attempts to obtain a lock and retries a fixed number of times before giving up.

B.2 DOT-LOCKING

The "test and set" locking technique requires the contending processes or threads to share some memory space where the lock variable is stored. How can this be done? There are essentially three choices. The processes could use shared memory if the operating system supports it. They could also use a system call, again if the operating system supports it. These two techniques were not widely available until recently.

A third option is available, thanks to a feature of most operating systems—a file semaphore. Basically, a file is used for the lock—if the system provides the ability to atomically create a file if, and only if, it doesn't already exist. In UNIX, this means that the O_CREAT and O_EXCL flags are available to the **open(2)** system call. If the call succeeds, the lock is acquired. The process can then perform its critical code and when done simply remove the lock file.

This technique is common on UNIX systems because many email environments on those platforms were designed before there were any reasonable alternatives for locking. In this case, the name of the lock file is constructed from the name of the file to be locked, with '.lock' appended. Hence the name *dot-locking*.

```
weekly-reports.lock
```

There are issues that must be dealt with when using dot-locking. For one thing, it's possible that the lock might not be removed, either from a coding error or premature abortion of the process. If the locking software doesn't take this into account, the resource will remain locked until the lock file is forcibly removed. A common solution is to have the cooperating processes forcibly remove the lock file, if it is considered stale, by establishing an expiration time. For example, it's often reasonable to expect that email programs can accomplish their critical code in less than 10 minutes. If the lock is older than 10 minutes, it is forcibly removed. This is not very rigorous, since it doesn't take into account heavily loaded machines or other extreme circumstances where 10 minutes would not be adequate. An alternative is to populate the lock file with the identifier of the process doing the locking. In this case, a process attempting to break the lock looks at the contents of the file and tries to determine whether the process using it is still running. If not, the file is definitely stale.

Another problem with dot-locking is that the O_EXCL flag for **open(2)** doesn't work with NFS, in which file creation is not atomic. This is equivalent to the nonatomic "test and set" problem mentioned earlier. There is a way to work around it that relies on the fact that linking a file *is* atomic in NFS.

Since the fundamental problem is the possibility of two processes trying to create the same filename at the same time, it can be avoided if the file being created is unique. If so, it is unlikely that the nonatomic nature of file creation in NFS will present a problem.

To perform dot-locking immune to NFS, a file is created that is unique in space and time. The de-facto convention is to build from the target lock filename, the current time, the process identifier, and the hostname of the process creating the file.

```
weekly-reports.lock.918790017.14922.tuba.example.com
```

This is called a *hitching-post* file, which the program then attempts to link to the desired lock filename. In the previous example, this would be 'weekly-reports.lock'. If the link fails, the lock wasn't acquired. If it succeeds, the status of the file is retrieved and the hitching-post file is removed. If the link count in the file status is equal to two, the lock succeeded; otherwise, it failed. When combined with the typical retry loop, this provides a file semaphore locking mechanism safe to use over NFS.

The primary problem with a dot-lock is that it is exclusive. Another problem is that creating a file is relatively expensive. While the mechanism is workable, other techniques are available that might be preferable.

B.3 FLOCK

Kernel locking provides an alternative to the rather inefficient dot-locking. Most, if not all, modern operating systems provide kernel-based locking in some form. There are two types available in UNIX: *flock,* and *fcntl,* named after the system calls that control the locking.

The **flock(2)** call is given two pieces of information: a file descriptor for an open file and an integer indicating the desired locking operation. Table B.1 lists the operations. The call normally blocks until it can obtain a lock. Adding the LOCK_NB flag causes the system call to return a EWOULDBLOCK error if the call would block, which allows the routine to be used in a retry loop.

TABLE B.1 flock Operations

Operation	Description
LOCK_SH	Shared lock
LOCK_EX	Exclusive lock
LOCK_UN	Unlock
LOCK_NB	Don't block when locking

Shared locks allow multiple processes to lock a file while preventing one from obtaining an exclusive lock on it. In email folders, this is most often to allow multiple processes to read a file while preventing any one from updating it. Without shared locks, every process that needs to read a file must lock it to prevent it from being updated while analyzing the contents.

Multiple processes may hold a shared lock on a file, but only one exclusive lock may be held on it at one time. An exclusive lock cannot be acquired on the file if there are any shared locks held on it. Shared locks are useful because they allow multiple processes to read a file at one time.

It's possible to create a shared lock and then promote it to an exclusive lock. Likewise, it's possible to demote an exclusive lock to a shared lock. However, there is one minor wrinkle. When promoting or demoting a lock, the original lock is released. Thus, a program runs the risk of losing its lock in the process. This can be accommodated in the code, but programmers need to be aware of it.

Losing a lock when promoting or demoting it is not the most serious problem with flock. The primary problem is that it doesn't work over NFS. It always succeeds, so it's useless for locking when a file is being accessed via NFS.

B.4 FCNTL AND LOCKF

The **fcntl(2)** system call provides the ability to manipulate several aspects of an open file descriptor. One of them is locking.

The operations related to locking that **fcntl(2)** provides are listed in Table B.2. Locking and unlocking are done with F_SETLK or F_SETLKW. The system call is

TABLE B.2   fcntl System Call

Operation	Description
F_SETLK	Set a lock; returns an error if a lock is already present
F_SETLKW	Like F_SETLK, but waits for the lock to be released
F_GETLK	Get lock information for process currently holding lock

TABLE B.3 **fcntl** Locking Operations

Operation	Description
LOCK_SH	Shared lock
LOCK_EX	Exclusive lock
LOCK_UN	Unlock
LOCK_NB	Don't block waiting for lock

passed a data structure containing the parameters to use for the locking operation, the elements of which include the flag to select which lock operation to perform, an offset into the file, a flag to indicate the reference point to calculate the offset from, the length of the region to lock, and the identifier for the process holding the lock.

Table B.3 lists the locking operations available in **fcntl(2).** Like the other locking mechanisms, **fcntl(2)** is not without its issues. For one thing, a process may have a file opened twice and be locked on one of the file descriptors. If a lock is acquired for the second descriptor, the first lock is released. This can be accommodated with code, but it's important to know its possible.

The **fcntl(2)** system call can be used for locking on NFS files if both the client and server are running the **statd** and **lockd** programs. These two programs provide a locking mechanism for NFS, which **fcntl(2)** can use. That's the good news; the bad news is that if the programs aren't running on the remote NFS server, the locking can hang indefinitely waiting for them to appear.

Some systems provide a **lockf(3)** C library routine, which is a wrapper around **fcntl(2);** however, it doesn't have the same functionality. For one thing, **lockf(3)** doesn't provide shared locks, only exclusive locks. It also lacks some of the options available in **fcntl(2)** for specifying the length of the locked region. The locking operations provided with **lockf(2)** are listed in Table B.4.

Some operating systems also implement **flock(2)** with **fcntl(2).** The documentation for **flock(2)** on those operating systems should indicate when this is true.

TABLE B.4 **lockf** Operations

Operation	Description
F_LOCK	Lock a region
F_ULOCK	Unlock a region
F_TEST	Test a region for locks
F_TLOCK	Test and lock a region

Locking can be an annoying problem for developers and system administrators. The design of a folder format has a strong impact on the locking requirements, as does the environment where the software is being used. Even if a developer or system administrator has a preference for a type of locking, none of the available locking techniques is optimal in all cases. To further complicate the problem, care must be taken that the types used by the participating programs are compatible. In fact, some email programs use a combination of locking techniques, just in case there are programs that only implement one.

If you've detected a pattern regarding NFS issues with file locking, you're right—NFS presents some serious problems.

Very few folder formats were designed to eliminate the need for file locking. In an NFS environment, **flock(2)** is unusable and **fcntl(2)** can hang under certain circumstances. This means that dot-locking is often the only dependable technique, which is unfortunate, since it is typically the most inefficient.

In general, NFS should be avoided for mail folder storage, except under carefully controlled circumstances and with a full understanding of the implications of the decision. While some folder formats are more tolerant of NFS, many are not. For storage of email on remote servers, IMAP often provides a better solution.

There is no magic formula for how the locking should be configured. Often the use of a particular folder format will drive locking choices. Other times, some hard decisions must be made, such as avoiding email folder access via NFS. System administrators, in particular, are encouraged to review the locking options for all email packages they use to determine whether they are the most appropriate.

Programming Languages

For anyone contemplating developing email software, one of the decisions to be faced is choosing a programming language. This section walks through some of the more common programming languages used for that purpose.

C.1 C

The C programming language is, arguably, the workhorse of the programming world, particularly for network protocols. It was originally designed as a *systems programming* language. This means it was intended for software such as operating systems, programming languages, and other low-level programming tasks. It is a compiled language—a C program is processed through a compiler to generate native code for a particular class of hardware.

Even as C has evolved, its roots as a systems programming language are still evident for those knowing what to look for. For example, it doesn't prevent a programmer from writing data past the end of a buffer or writing a floating-point number into the space occupied by some integers. However, the fact that the language allows such problems does not mean it is inappropriate for email software. In fact, its lack of certain constraints contributes to one of its main advantages. C programs are often considerably faster than programs written in many other languages. This is not always the case, but it's true often enough to make C a compelling option for email software.

A significant number of email programs are written in C, including most of the programs mentioned in this book. In fact, most of the programming languages mentioned in this appendix are written in C.

C.2 C++

C++ was designed as a superset of C. It retains the original C syntax while adding some new syntactic elements, most notably for object-oriented programming. Early in its history, some people thought C++ might replace C for some applications, particularly higher-level programs. This has not proven to be universally true.

Like C, C++ is a compiled language, producing native binary executables that can be executed on a particular class of hardware.

The object-oriented features of C++ are useful in many areas of email, particularly in MIME, where there are common underlying structures with variations at the higher levels. They are also useful with some of the newer protocols and security services, which are extremely modular and reuse many design elements. While C is sufficient, objected-oriented programming can be useful in these instances.

C.3 JAVA

Java was designed as a portable programming language. It is compiled, but the compiled data are not specific to a particular class of hardware. Instead, it is processed through a virtual machine, which insulates the programming language from the underlying hardware, including the graphics operations. In general, Java can be run on any machine where a Java virtual machine is available.

Java is object-oriented, with built-in support for graphics, networking, and file I/O. This makes it very interesting for email applications.

The most significant problems with Java are its speed and its youth. In general, Java programs run noticeably slower than C or C++ programs, but good programming and fast hardware can speed things up. Another problem for some programmers is that Java is still young and still undergoing changes, but this is expected to improve as it matures.

C.4 PERL

Perl was designed and originally implemented by Larry Wall. It has been described as the Swiss Army knife of programming languages. Perl has a very rich syntax, which is considered by some programmers to be a feature and by others to be a flaw. Its practical attitude toward getting the job done has made it one of the most widely used programming languages on the Internet.

Perl presents itself as an interpreted language, since it doesn't generate binary executables or virtual machine byte-code files, but it compiles program files into an internal representation in memory and acts on that representation.

While it didn't start out to be object-oriented, version 5 added the feature. This contributed significantly to Perl's ability to handle add-on modules in a rational manner. There are several third-party Perl modules available for processing email.

Very few end-user email applications are written in Perl, but it is very useful for writing tools for programmers and administrators. In fact, Perl gained much of its early popularity with administrators looking to write tools to get their job done.

C.5 PYTHON

Python is an object-oriented programming language, designed and implemented by Guido van Rossum. It provides several email-related modules as part of its base library.

Python might appeal to programmers put off by the syntax of Perl, as it has a much simpler syntax. Like Perl, Python gives the appearance of being an interpreted language, but it can automatically write byte-compiled data to disk the first time is executes a program file. After that, when asked to execute a program file, it checks for the compiled version. If one exists and is newer than the text version, it executes it. If the program file is newer, Python recompiles the program and saves the results to disk.

Python is useful as a tool language and as an application language. While not as popular as some of the other programming languages mentioned in this appendix, some readers might find it very useful.

C.6 EMACS

Emacs is a text editor. It's also proof of the **Law of Software Envelopment** coined by Jamie Zawinski: "Every program attempts to expand until it can read mail. Those programs which cannot so expand are replaced by ones which can."

Emacs is essentially a text editing engine with the Lisp programming language wrapped around it. The environment Emacs provides encourages users to extend its capabilities as well as use it as their primary tool. This was particularly true prior to the widespread availability of graphics terminals.

There are several MUAs available for Emacs, including rmail, vm, gnus, and mh-e. The latter three, in particular, provide very rich sets of MUA features.

Underneath the MUAs, several libraries are available that implement core email functions, including manipulation of RFC822 messages, and the client portion of SMTP. Most of this advanced functionality, like MIME processing, is provided by the individual MUAs.

One of the characteristics of Emacs development is that users are encouraged to extend existing Emacs programs. The Emacs MUAs are no exception. Each of the MUAs allows a user to extend its functionality by providing hooks at strategic locations in the code for adding features. Because of this, Emacs offers an excellent environment in which to experiment with email protocols and data structures.

There are a lot of programming languages to choose from. Like security algorithms, no one language is the best choice for all situations. This appendix surveys some of the more common or interesting ones with regard to Internet email.

C and C++ are compiled languages that are popular for large-scale email applications. Most of the email programs people use are written in one or both of these languages.

Perl and Python are useful for writing tools and experimenting. While they can be used for large-scale email applications, they are better suited for small- to medium-scale programs.

Emacs is a text editor with a programming language that is readily accessible to the user. In fact, the Emacs culture encourages extending the programs used with it. Since it is an interactive text editor, most email packages in Emacs are MUAs, but they are highly configurable. The level of configurability is far beyond what is available in most MUAs, providing a useful environment for email developers and administrators for experimenting with new features or ideas, well ahead of some software vendors.

Appendix D

IMSP

IMSP (Internet Message Support Protocol) is intended to enhance the services provided by IMAP. Its original Internet Draft was never published as an RFC, but a few commercial email packages support it, and successful deployments can be found around the world. The Internet Draft has long since expired, but a copy is still available from the Cyrus Mail project.[1]

IMSP provides three services: extended IMAP folder management, storage of client configuration information, and address books. Extended IMAP folder management includes the ability to manage folders on multiple IMAP servers from a single IMSP server. This makes it possible to store and update configuration information for MUAs. The address book mechanism allows user address books to be stored and maintained on a central IMSP server.

The protocol was designed to be used as an adjunct to IMAP. It runs on TCP port 403, but has provisions to allow a client to fall back to IMAP if IMSP is not available. IMSP is intentionally designed to be very similar to IMAP, the goal being to reuse as much IMAP code as possible when adding IMSP functionality to an email package. The syntax for the commands and responses is similar, as are the session states. The dissimilarities are mainly due to functional differences between the two services. For example, IMSP doesn't provide the ability to access or manipulate the contents of mail folders, so the protocol doesn't have a *selected* state. It also doesn't provide commands available in IMAP related to accessing or manipulating the contents of folders.

- capability
- noop
- logout

---

[1] ftp://ftp.andrew.cmu.edu/pub/cyrus-mail/draft-myers-imap-imsp-01.txt

TABLE D.1 IMSP Commands Not Present in IMAP

Command	Description
replace	Delete a mailbox and migrate subscriptions to new mailbox
move	Move a mailbox between servers or partitions
lmarked	List marked folders
get	Get configuration option data
set	Set a configuration option
unset	Delete or reset a configuration option
searchaddress	Search an address book
fetchaddress	Fetch address book entries
storeaddress	Store an address book entry
deleteaddress	Delete an address book entry
addressbook	List address books
createaddressbook	Create an address book
deleteaddressbook	Delete an address book
renameaddressbook	Rename an address book
lock	Lock a configuration option or address book
unlock	Unlock a configuration option or address book
setacl	Set the ACL on a mailbox or address book
deleteacl	Delete an ACL on a mailbox or address book
getacl	Retrieve the ACL on a mailbox or address book
myrights	List user's rights on a mailbox or address book

- authenticate
- login
- rename
- subscribe
- unsubscribe
- list
- lsub

Two commands, create and delete, are present in both protocols, but the syntax is slightly different in IMSP. The create command has an additional optional argument for specifying a server partition list, which is a parenthetical list of servers where the mailbox should be created. The delete command has an additional optional hostname argument that directs the IMSP server to delete the specified mailbox on the specified host.

All of the other commands available in IMAP are provided in IMSP. In addition, IMSP provides many commands, not available in IMSP, for configuration data management, access control list management, and address book management. They are summarized in Table D.1.

As an attempted enhancement to IMAP, IMSP is interesting, in that most enhancements are added to an existing protocol; whereas IMSP was designed separately but with a large overlap with its sister protocol.

IMSP's main claim to fame is that it served as a learning experience for the newer ACAP, which is described in Appendix E. Several aspects of IMSP were interesting to the Internet protocol design community, so many of its ideas were expanded and incorporated into ACAP. It is highly unlikely that IMSP will ever advance past its current state. Instead, work is focusing on ACAP development.

Appendix

E

ACAP

ACAP provides a client-server protocol for accessing remote program configuration and user preference information. It was designed in such a way that multiple client programs, even from multiple vendors, can use the same information on the server. This allows, for example, two separate email clients to share the same personal address book or two separate Web browsers to share the same set of bookmarks.

This appendix provides a summary of the protocol. The focus is on its overall design, with the hope that readers will explore the details on their own.

ACAP is defined in RFC2244 (ACAP—Application Configuration Access Protocol), which includes a description of how it works, its available commands, and how its data is structured. RFC2244, published in 1997, doesn't define the actual data elements that can be used in the protocol—this is left to subsequent RFCs. ACAP is relatively young. As of the writing of this book, there are no RFCs published that define configuration information manipulated by the protocol, but there are Internet Drafts in process. Several of these are expected to be promoted to RFCs soon.

Data in ACAP is organized as a hierarchical tree of entries, where each level is called a *dataset*. The name of a dataset is made up of zero or more UTF-8 characters other than '/', which is used as the separator when specifying a path down a tree of datasets. Each dataset contains a list of entries. This is analogous to directories and files, where a dataset can be viewed as a directory and an entry as a file.

Each entry has a unique name, specified as a series of UTF-8 characters. It can also contain an arbitrary number of attributes, each of which has a name and contains a single value or multiple values. Each attribute can also have metadata associated with it to help determine how it can be accessed or interpreted. A dataset inherits attributes from parent datasets.

The ACAP data model also supports the use of ACLs, to control data access, and quotas, to control the resource consumption of datasets. It also provides a mechanism called a context. When the client submits a search for data, it can specify that the results form a named context. This named context can then be used with some

TABLE E.1 ACAP Commands

Command	Description
noop	Do nothing
lang	Set preferred language
authenticate	Authenticate to the server
logout	Disconnect
search	Search for a subset of entries in a dataset
freecontext	Delete context
updatecontext	Ask server for updates in items in a context
store	Store entries in a dataset
deletedsince	List entries deleted since a specified date/time
setacl	Set ACL information on an object
deleteacl	Remove ACL information on an object
myrights	List rights current user has on an object
listrights	List rights a specified user has on an object
getquota	Show quota information for a dataset

commands to act on the set of entries contained in it. Contexts only exist for the duration of the session.

As with IMSP, the syntax of the ACAP commands and responses, as well as the overall protocol design, is very similar to IMAP. Unlike IMSP, the set of commands used in ACAP is very different from IMAP's. These commands are summarized in Table E.1.

While the protocol is still young, ACAP presents some interesting possibilities for Internet client software. Imagine only needing to give one piece of information to an email client—the name of your ACAP server. Once the client connects to the server, the user authenticates to the server, and the client can then configure itself based on the remote configuration data. Roaming users retain all their preferences, regardless of location. Multiple clients share the same configuration information, such as a personal address book. In addition, some configuration information is shared by packages from multiple vendors. Sound too good to be true? It might be, but ACAP does present some interesting possibilities.

LDAP

What do you do when you need to call someone, but don't know their phone number—the most obvious answer is to use the phone book or call directory assistance. The same is true with email addresses. Given a person's name or some other identifying characteristic, what is their email address or some other piece of information associated with them? Directory services is the collective name for mechanisms that allow a user, or program, to find this type of information.

There are several protocols that could technically be called directory services. DNS and Whois come to mind. DNS provides the ability to map a domain name into other types of information, including, in the case of email, A records, and MX records. In addition to the core record types it provides, DNS has also been successfully used to map for security certificates, point of contact information, and other useful information. Whois was designed to allow users to query the Internet registration database.

Neither of these protocols was designed for email directory services. In addition, neither was designed so that users can maintain their own information.

LDAP (Lightweight Directory Access Protocol) is the most widely used directory service used with email. It provides a distributed client-server protocol that programs can use to query servers for various types of information. In the case of email, the more common types of information include email addresses, group aliases, and security certificates. This appendix provides a brief overview of this protocol.

LDAP is a stripped-down version of X.500, designed for use over the Internet. X.500 is a CCITT protocol that provides a distributed, global directory service. It allows maintenance of the data in the directory to be decentralized, like DNS. It includes powerful searching capabilities, a single global namespace, security services, and extensibility.

The X.400 email services uses X.500 for their directory services. Like X.400, X.500 is a large, sophisticated protocol that is relatively difficult to implement, which has prevented it from gaining wide acceptance on the Internet. To address this, LDAP was created. It is much easier to implement and better suited for Internet use. Version 1 of the protocol was published in 1993 as RFC1487 (X.500 Lightweight Directory Access Protocol) and RFC1488 (The X.500 String Representation of Standard Attributes Syntaxes). As an adjunct, RFC1558 (A String Representation of LDAP Search Filters) was published to define how to notate search filters.

In 1995, version 2 of LDAP was published in RFC1777 (Lightweight Directory Access Protocol) and RFC1778 (A String Representation of Distinguished Names). Also in 1995 an API was defined for LDAP in RFC1823 (The LDAP Application Program Interface). In 1996, the notation for LDAP search filters was updated by RFC1960 (A String Representation of LDAP Search Filters); it was updated again in 1997 by RFC2254 (The String Representation of LDAP Search Filters).

In 1997, version 3 of the protocol was published in a series of RFCs.

- RFC2251—Lightweight Directory Access Protocol (v3)
- RFC2252—Lightweight Directory Access Protocol (v3): Attribute Syntax Definitions
- RFC2253—Lightweight Directory Access Protocol (v3): UTF-8 String Representation of Distinguished Names

Several companion RFCs were also published.

- RFC2254
- RFC2255 (The LDAP URL Format)
- RFC2256 (A Summary of the X.500(96) User Schema for use with LDAPv3)

LDAP uses TCP port 389. Like the email protocols, it is designed as a client-server protocol. Unlike the email protocols, it is not text-based but uses a subset of BER (Basic Encoding Rules) encoding. The protocol provides several commands for performing LDAP tasks, summarized in Table F.1.

In general, LDAP is asynchronous. Multiple commands may be sent by the client without waiting for the server to respond. In addition, the server can send unsolicited notifications to the client about server-side problems, such as an impending disconnection.

The data in an LDAP directory is called a DIT (Directory Information Tree). It consists of entries with names that consist of one or more concatenated attribute/value pairs. The name is referred to as the entry's DN (Distinguished Name) and is unique across the entire tree.

```
cn=Larry Ictus, o=Example Inc., c=US
```

Each entry contains a set of attribute pairs. An attribute pair consists of a data type name and one or more values associated with the attribute. For example, a

TABLE F.1 LDAP Commands

Command	Description
bind	Authenticate to the server
unbind	Terminate session and disconnect
search	Search for entries
modify	Modify an entry
add	Add an entry
delete	Delete an entry
modifyDN	Modify the DN for an entry
compare	Compare attributes of an entry to a template
abandon	Abort a pending command
extended operation	Send an command extension

"mail" attribute might be present, providing the email address associated with the entry. The data type name controls what type of data is contained in the attribute, the data syntax, and whether multiple values of the attribute can be present in an entry.

A schema contains the set of attribute data type definitions and object class definitions. It is a collection of attribute definitions, object class definitions, and other information, which a server uses to determine how the data in an entry can be processed.

Each entry has an object class attribute, which specifies what type of object the entry represents. Object classes also have parent classes, from which they inherit their attributes. Each object class has a specific set of required attributes, which must be present in an entry in that class, and a set of optional attributes.

The most popular use for LDAP is to provide information about people. In fact, several MUAs provide LDAP interfaces in their address book tools to allow users to query an LDAP server for address information. The user can query his or her local personal address book or one or more remote LDAP servers.

In addition to using it to distribute email address books for users, some experimentation is being done on LDAP as an alternative to MTA aliases files and as storage for user security credentials.

When populated with useful information, the services provided with LDAP are very popular with many end-users, particularly when combined with an MUA. LDAP is still evolving, but based on experience with current implementations and feedback from end-users, it appears to be developing into a useful addition to the collection of Internet protocols currently available.

Acronyms

A	Address
ABNF	Augmented Backus-Naur Form
ACAP	Application Configuration Access Protocol
ACL	Access Control List
AES	Advanced Encryption Standard
AOL	America Online
AS	Authentication Server
ASCII	American Standard Code for Information Interchange
ASID	Algorithms for SPAM Identification and Destruction
BCP	Best Current Practice
BER	Basic Encoding Rules
BITNET	Because It's Time Network
BNF	Backus-Naur Form
BOF	Birds of a Feather
CBC	Cipher Chaining Block
CCITT	Consultative Committee for International Telephone and Telegraph
CERT	Computer Emergency Response Team
CFB	Cipher Feedback
CNAME	Canonical Name
CR	Carriage Return
CRAM	Challenge-Response Authentication Mechanism
CRC	Cyclic Redundancy Check
CRLF	Carriage Return Line Feed
CSNET	Computer Science Network
DARPA	Defense Advanced Research Projects Agency
DES	Data Encryption Standard
DIT	Directory Information Tree
DN	Distinguished Name
DNS	Domain Name Service
DSN	Delivery Status Notification
DSSL	DynamicIP Spam Sources List
DUL	Dial-Up User List
EBCDIC	Extended Binary Coded Decimal Interchange Code

ECB	Electronic Code Book
FIPS	Federal Information Processing Standard
FQDN	Fully Qualified Domain Name
FTP	File Transfer Protocol
GMT	Greenwich Mean Time
GSS–API	Generic Security Service–Application Program Interface
GUI	Graphical User Interface
HTML	Hypertext Markup Language
IAB	Internet Architecture Board
IANA	Internet Assigned Numbers Authority
ICANN	Internet Corporation for Assigned Names and Numbers
IDEA	International Data Encryption Algorithm
IESG	Internet Engineering Steering Group
IETF	Internet Engineering Task Force
IMAP	Internet Message Access Protocol
IMSP	Internet Message Support Protocol
IP	Internet Protocol
IPv6	Internet Protocol—Version 6
ISO	International Organization for Standardization
ISOC	Internet Society
ISP	Internet Service Provider
ITU	International Telecommunications Union
KDC	Key Distribution Center
LDAP	Lightweight Directory Access Protocol
LF	Line Feed
LMTP	Local Mail Transfer Protocol
MAC	Message Authentication Code
MAPS	Mail Abuse Prevention System
MD4	Message Digest Algorithm 4
MD5	Message Digest Algorithm 5
MDA	Mail Delivery Agent
MIC	Message Integrity Check
MIME	Multipurpose Internet Mail Extensions
MOSS	MIME Object Security Services
MSA	Mail Submission Agent
MTA	Mail Transport Agent
MUA	Mail User Agent
MX	Mail Exchanger
NCSA	National Computational Science Alliance
NFS	Network File System
NIST	National Institute of Standards and Technology

NNTP	Network News Transfer Protocol
OFB	Output Feedback
ORBS	Open Relay Blocking System
OTP	One-Time Password
PCBC	Propagating Cipher Block Chaining
PDF	Portable Data Format
PEM	Privacy Enhanced Mail
PGP	Pretty Good Privacy
PKCS	Public-Key Cryptography Standards
PKI	Public-Key Infrastructure
PKIX	Public-Key Infrastructure (X.509)
POP	Post Office Protocol
PRNG	Pseudo-Random Number Generator
RBL	Realtime Blackhole List
RFC	Request for Comment
RNG	Random-Number Generator
RSA	Rivest, Shamir, and Adleman
RTT	Round-Trip Time
SASL	Simple Authentication and Security Layer
SGML	Standard Generalized Markup Language
SHA	Secure Hash Algorithm
SHS	Secure Hash Standard
S/MIME	Secure/Multipurpose Internet Mail Extensions
SMTP	Simple Mail Transfer Protocol
SSL	Secure Socket Layer
TCP	Transmission Control Protocol
TFTP	Trivial File Transfer Protocol
TGS	Ticket Granting Service
TGT	Ticket Granting Ticket
TLS	Transport Layer Security
UBE	Unsolicited Bulk Email
UCE	Unsolicited Commercial Email
UCS	Universal Character Set
URL	Uniform Resource Locator
UT	Universal Time
UTF	UCS Transformation Format
UTF-7	UCS Transformation Format 7
UTF-8	UCS Transformation Format 8
UUCP	UNIX to UNIX Copy
VERP	Variable Envelope Return Path
VPN	Virtual Private Network

WKS	Well-Known Service
WWW	World Wide Web
XBM	X11 Bitmap
XML	Extensible Markup Language
Y2K	Year 2000

INDEX

Note: Italicized index entries indicate a syntactical element. Entries that refer to field names, protocol commands, and protocol parameters are set in a monospace font.

CD-ROM Warranty

Addison Wesley Longman, Inc., warrants the enclosed disc to be free of defects in materials and faulty workmanship under normal use for a period of ninety days after purchase. If a defect is discovered in the disc during this warranty period, a replacement disc can be obtained at no charge by sending the defective disc, postage prepaid, with proof of purchase to:

Addison Wesley Longman
Editorial Department
One Jacob Way
Reading, MA 01867

After the ninety-day period, a replacement disc will be sent upon receipt of the defective disc and a check or money order for $10.00, payable to Addison Wesley Longman, Inc.

Addison Wesley Longman, Inc., makes no warranty or representation, either expressed or implied, with respect to this software, its quality, performance, merchantability, or fitness for a particular purpose. In no event will Addison Wesley Longman, its distributors, or dealers be liable for direct, indirect, special, incidental, or consequential damages arising out of the use or inability to use the software. The exclusion of implied warranties is not permitted in some states. Therefore, the above exclusion may not apply to you. This warranty provides you with specific legal rights. There may be other rights that you may have that vary from state to state.

More information and updates are available at
http://www.awl.com/cseng/titles/0-201-43288-9

Addison-Wesley Computer and Engineering Publishing Group

How to Interact with Us

1. Visit our Web site

http://www.awl.com/cseng

When you think you've read enough, there's always more content for you at Addison-Wesley's web site. Our web site contains a directory of complete product information including:

- Chapters
- Exclusive author interviews
- Links to authors' pages
- Tables of contents
- Source code

You can also discover what tradeshows and conferences Addison-Wesley will be attending, read what others are saying about our titles, and find out where and when you can meet our authors and have them sign your book.

2. Subscribe to Our Email Mailing Lists

Subscribe to our electronic mailing lists and be the first to know when new books are publishing. Here's how it works: Sign up for our electronic mailing at **http://www.awl.com/cseng/mailinglists.html**. Just select the subject areas that interest you and you will receive notification via email when we publish a book in that area.

3. Contact Us via Email

cepubprof@awl.com
Ask general questions about our books
Sign up for our electronic mailing list
Submit corrections for our web site

bexpress@awl.com
Request an Addison-Wesley catalog
Get answers to questions regarding your order or our products

innovations@awl.com
Request a current Innovations Newsletter

webmaster@awl.com
Send comments about our web site

cepubeditors@awl.com
Submit a book proposal
Send errata for an Addison-Wesley book

cepubpublicity@awl.com
Request a review copy for a member of the media interested in reviewing new Addison-Wesley titles

We encourage you to patronize the many fine retailers who stock Addison-Wesley titles. Visit our online directory to find stores near you or visit our online store: **http://store.awl.com/** or call **800-824-7799**.

Addison Wesley Longman
Computer and Engineering Publishing Group
One Jacob Way, Reading, Massachusetts 01867 USA
TEL 781-944-3700 • FAX 781-942-3076